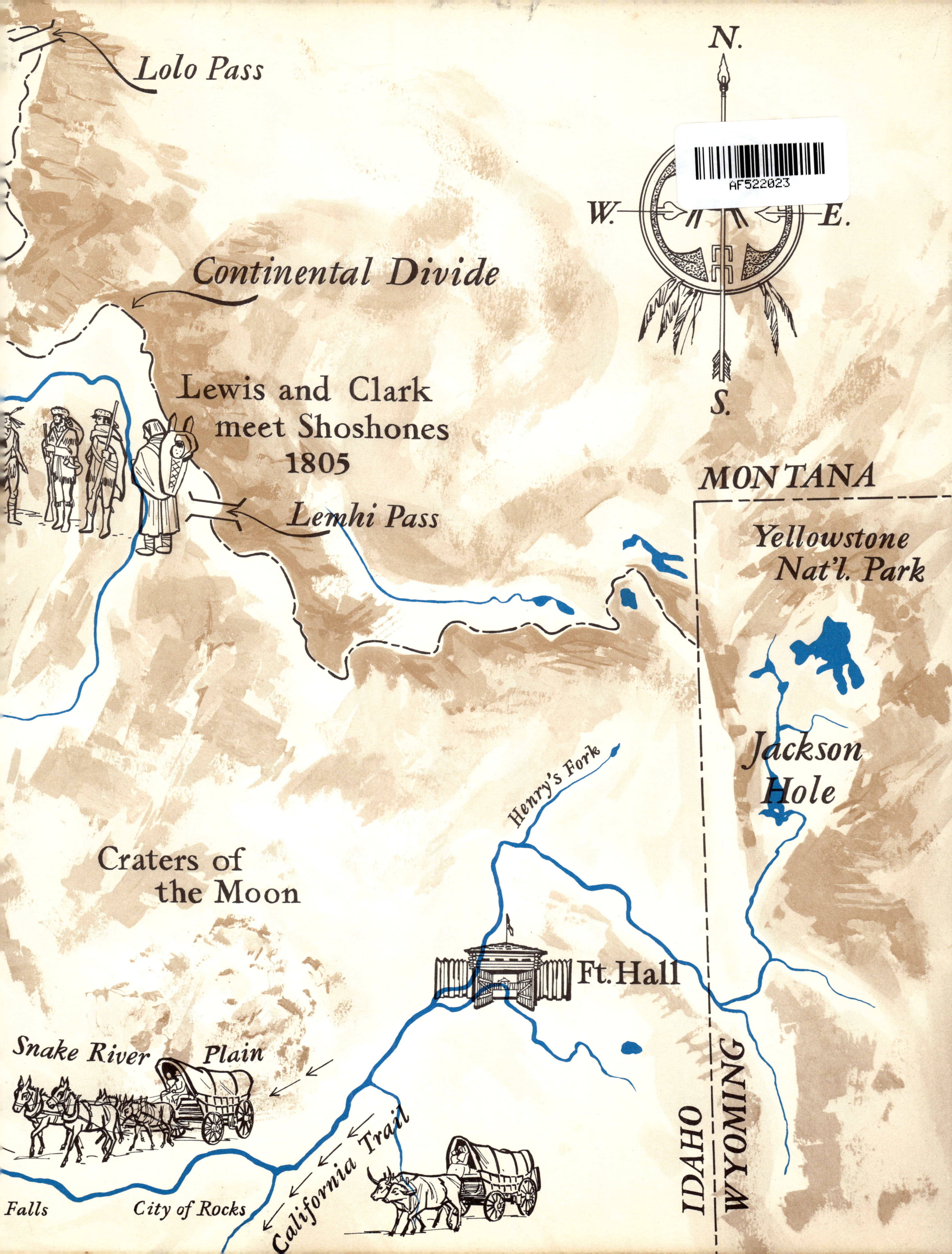

Lolo Pass
N.
AF522023
W.
E.
S.
Continental Divide
Lewis and Clark
meet Shoshones
1805
Lemhi Pass
MONTANA
Yellowstone
Nat'l. Park
Jackson
Hole
Henry's Fork
Craters of
the Moon
Ft. Hall
Snake River
Plain
California Trail
IDAHO
WYOMING
Falls
City of Rocks

SNAKE RIVER COUNTRY

SNAKE RIVER COUNTRY

by Bill Gulick

photography by Earl Roberge

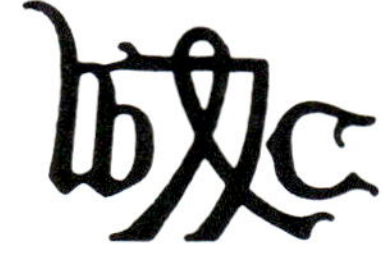

The CAXTON PRINTERS, Ltd.
CALDWELL, IDAHO 83605
1971

International Standard Book Number 0-87004-215-7

Library of Congress Catalog Card No. 71-140117

Lithographed and bound in the United States of America by
The CAXTON PRINTERS, Ltd.
Caldwell, Idaho 83605
114900

Dedicated to the memory of my father, Dr. Grover C. Gulick, who had a lifelong interest in the history of the West, and to my mother, Golda, who shared it.

Acknowledgments

Although I have explored most of the streams in the Snake River Country with fishing rod in hand, the facts and figures required to write a book of this nature do not rise like eager trout to skillfully dropped flies. Instead, they sulk like sullen steelhead in deep pools called libraries, public agencies, government bureaus, periodical files, and the minds of men engaged in highly specialized work. Thus, it pays to fish with experts who know where the big ones lie. With their help, I have wasted few hours on unproductive waters.

First, I must acknowledge a twenty-year debt to Penrose Memorial Library, Whitman College, Walla Walla, an important repository for source material available nowhere else. Currently, my debt is to Arley Jonish, Librarian; Larry Dodd, Curator of Manuscripts and Northwest Materials; Martha Jacky, Louise Humphrey, and the rest of the fine staff who have helped me on so many books in so many ways for so many years. In time past, Ruth Reynolds, retired librarian, Dr. Chester Maxey, President Emeritus, and Dr. Louis Perry, former president, treated me equally well.

Admittedly, the status of my wife Jeanne, who for ten years was Pacific Northwest Librarian at Penrose, quit at my urging to research Snake River Country for me, then went right back to Penrose to do it—*sans* pay—remains hazy to everyone except me. I miss her paycheck. But she set no precedent in quitting a paid job at Penrose and then going back to work there for free. Former research specialist, Marilyn Sparks, did this for a number of years. Ruth Reynolds, following her retirement, returned to undertake long-needed classification of priceless vault materials. When Jeanne asked them for assistance in assembling the index for this book, Marilyn and Ruth were delighted to help. For this, as well as many other past favors, I thank all three sincerely.

Dr. Donald Sheehan, current president of Whitman College, and Dr. Chester Maxey, President Emeritus, not only have put the library's facilities at my disposal; they have both endured being made auditory guinea pigs for two portions of the book while it was still in manuscript form. For their kind words of encouragement, I am grateful.

In the periodical section of the Portland Public Library, Alberta Byl, Ellen Byrnes, Marcella Holman, and Barbara Guyse saved me considerable time and travel by locating missing volumes of seventy-five-year-old magazines just when I had despaired of finding them.

At the Spokane Public Library, Bruce Carrick, Florence Johnson, and their capable staff responded to my sometimes odd requests as they have for years—with alacrity.

Justifiably proud of their sparkling new library in Walla Walla, John Carter and his staff cooperated in every possible way.

Useful though Subject Index files are and exotic as electronic memory banks may become, nothing yet invented is as valuable to the writer as the Director-Archivist of a State Historical Society. Not only does he know what has been written on a given subject; he knows what could and should be written on it, where prime source material is available, which pitfalls should be avoided, and which fruitful lines should be pursued. More often than not, he has just what the writer needs in an as yet unclassified box of material in the basement.

Dr. Thomas Vaughn, Director of the Oregon Historical Society in Portland, has for many years lent me this kind of inspiration, guidance, and assistance.

Dr. Merle Wells, Archivist for the Idaho State Library in Boise, has supplied me with so much microfilmed material (which I have turned over to Penrose) that on many subjects I can research Idaho's past as easily in Walla Walla as in Boise. Since Merle long has felt than the Snake River Country deserved a book, I can only hope he will agree that I have made a respectable use of the material he has given me so generously.

Professional associates in related fields have provided me with valuable tips, warnings, and bits of information. My long-time friend, teacher, and fellow writer, Foster Harris, University of Oklahoma School of Journalism, made several early suggestions, which I followed. Bill Burkhardt, editor of the official state publication, *Oklahoma Today*, generously shared his experiences regarding the uses of photographs and text, which helped me avoid serious missteps. Archie Satterfield, feature writer, and Roy Scully, photographer, Seattle *Times;* Jim Hutcheson, editor, Bill Lilley, photographer, and Vance Orchard, feature writer, Walla Walla *Union Bulletin;* and Nancy Stringfellow, former manager of the Boise Book Shop—all gave me helpful hints, though neither they nor I realized at the time that we were doing anything more than talking shop.

Most of the dams in the Snake River watershed are controlled to some degree by the Walla Walla District of the United States Army Corps of Engineers, a district which currently has the largest civil works load of any in the country. Colonel Robert Giesen (Retired), Colonel Richard M. Connell, Major Harold Matthias, Van Baldwin (Retired), Orville Murray, Robert H. Conway (Retired), and Frank King all went out of their way to supply me with detailed maps of the region, charts, statistics, or whatever else I needed. Equally helpful were John Oldfield, Henry McKinney, Merwin Jenkins, Floyd Shultz, Goldie Connell, and Emma Fagerstrom.

Don Basjen, who was Resident Engineer in charge of building Dworshak Dam when photographer Earl Roberge and I visited the site on several occasions, was most generous with his time and information. So was John Parvin, director of the nearby Fish Hatchery at Ahsahka, Idaho, the largest of its kind in the world.

In the Walla Walla office of the Bonneville Power Administration, William Kirkman (Retired), Harold Cantrell, Roy Nishi, and Mrs. Floyd Farris did me a number of favors which simplified my task.

In Portland, H. R. Richmond, Regional Administrator for BPA, Jessica Gilbert, his able secretary, Hector Durocher, and other staff members were most friendly and considerate.

To H. Calvert Anderson, executive vice-president of the Inland Empire Waterways Association, my thanks for material on Columbia-Snake barge traffic and the truck-barge side of past and present rate disputes.

To George Skorney, Director of Public Relations, Union Pacific Railroad, Portland, my appreciation for the loan and use of the ten-year file which he assembled and sent me on the Grain Rate War of the 1960s. And to Jerry Landau, Walla Walla manager of the Union Pacific, my thanks for several favors.

Charles F. Luce, chairman of the National Water Commission, New York City, and Executive Director Theodore Schad, have supplied me with bulletins and reports which have been very useful. Ray Holmes, E. J. Gullidge, and the staff of the Pacific Northwest River Basins Commission, Vancouver, Washington, have done likewise. Harry Stivers, Francis Warnick, and Gerry White, United States Bureau of Reclamation office in Boise, have lent me much appreciated assistance.

In the office of the Idaho Department of Commerce and Development, Boise, I owe a word of thanks to Al Minton, Dorine Goertzen, and staff. In the Portland office of the United States Fish and Wildlife Service, my thanks go to Walter Ray and Grant Woolley, whose prompt responses to my requests saved me a number of hours.

Robert McCaig, Montana Power Company, Great Falls, is too old a friend merely to thank in print; the rest shall be cared for later. Logan Lanham and Bob Brown, Idaho Power Company, Boise, who supplied me with rare historical material, I also hope to thank in person as well as in print.

To Dr. S. Thatcher Hubberd, Sierra Club, Spokane, I am grateful for several suggestions.

To Senator Henry M. Jackson for his quick work in supplying me with a transcript of the Middle Snake River Moratorium Hearing when I needed it in a hurry, I am most appreciative—as I am to Jeanne (and Dr. John) Bond for expediting matters under rather complicated circumstances.

Jim Kinney, who gave us several interesting hours as we flew and filmed the canyons of the lower Snake, hereby is fervently thanked for his skill as a pilot. Thanks also go to a group of personal friends, who, in the name of research, helped me explore the Snake, the Clearwater, and the Salmon by private and chartered boat. Whether running rapids, ascending navigation locks, going aground on mud flats, catching steelhead, losing steelhead, or enduring such hardships as open-air lunches of cold chicken, cheese, and chilled Chablis, Dr. Robert and Iris Beck, Warren and Sheila Bateman, of Walla Walla, and Miles and Clair McGovern, of Tulsa, Oklahoma, were good company; they came to appreciate, I'm sure, the dedication with which a writer must pursue truth.

I am also indebted to the professional rivermen who took us on research and picture-taking expeditions: Perk Lyda, Orofino; Guy Snyder and Everett Spaulding, Lewiston; and Jim Zanelli, Oxbow, Oregon. These white-water men—like others of their breed in the area—know how to demonstrate the uniqueness of a living river to the layman as no words or pictures can.

Bill Maxwell, of the J. R. Simplot Company, Pocatello, gave freely of his information and time; Ray Rostron, Twin Falls Chamber of Commerce, was helpful; and F. L. Sprague, United States Forest Service, Boise, conducted us on a fascinating tour of a twenty-million-tree nursery farm.

Special thanks for guidance through their logging operations go to Jack M. Gruber, Public Relations, Gordon Dickinson, Logging Superintendent, and Art Schultz, Safety Supervisor, Potlatch Forests, Inc., Lewiston, Idaho.

For the Atomic Energy Commission, Idaho Falls, Mack Corbett and Richard Blackledge, Public Relations Department, gave us a thorough briefing of what goes on at the National Reactor Testing Station before we undertook our tour of the EBR-II facility. Adrian Allen, our on-site guide next day, answered my questions with patience; Harry Lawroski, Superintendent of Reactor Operations for the Argonne National Laboratory, explained things without confusing me too much; while J. D. Bassett and Joe Davis were equally kind.

During the writing of the book, I asked two personal

friends to read certain sections in the manuscript. Part Five, "River of Treasure," was read by Dr. Walter H. Brattain, who had a special interest in it because his grandfather (from whose experiences I have quoted at length) was personally involved in the early gold strikes. I appreciate his helpful comments.

Colonel James H. Beddow (Retired) read Part Eight, "River of Power." Because of his years as a dam builder with the Army Engineers, his later experience as a consulting specialist with a private engineering firm, and currently as manager of the Walla Walla County Port District, I felt him well qualified to judge how badly or how well I had condensed a rather large technical subject into layman's terms. Whatever philosophy may have crept into the writing is mine, not his. But he was most helpful in clarifying a couple of murky spots.

I must give Jim Beddow further credit for what fishermen and golfers call "local knowledge." Ninety percent of a research problem is solved, I discovered, once the writer puts his question to the man best equipped to answer it. But finding that man may be difficult. Thanks to his broad acquaintance in the Pacific Northwest, Jim usually knew where the inquiry should be made—and I leaned upon this knowledge heavily.

So far as the photographs in the book are concerned, they speak for themselves. What is not evident are the energy, enthusiasm, and spirit with which Earl Roberge took them. As long as the light lasted, he was indefatigable, and my only serious problem was how to reduce the 1,500 color photographs he took to the hundred or so that could be used in this book. Credit should also be given to his wife Gertrude, and their daughter, Millie, who kept the studio going and a light burning in the window to greet him at the end of his many eighteen-hour days, and to Dr. George and Stella Faulkner, who took Earl on several back-country trips.

Since I have already thanked my wife Jeanne for the tremendous amount of work she did in researching and indexing the book, I suppose there is no point in admitting that it was fun having her along on the trips. Truth is, there was no way I could have left her at home. And I know she joins me in saying that much of the credit for whatever success SNAKE RIVER COUNTRY may have must go to Gordon Gipson, who had the vision to see what the book *could* be, to Kathy, who believed in it, too, and to all the rest of the Caxton Printers family—who have made this such a memorable experience for both of us.

BILL GULICK

Table of Contents

List of Illustrations

SNAKE RIVER COUNTRY

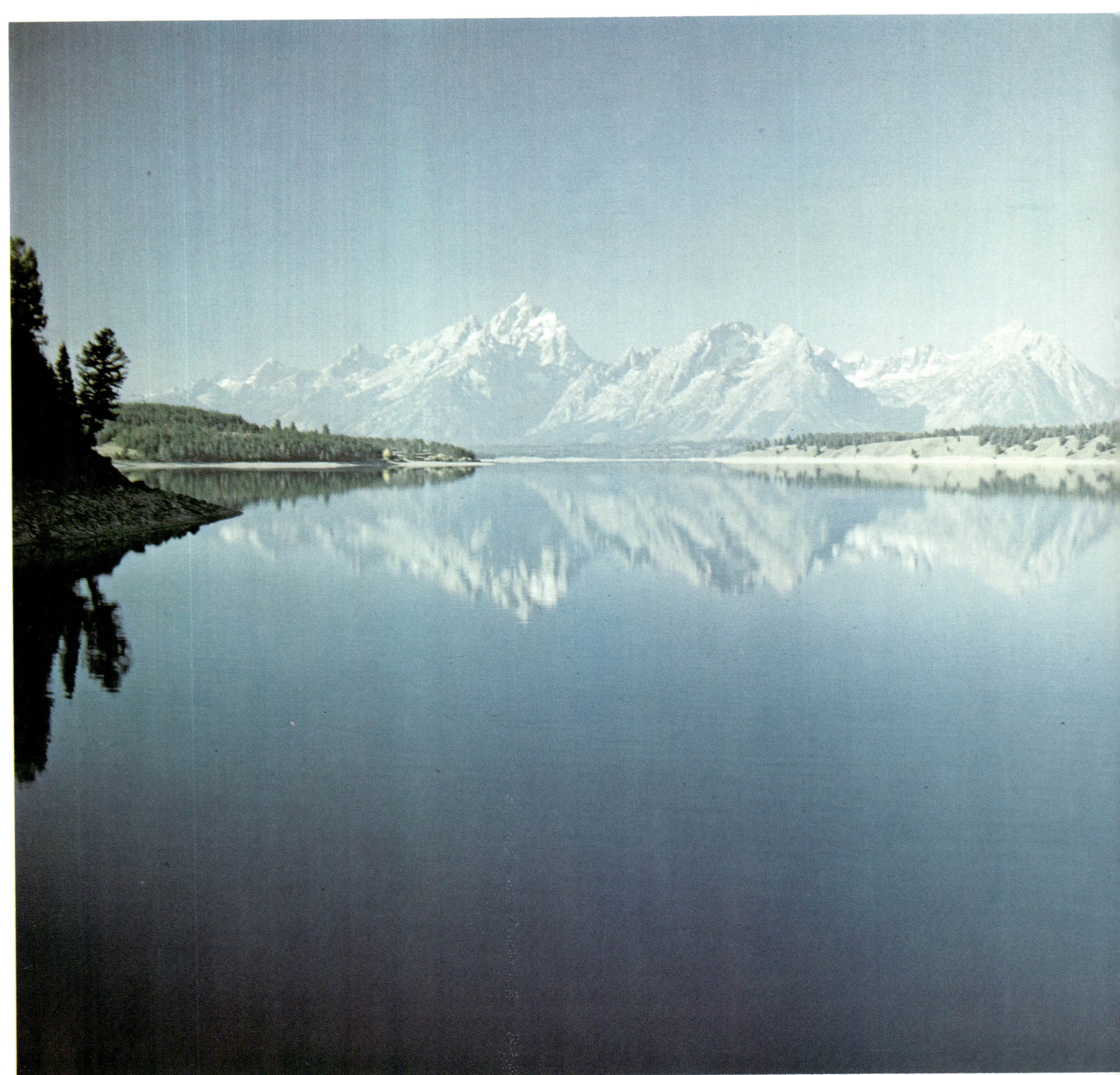

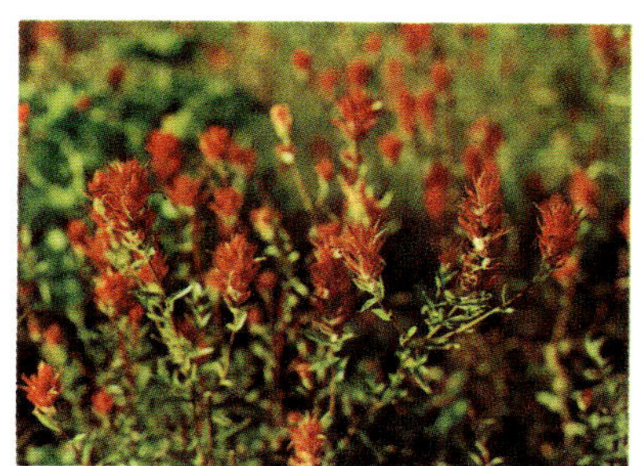

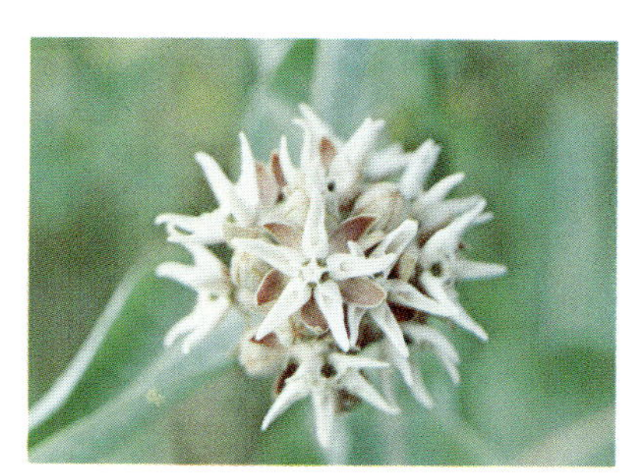

Introduction

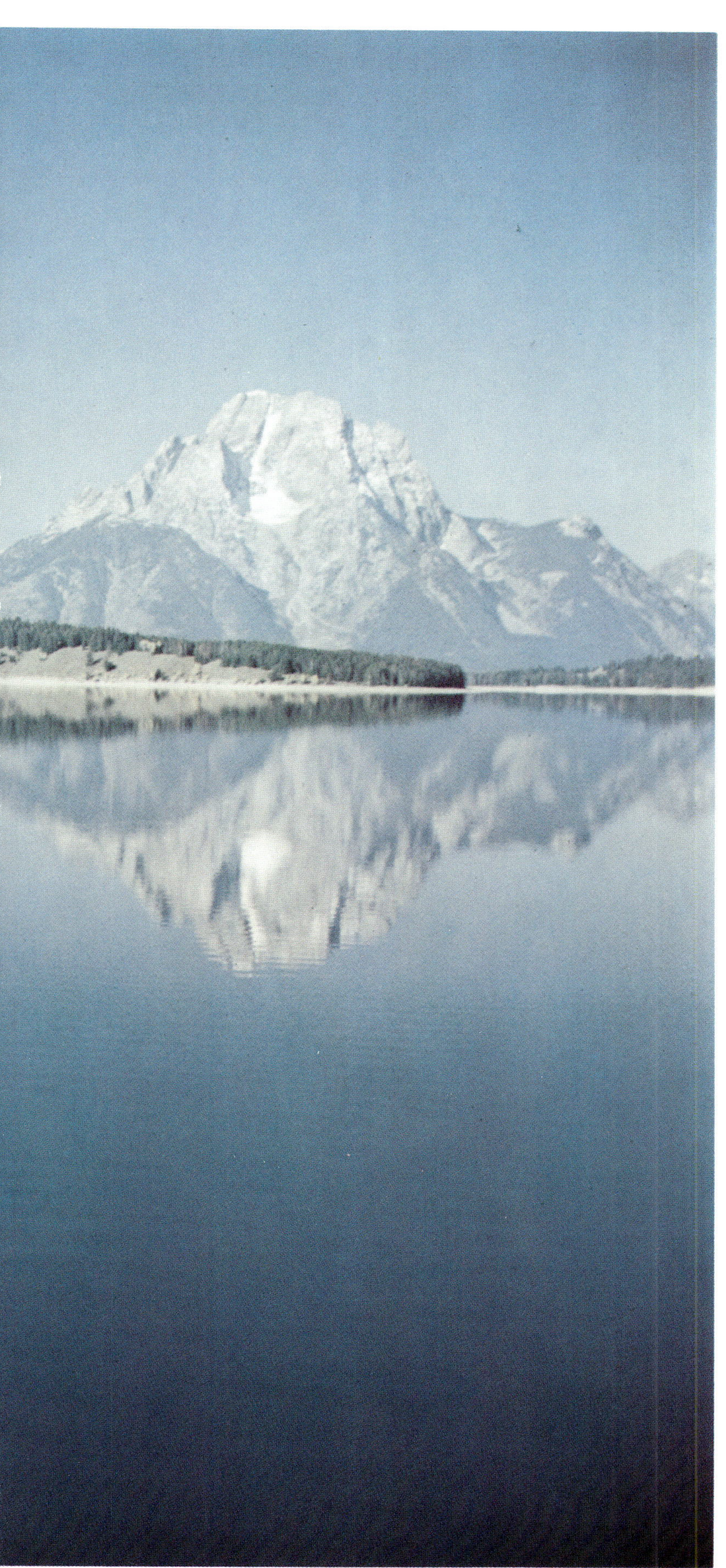

Born in incredible beauty,

Jackson Lake and the Grand Tetons, near the Birthplace of the Snake, on a Flawless September Day

flowing through incredible desolation,

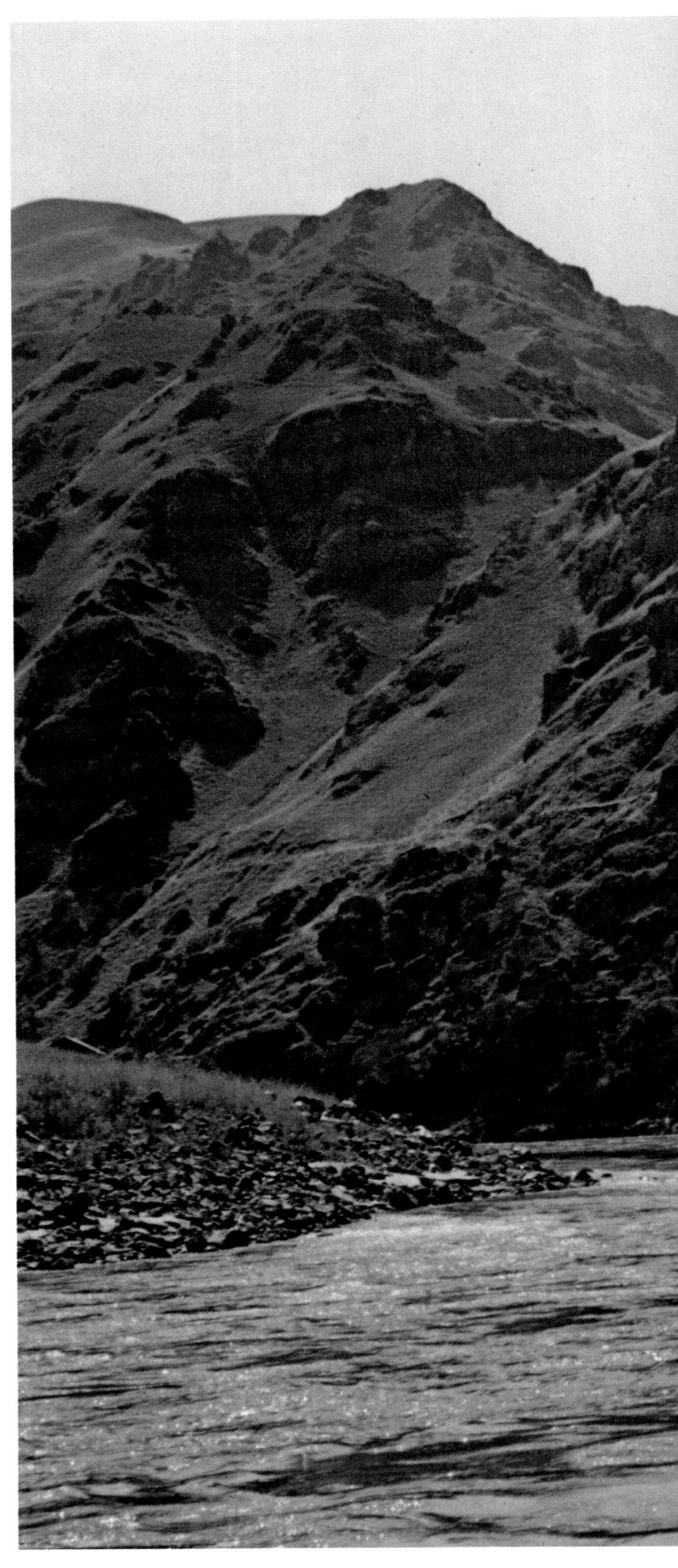

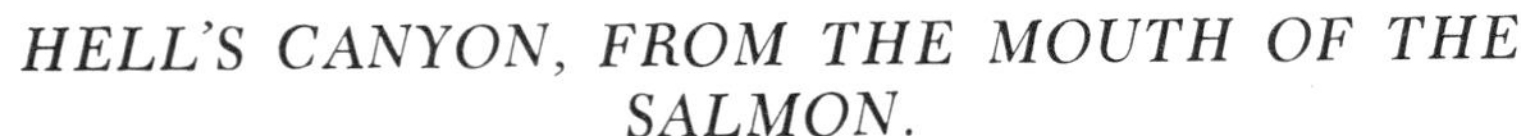

HELL'S CANYON, FROM THE MOUTH OF THE SALMON.

It is this one-hundred-mile stretch of free-flowing river that conservationists hope to preserve in its natural state, and that power advocates want to turn into a series of slackwater pools behind dams.

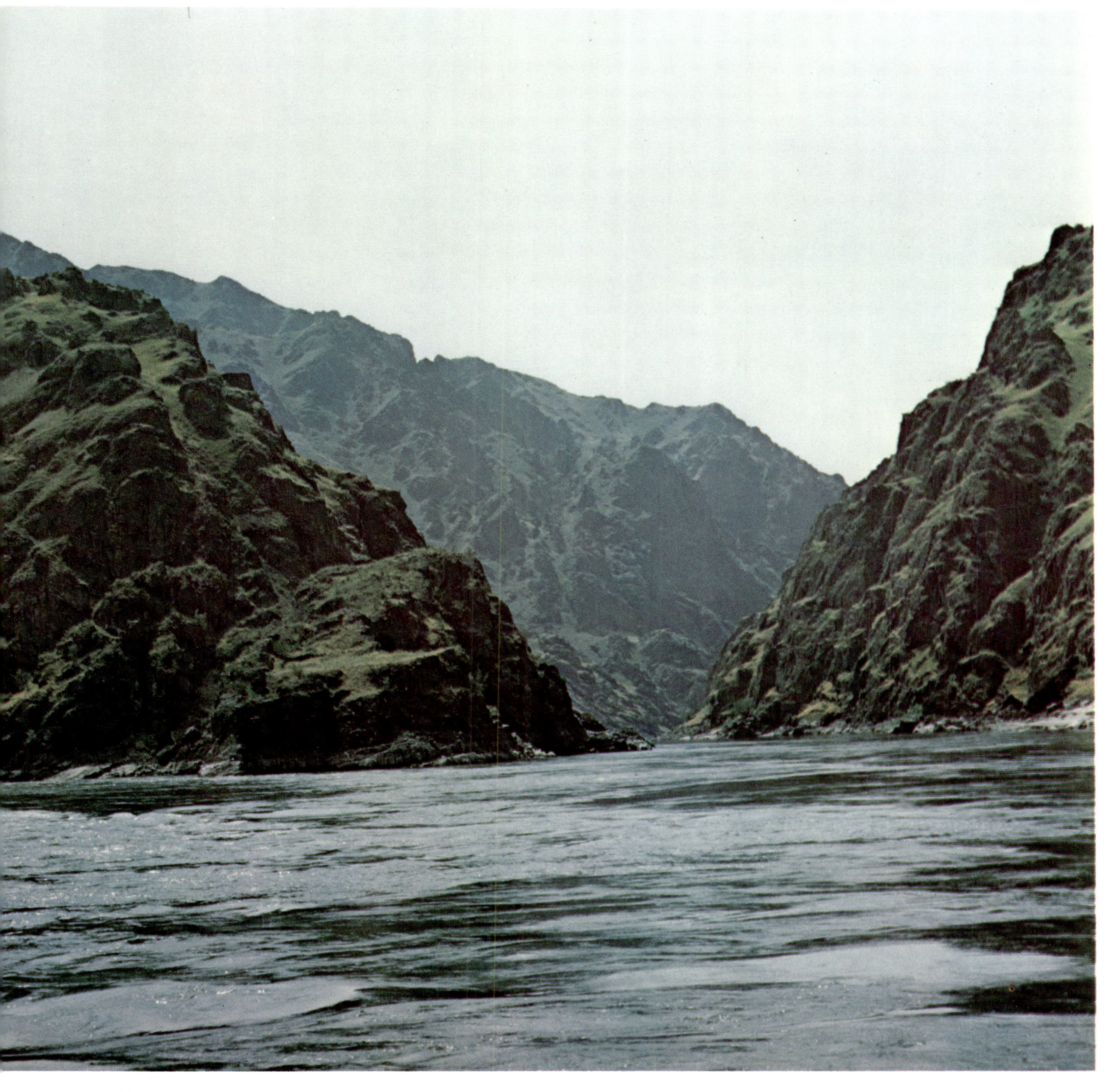

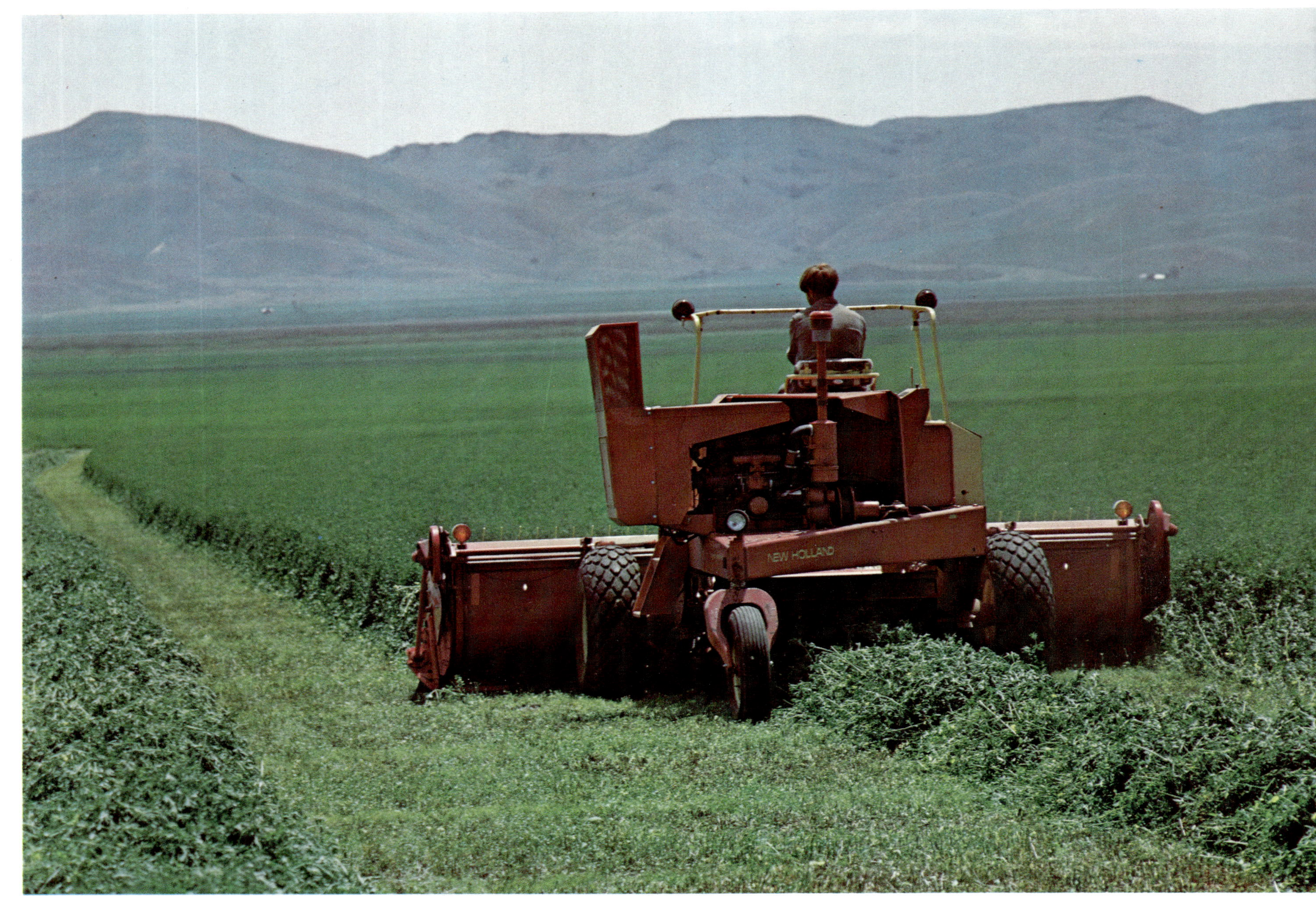

Cutting Alfalfa on Irrigated Farmland North of Gooding, Idaho

nourishing incredible fertility. . . .

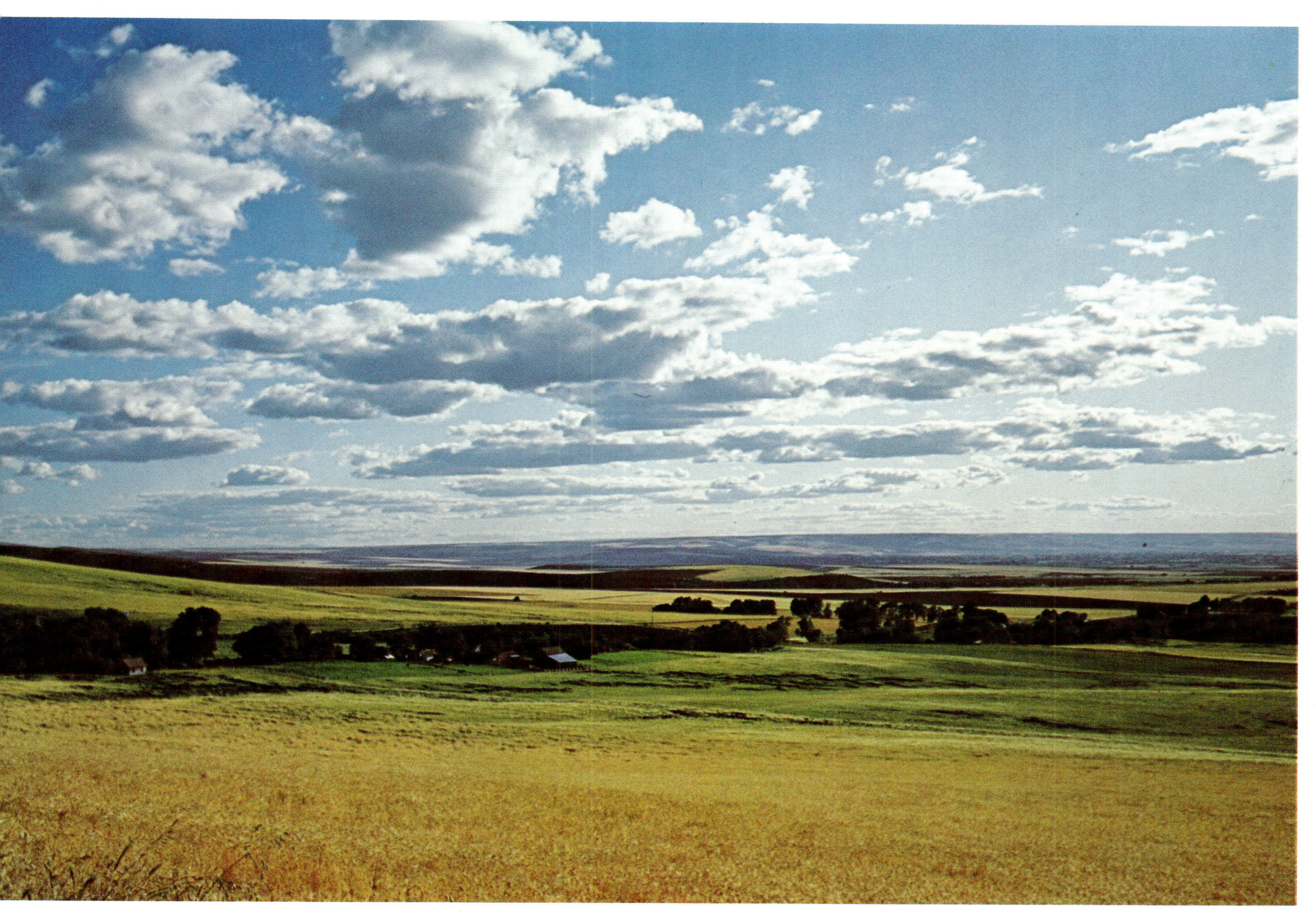

Wheat Fields in the Walla Walla Valley, Southeastern Washington

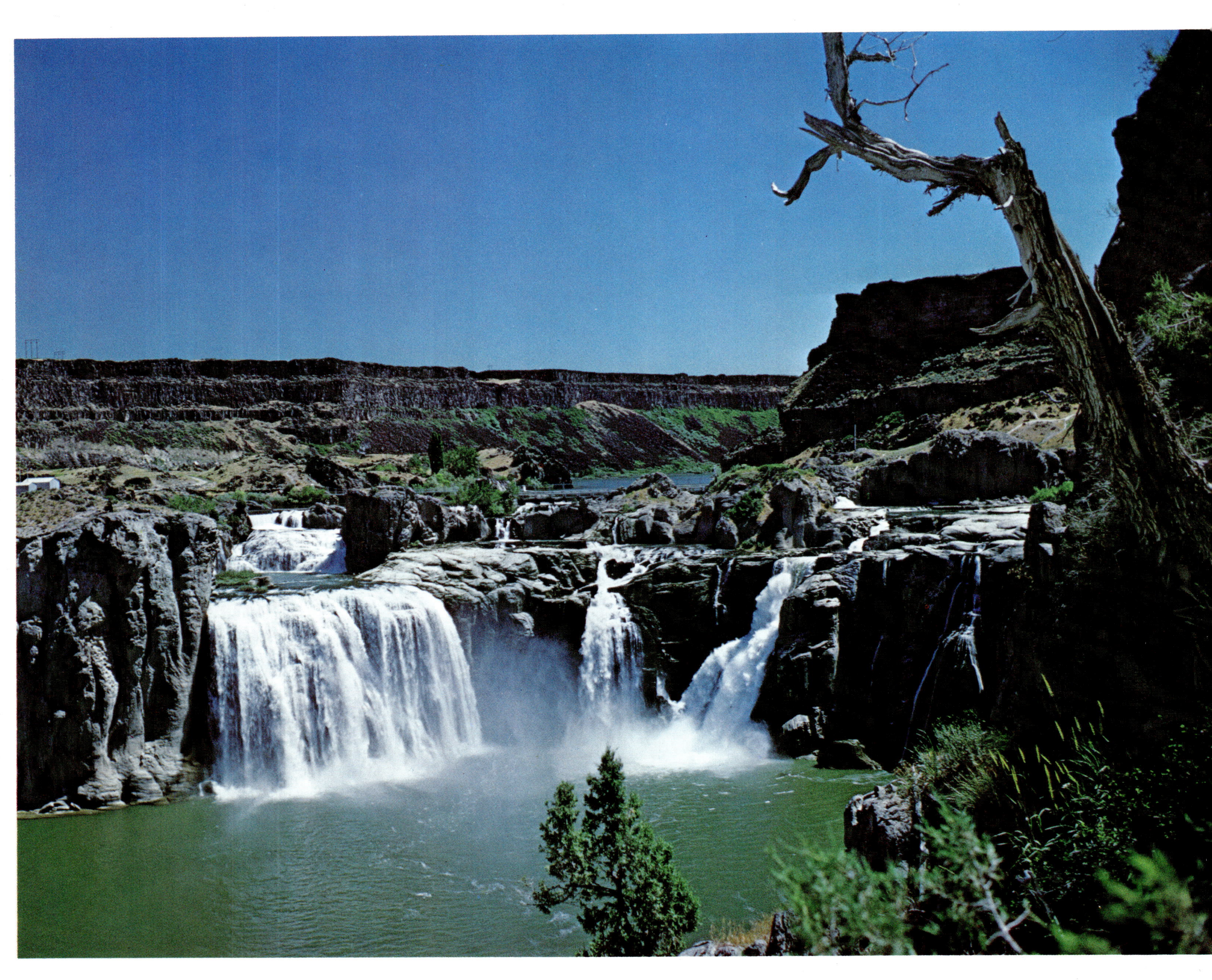

SHOSHONE FALLS, NEAR TWIN FALLS, IDAHO
On the mainstem Snake, they are 212 feet high, 35 feet higher than Niagara.

This is the Snake River.

GRAND TETON, JACKSON HOLE, WYOMING
Some of these peaks top 13,000 feet

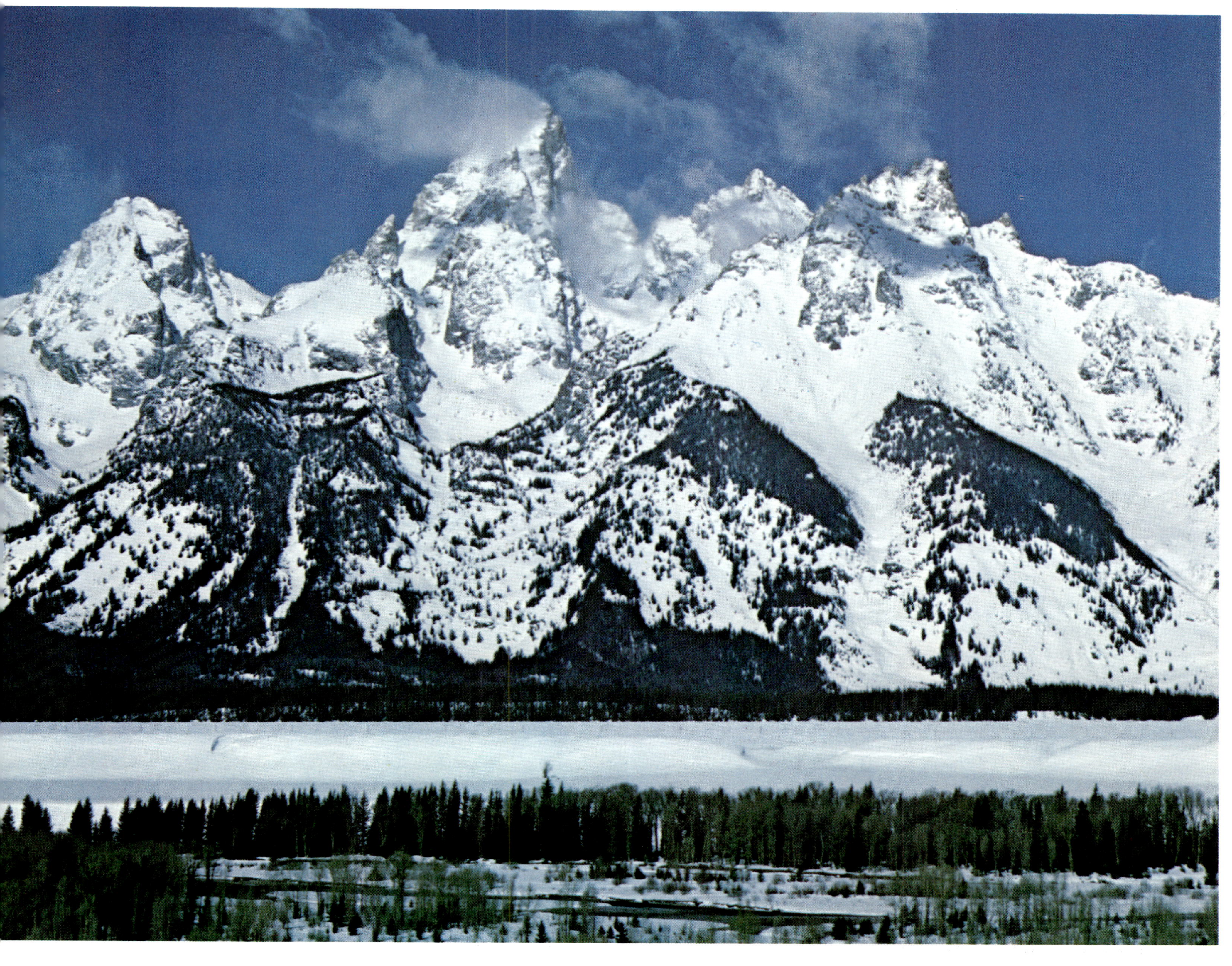

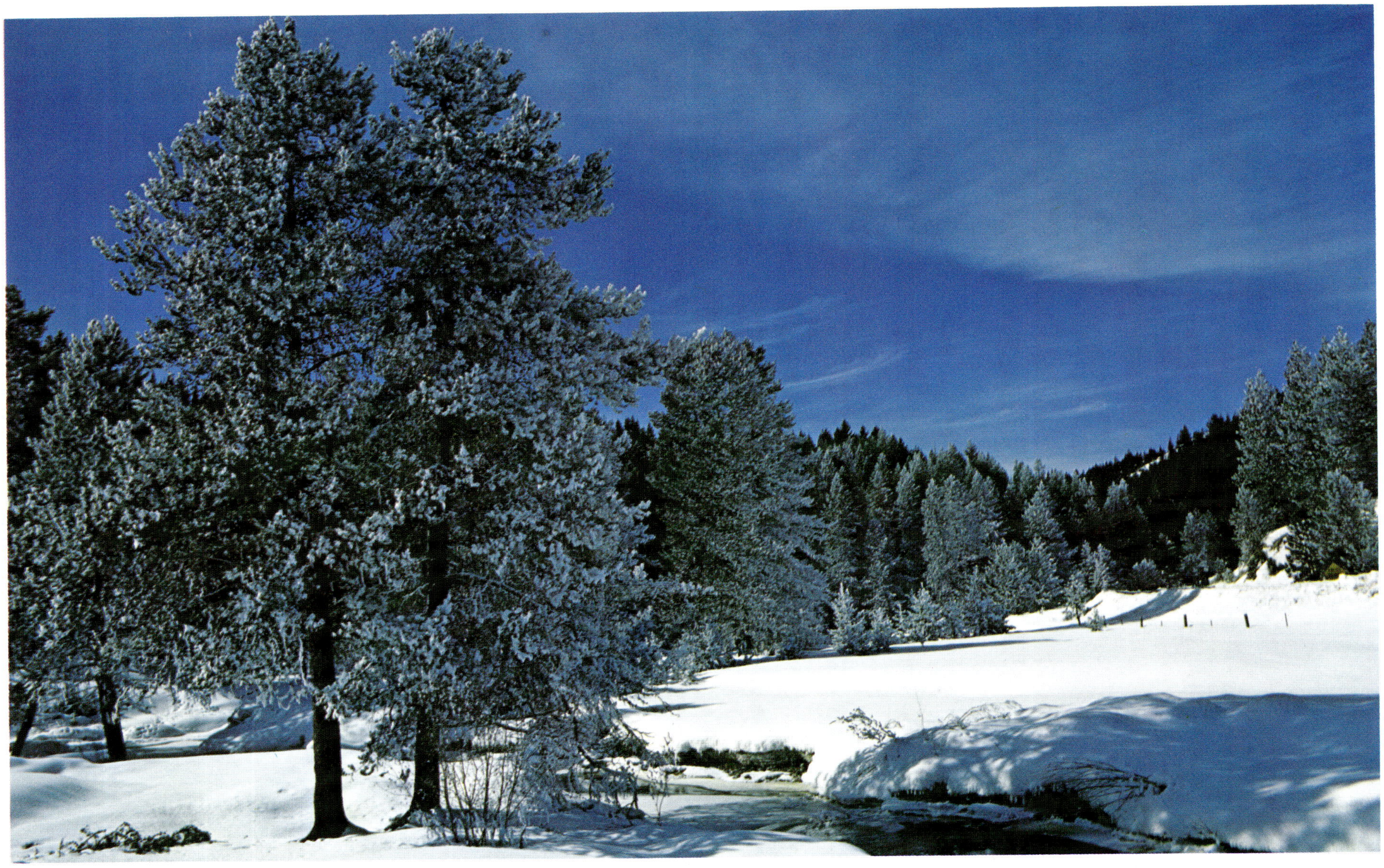

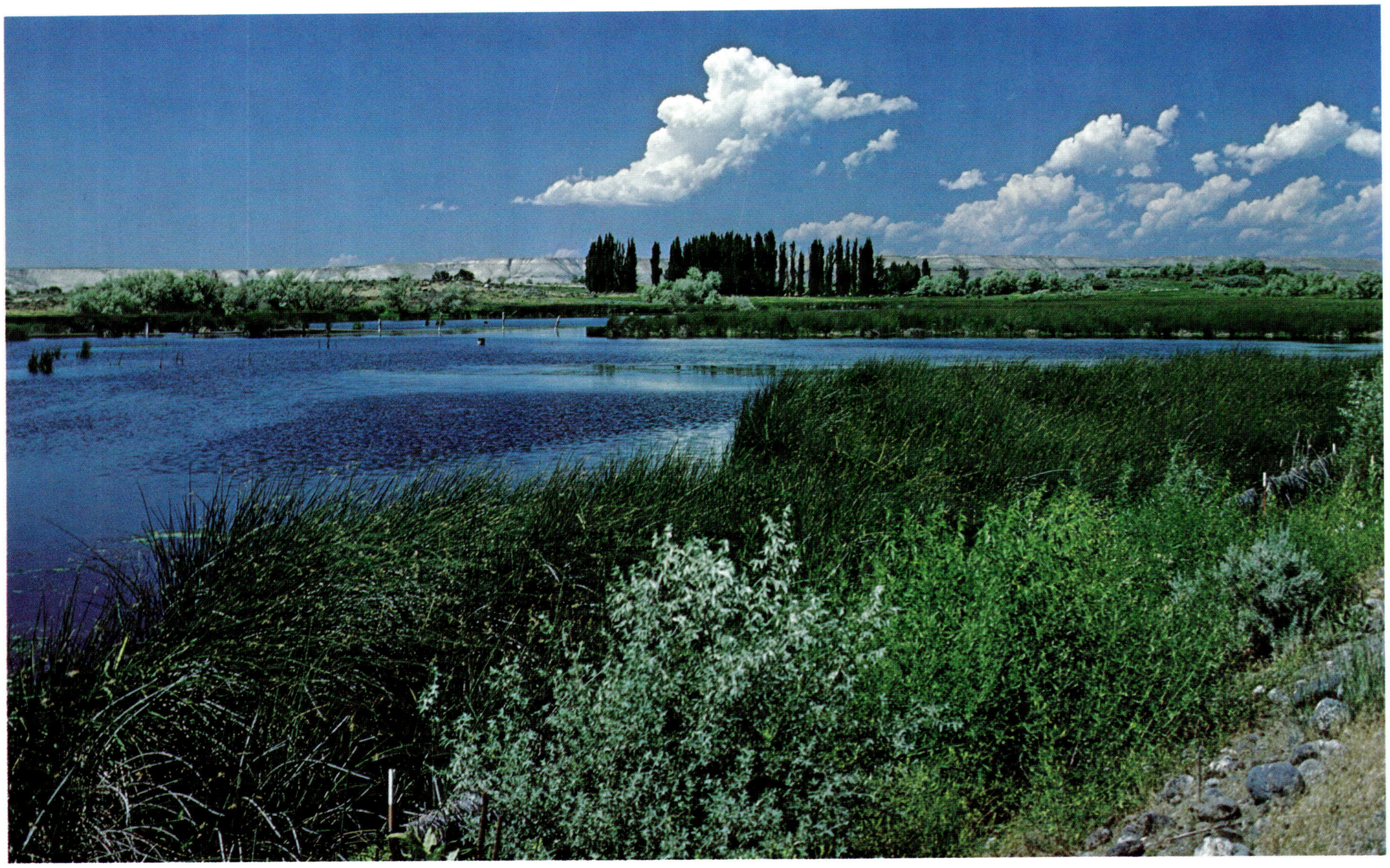

In all probability its name resulted from a misunderstanding between Plains Indians who lived east of the Continental Divide and Shoshone Indians who inhabited the Pacific Slope. When strangers met in olden times, I once was told by an elderly Nez Perce Indian,[1] their first concern was: "Are you friend or enemy?" If the stranger's intentions were peaceful, he raised his right hand, palm open and forward, to show it held no weapon. When a like response was given, he then moved the hand in a back and forth sideways gesture, asking while still at a safe distance: "Identify yourself."

On the Headwaters of the Payette River, near McCall, Idaho

Each Western tribe had its distinctive hand sign, the exact meaning and origin of which has long since been lost in the mists of time. When the white man came into the Snake River Country and started naming people and things, he translated those identifying gestures into his own tongue —English or French—in practical rather than scientific terms.

For example, the upper Missouri River Indian who pointed first at a dark-colored object, then at his lower extremities, became a "Blackfoot"; the one who passed an index finger under his nose, a "Nez Perce"; the one who pressed both palms to his forehead, a "Flathead"; and the one who made an oval gesture over his abdomen, a "Gros Ventre."[2] The fact that the Blackfoot's feet were red, the Nez Perce seldom if ever pierced his nose, the Flathead did not indulge in head-flattening, and the belly of the Gros Ventre was no bigger than that of any other Indian, had no bearing on the matter.[3] Nor was there any logical reason—other than common usage—why French names stuck with one tribe while English names clung to another.[4]

They had been named—and that was that.

When the white man came, the principal tribe occupying the Snake River Country was the Shoshone.[5] To identify themselves, these Indians held the right hand at waist level, palm toward the body, and then moved it forward in a sinuous gesture, like a fish swimming upstream. Undoubtedly, the sign meant "fish," for salmon formed a major portion of their diet. There were also many rattlesnakes in their country, which they may have eaten when no better food was available. By folding under two fingers and making the same sinuous gesture, the sign meant "snake."

The Hagerman Valley, near Buhl, Idaho

Being masters of saying with a single natural hand sign what the white man could say only with many words, the Shoshones probably were telling strangers: "We are the chosen people who live by the great river up which the big

1. Caleb Carter, Lapwai, Idaho, in 1955.

2. *Indian Sign Language*, by W. P. Clark, L. R. Hamersly & Co., 1885. Reprint by Rosicrucian Press, San Jose, California, 1959. Clark was a captain, Second Cavalry, who spent six years among the Indians.

3. A minority of early-day Indian and white historians say these tribes *were* named because of individual customs or traits, but a majority say no.

4. Usage Americanizes "Nez Perces," while "Gros Ventre" is given the French pronunciation.

5. Pluralize it "Shoshoni" if you like. But the early explorers wrote "Shoshone" or "Shoshones." Later, "Snake" or "Snakes" commonly denoted the same nation.

fish run," rather than: "We eat snakes."[6] But to the newcomers, this was an ominous, deadly country, filled with unaccustomed terrors: towering mountains, deep canyons, impassable lava flows, convoluted terrain that defied unraveling, and a brawny, treacherous, rapids-filled river that disdained to flow broad and tranquil to the sea as Eastern rivers did. So, of the many names by which this principal tributary to the Columbia was known from the first vague hint of its existence to its final definitive exploration, only the singularly appropriate name "Snake" stuck.

When I first saw the Snake through a rain-streaked train window twenty-six years ago, my feelings were akin to those expressed by the explorers, trappers, missionaries, emigrants, prospectors, and settlers whose journals I had read with so much interest, until I, too, was impelled to make the overland trek to Oregon. Awe, fascination, fear, puzzlement. This was no majestic Hudson, beautiful Ohio, muddy Missouri, or mighty Mississippi, which then—like the first explorers—were my models for rivers. Valleys of great rivers were filled with farms, industries, commerce, and cities; they were the cradles of civilization; they were the easy water-level pathways binding one part of the country to another. Every student of geography and history knew that.

But the Snake River did not fit the model.

During a long ride across Idaho that gray spring day, I got only brief glimpses of the river, of farms, and of populated places which, by liberal definition, could be called cities. Tumbled black lava flows cooled into immobility; flat, endless plains covered with sagebrush; snow-covered mountain peaks in the far distance to north and south; and an immensity of empty space through which flowed a mostly unseen river lost deep in a steep-walled gorge. For hours on end, except for an occasional whistle-stop station, a sheep-herder's wagon, or a horseback rider making his lonely way across Zane Grey landscape, there was nothing else visible.

A few months earlier, a New York friend of mine, who had made the trip I was making now, had written me: "So far as I am concerned, that's the bleakest country on earth. If they can't find some way to irrigate it, the Government ought to fence it off and keep people out. When you see it, you'll agree with me, I know. . . ."

He was almost right. Until four o'clock that afternoon, I did agree with him. Then the train stopped for a few min-

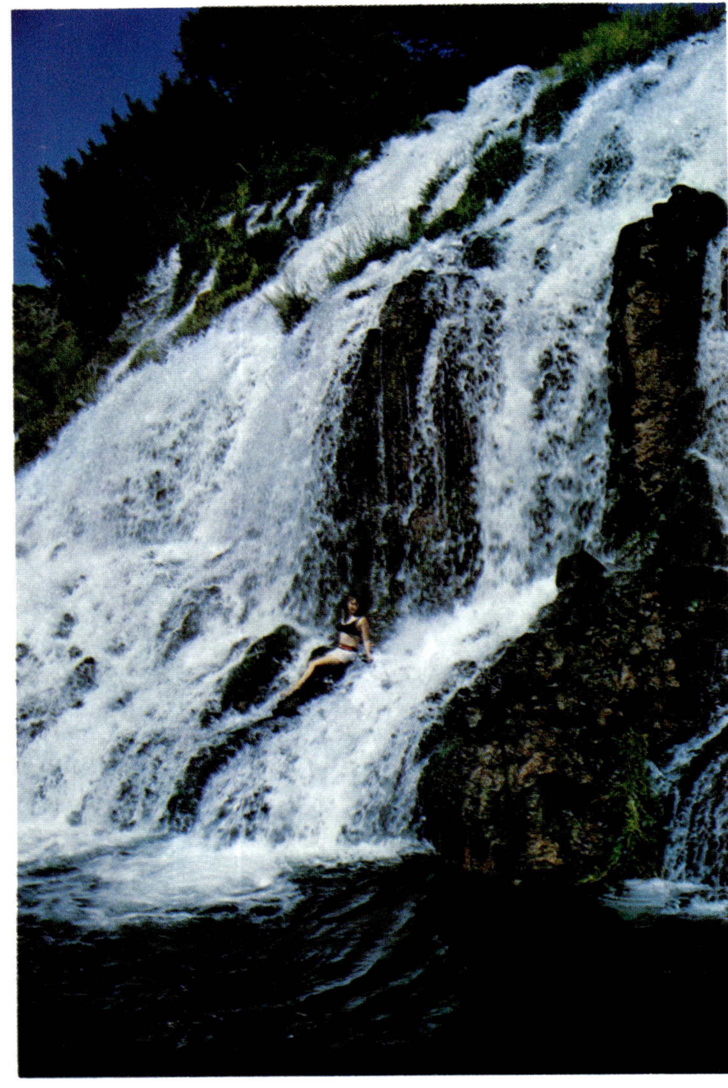

IDAHO AQUIFER

From the canyon wall of the Snake, near Buhl, Idaho, aquifers spew forth millions of gallons of water that has traveled many miles underground through broken lava formations. In one of the "Thousand Springs," as they are locally called, Millie Roberge shivers in forty-degree water on a 108-degree Fourth-of-July day.

---

6. In *Indian Sign Language,* p. 337, Captain Clark writes: "The Shoshone or, as they are usually called, Snake Nation, formerly occupied with the Bannacks (*sic*) an immense geographical area, including what is now known as Southeastern Oregon, Idaho, Western and Southern Montana, the northern part of Utah, Nevada, and Western Wyoming.

"In my investigations I was unable to ascertain positively why they were called Snakes, but one of their old men claimed that it was because they formerly ate serpents. . . ."

Dr. Merle Wells, Archivist for the Idaho Historical Society, says that the Indians were named "Snakes" by their Plains neighbors to the east, possibly because they reputedly used snakeheads painted on sticks to terrify their enemies. "In any event, the name used to identify the Snake Indians in various Siouan languages was the word for snake or rattlesnake. The French picked up the name from the Plains Indians, and the British, in turn, translated it from the French." (Reference Series No. 38, Idaho Historical Society, Boise.)

utes at Boise, I got out to stretch my legs in golden spring sunshine, and, from the heights upon which the railroad station set, beheld the greenest, loveliest valley I had ever seen. Though the Snake River itself lay thirty miles to the south, it was obvious that the miracle of irrigation had transformed this valley from bleak desert to fertile garden spot, and, as the train rolled westward toward Oregon during the next hour or so across flat, intensively cultivated country, I began to appreciate the extent of the miracle.

Then, quite suddenly, the miracle ended. Turning from west to north, the Snake had left its desert canyon, joined us, and flowed placidly alongside the rails for a while, behaving as an aging river should in its lower reaches. But now there were mountains ahead. Big mountains. After competing for space with the river for a few miles into an ever-deepening gorge, the train gave up, crossed its blue-green, swirling waters, and headed west. As I watched the Snake disappear into a dark, looming mass of barren, volcanic rock, the conductor came through the coach and paused nearby. I asked him why the rails did not follow the river.

He told me. For most of its length, he said, the route of the Union Pacific followed the Oregon Trail. At this point, like the emigrants themselves, the railroad surveyors had been forced to choose between the difficult and the impossible. Northward lay Hell's Canyon—deeper by five hundred feet than the Grand Canyon—through which only the river could pass. Westward lay the Blue Mountains, across which trail, rails, and highway had been laid only with great labor.

"Not far from here is a place called 'Farewell Bend'," he said. "The emigrants called it that because it was their last look at the Snake—and good riddance, they said. They hated the river. . . ."

Perhaps it was then—on that Portland-bound train laboriously climbing the Blue Mountains—that the character of the Snake River Country began to intrigue me.

It still intrigues me.

After I took my look at western Oregon and the Puget Sound area, I did what other people have done before me for a hundred years—retraced my steps and settled near the mouth of the Snake in eastern Washington. My justification for doing so was that I wanted to write a novel[7] dealing with the discovery of gold in Idaho Territory and the beginnings of navigation on the lower Snake River. Now, twenty-one years and quite a few novels later—half a dozen of which have dealt with the Snake River Country's historical past—I am still here—and more content with this part of the world than any other I have seen.

Somewhere along the way I learned that a great river influences the lives of the people in its watershed just as surely as the acts of those people influence the life of the river. Without water, people die. Without people's concern, a river dies.

Thus, this book.

Though there have been many studies of a technical nature on the resources of the Snake River Country, up until now no book has told the whole story of the river in layman's terms. All too often in talking to supposedly intelligent people living outside the Pacific Northwest, I have been appalled at their ignorance regarding the Snake and the problems unique to the country through which it flows. For that matter, most residents of the region know only a part of the story, dramatic though it is.

The late Stewart Holbrook, one of the Pacific Northwest's finest writers, used to say half in jest and half in earnest that we regional writers should not extol the wonders and virtues of our part of the country lest it be overrun by an influx of Easterners and Southern Californians who would spoil it for us. I agreed with him.

But bit by bit, the secret has leaked out.

Since it has, the time seems ripe to make a full confession, showing the beauties of the Snake River Country from Jackson Hole to its juncture with the Columbia by means of pictures, telling what the river has been, is, and may become in simple yet accurate words.

In length, drainage area, and volume of water carried, the Snake ranks sixth among the nation's rivers. To be more precise, it is 1,036 miles long, drains 109,000 square miles of country, and pours 36 million acre-feet of water a year into the Columbia—not quite half of the 85 million acre-feet which the Columbia is carrying at that point, and approximately one-fifth of the 198 million acre-feet which the Columbia contributes to the sea.[8]

Source of the Snake is Two Ocean Plateau at the 9,500-foot level in the southern part of Yellowstone Park, from whence it flows through Jackson Hole, the Hoback Mountains, and then crosses southern Idaho. Turning north, then, it moves through Hell's Canyon, Idaho, on its right, Oregon and Washington on its left, until it reaches Lewiston. There it swings west, flowing for 140 miles through southeastern Washington's fertile Palouse Hills until it joins the Columbia near Pasco at an elevation of 340 feet above sea level.

It is a river of many faces, many moods, and many uses, so I shall postpone detailed descriptions of it to later sections of this book. But there are a few items of general interest that should be mentioned here.

In the prehistoric past, the Snake may have flowed along a far different course than it now pursues. And its waters may never have reached the sea.

Professor Richard Clem,[9] Whitman College geologist,

———

7. *Bend of the Snake*, Houghton Mifflin, Boston, 1950. It was filmed as the movie, *Bend of the River*, starring James Stewart, Arthur Kennedy, and Rock Hudson by Universal-International and released in 1952. The resemblance between movie and novel was only coincidental.

8. These figures have been taken from *Upper Snake River Basin, Source to Powder River*, incl., Vol. 1, Summary Report, 1961, Bureau of Reclamation and Corps of Engineers; and *Water Resources, Appendix V, Columbia-North Pacific Region Comprehensive Framework Study, Vol. 1*, March, 1969, prepared by Pacific Northwest River Basins Commission, Vancouver, Washington.

9. Though it was Professor Clem who explained the "captured river" theory to me, he wishes to point out that he did not originate it. Credit for that goes to Harry E. Wheeler and Earl F. Cook, University of Washington and University of Idaho. For details, see their

thinks the Snake may be a "captured river"; that is, a river diverted from its original course by cataclysms of nature such as lava flows, ice ages, or the uplift or subsidence of land areas. In southwestern Idaho, where the Snake now turns north toward Hell's Canyon, Clem says, it may formerly have flowed in a southwesterly direction into what is now eastern Oregon and Nevada.

Where did its waters go from there? Perhaps into the Pacific by way of northern California's Feather River Canyon. Or perhaps nowhere. How could the waters of a great river go nowhere? By vanishing into thin air, drawn upward by the sun's incredible power of evaporation.

When I mentioned this possibility to a Corps of Engineers hydrologist, Robert Conway,[10] he nodded and said the idea was perfectly plausible. It fact, as a speculative exercise, he once had mentally plugged up the entire flow of the Columbia River near The Dalles—all 144 million acre-feet per year—applied the annual evaporation rate of standing water in the area, and, in imagination at least, stopped the river's flow to the sea forever.

"In this part of the country, water in a still pool evaporates at the rate of forty inches a year," he said. "According to my calculations, a plug rising to the 2,500 foot elevation level would spread the Columbia over a large enough area

-----

"Structural and Stratigraphic Significance of the Snake River Capture, Idaho-Oregon," *Journal of Geology*, Vol. 62, No. 6, November, 1954, pgs. 525-36.

10. Now retired. Since a lake of this size would inundate much of eastern Washington's fertile lands and thriving cities, we will never see it. But there is ample geologic evidence that in time past such lakes did exist.

that its entire flow would be taken up by evaporation, without a drop of water ever spilling over the top."

That plugs or lakes of the required size shall ever stop the flow of the Columbia or the Snake is beyond the realm of probability, of course. But merely speculating upon what *could* be done to a river by man—just as, in geological ages past, *has* been done by the forces of nature—brought home to me in dramatic fashion the awareness that if we are going to save and use our rivers in the best possible manner, we had better understand them.

Basic to the process of understanding is the destruction of myths, half-truths, and wishful thinking. Faced as our country now is with so many problems, we can build no solid solutions on the sands of fantasy. Yet for years we have attempted to do just that. To cite only one tragic example: As settlers came West and attempted to farm lands in regions of marginal moisture, some nameless promoter coined the happy phrase: "Rainfall follows the plough."[11] The theory, joyfully embraced by real-estate agents and sincerely believed by thousands of land-hungry little people, was that the breaking of ground and the planting of crops altered rainfall patterns for the better.

We learned different—but it took a long, painful while.

To tell the story of the Snake in simple, understandable terms requires treating it as nine distinct rivers. And the logical place to begin is with the myth—the river white men who never had seen it believed it to be—and how that myth was gradually dispelled. . . .

-----

11. Voiced as early as 1846 by expansionists such as William Gilpin. See *Virgin Land: the American West as Symbol and Myth*, by Henry Nash Smith, Harvard University Press, 1940. Also *Beyond the Hundreth Meridian*, by Wallace Stegner, Houghton Mifflin, 1954.

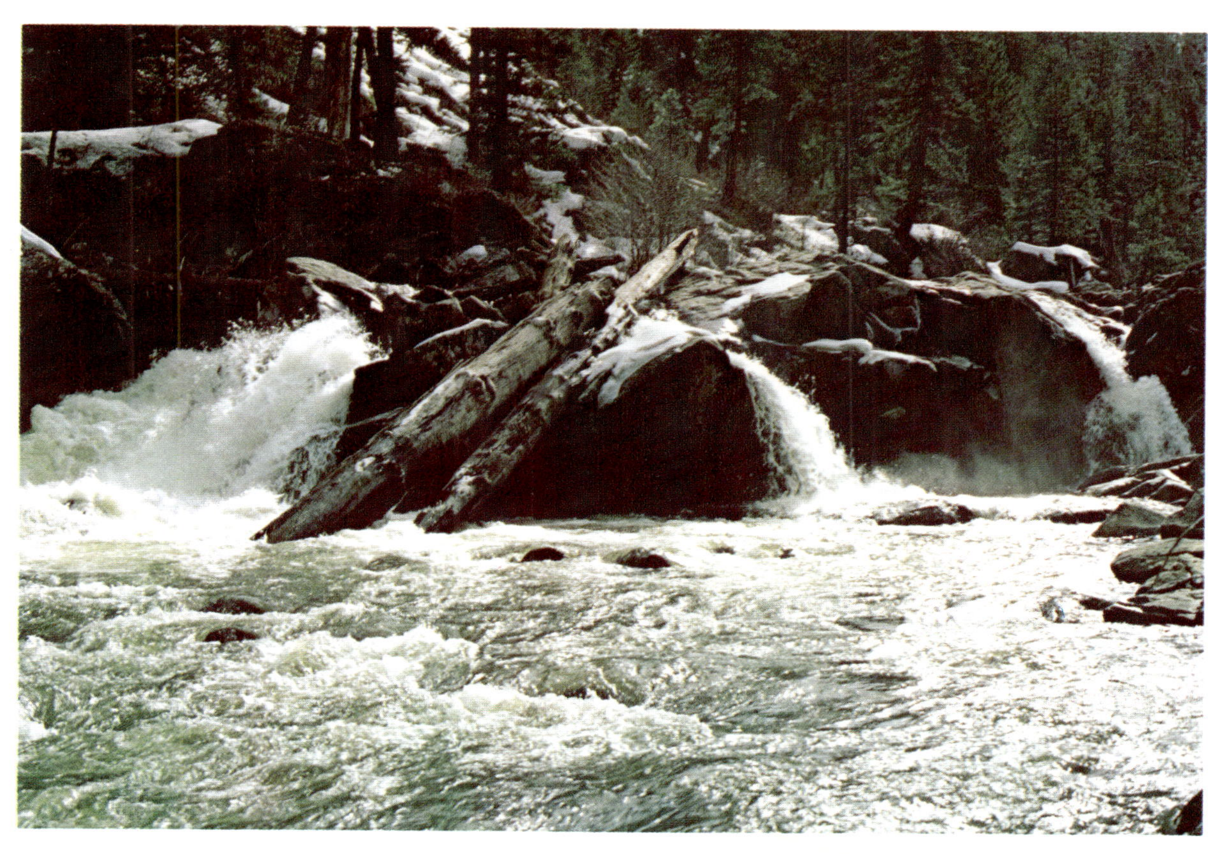

The Little Salmon River, North of New Meadows, Idaho.

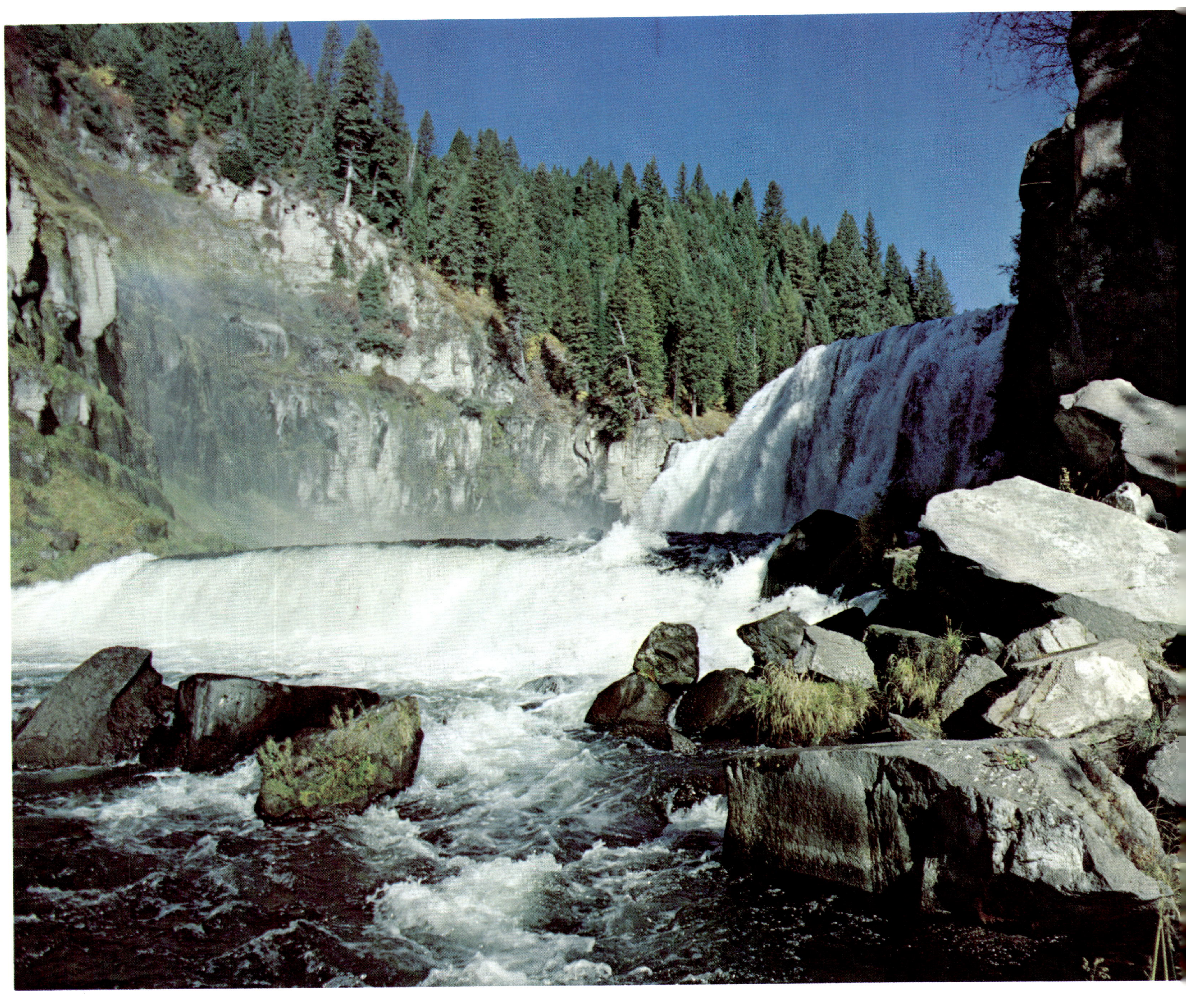

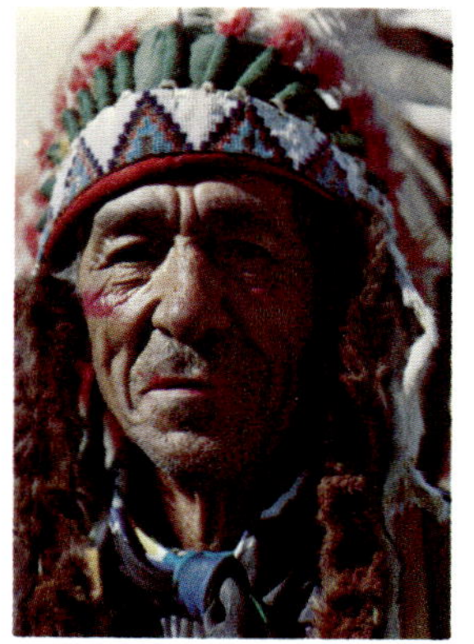

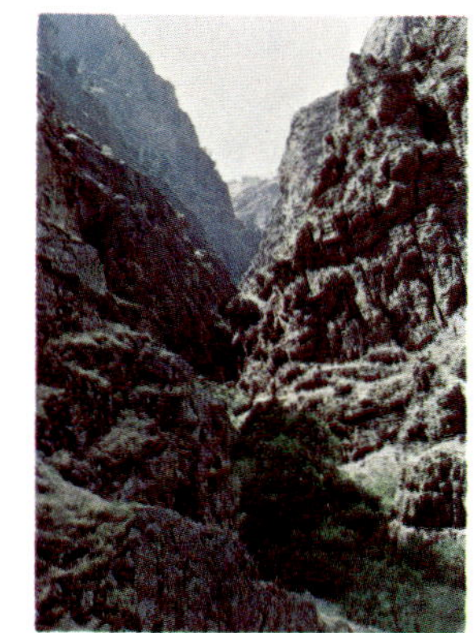

PART ONE

River of Exploration

1673-1813

1.

The dream of an easy water passage to the East Indies died hard. Since the Spanish and English explorers were having no luck finding a sea route through the North American continent, adventurers by land sought to make the dream a reality by discovering a river that would accomplish the same purpose. Some were honest men, who, in their writings, obviously were speculating upon meager bits of information they gleaned from the Indians. Others were self-promoters, who believed that hearing about a river was just as good as seeing it.

Let's take a sampling of both, bearing in mind that this was what passed for knowledge of the Snake River Country between the date of the landing of the Pilgrims and that of the Lewis and Clark expedition.

Father Jacques Marquette noted the mouth of the Missouri as he passed down the Mississippi in 1673. He wrote that the Indians spoke of a meadow, five or six days up the river, whence a stream ran westward. "Through this I hope to reach the gulf of California," he wrote, "and thence to the East Indies. If God gives me health, I do not despair of one day making the discovery. . . ."[1]

La Salle expressed a similar belief.

Mathieu Sageau, who had been with La Salle, told a tale so imaginatively untrue it must be admired. He claimed actually to have crossed the Western Mountains, descending a river to towns governed by a king blood-kin to Montezuma. Though he did not name the river, he saw gold there in greater abundance than in Peru; the King's apartment floor was paved with it. He saw a caravan of three thousand oxen laden with it, and while in that fabled land he and his French comrades were royally entertained. ". . . any woman who refused them was punished with death; and on their way thither they encountered lions, tigers and leopards, which offered them no harm. . . ."[2]

In the same vein, Baron Lahontan, in 1688, wrote of having traveled eight days up a tributary to the Mississippi called "Long River," during the course of which he passed natives more civilized than any in the East. He met four slaves, he claimed, who drew him a map on deerskin of their western country—which unfortunately he did not see—and told him of a river that emptied into a salt lake three hundred miles in circumference, and that ". . . the lower part of that river is adorned with six noble cities surrounded with stone. . . ."[3]

Of all the speculation, half-truths, exaggerations, and downright lies that were circulated during this period, the one credited to Daniel Coxe, published in 1722, probably gained the widest credence.[4] The Missouri, he wrote, was navigable to its source, thence less than a half day by horse or foot to the westward-flowing river. His authority? Apparently nothing more than a lively imagination and a facile pen.

In 1743, the French traders and explorers, the Vérendrye brothers, reached the eastern base of the Rocky Mountains in what is now Montana, heard of a great western river flowing into the Pacific, but did not see it.[5] A few years later, a Yazoo Indian living in the lower Mississippi area told a French writer a tale which, true or not, possessed a certain romantic charm.

In 1745, the Yazoo Indian claimed, he had ascended the Missouri for one moon, turned to the right, and, after several days, reached what he called the "Beautiful River," which flowed into the Western Ocean.

1. Bancroft, H. H., *History of the Northwest Coast,* San Francisco, 1884, Vol. 27, p. 111.

2. Ibid, p. 590.

3. Ibid., pp. 112, 589.

4. Ibid., p. 122.

5. *Oregon Historical Quarterly,* Vol. 26, No. 2, June 1925, p. 122.

Left: Mesa Falls, Henry's Fork, North of St. Anthony, Idaho

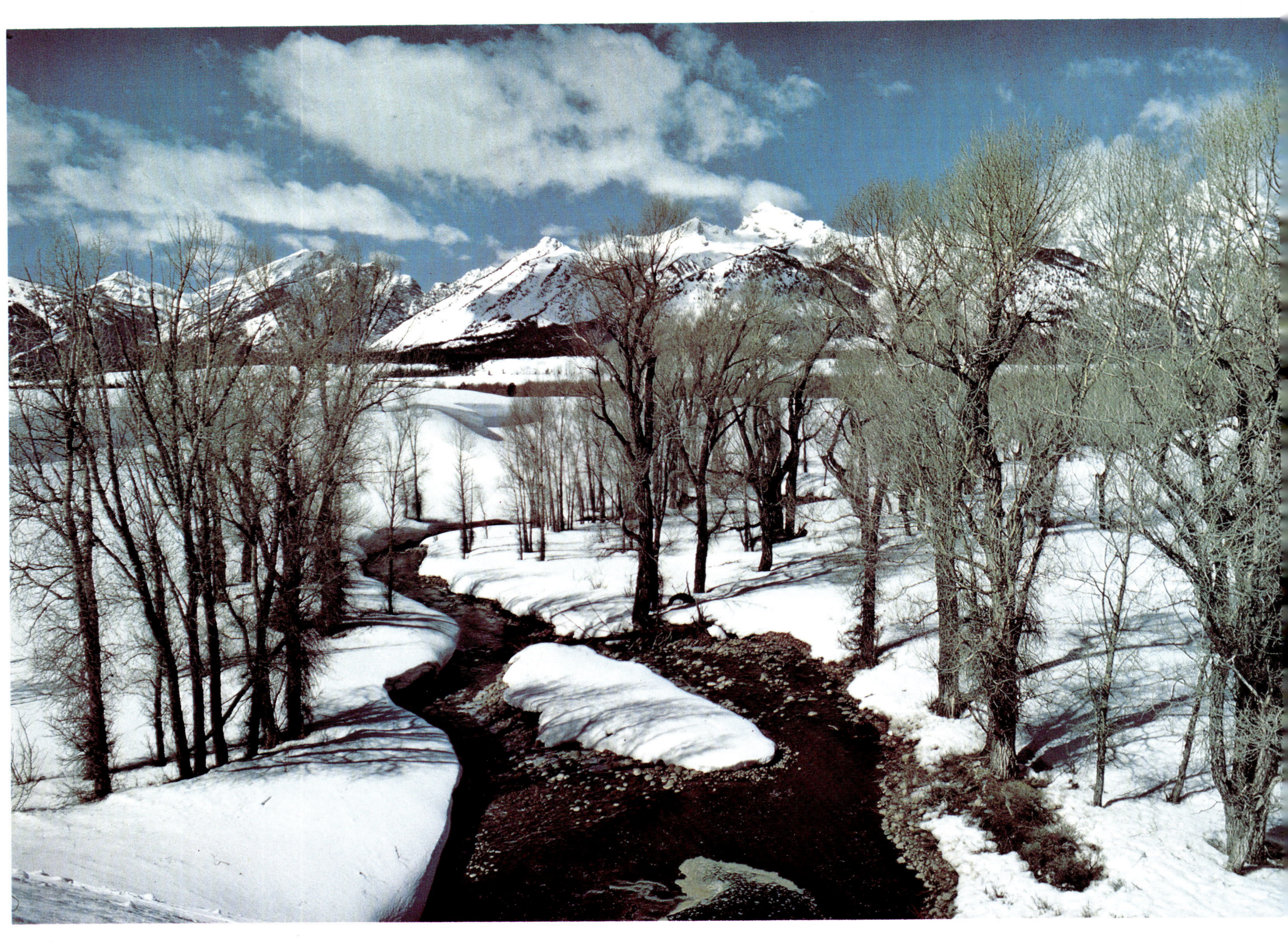

"I saw many mountains which I dared not cross for fear of blistering my feet," he related. Meeting some natives who invited him to swim with them in the Beautiful River, he replied that he needed bathing badly enough, but that he was afraid of the crocodiles. When informed that such monsters did not inhabit these northern waters, he bathed with pleasure.[6]

Whether it was Robert Rogers or Jonathan Carver who first used the word "Oregon" around 1765 is a question historians long have debated. Both did use it in one spelling or another; both claimed the Indians had told them of a river flowing into the Pacific; and both proposed exploring expeditions which never were made.[7] The terms "River of the West," "Mountains of Bright Stones," and "Shining Mountains" were used, and Carver wrote prophetically: "To the west of these mountains . . . may be found . . . countries full fraught with all the necessities or luxuries of life; and where future generations may find an asylum. . . ."[8]

* * *

2.

Soon after the American colonies won their freedom from Great Britain, the period of speculation regarding the geography of the Far West ended and the era of factual discovery began. By sea, the American, Captain Robert Gray, found the mouth of the River of the West in 1792, sailed up it twenty-five miles, and gave it a name that stuck—the Columbia. By land, a Britisher, Alexander Mackenzie, crossed Canada, discovered the Fraser River, and reached the Pacific in 1793.

Learning of these discoveries, John Ledyard, a former corporal of marines with the great English explorer Captain Cook, proposed to Thomas Jefferson, then United States Minister to France, and to John Paul Jones, America's naval hero, a wildly ambitious scheme entailing not only an overland journey across the North American continent but a trek across Siberia as well. Though both Jefferson and Jones liked the idea, nothing came of it, but this may have been the seed planted in Jefferson's mind out of which grew the purchase of the Louisiana Territory from France and the mounting of the Lewis and Clark expedition.

Judged by the standards of its time, this was a highly scientific expedition whose planning, leadership, and execution have no equal in American history. But it was based on a misconception of geography that would have led to disaster had less good judgment been shown by its leaders. For it relied on the existence of a river whose reality proved to be totally different from its myth.

It was believed in 1805 that the great rivers which drained the United States ran to cardinal points of the compass. The Saint Lawrence was the River of the East. The Mississippi was the River of the South. Since the Missouri flowed downhill from what must be the dividing range of the United States, it was assumed that just beyond that range there must be a River of the West. Judging from known rivers and mountains of the East, there should be no great obstacles between watersheds, and, once launched on the waters of the westward-flowing river, boats should experience little difficulty making their way to the sea.

President Jefferson accepted this idea, for it had been set forward by the best cartographers of the day. The divide had been called "a range of hills," a portage of "about twenty miles," or "a half day by horse or foot." Jefferson called the river "Oregon." In actuality, even after the incredible hardships of ascending the confusing maze of streams which eventually combine to form the Missouri, the "ridge of hills" proved to be two hundred and twenty miles of the cruelest kind of going before the waters of the "Oregon" were found navigable.

Moving ahead of the main party with several hunters, Meriwether Lewis crossed into the Snake River watershed August 13, 1805.[1] From Three Forks, where the Missouri proper begins, he had ascended the Jefferson and Beaverhead, reaching the Pacific slope through Lemhi Pass, a few miles southeast of Salmon, Idaho. Since the expedition's most pressing need was to establish friendly relations with the Indians of the region so that guides, food, boats, and horses could be obtained, he was delighted to encounter a band of Shoshones and made every effort to prove he came in peace.

The Indians took alarm and fled. But with typical canine curiosity their pets lingered for sniffs and looks at the white stranger.

"The dogs were less shye than their masters," Lewis wrote. "They came about me pretty close. I therefore thought of tying a handkerchief about one of their necks with some beads and other trinkets, but the dogs would not suffer me to take hold of them. . . ."

Cautiously proceeding down the valley, Lewis overtook three women, one of whom ran away in panic. The remaining pair, one elderly and the other a girl of twelve or so, sank down on the ground and gave up in abject despair, as if expecting to die.

"I took the elderly woman by the hand, raised her up [and] repeated the word '*tab-ba-bone*' [white man]," Lewis

6. Bancroft, p. 598.

7. Lavender, David, *Westward Vision*, McGraw-Hill, 1963, p. 53. Rogers spelled it "Ouragan" in a petition to the English Parliament in 1765. Carver visited the upper Mississippi, 1766-68, cribbing information from many sources, but his *Travels* were not published until 1788. He spelled it "Oregon." The often-repeated statement that the poet William Cullen Bryant first publicized the word in "Thanatopsis" is not true. This poem was not published until 1815.

8. Bancroft, Vol. 29, p. 134.

1. The rest of this chapter has been excerpted from *The Journals of Lewis and Clark* as edited and interpreted by Bernard DeVoto, Houghton Mifflin, 1953, pp. 189-206.

Left: Jackson Hole, Looking toward the Tetons, in February

wrote, "and strip[ped] up my shirt sleeve to s[h]ew her my skin . . . they appeared instantly reconciled."

The elderly woman fetched the one who had run away, Lewis painted her cheeks with vermillion—emblem of peace —and they had walked about two miles when a band of sixty warriors came galloping toward them at full speed. With cool-headed courage, Lewis laid down his rifle, walked away from it, and met them unarmed. The women spoke to the leaders of the band, who then ". . . advanced and embraced me in their way, applying cheek to cheek, and we were all besmeared with their grease and paint till I was heartily tired of the national hug. . . ."

Chief *Ca-me-ah-wait* of the Shoshones smoked a pipe with Lewis and gave him information about the country ahead.

This clear, rapid stream, the Lemhi, in a half day's journey discharged into one twice its size coming in from the southwest. The larger stream, the Salmon, presently turned west, but its current was so rapid and the canyon through which it flowed so precipitous "that it was impossible for us to pass either by land or water. . . ."

Receiving this unwelcome information, Lewis hoped Chief *Ca-me-ah-wait* was exaggerating.

The friendly Shoshones gave Lewis his first taste of salmon, which he liked, and agreed to furnish thirty horses to carry the baggage of the party behind. Lewis was pleased with the size and quality of the horses, which he described as equal to the best of Virginia, and he noted that some bore Spanish brands and bridle bits. Of the Shoshones, he wrote: "Notwithstanding the extreme poverty of these poor people, they are very merry. . . ."

They were also suspicious. To the west lay the country of their enemies, the Nez Perces; to the east, that of their enemies, the Blackfeet. Since this large party recently had passed through Blackfoot country, the stranger who had asked them for assistance might be leading them into a trap. When Lewis learned the reason for the chief's growing reluctance to keep the bargain he had made, he overcame it with a direct challenge to the Shoshone leader's pride.

White men considered luring friends into a trap a dishonorable thing to do, he said, but, conceding such a possibility, he hoped there were men among the Shoshones who were not afraid to die.

"I soon found that I had touched him on the right string," Lewis wrote. "To doubt the bravery of a savage is at once to put him on his metal. . . ."

Chief *Ca-me-ah-wait* and half a dozen braves rode back with Lewis and his companions to meet the main party, which, with its baggage, still was making its slow way up the east side of the divide. When George Drewyer, a hunter, killed two deer and an antelope and a feast was held, more Shoshones joined the group, and the Indians became so merry that they insisted on exchanging parts of their costumes with the clothes the white men were wearing. Word that in the party they were riding to meet were a woman of their tribe (Sacajawea) and a man with black skin (York) intensified their curiosity.

William Clark's surprise at seeing Drewyer and Lewis dressed like Indians, Chief *Ca-me-ah-wait* wearing Lewis's cocked hat with a feather in it, and Sacajawea jumping for joy as she attempted to convey the news that these were her people and the chief her brother, are pieces of real-life drama familiar to us all. But less well known is the fact that five days after he became the first white man to view the northern headwaters of the Snake River, Meriwether Lewis had a birthday.

On August 18, 1805, Lewis made this solemnly thoughtful entry in his journal:

> "This day I completed my thirty first year, and conceived that I had in all human probability now existed about half the period which I am to remain in this Sublunary world. I reflected that I had as yet done but little, very little, indeed, to further the happiness of the human race or to advance the information of the succeeding generation. I viewed with regret the many hours I have spent in indolence . . . and resolved in future . . . to live for *mankind,* as I have heretofore lived for myself. . . ."

* * *

3.

Lewis then turned his attention to practical problems, such as warning the men in the expedition to give Shoshone husbands, brothers, and sweethearts no cause for jealousy by their attentions to the "tawny damsels" (advice he doubted they would follow) and learning from Chief *Ca-me-ah-wait* the exact nature of the river he still hoped would afford an easy water passage to the Pacific.

Squatting on his heels, the chief drew a map on the ground and described the Salmon River in graphic sign language. Below the point at which the Lemhi entered the Salmon, that river flowed north for one day's march, and then inclined to the west for two days' march.

> ". . . here he placed a number of heaps of sand on each side, which he informed me represented the vast mountains of rock eternally covered with snow through which the river passed. [He said] that the perpendicular and even jutting rocks so closely hemmed in the river that there was no possibility of passing along the shore; that the bed of the river was so obstructed by sharp pointed rocks and the rapidity of the stream such that the whole surface of the river was beat into a perfect foam as far as the eye could reach; that the mountains were also inaccessible to man or horse. . . ."[1]

1. *Lewis and Clark Journals,* De Voto, pp. 208-50.

Right: A Meadow in Stanley Basin, on the Upper Salmon

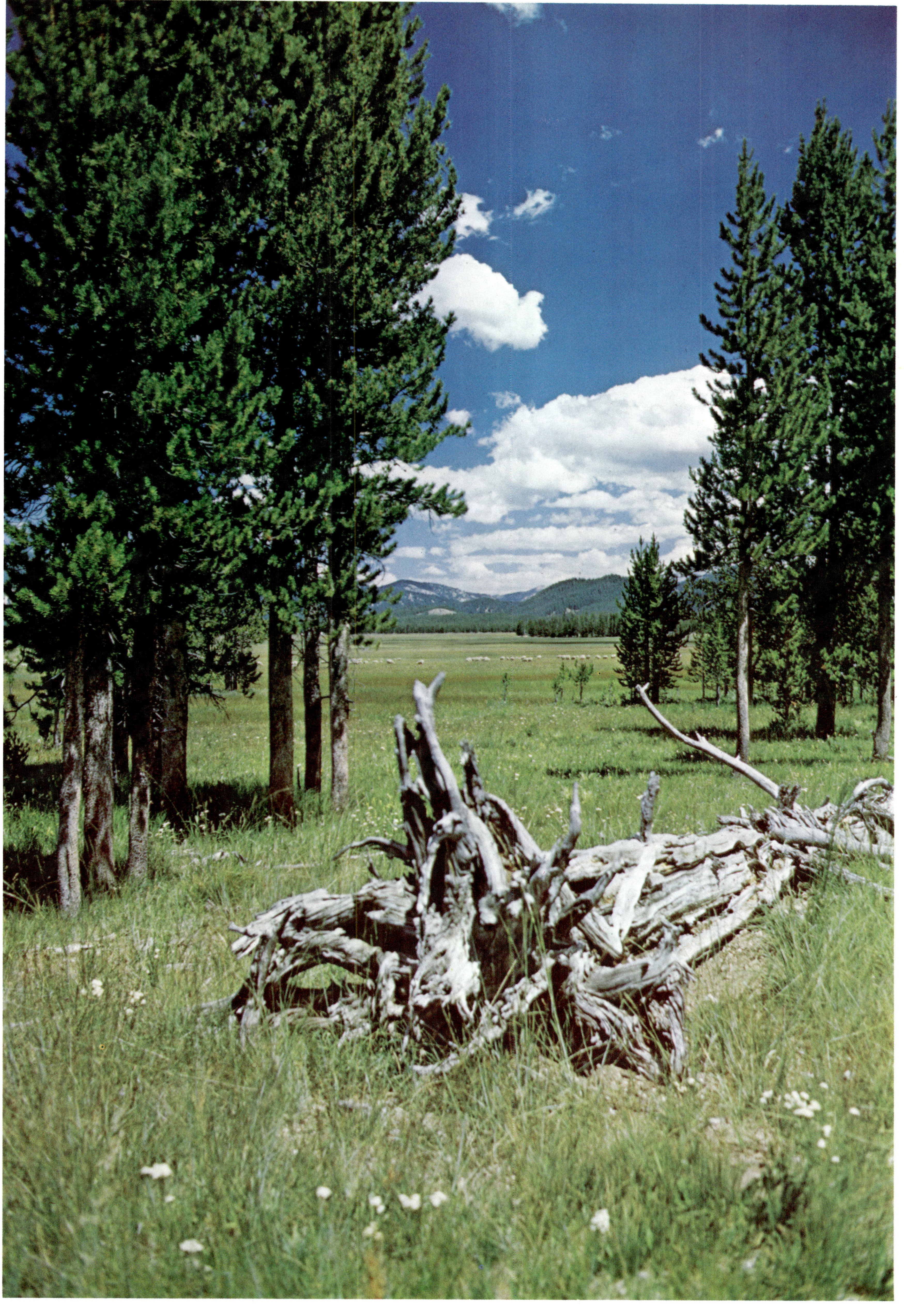

When asked about the country to the south and west, Chief *Ca-me-ah-wait* described it as rugged, mountainous, and very bad. The country to the north, then? This, too, was bad, he said, but some distance to the north the Nez Perces had a road by which they crossed the mountains to the buffalo country. To Lewis, this sounded like the most feasible route to the Columbia, for, if Indians with women and children could cross a range of mountains, surely the tough, seasoned men of the expedition could do the same. They would need horses, of course, but these could be acquired by trade.

William Clark, a man who must learn the impossibility of a task for himself before abandoning it, insisted on trying the river route. While on the upper Salmon, he wrote: "I shall in justice to Capt. Lewis, who was the first white man ever on this fork of the Columbia, call this Lewis's River. . . ."

In justice, the name should have stuck, for if ever an explorer earned his river, it was Meriwether Lewis. But the truth was, this was not the main tributary to the Columbia, and when, in later years, the Snake itself was discovered and mapped in its middle and upper reaches, the name "Lewis's River" fell into gradual disuse.

While Lewis and the helpful Shoshones brought the rest of the party over Lemhi Pass, Clark and a few men tested the canyon of the Salmon. Going proved to be as difficult as predicted—in a word, impossible. Clark wrote: ". . . without a road, over rocky hillsides where the horses were in perpetual danger of slipping to their certain destruction . . . with the greatest difficulty and risk made five miles and camped. . . ."

After losing three horses to injury or exhaustion, Clark gave up, rejoined Lewis and the main party, traded with the Shoshones for enough horses to carry the baggage, and the expedition turned north, seeking the Nez Perce road to the buffalo country. Their Shoshone guide, Toby, left them without waiting for his pay, and presently, near what is now Gibbon's Pass, they met another friendly tribe of Indians, the *Tushepau*, commonly called Flatheads.

The gurgling, throaty, extremely difficult to understand speech of these Indians inclined Lewis and Clark to believe that the tribe was of Welsh descent—a myth then hundreds of years old and still believed many years later.[2] Living as they did in a region bounded by larger, stronger nations—the Shoshones to the south, the Blackfeet to the east, and the Nez Perces to the west—the Flatheads tried to stay on reasonably friendly terms with all their neighbors. But their closest affiliation was with the Nez Perces, whom they called "cousins."

Yes, they told the white men, they knew the road which the Nez Perces took to the buffalo country and would guide the party to it. In fact, from Gates of the Mountains on the Missouri River to Lolo Pass, which was where the Nez Perce road crossed the mountains, it was just four days' easy travel. Clinging to the theory of ascending one river and then crossing to the headwaters of another, it had taken the Lewis and Clark party fifty-two days to traverse the distance between these same two points.

Thus, with much labor and wasted effort, the first lessons in Snake River Country geography were learned.

Accompanied by the Flatheads, and, later, by the Nez Perces, the Lewis and Clark party ascended Lolo Creek and crossed the mountains to the headwaters of a westward-flowing river. It was mid-September now, and, while rain and hail could be seen falling in the valley far below, up on the ridges along which the trail ran there was snow, and the going was dangerous.

There was little game to be found in this country, so the white men were forced to butcher and eat an occasional horse. This surprised the Nez Perces, who were a horse-loving people; their surprise turned to shock when they observed the white man's relish of dog meat, a dish the Nez Perces scorned. At the western foot of the mountains, the Lochsa River—which the trail was following—was joined by the Selway, coming in from the south, forming what the Indians called the *Koos-koos-kee*.[3] Near the present-day town of Orofino, the river became navigable at long last, and the party went into camp, cut down trees, and began making dugout canoes.

Chief Twisted Hair of the Nez Perces kindly supplied the explorers with salmon and dried camas, which made most of the white men sick. Clark treated them with emetics and salts. They managed to recover from both the malady and the cure.

At first, Clark did not think much of the Nez Perces. They were "stout, likely men, handsome women and very dressy in their way . . ." he admitted in his journal, but he thought them "selfish and stingy. . . ." Since their treatment of the party really was kind and hospitable, Clark's first judgment should be charged off to his weariness and illness. He soon changed his mind, calling the Nez Perces the most generous and likable tribe the explorers had met.

Launching their newly made dugouts, the party floated down the *Koos-koos-kee* without incident. After forty miles, it emptied into a much larger river coming in from the south. This, Clark decided, was Lewis's River, whose canyon the party had found impassable. From the Shoshones, he had heard of a river called the Snake, but it lay much farther to the south, he felt, and it did not occur to him that this might be it. So he put it down on the map as Lewis's River, describing its waters as greenish-blue, while those of the *Koos-koos-kee* were "clear as crystal. . . ."

Time was running short and the Pacific Ocean still lay a long way to the west. Below the flat, hill-surrounded plain where Lewis's River and the *Koos-koos-kee* melded their waters, the Nez Perces called the big river the *Ki-moo-e-nim*.[4] Chief Twisted Hair and Chief Tetoharsky, who had

2. *Across the Wide Missouri*, Houghton Mifflin, 1947. On p. 5, De Voto says: "Brigham Young was still looking for them in 1862. . . . George Catlin actually found them in 1832. . . ."

3. Like all Indian words, spelled many different ways.

4. The Snake. Lewiston, Idaho, is on the east side, Clarkston, Washington, on the west.

agreed to look after the party's horses, accompanied and guided the whites as the canoes floated on the swift current toward the Columbia. At this season, the water level was low and few of the rapids dangerous, though Clark admitted that some were run which would not have been attempted had the party not been so short of time.

There were a few upsets and dunkings, with valuable trade goods lost. But the amiable Nez Perces, a number of whom kept pace on horseback along the shore, always were there to help right and reload the dugouts. Their presence, that of the two chiefs, and the fact that the Shoshone woman, Sacajawea, always rode in the lead dugout, smoothed the way when new tribes of Indians were met. Sacajawea was particularly useful, for the inclusion of a woman was assurance of the party's peaceful intentions.

On October 16, 1805, the Lewis and Clark party reached the Columbia. Heartily sick of their fish diet, they shot some ducks, bought some dogs to eat, briefly explored the flat sagebrush desert in which the *Ki-moo-e-nim* placidly ended its existence,[5] and then moved on down the Columbia toward the sea. The party had been in the Snake River Country two months and three days.

* * *

4.

After building Fort Clatsop a few miles inland from the Oregon coast, the explorers spent a damp, miserable winter fighting fleas, flu, and boredom, and watching for a ship that never came.[1] Since trading ships were known to visit the mouth of the Columbia, President Jefferson had instructed Lewis and Clark to send two men home by sea with copies of all journals and maps, while the remainder of the party retraced the overland route. If the land traverse seemed "eminently dangerous," the entire party was to return by ship.

Why Jefferson made no arrangement to send a ship, instead of relying upon a chance meeting with one, is a lapse in planning that will always remain a mystery. But no ship appeared off that storm-swept coast.[2] With the party intact, the return trek overland began March 23, 1806.

By the time the party neared the mouth of the Snake, late April had come and the river was running in full spring flood. When the Walla Walla Indians described an overland route that would shorten the trip east, the white men gladly traded their boats for horses. To the southeast, snow-capped mountains were visible (the Blues),[3] and the Indians told Clark that beyond them a great river flowed westward across bleak, desert country.

This was the third time he had heard about the desert river: first, at the mouth of the Clearwater; again, at the mouth of the Willamette (near present-day Portland); and now here. Each time he failed to recognize it for what it was—the Snake. Calling it the "Multnomah," he theorized that it flowed from the Shining Mountains southwesterly across Spanish territory into either the Gulf of California or the Pacific Ocean.

Taking language difficulties and Indian conceptions of distance and geography into consideration, his error is understandable. But it would trouble cartographers for years to come.

Reaching the mouth of the Clearwater early in May, the whites camped with their Nez Perce friends in a pleasant, open prairie some miles up the river. Twisted Hair and Tetoharsky had taken good care of their horses, most of which were fat and strong. Indians with rheumatic aches, ulcerated sores, and eye troubles came frequently to Clark, the self-trained doctor of the party, for treatment. His medicants were salves, eye washes, and castile soap, and his philosophy of treatment closely akin to that of today's doctors: "We take care to give them no article which can possibly injure them. . . ."

This was a hungry season, for snow still lay deep in the high country, the salmon had not yet returned to the river, and food supplies dried for winter use were almost gone. But the Nez Perces gladly shared what food they had. On one occasion, the sharing was done in such an enthusiastic manner that Lewis lost his temper, a rare thing for him to do.

"While at dinner," Clark wrote, "an Indian fellow very impertinently threw a half starved puppy very nearly into the plate of Capt. Lewis by way of derision for our eating dogs and laughed heartily. . . . Much provoked, Capt. Lewis threw the puppy back, threatened the Indian with a tomahawk, and the fellow withdrew much mortified. . . ."

Aware that heavily laden horses could travel only a few days without food, the explorers impatiently waited for the snows to melt and the grass to come in the high country to the east. On May 17, with the snow four or five feet deep in the mountains, shoe deep on the lower plateaus, and long since gone at river level, Clark wrote: "Here we have summer, spring, and winter in the short space of twenty or thirty miles. . . ."

Finally, on June 10, the party broke camp and said farewell to their Nez Perce friends, disregarding the warnings that they were leaving too soon. The Indians were right. At first, the eight-foot drifts on the ridge trail were found firm enough to support the weight of the horses. But there was no grass, the horses weakened, and when the drifts deepened to twelve and then fifteen feet, it was impossible to be sure where the trail lay. Retracing their way, the party sent back to the Nez Perces for guides, offering the reward of a rifle to any Indian who would lead them across the mountains.

Three Nez Perces responded. With their help, the party

5. Near Pasco, Washington. Backwaters from McNary Dam now make both the Columbia and the Snake much wider at their juncture than they were in 1805.

1. *Journals of Lewis and Clark*, De Voto, pp. 279-412.

2. A ship did visit the coast while the explorers were there, but apparently the Indians saw no reason to inform either party of whites of the other's presence.

3. Waters from the western slope of the Blue Mountains drain into the Columbia, those from the eastern slope into the Snake.

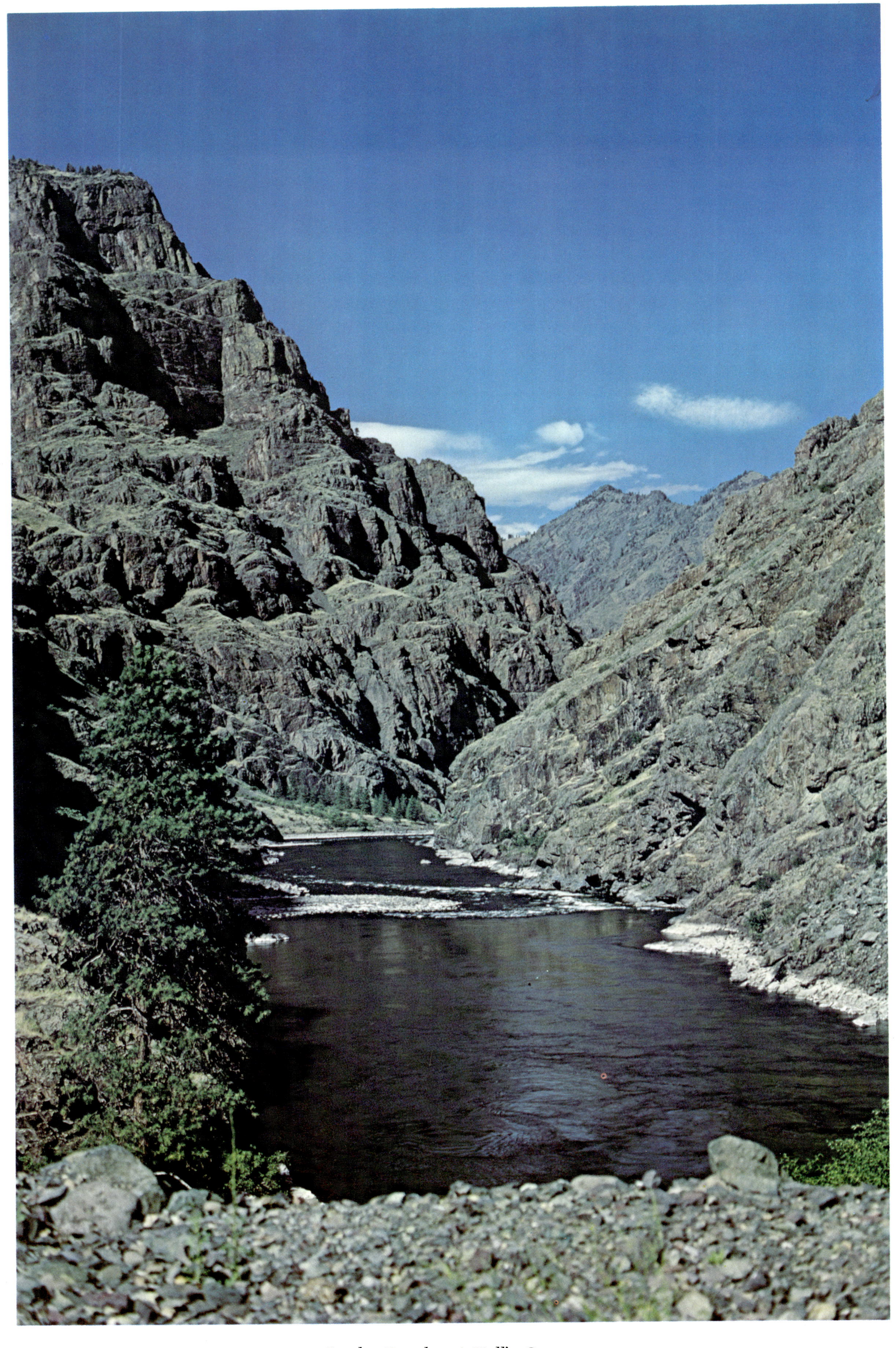

In the Depths of Hell's Canyon

The Selway, an Upper Tributary to the Clearwater, Shows How the Latter Stream Got Its Name.

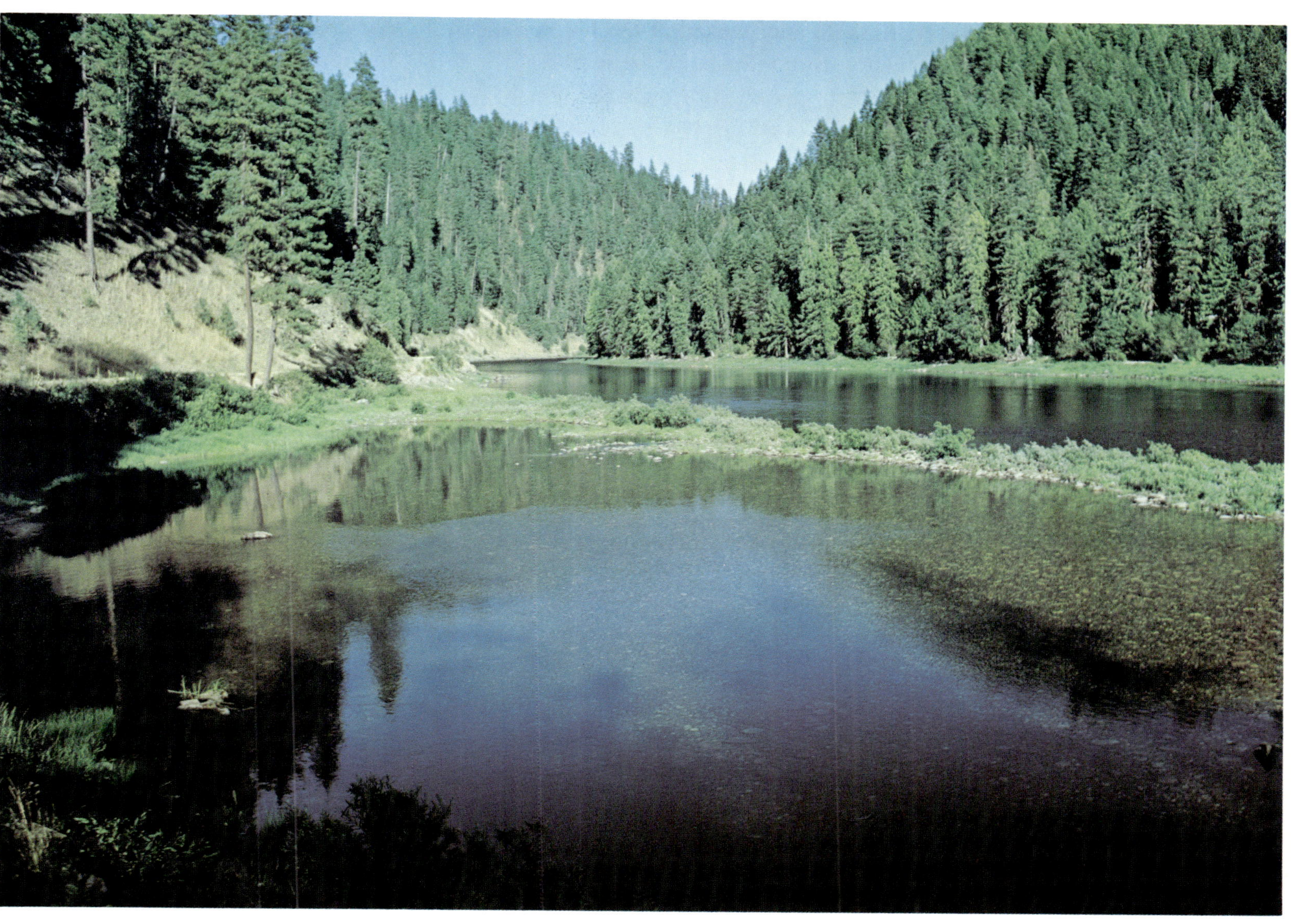

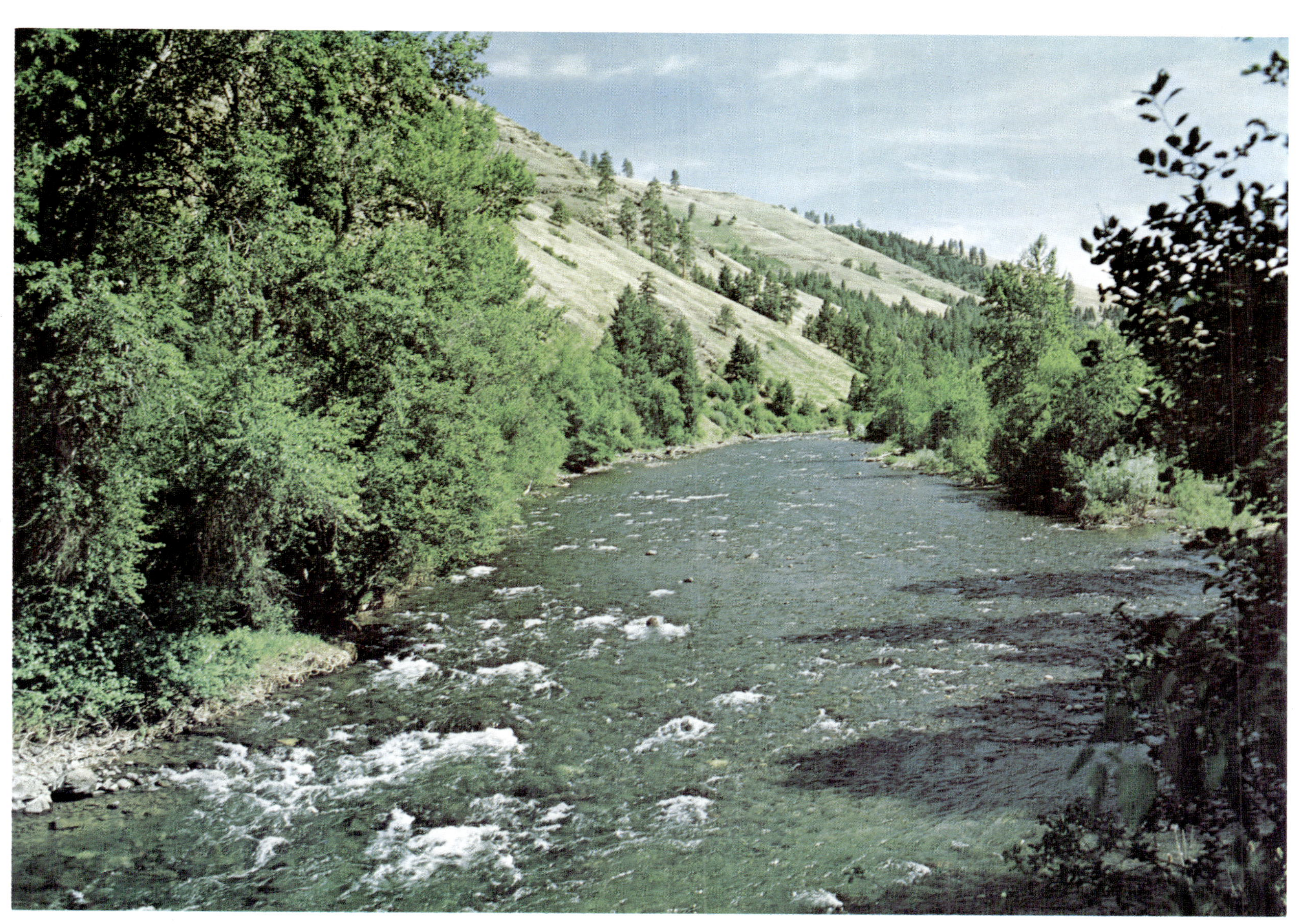

THE MINAM RIVER, IN NORTH-EASTERN OREGON

This lovely stream now is classified as a Wilderness River and will be preserved in its natural state.

crossed Lolo Pass on June 29 and paused at the hot springs on the eastern slope of the Bitter Roots, to recuperate their strength. One of the Indian guides did Lewis the honor of trading names, calling him *Yo-me-ko-lick*, which freely translated meant "grizzly bear."

Before the Indians set out for home, promises of eternal friendship between the white and Nez Perce people were made—promises that would be kept for seventy years.

During its return trip from the Pacific, the Lewis and Clark party had spent two months in the Snake River Country. They had put its two main northern tributaries, the Clearwater and the Salmon, on the map, and had gained firsthand knowledge of the lower third of the river. So far as the middle river was concerned, they misconceived it to be the Salmon (Lewis's River); and of the upper river to its source what they thought they knew was totally wrong.

They are not to be faulted, of course. Their mission was to follow the Missouri River to its source and trace a route thence to the Pacific—and their success in this was a notable one. True, they found no easy way West—but they did find a way, and lost no lives in doing so.

Explorers who followed them, seeking other ways across the Snake River Country, were not so fortunate.

The first was the overland section of the Astor expedition, led by Wilson Price Hunt. . . .

* * *

5.

In concept, the plan of the New York fur magnate, John Jacob Astor, was sound.[1] By sea, he would send a well-equipped party to the mouth of the Columbia to build a trading post, collect furs from the interior, and engage in the highly profitable tea and spice trade with the Orient. By land, he would send another party up the Missouri and across the Continental Divide along the route followed by Lewis and Clark, with some of its members dropping off en route to trap the beaver-rich streams of the high country while the rest transported supplies to the new post and encouraged Indians encountered along the way to trade ten-dollar beaver plews for ten-cent strings of beads.[2]

A simple, practical plan. But in leadership and execution, it went sour.

Wilson Price Hunt, a partner in the company, left St. Louis on March 12, 1811, with a large group of men and a great deal of baggage. Though he must have had access to the journals and maps of the Lewis and Clark expedition,[3] his time and distance senses were faulty. The party traveled at far too slow a pace. By the time it reached the upriver country, August had come and the Pacific slope still was far away. Since the party included one hundred and eighteen horses and sixty-four people, many of whom were seasoned frontiersmen, it should have been able to defend itself against any conceivable Indian attack, for at that time very few natives possessed firearms. But Hunt, impressed by tales of the ferocity of the Blackfeet, took alarm, and, in order to bypass hostile country, left the Missouri and sought a more southerly route to the coast.

The trail led through the Snake River Country—terrain more brutal and deadly than any human foe.

Jackson Hole, in northwestern Wyoming, lies directly south of Yellowstone Park, is bordered on the west by spectacularly beautiful mountains, and is drained by the Snake River. Because of the 6,500 foot elevation, its tourist season ends in mid-September. The Hunt party—its first white tourists—arrived September 25, coming in from the east by way of Hoback River. Like tardy tourists today, they were in too much of a hurry to do justice to the magnificent scenery.

Viewing the jagged peaks we now call the Grand Tetons, they named them the "Pilot Knobs," then, impatiently dropping their eyes to the ground, considered abandoning their horses, building boats, and floating downstream to the Pacific on the waters of the stream into which Hoback River flowed. An examination of the rapids, rocks, and hazards of that stream, which here entered a fearsome gorge, convinced them that no boat could survive in its current. They first named it "Mad River," then, after testing its strength farther downstream, rechristened it in more eloquent terms *La Maudite Rivière Enragée*, which is French for "The Accursed Mad River."

By any name, this was the true Snake nine hundred miles above its mouth and twelve hundred and fifty miles from the sea. Autumn was at hand. Having heard of a trading post recently established to the west of the Tetons, Hunt led his party through the mountains over an old Indian trail, making for Henry's Fort near the present-day town of St. Anthony, Idaho.

To his great disappointment, he found the post deserted. Andrew Henry, who had moved to this spot because of Blackfoot hostility in the Three Forks area, had found neither peace nor trade here, so had given up and departed. The strong, dark, rapid stream flowing in a southwesterly direction bore his name, Henry's Fork. To the weary travelers, now seven long months from St. Louis, it looked navigable; and to one of the party's leaders ". . . with an ailment

1. My sources for this chapter are Washington Irving's *Astoria* and Hiram Chittenden's *American Fur Trade*, Academic Reprints edition, Stanford, California, 1954, which first was published in 1902. Irving had access to the original journals and records, but, never having seen the country, is hazy on distances and terrain. Chittenden (1858-1917) graduated from West Point in 1884 and from the Army Engineering School three years later, retiring as a Brigadier-General in 1910. He did know the country and his *Fur Trade* still is regarded as authoritative.

2. An approximation. Traders paid as little as they could or as much as they had to. But they usually made a tremendous profit.

3. Perhaps he did not, for first publication was in 1814. But the information they contained surely would be a "must" to a leader with his mission, and one would assume he would make every effort to obtain them.

Right: On the North Fork of the Payette

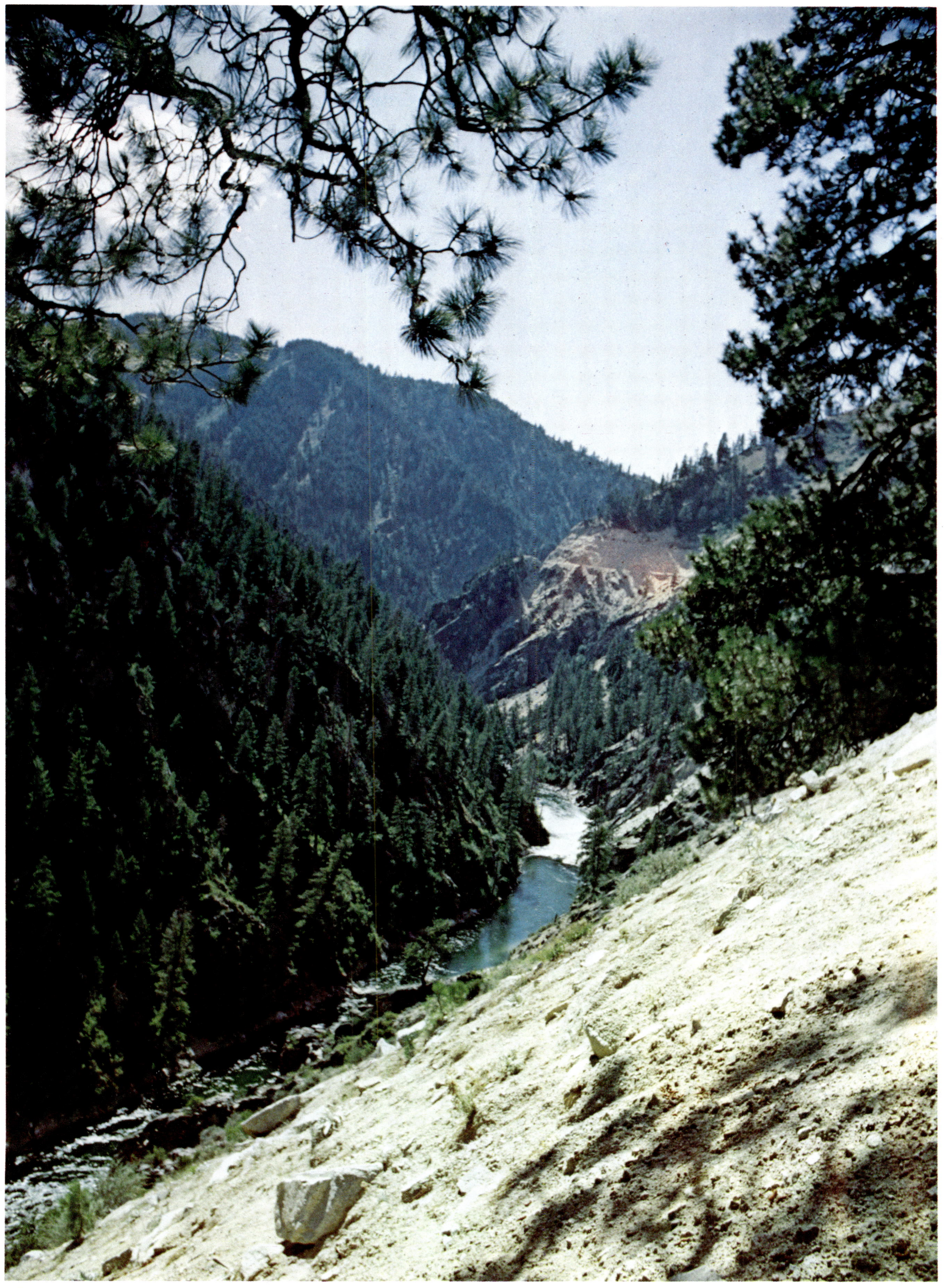

that made riding a horse torture . . ." the prospect of floating serenely to the sea was irresistible.

Wilson Hunt here committed ". . . the great mistake of the expedition. . . ."[4] Only a hundred comparatively easy miles to the northwest lay the Lemhi River and the trail blazed by Lewis and Clark through country controlled by friendly Indians. But he feared their Blackfoot neighbors. So despite the fact that he possessed no reliable information regarding the river route west, he built boats and committed his people and baggage to the currents of Henry's Fork.

It was October 19 by the time the fifteen boats were completed. Leaving the horses in the care of a pair of Snake Indians, the party embarked, and found the first day's travel ". . . a delightful change. . . ." But now Henry's Fork joined the Snake, and, in the days that followed, "The "Accursed Mad River" showed its true character. In rock-strewn gorges and white-water rapids expressively named the "Devil's Scuttle Hole" and "Caldron Linn" a boat was wrecked and one of the men, Antoine Clappine, drowned. Belatedly, Hunt suspended further attempts at navigation until the downstream hazards could be appraised.

His own inspection of a forty-mile stretch convinced him that the rapids could not be negotiated. Other members of the party thought differently, made the attempt with four boats—and lost them all. Faced with the grim reality of being set afoot in the midst of the Snake River Desert (probably in the vicinity of Twin Falls), Hunt called ". . . a bewildered counsel . . ." out of which came the desperation-inspired decision to fragment the party into four smaller groups.

One would dig caves in which to cache excess supplies; one would head northwest toward the Nez Perce country; one would return to Henry's Fork for the horses left there; one would proceed downriver. Where and when the groups would reunite in the bleak, unknown terrain ahead was left mostly to chance.

After three days, the group sent back for the horses declared their mission too risky, turned around, and rejoined the men digging caches. Five days later, the group sent downriver came back, reported the Snake's waters absolutely unnavigable, and the final decision was made to travel afoot. Dividing the party into two groups now, one to follow the right and the other the left bank of the Snake, Hunt gave the order to march. It was November 9—and winter had come.

The wanderings, retrograde marches, and sufferings from cold, starvation, and illness were too prolonged and involved to be detailed here. Donald McKenzie, Robert McClellan and John Reed, the most fortunate group, made their way across the mountains to the Clearwater in twenty-one days, and, with the help of the friendly Nez Perces, floated down the Snake and Columbia without serious incident, reaching Astoria January 18, 1812.

Finding it impossible to follow the Snake through Hell's Canyon, the right and left bank parties reunited, made a midwinter crossing of the Blue Mountains over what would become the Oregon Trail, and reached the mouth of the Columbia on February 15. Behind, near Farewell Bend, they had left half a dozen party members too weak or ill to travel, two men who had gotten lost, and the body of Jean Baptiste Prevost, who had become so frenzied at the sight of food, he had ". . . danced in a delirium of joy . . ." in a canoe, upset it, and drowned.

In May, 1812, the two lost men, Ramsay Crooks and John Day, were found wandering, naked, starving, and destitute, on the banks of the Columbia. One band of Indians, the Umatillas, had treated them kindly, fed them, and sent them on their way. Another, the Wishrams, had robbed them, stripped them, and turned them loose to die. Eventually found by white friends and taken to Astoria, Crooks recovered, but John Day, a tall, strapping, vigorous man a year earlier, soon went mad and died.

Costly in lives, goods, and suffering though the expedition led by Wilson Price Hunt was, it filled many blanks on the map so far as the Snake River Country was concerned. It was clear now that there was no feasible water route west. Since the success of the Astor enterprise required that a line of communication be established between the post at the mouth of the Columbia and St. Louis, Robert Stuart[5] and a party of men set out for the East in the spring of 1812, traveling overland and carrying messages regarding the successes and failures of the first American business effort in the Pacific Northwest.

The most important message was that competition was in the field. Only three months after the arrival of the Astorians, the British North West Company showed up. Disappointed in their effort to be first on the lower Columbia, the Nor'westers planted a flagpole and posted a sign at the mouth of the Snake, laying claim to the country in the name of Great Britain. In retaliation, the Astorians sent parties north to the Okanogan and east up the Snake, to build posts and trade with the Indians.

The battle for beaver had begun.

Other messages Robert Stuart and his companions carried east concerned the loss of the *Tonquin,* Astor's supply ship, the pilfering of the supplies cached at Caldron Linn, and the bad luck of the trapping parties left in the high country of the interior, all of which had been relieved of their furs by thieving Crows.

In the route followed, as well as the hardships endured,

-----

4. Chittenden's comment.

5. *On the Oregon Trail: Robert Stuart's Journey of Discovery (1812-1813),* edited and with an introduction by Kenneth A. Spaulding, University of Oklahoma Press, 1953.

Right:
DESERT COUNTRY, SOUTHEASTERN, WASHINGTON
Here, near the mouth of the Snake, the rainfall may be as low as seven inches a year. But the land, when irrigated, yields tremendously.

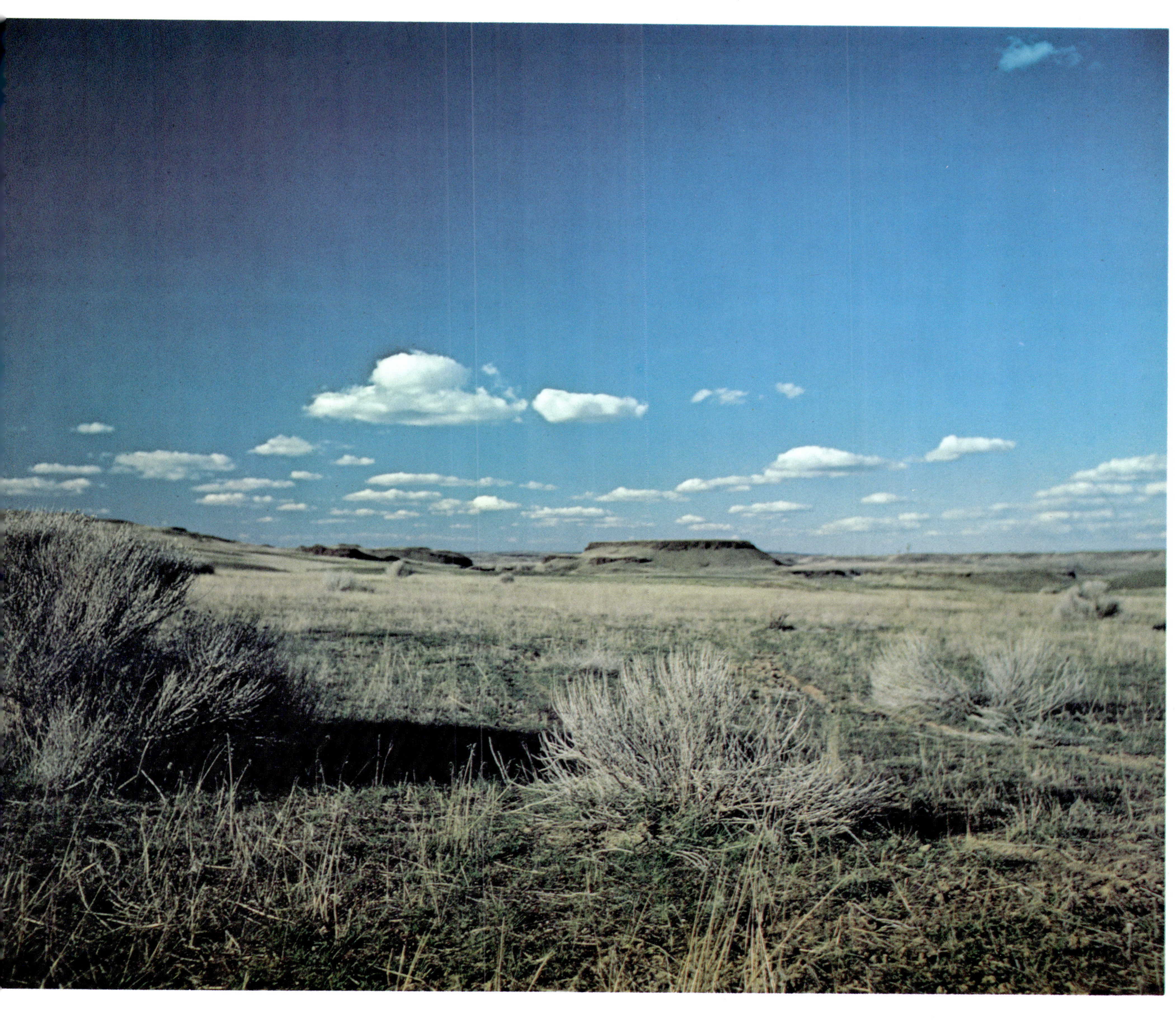

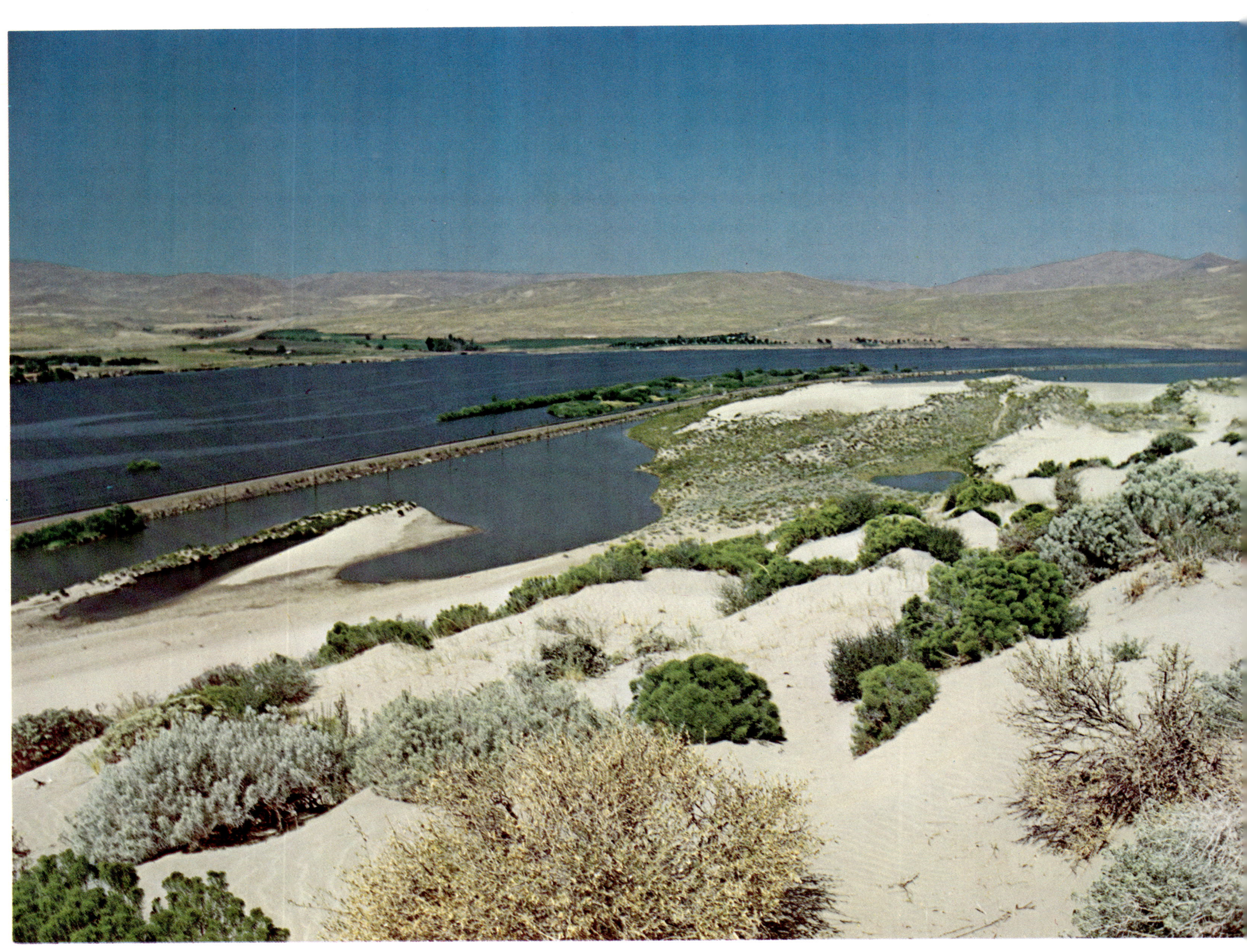

the eastbound Stuart party duplicated the experiences of the Hunt party so closely that they need not be detailed here. But two route deviations later proved to be very important.

Where Hunt traveled south along Henry's Fork to its juncture with the Snake, Stuart took a much more southerly route into the Bear River country, whose terrain totally confused him. In attempting to correct his supposed error, he made a wide, retrograde loop northwest into Jackson Hole, turned east, then south, and completely forsook Hunt's trail along the Hoback and through the Wind River Mountains. As he again turned east, he found a wide, flat trough across the Continental Divide, a trail devoid of any serious obstacles, and suddenly found himself upon the headwaters of the North Platte.

Give or take a few miles, he had discovered South Pass. The date was October 26, 1812.

For all practical purposes, the era of exploration in the Snake River Country was finished now, the curtain was down on the first act of the drama, and the cast of characters was assembled for Act Two.

The leading actors would be Great Britain and the United States, with supporting roles to be played by the Indians native to the watershed. As in all epic plays, the tangible prize fought for would be but a symbol of a much larger stake.

The prize?

The harmless, hard-working beaver, whose pelt made such fine hats.

The larger stake?

An empire, whose winning would transform a young, weak nation into a world power.

Stage for the drama would be the 109,000 square miles of mountain, plain, desert, and valley drained by the Snake River.

The curtain rises. . . .

Left:

FAREWELL BEND

As the Oregon-bound emigrants saw it from the Idaho side of the river. Here the trail left the river and began its tortuous climb over the Blue Mountains.

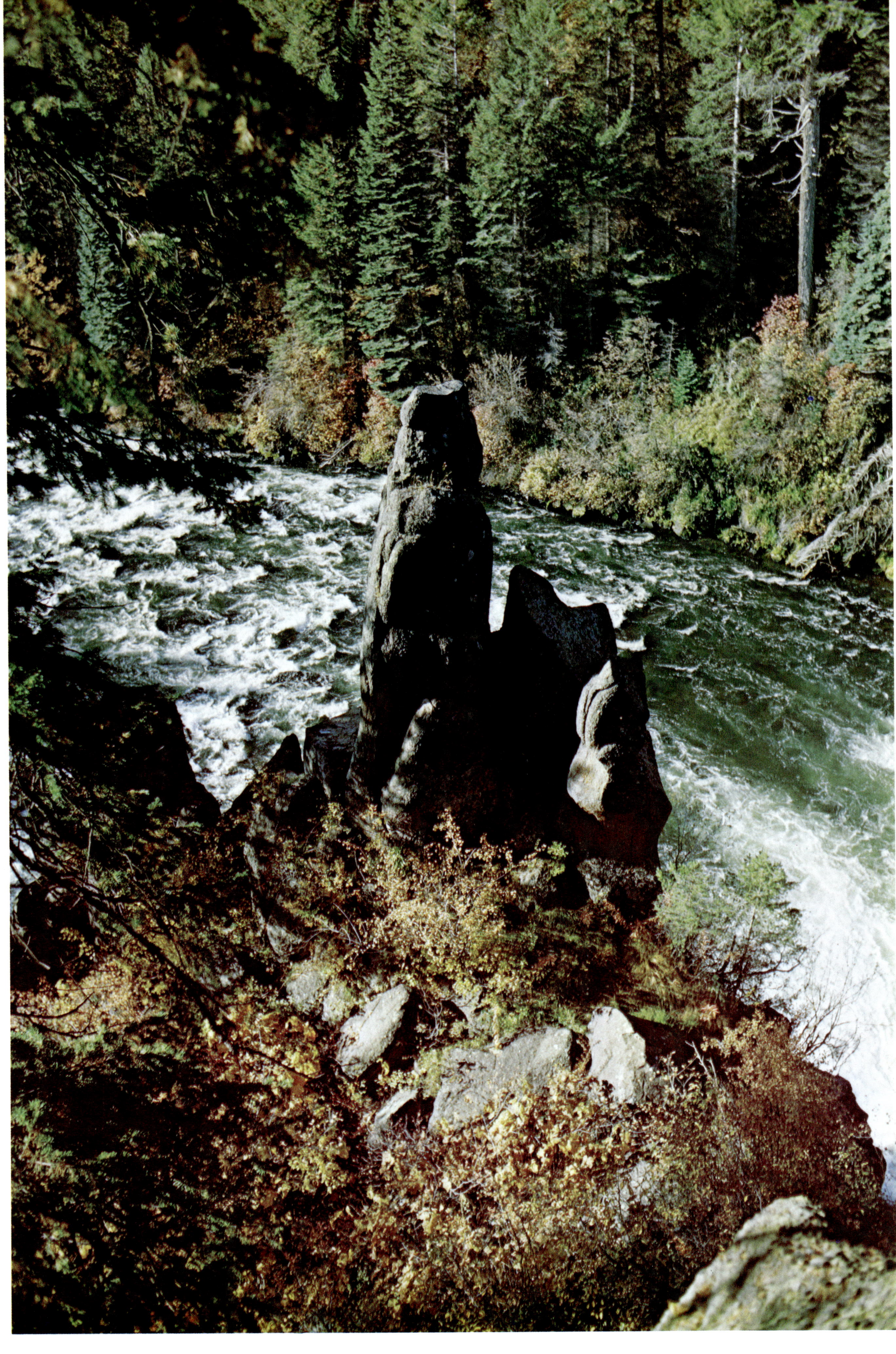

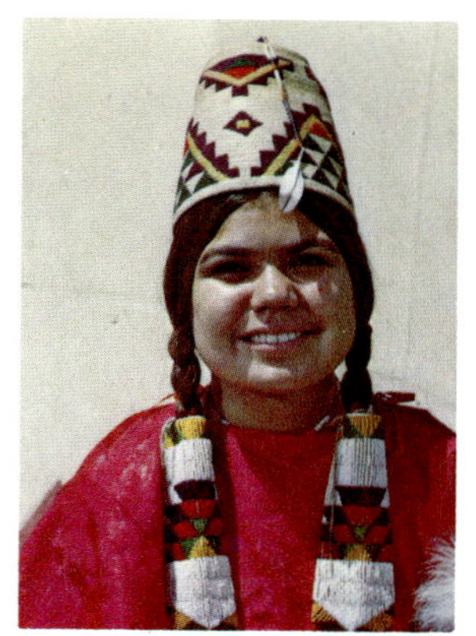

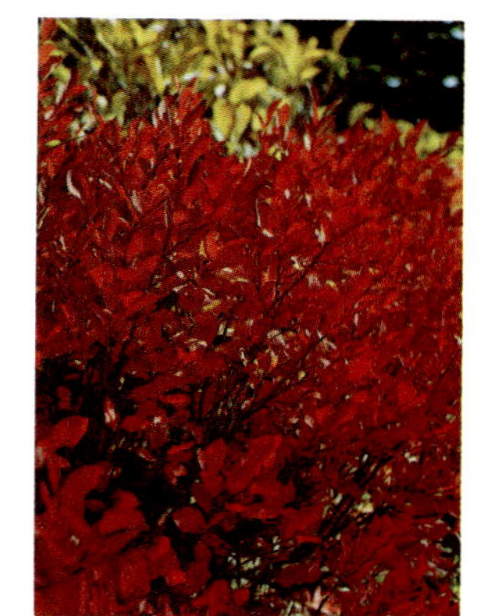

PART TWO

River of Empire

1813-1830

1.

In order to understand the scope and ground rules of the conflict about to take place in the Snake River Country, we must step outside the region for a moment and take a broader view of the relations between Great Britain and the United States.

As disaster piled on disaster, the partners in charge of Astoria decided that they had no alternative but to sell out to their British competition, the North West Company. Shortly after the Americans closed the deal and transferred the property, a British man-of-war, the *Raccoon,* dropped anchor and its captain came ashore. A state of war now existed between Great Britain and the United States, he told the traders, and he had orders to seize the post. It's already British property, you say? No matter. He would seize it anyway.[1]

When the war ended, one of the peace treaty terms required that all property seized by Great Britain must be returned to the United States.[2] The question arose: did sale or seizure take precedence? It was decided that seizure did. In a comic-opera scene, Fort Astoria—which had been renamed Fort George—was solemnly given back to a representative of its former American owners, who then, having gone to work for the Nor'westers, reaffirmed its sale and solemnly turned it over to the British company.

Thus, on a technicality, Astor managed to sell out and withdraw from the fur business in the Pacific Northwest without compromising his country's political claims to sovereignty in the region. Now the American government took steps to solidify those claims.

-----

1. Bancroft, H. H., *History of the Northwest Coast,* Vol. 28, p. 331.
2. Treaty of Ghent, 1814.

Left: Henry's Fork, Downstream from Mesa Falls

The area in dispute lay between the forty-second and forty-ninth parallels and extended from the Continental Divide westward to the Pacific Ocean. In a treaty made with Spain, the United States persuaded that nation to set its northern limits at the forty-second parallel.[3] But Great Britain, a more stubborn bargainer, refused to give up its claims to the Snake and Columbia rivers. The result was the Joint Occupancy Treaty of 1818, which granted access to the area to citizens of both English-speaking countries for ten years. Given this period of grace, future diplomats might be able to settle the question peacefully. If not, there was always war.

With Astoria sold, the American trading posts in the Snake River Country abandoned, and only an occasional trapper venturing across the Rockies during the years between 1813 and 1823, the chances that this vast region would fall into American hands on a "squatters' rights" basis seemed remote. But to make absolutely sure the area became British, George Simpson, head of the gigantic Crown-chartered Hudson's Bay Company, which had absorbed the North West Company after a bitter struggle, took ruthless measures. As a conservation policy, it was usual Company practice to trap a fur-bearing district only once every five years, so as not to wipe out its beaver population. But Simpson decided the surest way to keep Americans out of the Snake River watershed was to eradicate its only attraction —beaver. With that goal in mind, he ordered yearly parties to go out and "strip the country bare. . . ."

Between 1818 and 1827, they did exactly that.

A post was built near the mouth of the Snake,[4] another near present-day Spokane,[5] and still another in the Flathead country to the east.[6] From these each year expeditions were sent out as soon as the beaver plews (as the pelts were

-----

3. February 22, 1819.
4. Fort Nez Perce.
5. Spokane House.
6. Flathead Post.

called) turned prime in the fall and were kept in the field until summer made them valueless.

To anyone familiar with the ruggedness, deep snows, and frigid high-country winters of the Snake River Country, it is difficult to believe that a large body of men and horses laden with traps and baggage could traverse it from end to end from November until June and survive by living off the land, let alone wade icy ponds and creeks and make a substantial catch of beaver. Add the fact that hostile Blackfeet, thieving Crows, and Snakes made treacherous by hunger were an ever-present danger, and the feats accomplished by the trapping parties become incredible.

We will presently discuss these expeditions and the men who led them, but, for the moment, one example of the hardships suffered will suffice.

In 1823, a dour Scot named Finan McDonald spent several months leading a British party through the country. Upon his return, he reported four thousand skins collected, six white men and sixty-eight Indians killed, then added this bitter comment:

> "I got Safe home from the Snake Cuntre, thank God, and when that Cuntre will see me agane the Beaver will have Goulde Skin. . . ."[7]

What were the Americans doing during this period? Most of the time they were trapping beaver and fighting Indians on the other side of the Divide. Since beaver were plentiful there and the unhappy experiences of Andrew Henry and Wilson Price Hunt had given the upper Snake a bad reputation, no magnet existed to draw them west, though on occasion they did make brief hunts in the vicinity of the Tetons. Certainly, descriptions of the Snake River Country below the Henry's Fork juncture gave it negative appeal.

> "It [the Snake] has now acquired those peculiar qualities which give it a distinct character among the streams of the West. Starting from the same elevation as does the Missouri, and reaching the sea in half the distance, it is much more rapid and torrential than the eastern stream. It flows with a strong current almost from the start, and its dark gloomy waters, moving here in silent but dreadful power, there in loud and violent impetuosity, breathe danger and treachery at every step. Many indeed have been the lives lost in its uncertain crossings.
>
> "For a great distance in Southern Idaho it flows through ancient lava fields in a narrow gorge of varying depth, and over a constant succession of rapids and cascades. In many places not even the usual trees line the water's edge, and a traveler two hundred yards away would never suspect the presence of a great river, for the narrow cleft in the even plain is quite indiscernible unless [sighted] from some neighboring elevation.
>
> "Through portions of this gorge the river has wrought a most weird and fantastic channel, with winding and broken shoreline and rocky islets, all

7. *Peter Skene Ogden's Journals, 1824-25 and 1825-26.* Edited by E. E. Rich, London, The Hudson's Bay Company Record Society, 1950, Vol. 1, p. xxxvi.

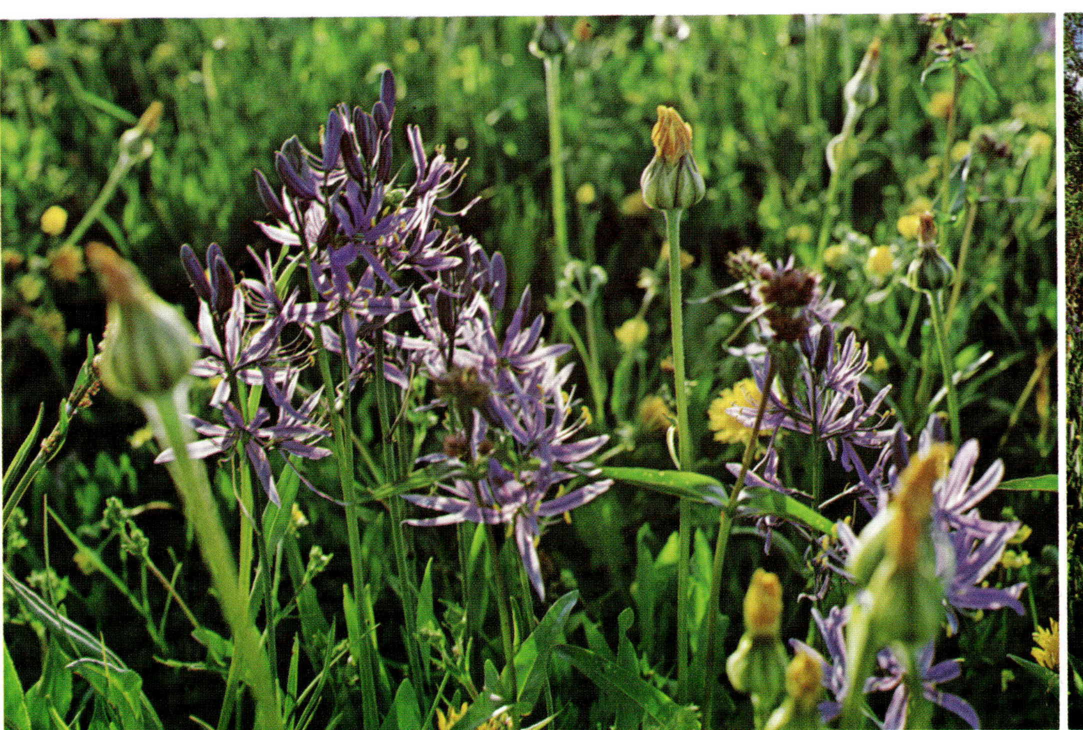

CAMAS IN BLOOM

The small bulblike root, which was dug when the plant flowered, was a staple in the Indian diet. On one occasion, it caused a war when what should have been written "Camas Prairie" was transcribed by a bureaucrat as "Kansas Prairie" and a marshy basin meant to be set aside for the Bannock Indians became a feedlot for a white farmer's hogs.

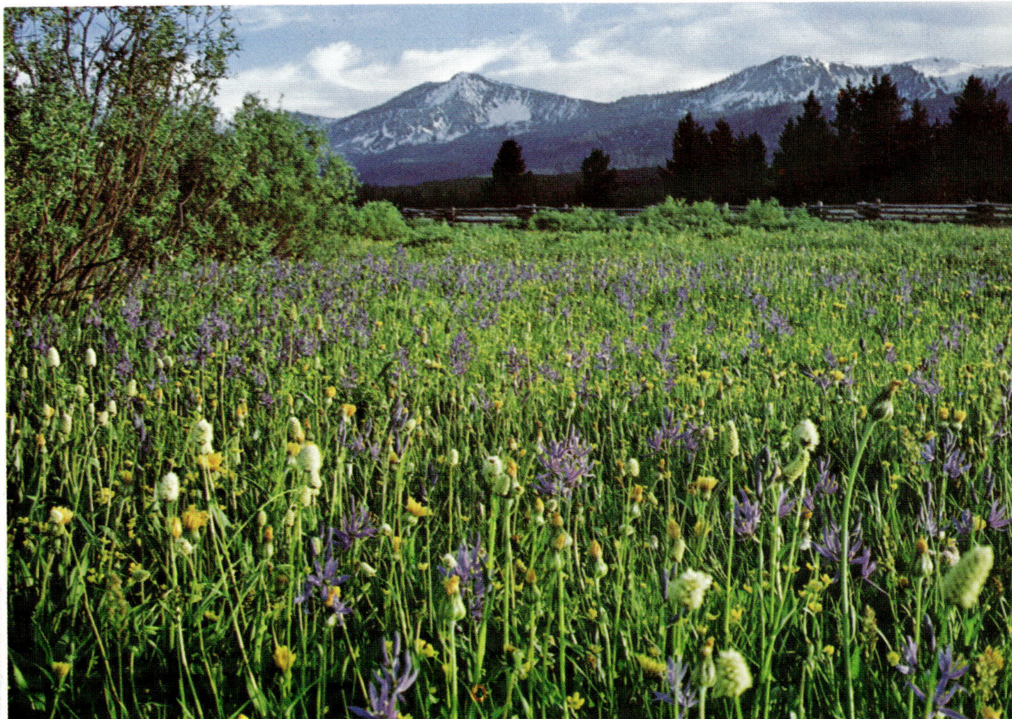

A FIELD OF CAMAS IN FULL BLOOM

What the camera fails to show are the millions of vicious mosquitoes that infest these marshy areas a few miles west of Stanley, Idaho, following the snowmelt of early summer.

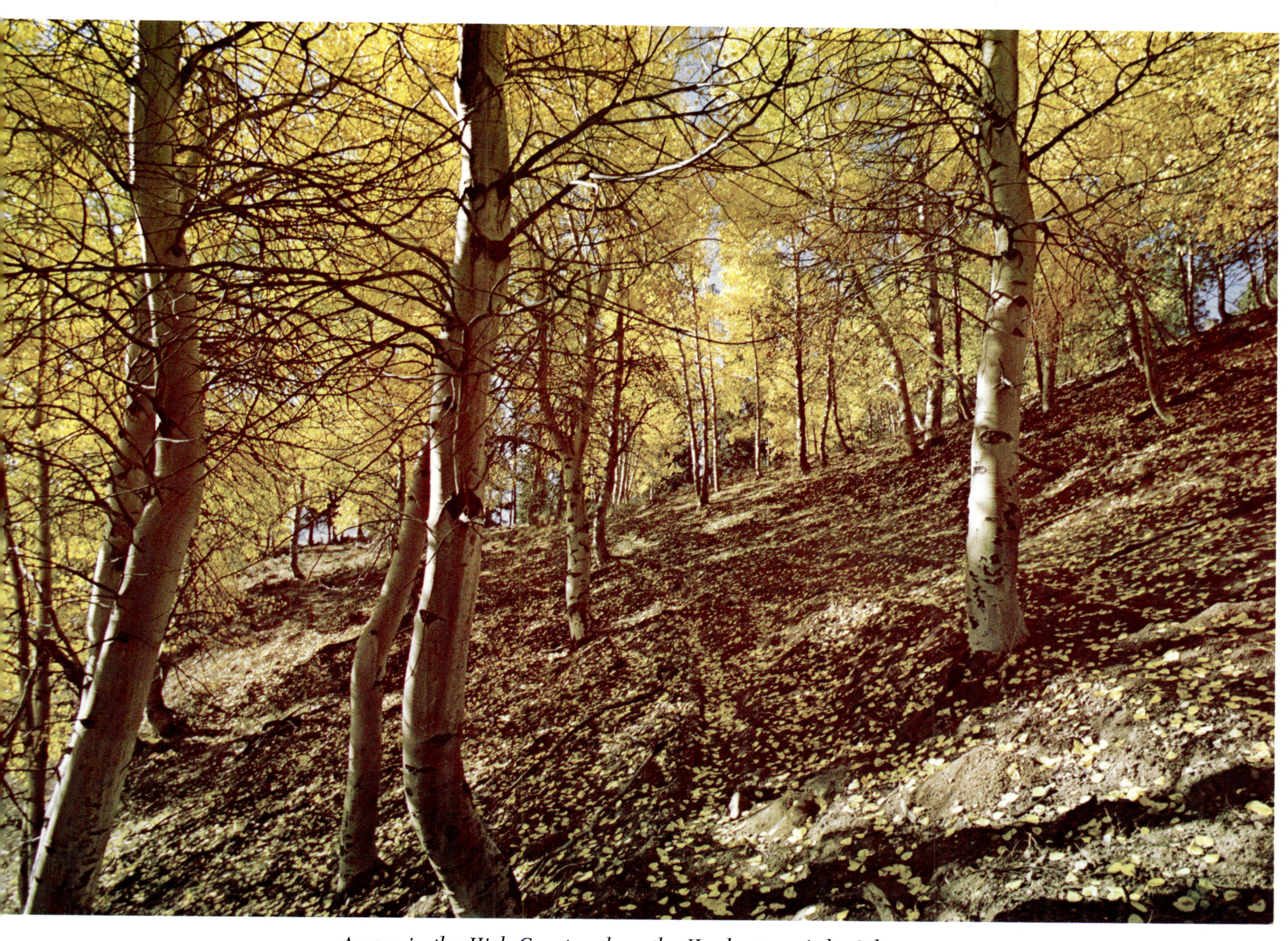

Aspens in the High Country along the Headwaters of the Salmon

black and dismal like the aspect of the surrounding country. . . .

"It is all the way an unnavigable stream. . . ."[8]

Logistics and differing business methods also tended to prevent direct competition between trapping parties of the two nations. Being a monopoly and possessing permanent posts within the watershed, the Hudson's Bay Company exercised rigid control over wages paid its employees and prices paid for pelts. Its supply lines were relatively short. The Americans, on the other hand, practiced free enterprise in the broadest sense of the term, repeatedly failed to establish posts in the upriver country because of Indian hostility, and had no base of supply west of St. Louis.

So it is not surprising that during the years of contention for beaver in the Snake River Country between American and British trappers only one major and a few minor clashes occurred. Before detailing those clashes we should take a closer look at the prize being fought for—the beaver itself. . . .

* * *

2.

Nine miles above its confluence with the Columbia, the Snake has recently been tamed by a 130-million-dollar structure of concrete and steel called Ice Harbor Dam. In addition to its power-generating and fish-passage facilities, a navigation lock 675 feet long and 100 feet high has been built to handle boat and barge traffic. One day toward the end of the construction period, a workman observed a dark-brown, furry animal determinedly swimming toward the downstream side of the huge lock gates, bearing a three foot stick in his mouth.

Benny Beaver was reporting for work.

Without blueprints, core-drilling samples, rate-of-flow statistics, or cost-benefit-ratio studies, Benny was obeying his natural instincts—the regulation of flowing water so that the survival of his species would be assured.

After several weeks of valiant effort, applauded equally by nature lovers, children raised on Walt Disney movies, and hard-hat construction men, Benny gave up and departed. But his labors were typical of his kind. Where water flows in the Snake River Country, sooner or later some eager beaver attempts to build a dam.

Biologically, the beaver is a rodent, the largest of his species found on the North American continent.[1] Though most people think of him as an inhabitant of remote mountain meadows, he is found along all streams from the shores of the Arctic Ocean to the Gulf of California. Usually he builds his lodge in a quiet pond, but, if the stream is too large or swift to be dammed, he will make his home by tunneling into its shores. There, he is called a "bank" beaver.

Though his food is primarily the bark of aspen, poplar, cottonwood, and willow, he loves to dam irrigation ditches and eat sugar beets. Though he is a home lover, a conservationist, and a pacifist, he can defend himself when need be, for long, chisel-like teeth capable of cutting through a four-inch aspen in fifteen minutes or downing a tree five feet thick and a hundred feet tall in a night are deadly weapons against flesh and bone.

Excluding man, his only natural enemies are the grizzly bear and the wolverine, both of whom he can evade by taking to water. When they attempt to dig into his lodge from above, as they sometimes do, he has two underwater escape hatches; and, should the season be winter, he has taken the precaution of coating the exposed portion of his lodge with wet mud just before freezing weather came, making a concrete-like surface impenetrable even to grizzly and wolverine claws.

When full grown, he weighs an average forty pounds, though sometimes his weight will top one hundred. His life span may extend to fifteen years, he will measure three or four feet in length from nose to tail tip, and one-third of his length *is* tail. His hind feet are webbed, his forefeet very much like human hands, and he can stay under water fifteen minutes at a stretch. He mates for life, and, except for a brief period when his wife runs him out of the house as she prepares to present him with a new batch of kittens, he is a good family man.

Since his safety depends upon both entrances to his lodge being under water, while its interior remains high and dry, he must stabilize the level of his pond. Thus, he builds dams. Naturalists say it is instinct, not intelligence, that causes him to do this, but the results in controlling stream flow and creating pools to benefit fish and wildlife are intelligent indeed. Though most dams are only four or five feet high and twenty or thirty feet long, some have been found twelve feet or more in height and up to two thousand feet long. Like human dams, the larger ones represent the work of many cooperating beaver.

When stream flow dwindles and the pond shows signs of running dry, beaver have been known to dig long canals to other sources of water. Sometimes they use these canals to transport logs too heavy to be carried; on occasion, there are primitive lock systems in the canals.

In the Snake River Country when the white man came, trapping beaver was an unknown art to the Indians. If they wished to kill the animal, they had to catch it out of the water (which was not easy, for the beaver labors at night) or plug both exits to its lodge with the beaver inside, then chop through the tough, five-inch layer of mud and sticks from the top (which was hard work). As a consequence, few Indians depended upon beaver for fur or food before the white man came. And afterwards, few had the patience or ambition to learn trapping white man style, nor could they acquire the expensive traps with which to pursue the trade unless they stole them—which they sometimes did.

8. Chittenden, *Fur Trade,* Vol. 2, p. 784.

1. *The Animal Kingdom, Mammals,* Frederick Drimmer, ed., "North American Beaver," New York: Greystone Press, 1954, pp. 294-300.

Since a full-grown beaver is a powerful animal, it takes a strong trap to hold him. One constant complaint expressed by the Hudson's Bay Company men was that the iron in the traps furnished them was inferior to that in the traps used by their American competitors.[2] Since a beaver caught by a leg invariably would gnaw off the leg to free himself, if given the opportunity, it took an expert to set the trap in such a way that the animal's first struggles would pull it into deep water, where it would drown.

This meant that the trapper must make his set along natural beaver pathways, in water a few inches deep, then wade into deeper water, drive a stout pole through the ring at the end of the five-foot chain, and make sure that the pole would hold.[3] Each trap weighed five pounds. Even in early fall and late spring, mountain streams were cold. In winter, they were frigid. Burdened with sacks of traps, a gun, and a hatchet, staying in the icy water most of his working day, and constantly watching for hostile Indians, the trapper led a hard, precarious life. One authority estimates that four years was the average life-span of a trapper in the western wilderness. Peter Skene Ogden, a Hudson's Bay Company factor, wrote: "A convict in Botany Bay is a Gent living at his ease compared to a trapper."[4]

The average price paid the trapper for a prime beaver plew was six dollars by American traders, two-fifty by British. Because of the durability of a properly cured skin and the utility of the closely knit underfur as felting material after the coarse outer guard-hairs were trimmed off, beaver was in great demand for men's hats, men's and women's coats, and other wearing apparel.

Each time the plew was traded or processed, its price went up, with the lowly trapper making a bare subsistence wage while an elite few at the top of the pyramid reaped fortunes. Among the Americans, John Jacob Astor and William Henry Ashley turned beaver into "Goulde Skin. . . ." while during the trade's most prosperous years, 1820-40, the Hudson's Bay Company is said to have paid its stockholders 40 percent annual dividends.

* * *

3.

The basic ground rule of the British-American conflict for beaver in the Snake River Country was: "Use any means short of violence."

The Americans blustered, threatened, and encouraged defection of Hudson's Bay Company employees by paying higher prices for pelts. The British complained that the Americans were not gentlemen. The Americans accused the British of inciting Indians to attack their trapping parties. Quite the contrary, replied the British, and then pointed out

------

2. *Ogden's Journals*, p. 72. (Hereafter, *O.J.*)
3. DeVoto, *Across the Wide Missouri*, pp. 156-58.
4. *O.J.*, p. 94.

the several times they had protected American trappers and punished Indians who stole from them.

For the British, Peter Skene Ogden, who had been born a gentleman but became the toughest, most durable field man the Hudson's Bay Company had, took the brunt of the conflict. A short, stocky, powerful man, he was a veteran of Canada's bitter fur company wars and capable of drubbing any three men in his employ. Of himself, he wrote at the age of twenty-three: "My legal primer says that necessity has no laws." An associate wrote of him: "We bid adieu to the humorous, honest, eccentric, law-defying Peter Ogden, the terror of the Indians, and the delight of all gay fellows. . . ."[1]

Whatever Ogden's good or bad qualities were, his loyalty to the Company was complete. Even when he detested tasks assigned him by his superior, George Simpson, and disliked instructions given him by the Fort Vancouver factor, Dr. John McLoughlin, the thought of failing to execute them never entered his head.

> "In regard to the Snake Country Expedition, we mean to continue it. The more we impoverish the country the less likelihood is there of being assailed by the opposition. . . . The route now pursued will lead you into trouble in other respects, as 'tis probable you may fall in with the Americans, in which case I am satisfied more than half of your people will desert you. . . ."[2]
>
> "Though we should by no means infringe on the Rights of Others, still they must have surer foundation than mere assertion on their part. . . . However, it is proper you should avoid any collision either with Americans or Spaniards, as it must be attended with difficulties, trouble, and expense. . . ."[3]

Running into a party of American trappers in the Blackfoot River country (southeastern Idaho) in 1825, Ogden confided to his journal:

> "We must endeavor to annoy them as much as we possibly can. We will try to get them to steer another course. . . . The Americans have taken nearly all the Beaver. They are a selfish lot; they leave nothing for their friends. We act differently. . . ."[4]

After seeing a number of his men desert to the Americans, engaging in a fight with a roving band of Blackfeet, and receiving a tongue-lashing from a belligerent American who called him a trespasser, Ogden controlled his impulse to respond physically, but his pen scorched the page. "Cursed Country! I wish to God all these Villains were burning in Hell, if there be such a place. . . ."[5]

------

1. *O.J.*, p. xix.
2. Ibid., pp. 253-55. From Simpson.
3. Ibid., p. 139. From McLoughlin.
4. Ibid., pp. 37, 39, 44.
5. Ibid., p. 79.

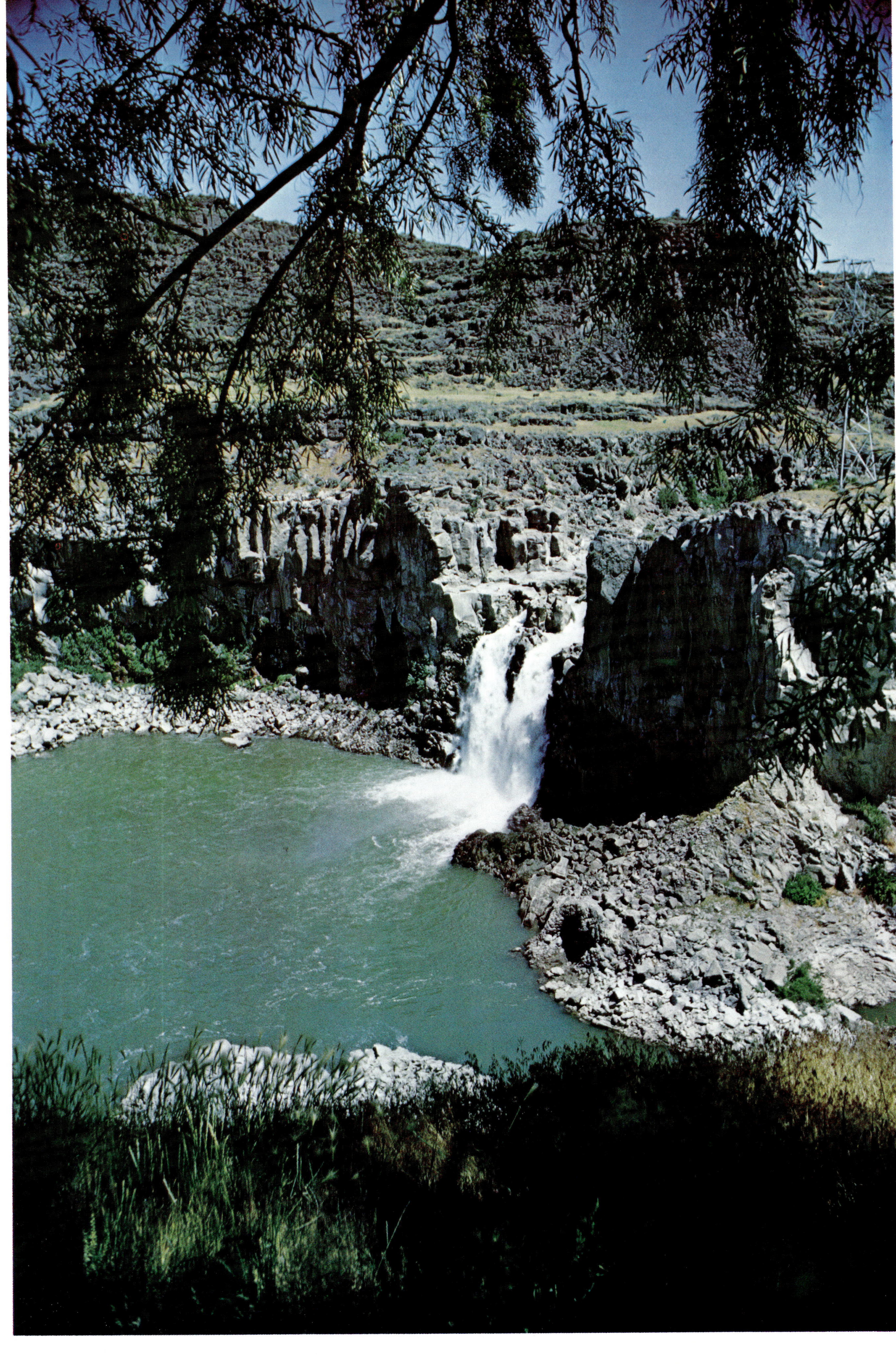

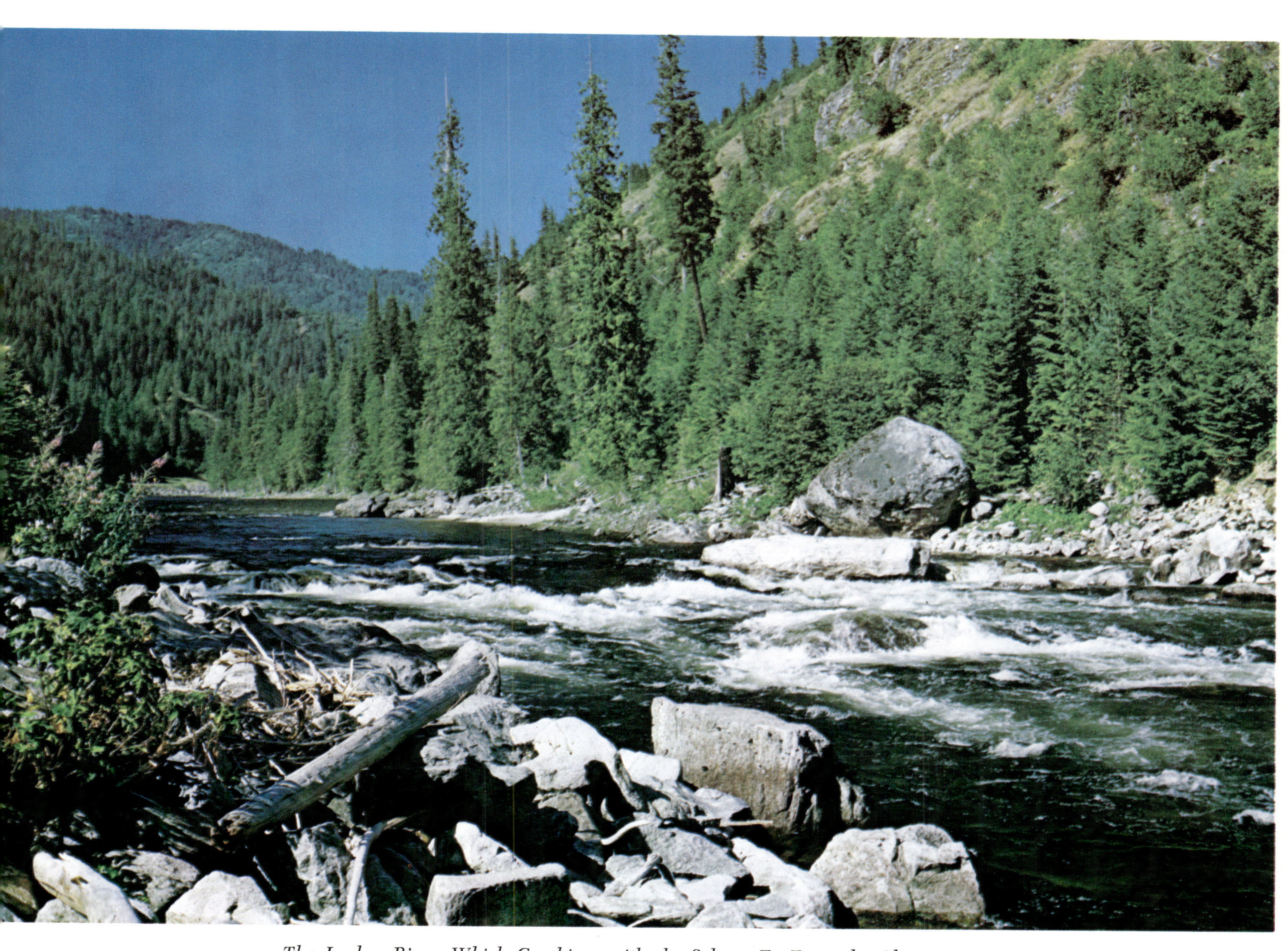

The Lochsa River, Which Combines with the Selway To Form the Clearwater.

Left:

TWIN FALLS, ON THE MAIN SNAKE

Upstream from the city of the same name, only one of the "twins" drops freely now. The other has been dammed.

Whether "Villains" referred to the Americans, the Blackfeet, or to his own deserters is unclear; but it seems a safe assumption that the word was used as a collective noun.

We have already noted that there were important differences in the trapping systems of the two countries. Since Astor's aborted attempt to establish a monopolistic fur enterprise in the West, a series of St. Louis-based American companies had been formed, fragmented, and undergone changes in ownership almost yearly. In typically American style, rising from working trapper to partner in the company was achieved not by a slow, steady climb up the ladder but by an enthusiastic leap into the blue, with the brass ring of a sizable fortune the reward if one could only grasp it, the cold waters of bankruptcy the penalty if one missed.

Each year, traps, gunpowder, salt, sugar, alcohol and other necessities were purchased on credit in St. Louis and transported by mule or horse to some spot of rendezvous in the mountains. There, "free" trappers and Indians traded in the furs they had gathered for the supplies they required during the coming year. Usually the free trappers ended up in debt to the traders, a debt hopefully to be paid in plews at the next rendezvous.

Competition and the laws of supply and demand governed prices. By law, it was illegal to give alcohol to the Indians; but law enforcement officers were seldom at hand. If an Indian possessed furs, no questions were asked as to whether he had trapped or stolen them; if he proved to be an obstinate bargainer, a few ounces of alcohol diluted with water could be depended upon to put him in a more genial mood.

In contrast, the Hudson's Bay Company had been in existence a long while, expected to make a profit each year, and usually did. If, in its corporate wisdom, it decided in London that ten shillings was a fair price for a prime beaver plew, then that was the highest price Peter Skene Ogden could pay. The discrepancy between his two-fifty top and the American's six dollars was *his* problem. But one way or another, he must get the pelts.

After long and faithful service, Ogden could expect to be rewarded with a share of the profits he had produced for the Company. Under him during his fur-gathering expeditions were two classes of men: *engagées,* who were paid a yearly wage of sixty dollars, and "freemen," who, in exchange for their credit-purchased arms, ammunition, and supplies, traded the pelts they gathered at ten shillings each and were privileged to keep the cash profits—if any. Most stayed in debt all their working lives.

Ogden had constant trouble with the freemen. As a class, they were a happy-go-lucky, improvident lot, who, even in an area known to be swarming with hostiles, required ". . . an alarm every eight days . . ." to keep them alert.[6]

From their names, we know that many had French blood in their veins, and since most of them had Indian women along to do the cooking, care for the pelts, and give birth to a baby now and then, it is possible that the blood of both races had run in their veins for generations.[7] In canoe country, they would have been *voyageurs,* the best boatmen and most prodigious eaters alive. This was not canoe country; still, they insisted on eating like *voyageurs.* When fresh meat was available, eight pounds per man was considered a normal meal.

Where Indian women were concerned, they got along famously. They did not like to fight, stand watch, or guard horses. But they dearly loved to ride, shoot, and hunt deer, elk, and buffalo.

> "Many a buffalo has been killed today (on the Snake River Plain) but little or no meat brought into camp. It is the way of freemen they care little how hard they run their poor horses provided they have the pleasure of destroying animals, the meat of which they leave to the wolves. . . . They merely supply themselves for a couple of days, then run again. . . . Today great demands were made for ammunition, but Mr. Ogden thought proper not to give any; they would find ways and means to waste it. . . ."[8]

In vain, Ogden cajoled, threatened, and on one occasion gave one of them ". . . for his impudence a drubbing . . ." in an effort to make the freemen take care of their horses, quit wasting meat and ammunition, and give a better account of themselves during encounters with hostile Indians. But they paid no heed. Even after one of their number, Antoine Benoit, was killed and scalped by Blackfeet, they refused to stick together;[9] and though solemnly agreeing to obey sensible safety rules, lost twenty-seven horses to another party of the same tribe two weeks later.

To Ogden, their waste of ammunition was criminal. Before their contact with the Americans, the freemen were equipped and content with smooth-bored fusils, which Ogden calls "guns"; afterwards, they insisted on obtaining and using the long-barreled rifles with which American frontiersmen were so adept. Ogden writes:

> "With our wretched hunters, we cannot afford to live on deer and elk. Even allowing we had double our present supply of ammunition, each animal costs one-half pound of lead and powder; whereas, one good hunter with the same quantity could supply us with provisions for a month.
>
> "Rifles are supposed by many to cause a saving of ammunition, but I am now fully convinced of the contrary. So vain are the hunters as to their ability as marksmen, they never take into consideration the distance they fire nor the uneven ground; according to

6. Ibid., p. 184.

7. Some were Iroquois, Eastern Indians who had acquired all the white man's vices.

8. *O.J.,* pp. 219-21. William Kittson.

9. Ibid., p. 226.

their erroneous ideas, a ball from a rifle can reach almost any distance.

"Far different is the case with the gun. Here the hunter is fully impressed with the idea that he must be within twenty yards of his object. To effect this, he takes every care and precaution and is seldom disappointed. From a gun, six shots out of every ten will kill. But from a rifle—including the shots fired at a mark to keep it in order—only one shot in ten will kill.

"Three years sojourn with hunters has fully convinced me of the correctness of the above calculations. We are indebted to the late American Fur Company for introducing rifles to the Columbia, and I for one do not feel obliged to them for it. . . ."[10]

Despite his lack of gratitude for their introduction of ammunition-wasting weapons, there is reason to believe Peter Skene Ogden had a special spot in his heart for Americans. Four generations of his own ancestors had been Americans. The first settled on Long Island in 1640. But his father, Isaac, a prosperous New York lawyer, held to the Loyalist cause during the Revolutionary War, took his family to England in 1783, spent several years there, then moved back to the New World, settling in Quebec. Peter, the last child in a large family, was born in Montreal in 1794.[11]

During his 1824-25 expedition into the Snake River Country, Ogden encountered the largest, most aggressive band of American adventurers he ever had the displeasure to meet. The confrontation led to the very brink of an act of violence that might well have caused a war. . . .

° ° °

4.

Before engaging in the fur trade, William Henry Ashley had been a prominent figure in American frontier politics and military affairs. A Virginian by birth, he moved to St. Louis in 1802, took an active part in organizing the state militia, attained the rank of captain in 1813, colonel in 1819, and commanding general in 1822. In 1820, he was elected the first lieutenant-governor of the newly admitted state of Missouri, and, following his six active years in the fur-gathering business, served seven years in Congress.[1]

Beaver made him a rich man, we know, and much of it came from the Snake River Country. Whether he acquired it legitimately, stole it, or stubbed his toe on it, has been a question long debated by historians. Recent publication of his journals, records, and letters appears to have solved the mystery, but, for the moment, we shall relate only the facts known to his competitors at the time.[2]

Planning to develop the upper Missouri River trade, Ashley first went into partnership with Andrew Henry in 1822. Bad luck dogged the venture from the start. A keelboat containing ten thousand dollars' worth of trade goods was lost, pitched battles were fought with hostile Aricaras and Blackfeet, and, after two financially disastrous years, the partnership folded and Ashley went back to St. Louis and ran for governor. Defeat was his lot here, too; so, in desperation, he mortgaged everything he owned, put together another fur brigade, and set out for the Rocky Mountains on what he must have regarded as his last leap into the blue for the brass ring of fortune. This was in the autumn of 1824.

Determined to avoid the scenes of his earlier failures, Ashley and his aide, Etienne Provost, led the trapping and exploring party into more southerly country, dipping down into Spanish territory along the hitherto unmapped reaches of the lower Green River. Tradition credits Provost with the discovery of South Pass, though there is no proof.[3]

Late in May, 1825, the party turned north, traveling toward the appointed rendezvous spot. Then, as Chittenden writes:

> "At some point north of Great Salt Lake, and possibly in the beautiful mountain park known as Cache Valley, an event took place which marked the turning point in Ashley's fortunes. . . ."[4]

Before detailing that event, we must go back a bit in time and space and introduce another American adventurer, Jedediah S. Smith. He has rightly been called ". . . one of the most remarkable men that ever engaged in the American fur trade." Though he went to work for Ashley at the age of eighteen, proved his courage in dangerous circumstances at nineteen, and became a trusted leader of men at twenty, it was neither his youth nor his enterprise that made him stand out from the crowd.

It was his religion.

> "Smith was a bold, outspoken, professing, and consistent Christian, the first and only one known among the early Rocky Mountain trappers and hunters. No one who knew him well doubted his piety. . . ."[5]

With six men, Jedediah Smith had spent the previous summer and fall along the headwaters of the Snake. By accident or design, his group showed up at Flathead Post shortly before Peter Skene Ogden set out December 20,

10. *O.J.*, p. 60. I have clarified and punctuated Ogden's difficult to follow phrasing.

11. An excellent biography, *Peter Skene Ogden*, by Archie Binns, Binfords & Mort, Portland, Ore., was published in 1968.

1. Chittenden, *Fur Trade*, Vol. 1, pp. 247-48.

2. *The West of William Ashley*, edited by Dale L. Morgan, Denver, 1964. This work fills in blank spots and corrects misconceptions made by Chittenden.

3. Chittenden, *Fur Trade*, Vol. 1, p. 271. Robert Stuart and his eastbound party in 1812 probably crossed the divide some miles south of the pass.

4. Ibid., p. 277. Morgan places it fifty miles farther south.

5. Ibid., p. 253. Quoted from William Waldo MS No. 135, Missouri Historical Society, St. Louis.

1824, on a trapping expedition which would run head-on, next May, into the Ashley party on its way to rendezvous. Since the seven Americans and the twenty-two lodges of Hudson's Bay Company *engagées*, freemen, Indian guides, and women camp helpers all planned to travel in the same direction, it seemed a good idea to travel together.

At least, to the Americans, it did. Being a gentleman and familiar with the ground rules, Ogden did not protest, but one of his assistants, William Kittson, thought good manners should have their limits. After moving up the Bitter Root Valley, crossing over to the North Fork of the Salmon, finding buffalo grazing on a level plain, and "... the river as in summer ..." February 11, 1825, Kittson was happy to report, at long last, the imminent separation with the Americans:

> "The seven Americans are preparing to leave us and try to make their way to Snake River ... well satisfied, I hope, with the care and attention we paid them.... One Jedediah S. Smith is at the head of them, a sly, cunning Yankey.... Mr. Ogden has ordered me to notice the way they went...."[6]

Now there began a game common to trappers, gold prospectors, and trout fishermen: a game of fool the other fellow, fake him into unproductive territory, or, if he does make a strike, move in quickly and get your share. When in beaver country, trappers worked in teams of two or three, one team working this creek, another that, with meeting places arranged from whence the party as a whole would move on once the area was trapped out. Since this was on the edge of Blackfoot country, a constant watch must be kept for hostiles.

A party of seven men was more mobile than one of twenty-two lodges; it was also more vulnerable. The ground rules did not permit the betrayal of one party to hostiles by the other; still, if the rival trappers got careless and lost their scalps, it was *their* hair to lose.

Trailing the Americans to notice the way they went, Kittson very nearly did lose his topknot. On April 1, Ogden detached Francois Payette and thirteen trappers to start for the Snake "... to oppose the Americans and get a share of the beaver."[7] A week later, the Hudson's Bay Company party was chagrined to learn the Americans had taken eighty beaver. Next day, forty Blackfeet attacked the Britishers, killed and scalped Benoit, and Ogden judged it wise to have a meeting with the Americans for the purpose of discussing mutual security. Apparently Smith told him he and his men could take care of themselves, thank you, so the opposing groups parted. Ten days later, Ogden's freemen, through "laziness ...," lost another batch of horses to raiding Bloods.

Thus, the small American and large British party trapped, fought Indians, and moved in a general southeasterly direction across Snake River Plain, over the divide to the Bear River watershed, where they would meet General William Ashley's party and participate in the turning point of his fortunes....

Like all confrontations, this one must be viewed from many angles before we can understand what really happened. Chittenden writes:

> "There was in this neighborhood at the time a party of Hudson's Bay trappers under the leadership of the well-known trader, Peter Skene Ogden. They were in possession of a large quantity of beaver fur variously estimated at from seventy to two hundred thousand dollars' worth. These furs, through some transaction not positively known, came into Ashley's possession at an insignificant price—some say by looting a cache in which they were concealed, and some by a voluntary sale to Ashley by Ogden to relieve the latter's necessities. Be that as it may, the event was an important one to Ashley ... the returns of this year enabled him to pay off his debts and lay the foundations of a goodly fortune...."[8]

That *any* necessity could force a man like Peter Ogden into making a shady deal is as flatly incredible as the possibility that a man like Ashley could loot a gigantic cache and get away with it. But the presumed swindle of a Britisher by an American held such appeal to popular fancy in St. Louis that it became a word-of-mouth tradition in the fur trade. Like a man who catches a record fish by having it jump into his boat, Ashley did nothing to disillusion the believers. And Ogden's reports to his superiors have remained locked in the Hudson's Bay Company archives until a recent day.

This is the British side of the story:

Neither Ogden nor his aide, Kittson, mentions Ashley in their journals. Kittson says twelve freemen deserted to the Americans, taking with them 454 beaver pelts. At American prices, this totals only $2,700. Upon the conclusion of the season's trapping expedition a few months later, Ogden turned in four thousand skins, a figure that compares favorably with catches made in the same region in other years.

Kittson records meeting:

> "... a strong party of Americans bearing flags and under different heads. One of them proclaimed in the camp the freedom of the country they were on, being, as he said, American Territories, and that whomsoever wished to go with him they were welcome...."[9]

Twice, guns were cocked and pointed at him, Ogden says, in attempts to provoke a fight. Once, he picked up a rifle himself and came very close to using it.

> "I cannot but consider it a fortunate circumstance

6. *O.J.*, p. 221. Kittson.
7. Ibid., p. 224.
8. Chittenden, *Fur Trade,* Vol. 1, p. 277.
9. *O.J.*, pp. 233-34. Kittson.

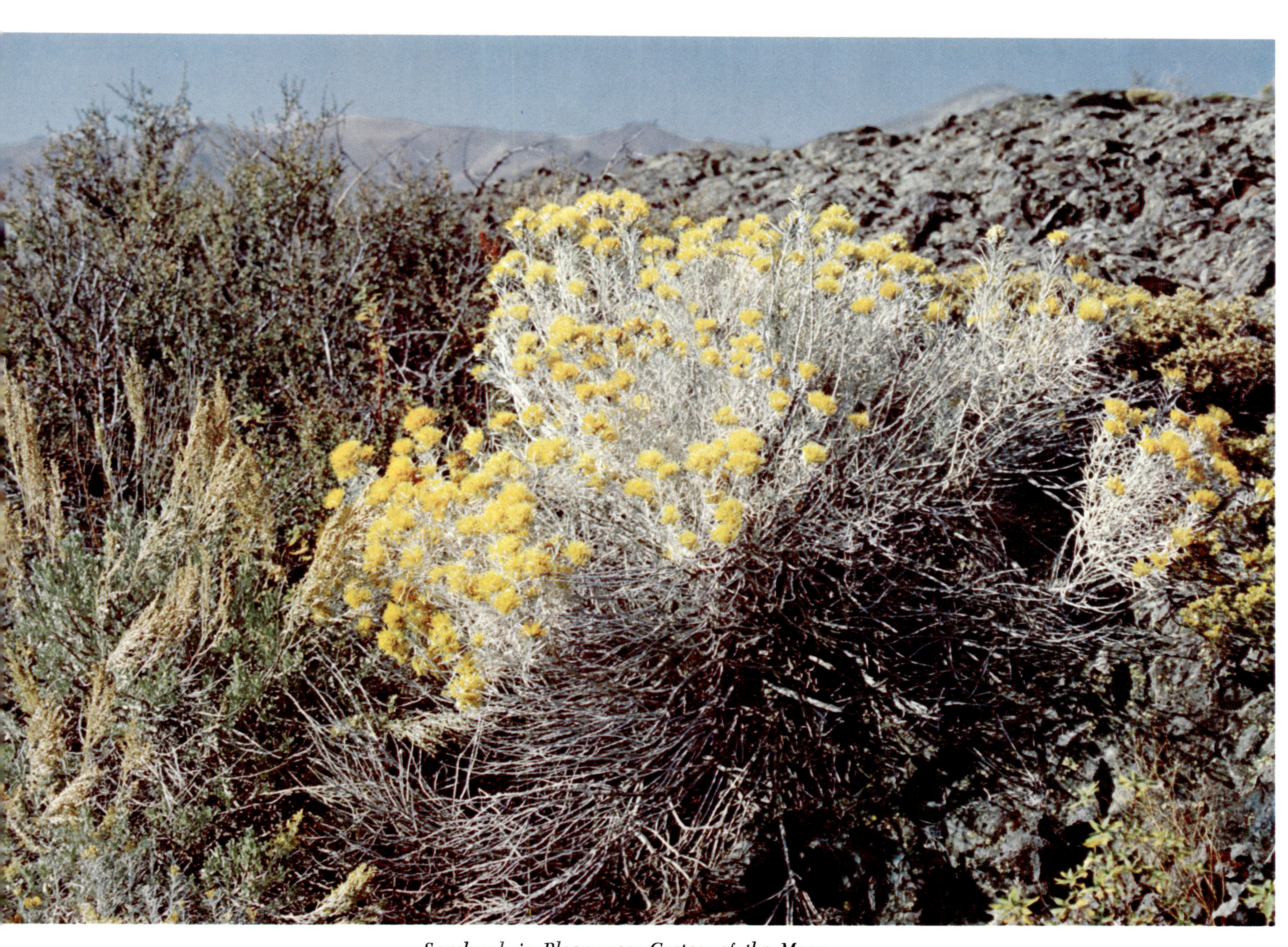

Sagebrush in Bloom near Craters of the Moon

that I did not fire, for, had I, I have not the least doubt all was gone, property and furs . . . assuredly they did all they could to make me, but I was fully aware of their plan, and by that means saved what remains. . . ."

On the morning of May 24, 1825, one of the Americans, Johnson Gardener, came to Ogden's tent.

> ". . . he questioned me as follows. Do you know in whose Country you are? To which I made answer that I did not, as it was not determined between Great Britain and America to whom it belonged. To which he made answer that it had been ceded to the latter, and, as I had no license to trap or trade, to return from whence I came. To this I made answer, when we receive orders from the British Government we shall obey. Then he replied: Remain at your peril. . . ."[10]

Gardener, who appears to have been a super-patriot, boasted to Ogden that before the year ended, American "troops" would move into the Flathead and Columbia River country,[11] take over, and drive the British out. With his own party now reduced to twenty men and badly outnumbered by the Americans, Ogden was not inclined to do much flag-waving himself. Nor did he bother to point out that Gardener was making his brag on Spanish soil, where both parties were trespassers.

Prudently, Ogden gave orders to break camp, and, anxiously watching his back trail for the attack he feared would come, set out for more friendly country.

For the first time in his life, this Britisher with four generations of American ancestors had backed off from a fight. The uncharacteristic act would have odd repercussions. . . .

Now for William Ashley's side of the story. At the time of the confrontation, he was on the lower Green River, about to turn north and head for rendezvous. This places him about 140 miles to the southeast.[12] He heard about the fracas when he met his aides, of course, and in a letter written two and a half years later, said:

> "Some of the American hunters, who were then in my employ, went to the British camp, which consisted of sixty men. The circumstances very nearly led to serious consequences. Jedediah Smith, William Sublette, and other Americans, intelligent men of strict veracity, reported to their comrades that the British flag had been repeatedly hoisted.
>
> "The Americans, indignant at such impertinence, resolved to tear down the flag, even at the risk of their lives. Twenty-two of them, with the American flag hoisted, advanced to the spot, but no British flag was to be seen. They made known their business to Mr. Ogden, and protested in threatening language against a recurrence of the insult; they also required Mr. Ogden to remove his party from the vicinity without delay. . . ."[13]

In the same letter, Ashley admits that he did not see Ogden.

> "I was informed, however, that they had about six thousand pounds of beaver with them . . . and, in the course of several hunts, had taken 85,000 beaver; say, 150,000 pounds, worth about $600,000. . . ."

Obviously, the totals Ashley quoted here were rough estimates of the amount and value of beaver taken by the Hudson's Bay Company in the entire Snake River watershed over a period of years. By his own account books, he obtained only 675 plews from the freemen deserters, whose number he placed at twenty-nine.

Also, by his own account books, in the autumn of 1825, he brought back to St. Louis 8,829 skins, worth $52,934;[14] in 1826, 125 packs, worth $60,000;[15] and, in 1827, an unspecified quantity of furs valued at $60,000 to $70,000.[16]

By perserverance and hard work, he had become a rich man. If it tickled the fancy of his contemporaries to believe that he had laid the foundation for his fortune by tricking a Britisher, that was all right with him. But we know now it didn't happen that way.

The way it happened was this: Helped by a "sly, cunning Yankey . . ." with a penchant for seeing what lay on the far side of the next hill, he had stumbled into a region so rich in beaver that three years of trapping it could make a trader wealthy. Why broadcast the news to the competition?

* * *

5.

Consistent Christian though he was, Jedediah Smith had the instincts of a Yankee trader. During his first trip into the Snake River Country in 1824, he ran into a party of Hudson's Bay Company traders which, while working the streams south of the Snake, had been attacked by Indians, saved their scalps, and then gotten themselves hopelessly lost. Would he guide them north to Pierre's Hole? Certainly, he would. A consistent Christian could do no less. However, since they had managed to save a hundred beaver plews, he would charge a slight fee for his services. Say, a hundred beaver plews?

The lost trappers paid the fee gladly enough; Smith

-----

10. Ibid., p. 53. I have supplied a few badly needed punctuation marks and capital letters.

11. Ibid., p. 54.

12. Morgan, *West of Ashley,* p. 114.

13. Ibid., p. 177.

14. Ibid., p. 126.

15. Ibid., p. 153.

16. Ibid., p. 176.

cached the pelts, and then led the men back to their commander, Alexander Ross, who was not pleased with the bargain. Ironically, the lost trappers were Indians themselves, Iroquois from Eastern Canada, unfamiliar with this western country.[1]

Ross uncharitably called Smith and his men "spies." In a sense, they were, for following their sojourn at Flathead Post, where they observed and listened intently, Smith made a report through Ashley to General Henry Atkinson in St. Louis of such interest and importance that the Army officer wasted no time forwarding it to the War Department, noting in the letter of transmittal that Smith was ". . . an intelligent young man who was employed by General Ashley beyond the Rocky Mountains. . . ."[2] Among other items, Smith noted that the Hudson's Bay Company had sixty trappers working the Snake River Country, from which they had taken half a million dollars' worth of beaver.[3]

Smith liked the Flatheads, the Indians Lewis and Clark thought to be of Welsh descent, and, since he customarily carried a Bible and hymn book on his person, he may have told them something about his religion. He was a Wesleyan Methodist, a breed new to the Flatheads, though, from the Iroquois and the Canadians, they had heard of Catholic priests, whom they called "Black Robes." That both Methodists and Catholics believed a person should not steal, lie, or speak ill of his fellowman, did not surprise these western Indians, for they held the same beliefs themselves.

But could only Christians possess the secret of gunpowder? This was a thought to brood on. . . .

Meanwhile, back in St. Louis, William Ashley decided to quit the game and run for Congress.[4] New owners of the business would be the firm of Smith, Sublette, and Jackson. After a profitable season of trapping along the headwaters of the Green and Snake, Smith proposed an ambitious journey which hopefully would open up new territory.

Despite the protests of expansion-minded Americans, the Joint Occupancy Treaty with Great Britain had been renewed in 1827 for another ten years. South of the forty-second parallel, the Spaniards had no interest in beaver. Smith believed that the streams of what would become Utah, Arizona, Nevada, California, and western Oregon were rich in beaver. Yes, the treaty with Spain excluded Americans from the region. But since when did a Yankee trader pay any attention to a treaty, if a profit could be made?

David Jackson would stay in the mountains, trapping and wintering in the beautiful valley that now bore his name. William Sublette would lead the brigade transporting supplies west from St. Louis each year. With twenty or so men, Jedediah Smith would spend two years exploring, trapping, and opening up trade with the Indians and Spaniards of the Great Southwest. Eventually, he and his men would come up the Oregon coast, scare the living daylights out of the British traders along the lower Columbia with a threat of competition, and then join the other partners on Henry's Lake, directly west of the Tetons.

Smith's saga of exploration, Indian fights, and run-ins with the Spanish authorities can be considered here only in its effect on the political future of the Snake River Country. Midsummer of 1828 found Jedediah Smith, Arthur Black, and fifteen men camped on the Umpqua River, in western Oregon. They had a large number of furs and were looking forward to their arrival in a few days at Fort Vancouver, then the most civilized post in the Pacific Northwest. True, it was a British post. But its factor, Dr. John McLoughlin, was a gentleman, and knew the ground rules.

Then tragedy struck. In a wild, bloody melee, Indians attacked and killed every member of the party except Jedediah Smith and Arthur Black. By some miracle, the two leaders escaped, found their way to Fort Vancouver, and told their tale of horror to McLoughlin. With the approval of his superior, George Simpson, who was visiting the post at the time, the Hudson's Bay Company factor organized an expedition, sent it in pursuit of the Indians, caught them, punished them, and retrieved most of Smith's furs.

> "Dr. McLoughlin charged for this service only at the value of the men's time at the rate of sixty dollars a year and four dollars apiece for such horses as were lost on the trip. He purchased Smith's furs, amounting to $20,000 worth, at the market price, giving him a draft on London in payment.
>
> "Smith remained at Vancouver until March 12, 1829, then he set out for the East to rejoin his partners. . . ."[5]

Again, Smith stopped for a visit with his favorite Indians, the Flatheads, and again they may have chatted about religion. Then Smith and his associate, Arthur Black, journeyed on to Henry's Fork of the Snake, where David Jackson and William Sublette were anxiously waiting.

Trapping had been good along the headwaters of the Snake. Both Sublette and Jackson were eager to extend their operations over the entire Snake River watershed farther west, competing head to head for beaver with the Hudson's Bay Company. But Jedediah Smith, who had seen how scrupulously Peter Skene Ogden, Dr. John McLoughlin, and George Simpson himself obeyed the ground rules, had other ideas.

> "Smith's Christian nature would not permit McLoughlin to outdo him in generosity, and he insisted that the fall hunt of himself and his associates be made east of the Continental Divide, so as not to trespass upon the territory which the Hudson's Bay

1. *Jedediah Smith, Trader and Trailbreaker,* by Maurice S. Sullivan, Press of the Pioneers, N.Y., 1936, p. 59.

2. Chittenden, *Fur Trade,* Vol. 1, p. 272.

3. Sullivan, *Jed Smith,* p. 60.

4. Chittenden, *Fur Trade,* Vol. 1, p. 281

5. Ibid., p. 286.

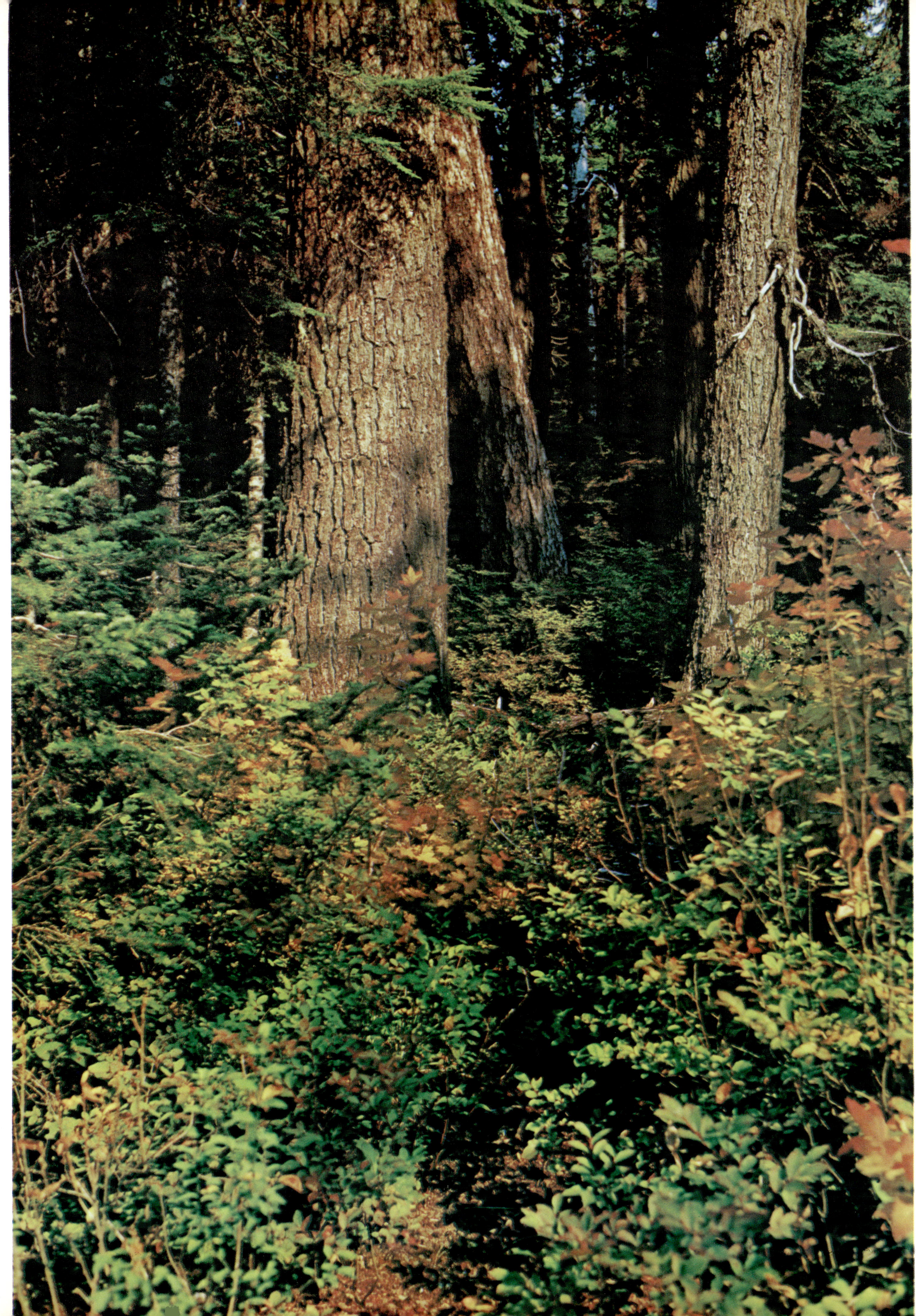

Company claimed as belonging commercially to them. . . ."[6]

Unilaterally, Jedediah S. Smith had abrogated the Joint Occupancy Treaty and resigned from the competition. Even a ". . . sly, cunning Yankey . . ." could be a gentleman.

Thus, the harvesting of the Snake River Country's rich beaver crop was left in the capable hands of Peter Skene Ogden. In carrying out Simpson's scorched-earth policy, he and his men waded every creek, crossed every mountain, and made their tortured way across every barren mile of desert in the watershed. They suffered from heat, cold, and starvation. And many of them died.

> "It is certainly gloomy to reflect the number of lives lost in this quarter," Ogden wrote, "and without the death of one being revenged. . . ."[7]

His somber reflection took place in southwestern Idaho, where the Boise River joins the Snake. Here, a few years earlier, John Reed and eleven companions had been killed by Indians; here, two Canadians had suffered the same fate; and here, a river coming into the Snake from the bleak Oregon desert had appropriately been named the *Malheur*, or, as Ogden called it, the "Unfortunate River." In any tongue, this was a bad-luck place.

Ogden and his trappers put names on the land as they trapped and explored. Bruneau, Raft, Boise, Payette, Godin, Weiser, Burnt, Powder, Grande Ronde, Imnaha, Palouse, Wallowa—all names given to rivers in French, English and Indian tongues, as one would expect. But suddenly on the map in southwestern Idaho there appears a range of mountains and a river named "Owyhee." Where did *that* name come from? From three Sandwich Island natives killed in the area in 1819, Ogden says, not troubling to explain that in the Sandwich Islands there is an isle called Hawaii—and a hard-working trapper cannot be expected to spell perfectly.[8]

In those days, most sailing ships engaged in the England, China, Columbia River trade made Hawaii a port of call.

> "Captains augmented their crews with Owyhees and the inland traders adopted them," Alexander Ross writes. "They are submissive to their masters, honest and trustworthy, and willingly perform as much duty as lies within their power . . . they are not wanting in courage . . . if let loose against Indians, they rush upon them like tigers . . . they are expert swimmers, it is next to impossible for a person to drown if one is at hand. . . ."[9]

------

6. Ibid., p. 288.
7. *O.J.*, p. 130.
8. Ibid., p. 130.
9. *O.J.*, Vol. 2, p. 145.

Left: Fall Colors, Stanley Basin

At the time Ross wrote (1821), he estimated that a score or so Hawaiians were in the interior country. But they were not happy. In their own country, he thought them the most active people he ever had seen. But ". . . transplanted to the snows and cold of the Rocky Mountains, they become consumptive and find their graves in the stranger's land. . . ."

For their monuments, only the river and a range of mountains remain.

Ogden was growing weary. For four years now, he had led trapping parties over the Snake River watershed, southeast to Great Salt Lake, southwest into central Oregon, Nevada, and California, suffering hardships with his men. Once, on Raft River, he and his men became deathly ill by eating flesh from the tails of beaver which had been feeding on poison hemlock. The diet did not affect the health of the beaver and gave the flesh no warning taste, but it came close to killing the men.[10]

Horses too weak and footsore to travel were butchered and eaten for food. His men would not eat rattlesnakes, he wrote, though the Americans "relished " them. At one time, scarcely three of his trappers had shoes on their feet. This was such a barren, brutal country, he observed, that few Indian babies survived for long; in one poor band of starving Snakes, he saw only three children among a hundred adults.[11]

Iron-natured though he was, Ogden felt sympathy for his men.

> ". . . obliged to sleep out, and two-thirds without a blanket to cover them. Still, not one complains. Poor fellows, drenched with rain, shivering with cold, wading in cold water two-thirds of the day, and sleeping often without fire. In four years, this life makes a man look as if he had reached the advanced age of sixty . . .
>
> "Still, they are happy amidst all their sufferings. A roving life pleases them, and with nearly all it would be viewed more as a punishment than a favor to send them to Canada. . . .[12]

Both natural disaster and the Snake Indians were lending assistance in eradicating the beaver of the watershed. Fire sweeping over the upper Goose and Bruneau rivers ruined beaver habitat there for years to come.[13] Deciding to go in business for themselves, the Snakes plundered 180 traps from the Americans, killing thirteen of them in the process.[14] Where a few years ago beaver had been plentiful along the Payette, now there were practically none. And the wanton destruction of females and their unborn kittens sickened Ogden.

> "It is almost a sin to see the number of Small Beaver we destroy, to no purpose. Some of the Females

------

10. *O.J.*, Vol. 1, pp. 163-65.
11. Ibid., p. 134.
12. *O.J.*, Vol. 2, p. 94.
13. *O.J.*, Vol. 1, p. 166.
14. Ibid., p. 179.

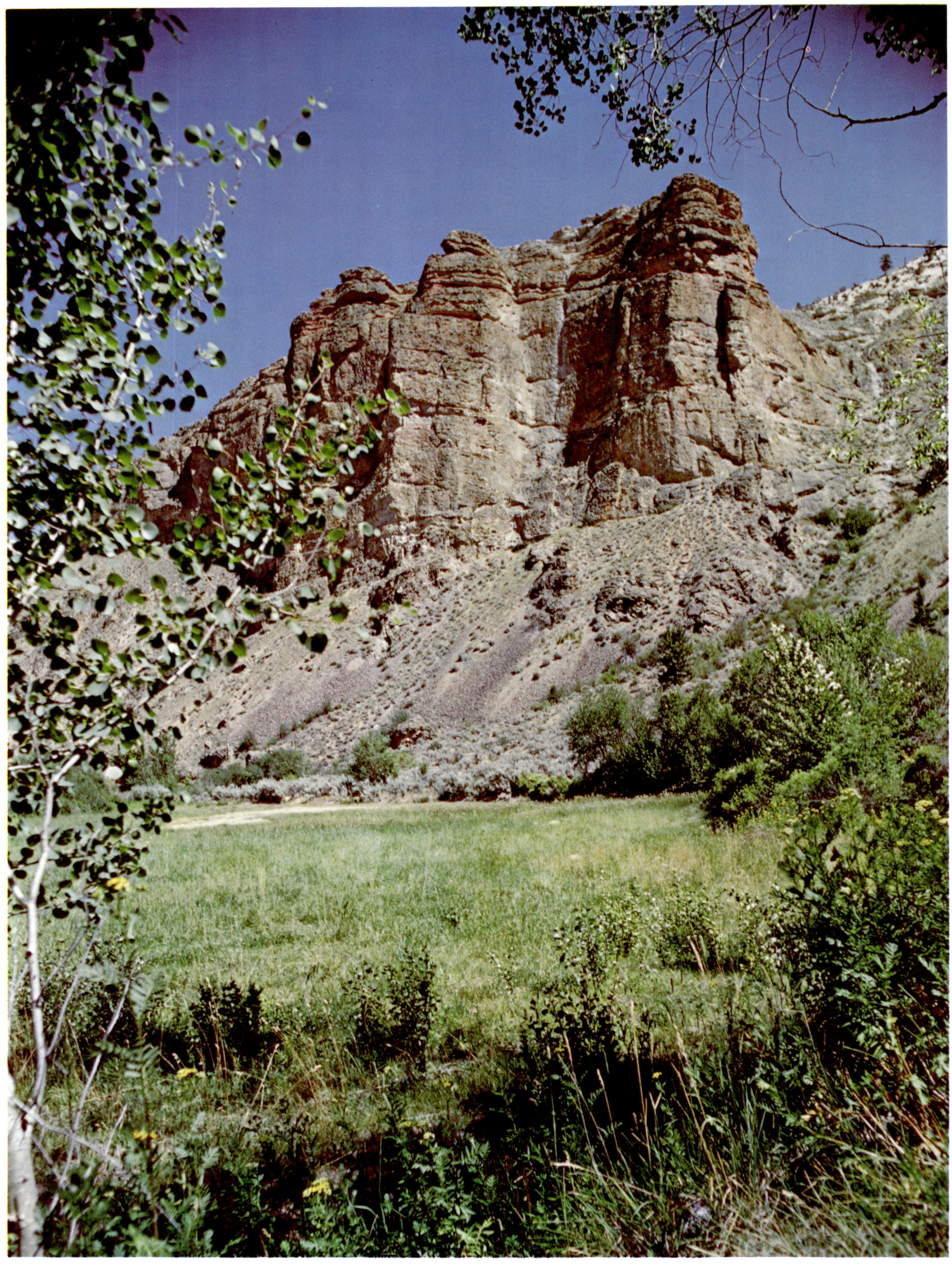

taken have no less than five young, which, a month hence, would be sent out into the world. This is the effect of Traps . . . all are destroyed. . . ."[15]

With most of the Americans gone from the Snake River Country and the watershed trapped out, Peter Skene Ogden's job was done. To give him a badly needed rest, George Simpson sent him north to take charge of a new post in British Columbia. In time, he would return and play one final dramatic scene—the most important role of his life, so far as the Americans were concerned. But for now, we can best sum up his labors in the Snake River Country by saying:

15. *O.J.*, Vol. 2, p. 91.

"It was his task to hunt beaver. It was his mission to explore."[16]

In 1830, it appeared that George Simpson's plan to impoverish the country so that the Americans would have no incentive to come West had worked beautifully. But the forces that motivate men are not always measured in dollars and cents.

Even now, up in the Flathead country, Jedediah Smith's favorite Indians were conferring with their cousins, the Nez Perces, over a question that long had been on their minds.

Must one become a Christian to possess the secret of gunpowder . . . ?

16. Ibid., p. xxiv.

Left: On the Lower Salmon, Stark Lava Buttes Contrast Grimly with the Soft Greens of the Countryside.

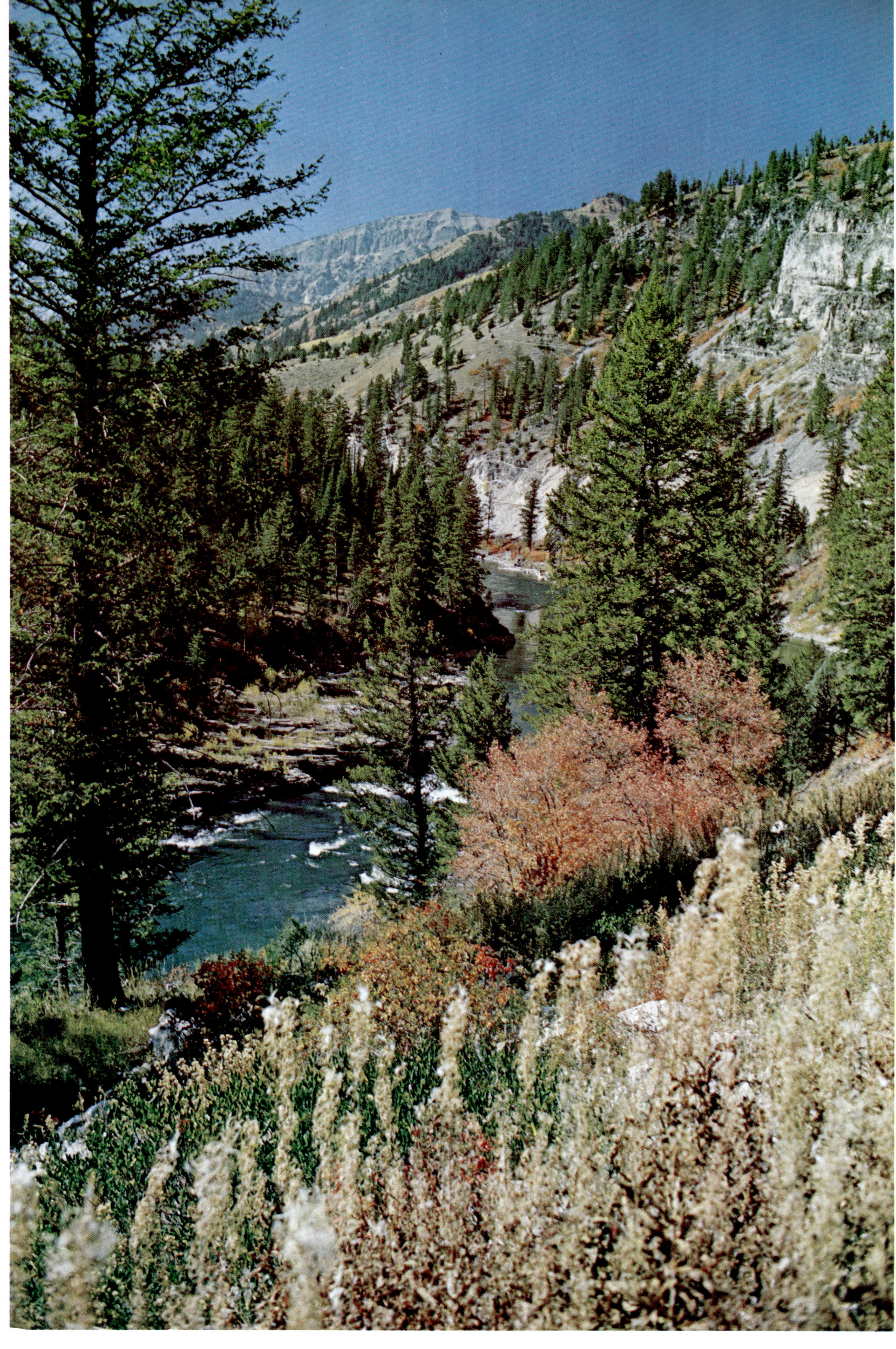

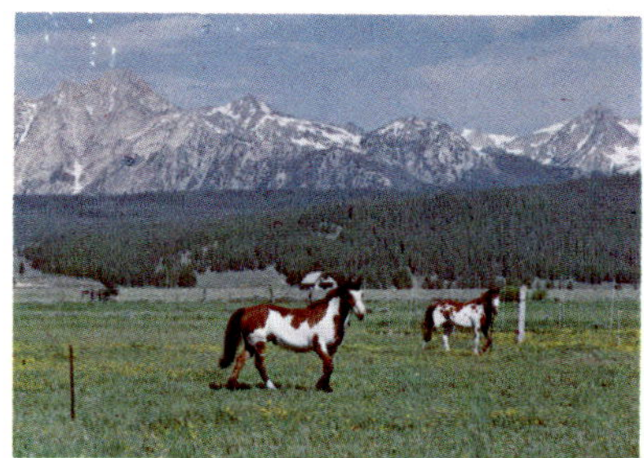

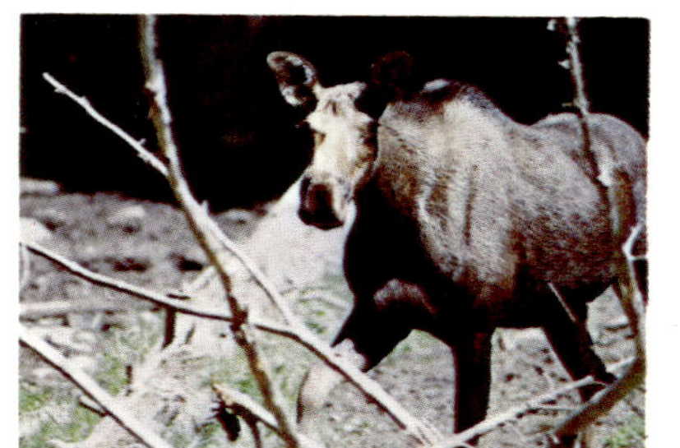

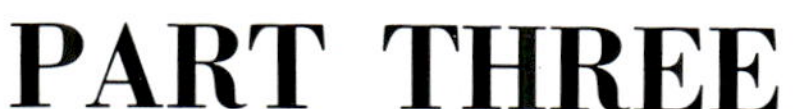

PART THREE

River of Settlement

1831-1842

1.

If the native races of North America had begun recording their history in writing at the same time the Europeans did, it would make fascinating reading today. Marks scratched on paper last. Words passed from the lips of the old to the ears of the young vanish like smoke on a rising wind.

From the viewpoint of the white man, the most important event in the history of the Snake River Country was the Lewis and Clark expedition. Far less well known, though of equal importance from the viewpoint of the Indian, was the epic journey of four red men to St. Louis during the summer of 1831.

Since they kept no diaries, wrote no letters, and made no statements for historians to analyze, their motives for making the trip must remain forever obscure. Among their descendants, tradition verbally passed down through the generations tells us they went out of "simple curiosity." Which covers a lot of ground. Stripped to fundamentals, it was simple curiosity that impelled Columbus to the New World, Lewis and Clark to the Pacific, and adventurers of our day to the moon.

Imaginative writers of the 1830s, some of whom had specific axes to grind, waxed lyrical as they compared the trek of the four Indians with that of "The Wise Men of the East" and insisted that theirs was a quest for "The White Man's Book of Heaven."

> ". . . It appeared that some white man had penetrated into their country," wrote one enthusiast, "and happened to be a spectator at one of their religious services. . . . He informed them that their mode of worshipping the Supreme Being was radically wrong . . . that the white people away toward the rising of the sun had been put in possession of a book containing directions how to conduct themselves. . . .
>
> "They called a national council to take this subject into consideration . . . some said if this be true it is certainly high time we were put in possession of this mode. . . . They accordingly deputed four chiefs to proceed to St. Louis to see their great father, General Clark. . . ."[1]

Left: The Snake River, near Jackson Hole, Wyoming

The facts known beyond reasonable doubt are that four Far Western Indians did reach St. Louis in September, 1831, talked to General William Clark, who was Superintendent of Indian Affairs, and spent several months there. One apparently was a Flathead, the other three Nez Perces. The two older Indians, Man-of-the-Morning and Black Eagle, sickened, were given the rites of the Catholic Church, died, and were buried in St. Louis. The two younger Indians, Rabbit-Skin-Leggins and No-Horns-on-His-Head, sailed up the Missouri next spring on the steamer *Yellowstone* and were sketched by the wandering American artist, George Catlin, who did not learn of their mission until some months later. One of the younger Indians died while on the Missouri River; the other, aided by friendly Sioux, set out overland for home.

And the rest is silence. . . .

We can speculate, as many historians have done, that recent contact with the white man's superior tools, weapons, and knowledge had made a great impression on Far Western Indians. Only a few generations earlier, this Stone Age race of people had acquired the horse, which drastically altered their way of life. Lewis and Clark introduced the miracle of gunpowder; the Astorians, the Nor'westers, and the Hudson's Bay Company brought in highly efficient metal traps; the Indians fingered, admired, and obtained by

1. *American Fur Trade*, Chittenden, Vol. 2, pp. 916, 917. He is quoting from William Walker's letter to G. P. Disosway, published in the *Christian Advocate and Journal and Zion's Herald*, March 1, 1833.

trade brightly colored cloth garments, hawks'-bells, manufactured beads, hatchets, kettles, and a whole glittering array of civilized trinkets and hardware new to them.

What manner of people could make such things? How did they live in their country? Could their magic be acquired?

From many sources, they had heard about the white man's religion. Most of the Hudson's Bay Company employees were Catholic and had told them about the Black Robes. William Clark was a religious man. Jedediah Smith was a "bold, outspoken Christian," who customarily carried a Bible and hymn book with him. As early as 1825, Canadian factors had taken an occasional Indian youth back East with them; at least one, Spokane Garry, had gone to school in the Red River settlements, learned English, become a Christian, and remained one until disappointment and disillusionment turned him sour. As a number of travelers commented, the Flatheads and Nez Perces were superior Indians with high moral standards and a well-developed religion of their own.

Even so, it is seriously to be doubted that such a people would travel thousands of miles through dangerous, unknown country in search of a Book that would tell them how to conduct their spiritual lives. Of course, if the Book were "Big Medicine," containing the secrets of the white man's tools, weapons, and knowledge—*that* would be a Book worth possessing, if only they could get someone to interpret it to them.

Whatever their motives, the mission of the Four Red Wise Men apparently had failed, so far as the Flatheads and the Nez Perces were concerned. But in the white man's world back East, marks scratched on paper were setting the souls of religious people afire. Not with exact truth, necessarily, but with a vision, a call, a dramatic pealing of a distant bell that no missionary of spirit could ignore.

It is doubtful if William Walker, a Christianized Wyandot from the East, even saw the visiting Indians in St. Louis; it is almost certain that none of them had deformed heads. Nevertheless, he drew a sketch of an extremely flat-headed Indian, described this gruesome practice in vivid detail, and enclosed the sketch with a letter to a friend, adding the observation: "It is impossible for me to describe to you my feelings. . . ."

In passing sketch and letter on to the Eastern religious publication in which they were soon printed, the friend, G. P. Disosway, managed to be more articulate:

> "How deeply touching is the circumstance of the four natives traveling on foot 3,000 miles through thick forests and extensive prairies, sincere searchers after truth! The story has scarcely a parallel in history. May we not indulge the hope that the day is not far distant when the missionaries will penetrate into these wilds where the Sabbath bell has never yet tolled since the world began! . . ."[2]

2. *Fur Trade*, Vol. 2, p. 919.

An answer to that question was not long in coming.

> "We will not cease," proclaimed one evangelist, "until we shall have planted the standard of Christianity high on the summit of the Stony Mountains. . . ."

Shrewd businessman though he was, George Simpson had been wrong in thinking that beaver was the only thing of value in the Snake River Country. Now Americans in the East knew it contained a far more precious commodity, poor benighted heathens with flattened heads and souls to be saved, who were eager to hear the Word.

All over the East, church bells began to ring. . . .[3]

* * *

2.

While missionary societies of several denominations were holding meetings and making plans, three men impelled by other motives played vital roles in the settlement of the region. One, a Boston schoolteacher named Hall J. Kelley, was a talker. The other two, Nathaniel J. Wyeth and Captain Benjamin Louis Eulalie de Bonneville, were doers.

Hall Kelley, the talker, never set foot in the Snake River Country, knew next to nothing about it, and spent most of

3. For a full discussion of the many accounts of the Indian trek to St. Louis and its aftermath, read *The Evolution of A Lament*, by C. T. Johnson, *Washington Historical Quarterly*, Vol. II, No. 3, April, 1908. Before the Indians left St. Louis, legend has it, one of them made a touching speech which was copied by a listener who happened to be in an adjacent room. But legend, as usual, is wrong. As Johnson points out, the supposed speech did not see the light of print until February, 1866, in the Walla Walla *Statesman*, and then it came from the not very accurate pen of Henry Spalding. But it made such a big hit, it was later revised, refined, and finally accepted as authentic by some writers. The 1883 version, composed in pure *McGuffey Reader* style, has been the most widely quoted, so we'll give it to you here:

"I came to you across the trail of many moons from the setting sun. You were the friend of my fathers, who have all gone the long way. I came with one eye partly opened, for more light for my people, who sit in darkness. I go back with both eyes closed. How can I go back blind to my blind people? I made my way to you with strong arms, through many enemies and strange lands, that I might carry back much to them. I go back with both arms broken and empty. The two fathers who came with me—the braves of many winters and wars—we leave asleep here by your great water. They were tired in many moons and their moccasins wore out. My people sent me to get the white man's Book from Heaven. You took me where you allow your women to dance as we do not ours, and the Book was not there. You took me where they worship the Great Spirit with candles, and the Book was not there. You showed me the images of good spirits and pictures of the Good Land beyond, but the Book was not among them. I am going back the long, sad trail to my people in the dark land. You make my feet heavy with burdens of gifts, and my moccasins will grow old in carrying them, but the Book is not among them. When I tell my poor, blind people, after one more snow, in the big council, that I did not bring the Book, no word will be spoken by our old men or by our young braves. One by one they will rise up and go out in silence. My people will die in darkness, and they will go on the long path to other hunting grounds. No white man will go with them and no white man's Book to make the way plain. I have no more words."

his long life making wild speeches, publishing inaccurate tracts, and bombarding Congress with fanatical petitions. Patriotism, expansion, and American colonization of the Far West were his personal dreams—and he promulgated them with the single-minded intensity of a madman. Of the three trips he attempted to make to the Oregon country, two were aborted and the third ended in comic-opera fashion. Still, he laid claim, during his twilight years, to being the originator of the Manifest Destiny philosophy. He also claimed that the neighborhood rowdies who made his later life miserable by throwing rocks at his New England house were put up to their mischief by the Hudson's Bay Company, the arch-villain whose plot to steal an Empire he took sole credit for bringing to naught.[1]

By then, nobody was listening to him. But in 1831, when he was proposing grandiose expeditions and enlisting members in his Oregon Colonization Society, quite a few intelligent people were listening carefully. One of them was a practical, prosperous, thirty-year-old Cambridge farm manager and ice seller, Nathaniel Wyeth.

As a successful businessman, Wyeth was more interested in profits than in will-o-the-wisp colonization dreams; so, though he first joined the Society, he soon parted company with Kelley and initiated a plan of his own. He felt sure that the Joint Occupancy Treaty with Great Britain, due to expire in 1838, would not be renewed. The district north of the Columbia River would become British, he reasoned; that to the south, American; with the Snake River Country commercially up for grabs to the merchant bold enough to move in and seize its trade.

Organizing a company for that purpose, he filled a ship, the *Sultana,* with supplies, trade goods, and empty barrels in which to bring back a cargo of furs and salted salmon, and dispatched it from the East coast around the Horn to the mouth of the Columbia. By the time it completed the voyage, he and the twenty-three local adventurers he had persuaded to enlist in his overland brigade would have crossed the continent, established trade relations with the Indians of the Snake River Country and fisheries on the lower Columbia. The company would be in business and the profits would start rolling in.

Since discipline would be important in the Western wilderness, he organized his party in semi-military fashion, making the men wear uniforms, agree to obey orders, and undergo a ten-day camp-out to get used to the rugged life. Since he knew there would be plains and rivers to cross, he had ingenious boat-wagons built, theoretically suitable to both land and water. Practically, they proved suitable to neither, so were abandoned at Independence in favor of horses.

There, Wyeth and his band of greenhorns, who by now had abandoned their semi-military discipline, fell in with the veteran trader, William Sublette, who, with sixty-two men of the Rocky Mountain Fur Company, was headed for the mountains. Crossing the Continental Divide, Jackson Hole, and Teton Pass, the combined parties reached rendezvous grounds in Pierre's Hole on July 8, 1832.

Here they found one hundred and twenty lodges of Flatheads. Here, also, were gathered men whose names would become legend in the West—Jim Bridger, Joe Meek, Kit Carson, Robert Newell, William Craig. And, here, was assembled formidable competition—ninety men employed by the American Fur Company, the Astor-backed enterprise which soon would demand nothing less than total monopoly of the Western fur trade.

Wyeth was growing impatient to move on down the Snake and Columbia to meet his supply ship. But some of his men, tempted by employment offers from the Rocky Mountain and American Fur Companies, threatened mutiny. Of these men, John Ball, a party member loyal to Wyeth, later wrote:

> ". . . [They] were such loafers and laborers as he had picked up in and about Boston . . . none of them showed any understanding of what they were going into. . . ."[2]

After making demands which Wyeth refused to meet, half of his "loafers" quit him, some to return East, others to work for the rival companies. Down now to eleven men, Wyeth broke camp on July 17, and, traveling with Milton Sublette's party, got a baptism in blood next morning in a conflict typical of the upper Snake River Country.

In addition to being a convenient meeting place for Indians and white traders, Pierre's Hole was a major crossroads for north-south, east-west traffic. From time immemorial, Shoshones, Flatheads, Nez Perces, Bannocks, and other tribes passed through the area, sometimes keeping an uneasy peace when they encountered one another, sometimes engaging in bitter conflict.[3] When the Blackfeet appeared, as they did now and then, there was always serious trouble.

That happened now. Apparently unaware that large numbers of red and white enemies were in the vicinity, a band of Blackfeet, with women and children along, blundered into the breakup of rendezvous. Too encumbered to flee and too outnumbered to fight, the normally hostile Indians responded favorably to overtures of peace, prudently moving women, children, and horses into a marsh covered with bushes and scrub timber, while the Blackfoot chief came forward to parley and stall for time.

1. *Hall Jackson Kelley,* by F. W. Powell, *Oregon Historical Quarterly,* Vol. 18, No. 3, Sept., 1917, pp. 167-224.

2. *Autobiography of John Ball,* compiled by His Daughters, Kate Ball Powers, Flora Ball Hopkins, and Lucy Ball, The Dean-Hicks Company, Grand Rapids, Michigan, 1925. p. 60.

3. During this period, the mountain men usually divided the Shoshonean Nation into three groups: (1) Shoshones, mountain Indians whose range included the upper Snake River and Henry's Fork; (2) Bannocks, ranging along the southern slopes of the Sawtooths from eastern Idaho to the lower Boise Valley; and (3) Snakes, those Indians who normally stuck to the river's main valley. But the terms were very elastic, as was the range of the Indians. To further confuse the nomenclature problem, any poor, starving Indian subsisting on roots and a meager insect diet often was called a "Digger," simply because he dug.

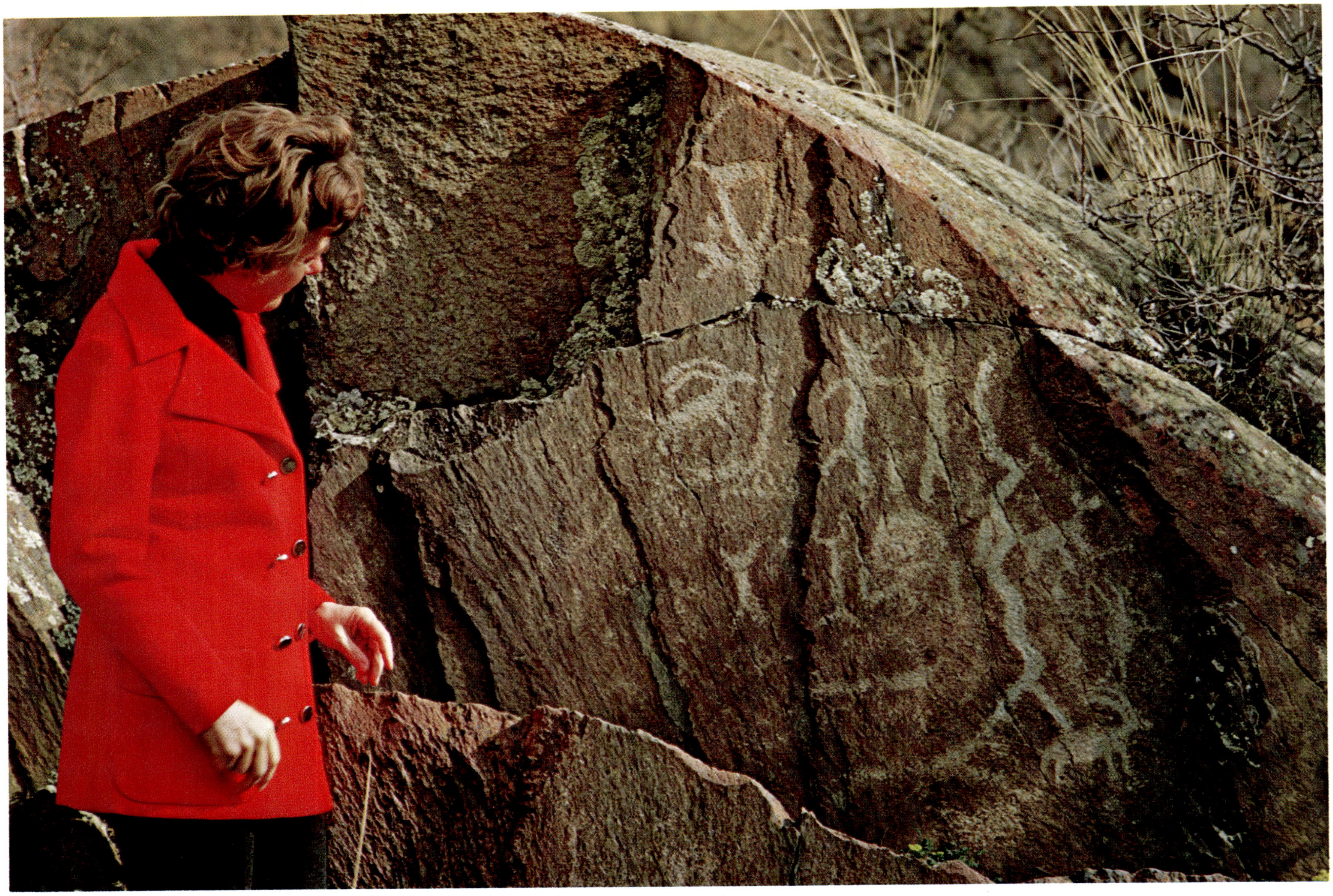

Above:

INDIAN WRITINGS

Many visitors making the trip by boat from Lewiston upriver into Hell's Canyon pause to examine these Indian writings on the rocks on the Idaho side of the river. Thought to be 8,000 years old or more, they will be buried if proposed dams are built. The lady studying the pictographs is Iris Beck, Walla Walla.

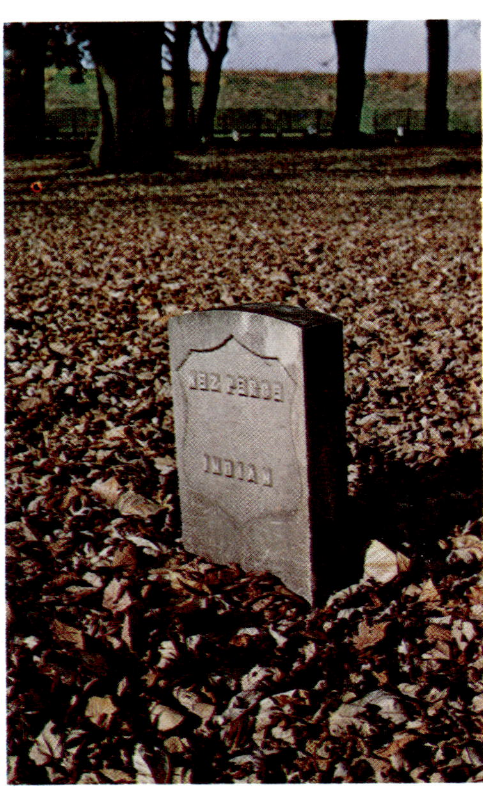

Left:

UNNAMED GRAVE

In an old military cemetery, Fort Walla Walla. From this post, which was established in 1856, many of the campaigns against "hostiles" were mounted. Probably the nameless Nez Perce Indian was a scout for the whites, for this tribe long gave its friendship to the bluecoats.

Right: The Upper Salmon River near Stanley Basin

records for a thousand dollars (papers which Irving destroyed after completing his best-selling book), and thus became famous.

The historian, Hiram M. Chittenden, calls Irving's *Adventures of Captain Bonneville* "stirring and in most instances accurate. . . ." Bancroft dubs the book "an elegant romance, full of lies. . . ." Since we lack access to the papers from which Irving worked and respect him as a writer, we'll tell the tale as he told it.

Bonneville headed west from Independence in May, 1832, and is credited with being the first man to take wagons across South Pass. Through Irving, he gives us a vivid description of the American mountain man as seen at rendezvous:

> "You cannot pay a free trapper a greater compliment than to persuade him you have mistaken him for an Indian brave; and in truth the counterfeit is complete. His hair, suffered to attain to a great length, is carefully combed out, and either left to fall carelessly over his shoulders, or plaited neatly and tied up in otter skins or part-colored ribbons.
>
> "A hunting shirt of ruffled calico of bright dyes, or of ornamented leather, falls to his knees; below which, curiously fashioned leggins, ornamented with strings, fringes, and a profusion of hawks'-bells, reach to a costly pair of moccasins of the finest Indian fabric, richly embroidered with beads.
>
> "A blanket of scarlet, or some other bright color, hangs from his shoulders, and is girt around his waist with a red sash, in which he bestows his pistols, knife, and the stem of his Indian pipe; preparations either for peace or war. His gun is lavishly decorated with brass tacks and vermillion, and provided with a fringed cover, occasionally of buckskin, ornamented here and there with a feather.
>
> "His horse, the noble minister to the pride, pleasure, and profit of the mountaineer, is selected for his speed and gait, and holds a place in his estimation second only to himself. . . ."[1]

At rendezvous, Bonneville took such a liking to the Flatheads and Nez Perces that he decided to winter with them on the upper Salmon River, leaving the duller task of trapping beaver along the Snake River Plain to a detachment sent in that direction. Camping with his genial Indian friends near the present-day town of Salmon, Idaho, he found them generous, easygoing hosts. So did raiding parties of Blackfeet, who repeatedly stole horses which the Flatheads and Nez Perces indifferently guarded.

Observing the perpetual state of war that existed between his hosts and the Blackfeet, Captain Bonneville put forward a suggestion: Why not make peace? This thought struck the Flatheads and Nez Perces as so novel that the head men called a council, debated the idea for two days, then rejected it on these grounds:

> "War is a bloody business and full of evil; but it keeps the eyes of the chiefs always open, and makes the limbs of the young men strong and supple. In war, everyone is on the alert. If we see a trail, we know it must be an enemy. If the Blackfeet come to us, we know it is for war, and we are ready.
>
> "Peace, on the other hand, sounds no alarm; the eyes of the chiefs are closed in sleep, and the young men are sleek and lazy. The horses stray into the mountains; the women and their little babes go about alone.
>
> "But the heart of a Blackfoot is a lie, and his tongue is a trap. If he says peace, it is to deceive. He comes to us as a brother; he smokes the pipe with us; but when he sees us weak and off our guard, he will slay and steal. We will have no such peace; let there be war!"[2]

Because of the mild winter, raiding Blackfeet, and vanishing game, the village was moved into the steep, narrow canyon of the North Fork of the Salmon. Here, game was plentiful and horses and people could be protected with a minimum of effort. Captain Bonneville settled down to enjoy life, which was the thing he did best. Described as "a compact, muscular man with a merry eye . . ." he was well liked by Indians and whites, spoke fluent French, had a knack for leadership, and was prematurely bald. At this moment, he was a bachelor—and sick and tired of it.

Without impugning the integrity of Irving as a writer, it seems safe to assume that the Bald-Headed Captain did *not* tell his friend, Chief Kowsoter, his feelings in the words Irving puts in his mouth: "I want a wife who will share my lot without flinching and be a helpmate to me in the wilderness. . . ."

But whatever Bonneville said, Chief Kowsoter got the message. After looking over the helpmates available and doing a bit of bargaining, the chief found a willing maiden.

> "At the appointed time, he approached, leading the bride, a comely copper colored dame attired in all her Indian finery. Her father, mother, brothers by the half dozen and cousins by the score, all followed to grace the ceremony and greet the new relative. . . ."[3]

If Captain Bonneville did not realize that when a white man married an Indian girl, he also married her family, he soon would learn that fact of life. He also would learn:

> "The free trapper, while a bachelor, has no greater pet than his horse; but the moment he takes a wife, he discovers that he has a still more fanciful and ca-

-----

1. *Adventures of Captain Bonneville,* by Washington Irving, first published in 1837. Reprint by Binfords & Mort, Portland, Oregon, 1954, with foreword by Alfred Powers, p. 58.

2. Ibid., p. 91.

3. Ibid., p. 103.

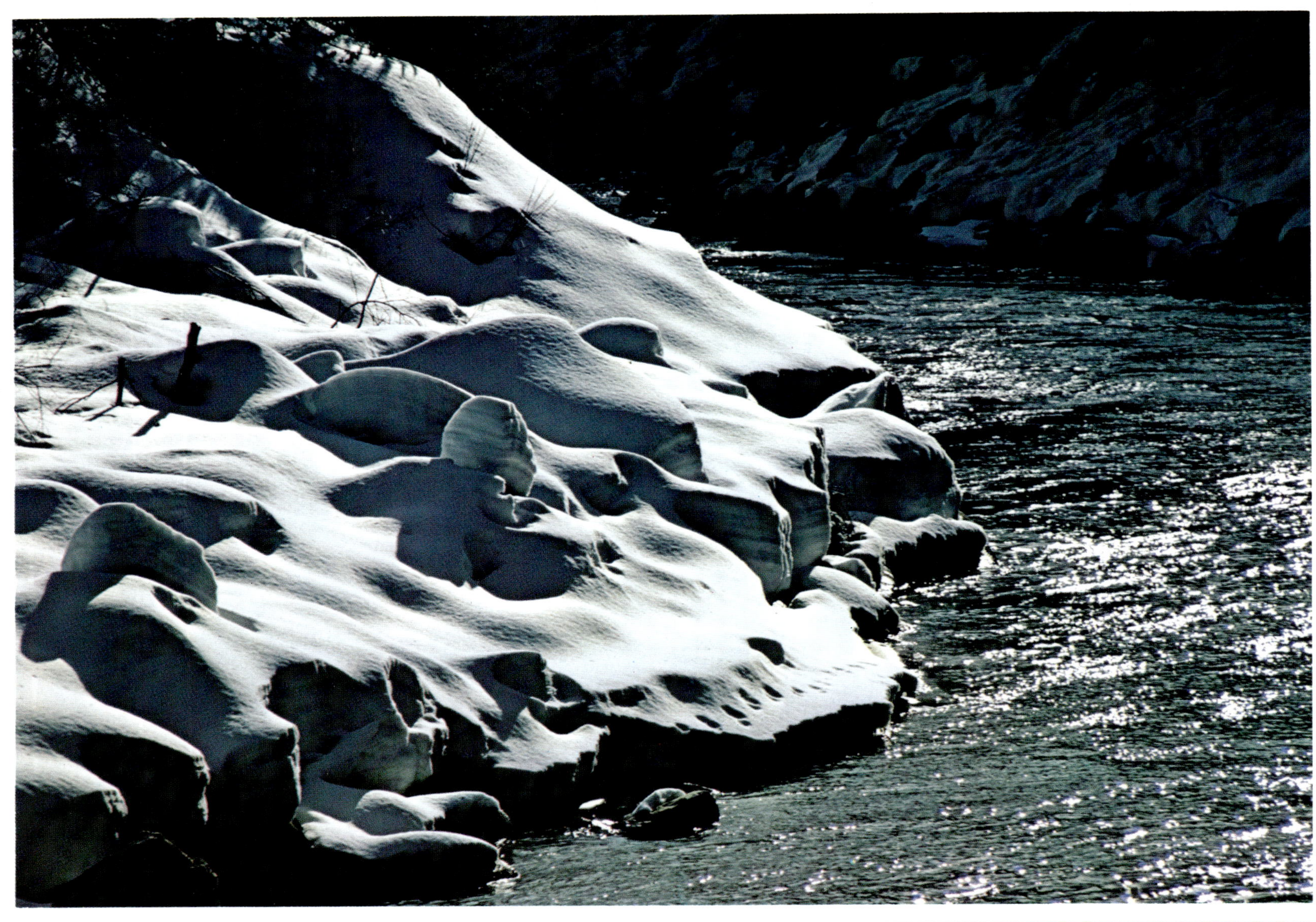

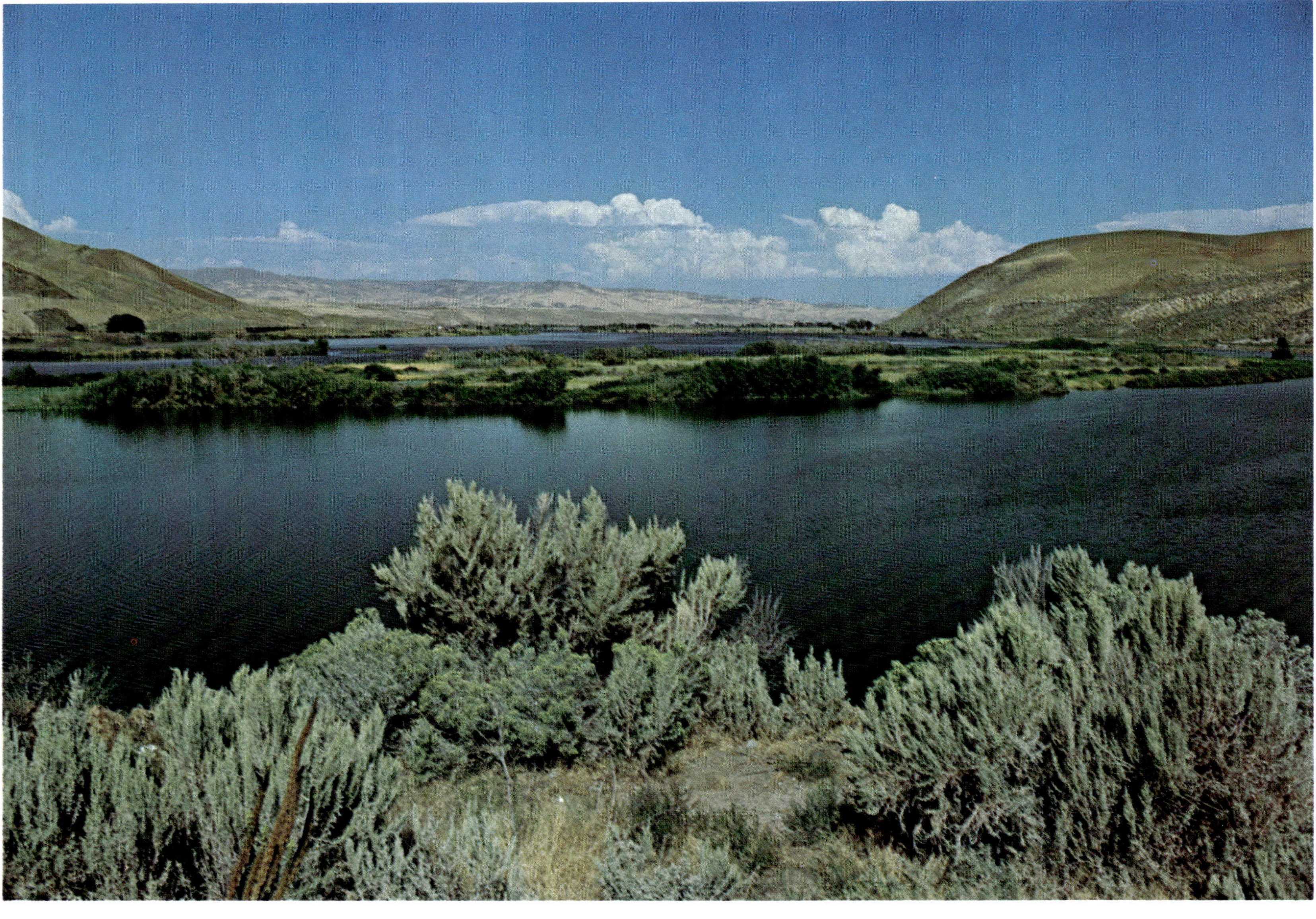

pricious animal on which to lavish his expenses. . . .

"It is worthy of mention that wherever there are several wives of free trappers in camp, the keenest rivalry exists between them, to the sore detriment of their husbands' purses. . . ."[4]

Perhaps there was no connection between the two events, but a month after his wedding Captain Bonneville began to worry about the detachment of trappers he had sent toward the Snake and decided to go in search of it. In January, 1833, as he traveled south up the Lemhi Valley, then down to Snake River Plain, the weather turned bitter cold and snow lay thirty inches deep. His wanderings took him over country drained by what then were called Malade (Sickly) and Godin's rivers, later named Big Wood and Big Lost rivers. In the midst of the immense lava flows covering this region, both the Big Lost and Little Lost rivers vanish from sight and become part of the underground water table—thus their names.

His concern for the detachment of trappers proved justified. Finding it at long last in the Bear River country, he learned it had been attacked by Indians, lost many horses and supplies, and was on the verge of starvation. Needless to say, its beaver catch was small.

The coming of spring brought milder weather and more endurable living conditions, but, as the combined parties began to work the tributary streams of the Snake along the south slopes of the Sawtooth Mountains between the Lost rivers and the lower Boise valley, it brought fierce competition, too. Pinched between the veteran Hudson's Bay Company brigades moving in from the west and fiercely competing Rocky Mountain Fur and American Fur Company bands coming in from the east, Bonneville was an amateur playing against seasoned pros, putting more chips into the pot than he raked out. But, through Irving, he does make some interesting comments on the scenery.

West of Idaho Falls, in the area which now includes Hell's Half Acre, Craters of the Moon National Monument, and the sinks of the two Lost rivers, Irving says:

"Here occur some of the striking phenomena of this wild and sublime region. The plain is gashed with numerous and dangerous chasms, from four to ten feet wide, and of great depth. Captain Bonneville attempted to sound some of these openings, but without any satisfactory results. A stone dropped into one of them reverberated against the sides for apparently a great depth. It is sometimes necessary to travel fifty or sixty miles to get around one of these tremendous ravines. Considerable streams lose themselves in this plain; some of them end in swamps, others suddenly disappear. . . .

"The volcanic plain in question forms an area of about sixty miles in diameter, where nothing meets the eye but a desolate and awful waste; where no grass grows nor water runs, and where nothing is to be seen but lava. Ranges of mountains skirt this plain, and far to the east the Three Tetons lift their heads sublimely—one of the most striking features of a wilderness where everything seems on a scale of stern and simple grandeur. . . ."

Viewing the Boise Valley, farther west, Bonneville calls it: "The most enchanting he had seen in the Far West. . . ."[5]

Following an attempt to persuade Hudson's Bay Company trappers and Indians to trade with him by plying them with alcohol, only to find that the binge resulted in his *own* men almost deserting, the merry-eyed Captain took what few furs he had gathered to rendezvous, shipped them East, then, after some months of wandering, established winter camp on the Portneuf. Ere long, he became restless. What he should do, he decided, was go down the Snake and Columbia and look into the possibility of establishing a post in direct competition with the British.

No sooner decided than done. On Christmas Day, 1833, with three companions, he rode away from the Portneuf camp, blithely telling the detachment left behind that he would return in early March.

"They were obliged to travel slowly," Irving wrote, "to spare the horses; for the snow had increased in depth to eighteen inches; and though somewhat packed and frozen, was not sufficiently so to yield firm footing. . . ."[6]

Thus began one of the most incredible journeys ever taken across the Snake River Country. Because Irving never saw the region, he misplaces streams and landmarks, but since he is specific on dates we can trace Bonneville's route with reasonable accuracy. Moving along the south and west bank of the Snake, he reached the vicinity of Farewell Bend January 12, 1834. There, instead of crossing the Blues by the route taken by Robert Stuart, Wyeth, and many Hudson's Bay Company brigades, Bonneville hired an Indian guide, who gave him a bad piece of advice.

"Stick to the river; there will be less snow."

This was true. But the guide neglected to add that the river route led into Hell's Canyon—impassable in any season. After a few days, the guide deserted, and Captain Bonneville found himself and his three companions in serious trouble.

"The river forced its way into the heart of the

Left, above: The Snake in winter, just below the mouth of the Hoback where it enters ". . . a fearsome gorge. . . ."

Left, below: The Snake near Weiser, Idaho

-----
4. Ibid., pp. 104, 105.

5. Ibid., p. 126.
6. Ibid., p. 208.

> mountains, winding between tremendous walls of basaltic rock . . . the snow was from two to three feet deep, but soft and yielding, so that the horses had no foothold . . . sometimes the crags and promotories forced them onto the narrow ribbon of ice that bordered the shore . . . to scramble over vast masses of rock that had tumbled from the impending precipices . . .to cross streams on bridges of ice and snow . . . to pass along narrow cornices . . . two of their horses fell into the river, one saved, the other lost. . . ."[7]

In desperation, the four men considered killing and skinning their horses, making bullboats of the hides, and committing themselves to the mercies of the river. If they had done so, Washington Irving would not have written his book. For in Hell's Canyon, the Snake is a merciless river.

Deserting the water's edge, the freezing, exhausted, starving men climbed out of the canyon, probably in the vicinity of Oxbow Dam. It is likely that they ascended North Pine Creek, crossed a six thousand foot high spur of the Wallowa Mountains to the headwaters of the Imnaha, descended that river to its lower valley, climbed again until the towering ridge dividing the watersheds of the Imnaha and Grande Ronde rivers had been crested, and at last descended into gentler country near the present-day border between Oregon and Washington.

They were fifty-three days from camp on the Portneuf; twenty from Farewell Bend.

This was the winter home of Chief *Tu-eka-kas'* band of Nez Perces, and, as always the Indians treated the whites hospitably, providing food, shelter, guides and an escort.[8] Heading west toward Fort Walla Walla:

> "They now traversed a gently undulating country, of such fertility that it excited the rapturous admiration of two of the Captain's followers, a Kentuckian and a native of Ohio. They declared that it surpassed any land that they had ever seen and often exclaimed what a delight it would be just to run a plough through such a rich and teeming soil. . . ."[9]

Early in March, 1834, Bonneville and his men reached Fort Walla Walla near the mouth of the Snake, where Hudson's Bay Company Factor Pierre Pambrun treated them with a cold politeness. Bonneville told Irving that he was not permitted to trade even for the necessities, but in a letter later written to Pambrun, Dr. McLoughlin chided the factor for selling the Americans "A Roll of Tobacco and some Dry Goods at Freemen's prices . . . I explained the error, and I am certain he will not do the like again. . . ."[10]

This was not the time to go into competition with the British, Bonneville decided; so, still accompanied by the genial Nez Perces, he turned back, and headed for the Portneuf along the same route he had taken west. All he had to show for his incredible hardships was the good will of the Nez Perces, who told him they would prefer trading with Americans rather than British and urged him to establish a post in their country.

Spring comes late in the high Wallowas, some of whose peaks rise to ten thousand feet. Even with guides to help, the retrograde march was gruelling. Snowdrifts lay deep on the northern slopes; steps had to be hacked in sheer ice for the horses, one of which was lost. But the crossing was made.

Reaching the Portneuf May 12, 1834, Bonneville rejoined the detachment left there, went to rendezvous on the upper Bear River a month later, and met the party just returned from its expedition to California. Except in exploration, adventure, and fuel for campfire tall tales, it had not been commercially successful. But, with typical energy, Captain Bonneville sent furs East, wrote a letter requesting an extension to his leave of absence, then, with a party of twenty-three men, set out once more for the lower Columbia.

This time, he shunned the Hell's Canyon route, crossing the Blue Mountains by leaving the Snake and ascending Burnt River (Irving calls it "Gun Creek") to the upper valley of the Grande Ronde. Late August had come after a hot, rainless summer, and the carelessness of man or bolts of lightning during thunderstorms had set the countryside afire.

> "Here they found all the plains and valleys wrapped in one vast conflagration, which swept over the long grass in billows of flame, shot up every bush and tree, rose in great columns from the groves, and sent up clouds of smoke that darkened the atmosphere. . . ."[11]

Even at high noon, the smoke was so thick that men separated from the party could find their companions only by shouting. For days they wandered aimlessly through the eye-smarting haze, until at last encountering friendly Indians, the Cayuses, who led them on across the Blues and down onto the Columbia River Plain.

Now they were out of the fire and into the frying pan, Bonneville found, for the farther west they proceeded along the Columbia, the more hostile the Hudson's Bay Company and the Indians became. Somewhere in the vicinity of The Dalles, a hundred miles upriver from Fort Vancouver, he gave up reaching it for the second time, turned around, and headed for the interior.

After one more winter in the West, he would forsake trading, return to the East, and meet Washington Irving.

-----

7. Ibid., p. 219.

8. This was Chief Joseph, the elder, who would not receive his Christian name until taken into the church a few years later. It would be his son, Chief Joseph, who would lead the Nez Perces in their classic battles against white soldiers in 1877.

9. *Bonneville,* Irving, p. 248. These are the fertile Palouse Hills.

10. *Letter,* McLoughlin to Simpson, October 31, 1837.

11. *Bonneville,* Irving, p. 324.

The writer would praise him as a leader, pointing out that during his four years in the wilderness, he never lost a man. But it is to be doubted that Irving's summation of the character of the Snake River Country came from Bonneville's lips:

> "An immense belt of rocky mountains and volcanic plains, several hundred miles in width, must ever remain an irreclaimable wilderness, intervening between the abodes of civilization, and affording a last refuge to the Indian. . . . Here, in time, the Indians and white men of every nation will produce hybrid races like the mountain Tartars of the Caucasus, who will become a scourge to the civilized frontiers. . . ."[12]

Like George Simpson, Irving labored under the delusion that beaver was the only thing of value in the Snake River Country. As other writers had done, he noted the religious nature of the Flatheads and Nez Perces and thought American missionaries would be welcomed by them. But in a region so vast, bleak, and filled with violence, what could missionaries accomplish beyond saving a few heathen souls?

That they might also save an empire-sized watershed for their country never entered the writer's mind. . . .

* * *

4.

With the three thousand dollars' worth of trade goods he had contracted to the Rocky Mountain Fur Company, Nathaniel Wyeth and a well-equipped party of men reached Green River rendezvous grounds in early July, 1834. He had chartered another ship, the *May Dacre,* which he planned to meet on the lower Columbia. Accompanying him, two scientists, Thomas Nuttall, a Harvard botanist, and John K. Townsend, a Philadelphia physician and ornithologist, rapturously classified flora, fauna, and birds, filled journals with copious notes, and behaved with such reckless disregard for their scalps while passing through dangerous Indian country that the hostiles, thinking them mad, left them strictly alone.

Also included in the party were the first men of the cloth to respond to the Indians' plea for missionaries: the Methodist minister, Jason Lee; his nephew, Daniel; and three lay brethren. Observing the stars, shooting the sun, and making accurate recordings of longitude and latitude with his feet set firmly upon the ground rather than on the heaving deck of a ship, was Wyeth's second in command, an old sea dog, Captain Joseph Thing.

Rendezvous was bigger and more riotous than ever, that summer, for, in addition to many lodges of Flatheads, Nez Perces, and Snakes, Bonneville's men, Wyeth's men, Rocky Mountain Fur Company trappers, men employed by the American Fur Company, deserters from the Hudson's Bay Company, and free trappers owing allegiance to no one but themselves—all were there. Perhaps it was Wyeth's New England sense of order and morality, but he respected British traders more than he did American. In a letter to Francis Ermatinger, a Hudson's Bay Company man, he wrote:

> "I have again to repeat to you the advice which I before gave you—not to come with a small party to the American Rendezvous. There are here a great collection of scoundrels. . . ."[1]

Seeing the missionaries, the Flatheads and Nez Perces first were delighted, then disappointed. Sorry, Jason Lee said, we do not plan to establish a mission in your country, which we hear is uncivilized. We're going on west to the Willamette Valley, near Fort Vancouver. Perhaps later. . . .

Now it was Wyeth's turn to be disappointed. Locked in a dog-eat-dog conflict with the American Fur Company, the Rocky Mountain Fur Company was being driven to the wall. Milton Sublette, who had signed the contract with Wyeth, had turned back short of Green River because of an increasingly painful leg injury. William Sublette, his brother, refused to honor the contract, accepting only a small part of the trade goods at bargain-basement prices.

Wyeth was furious. In retaliation for the breach of contract, he would "roll a stone into the garden of the Rocky Mountain Fur Company that they could never dislodge. . . ."

Leaving rendezvous and crossing over into the Snake River watershed, he chose a site ". . . in the low, rich bottom of a valley formed by the confluence of Portneuf River with the Snake, which it enters about nine miles below . . ." and commenced building a trading post July 15, 1834. Among the interested observers was Thomas McKay, leader of a Hudson's Bay Company brigade which happened to be in the neighborhood. It was McKay who had convinced Jason Lee that the Willamette Valley would be a more logical place to establish a mission than the country of the Flatheads and Nez Perces. After all, he no doubt told Lee, when the Joint Occupancy matter is settled, the Snake River Country will become British while the Willamette Valley becomes American.

Lee did consent to preach a sermon Sunday afternoon, July 27, to the Indians, whites, half-breeds, Americans, British, and combinations thereof assembled near Wyeth's still-building fort. The listeners were most attentive. Afterwards, the Sabbath was broken by a series of horse races, in the last of which a French-Canadian named Kanseau was tragically thrown and killed.

Next day, Jason Lee participated in a three-denominational burial service, reading the Ninth Psalm, which begins: "I will praise thee, O Lord, with my whole heart. . . ."

Wyeth wrote:

---

12. Ibid, p. 355.

1. *Fort Hall,* Brown, p. 136.

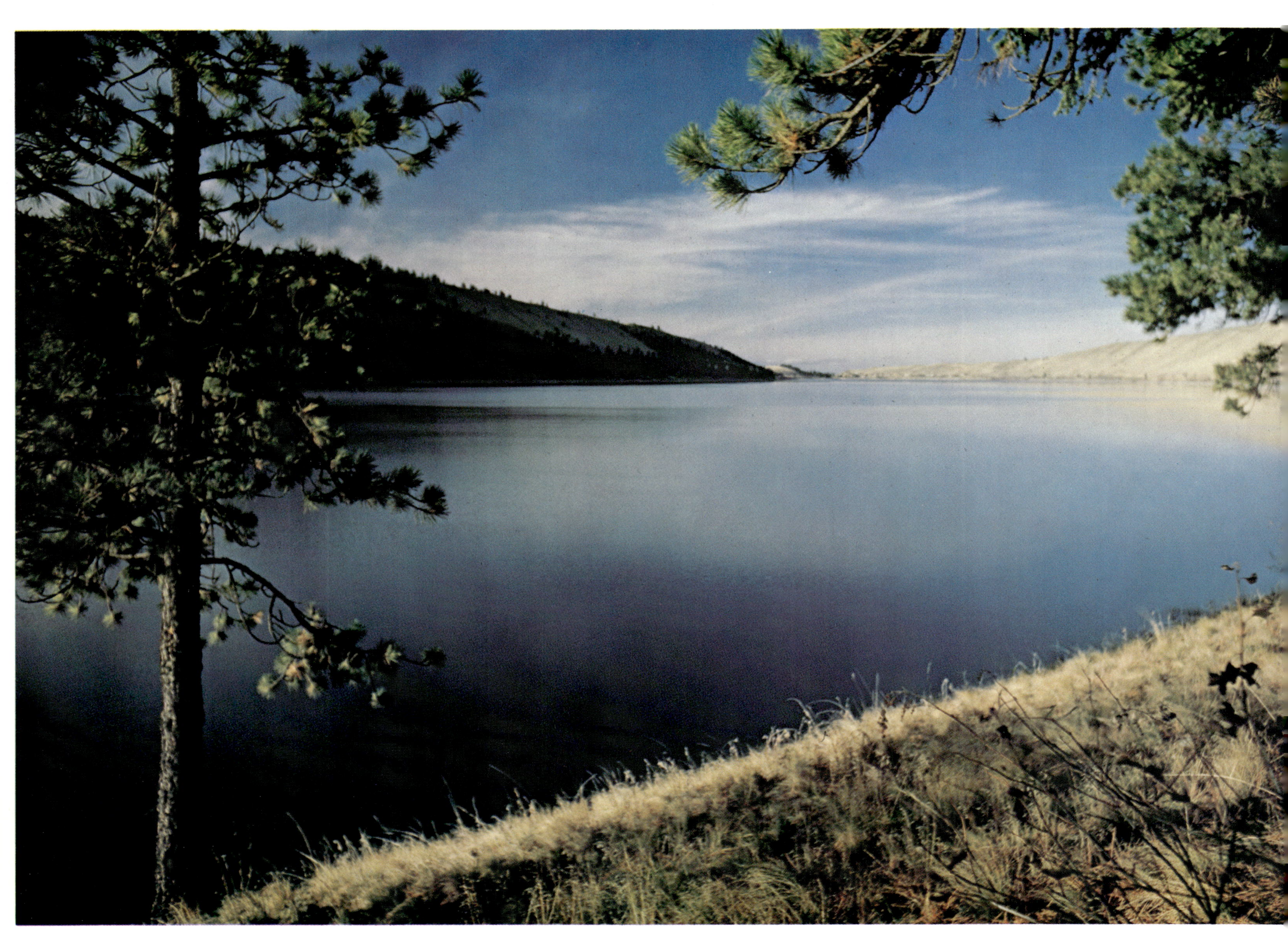

"Services for him were performed by the Canadians in the Catholic form, by Mr. Lee in the Protestant form, and by the Indians in their form, as he had an Indian family. He at least was well buried. . . ."[2]

Accompanied by the Hudson's Bay Company brigade, which had offered to see it through to the lower Columbia, the Lee party set out shortly thereafter. The building of the post, which Wyeth named after his principal backer, Henry Hall, went on. The morning of August 5, 1834, a homemade American flag was raised over Fort Hall, one of the three barrels of alcohol Wyeth had brought along was tapped, and the day was spent in celebration.

Townsend, the physician and naturalist, viewed it with disapproving eyes:

"At sunrise this morning the *Star Spangled Banner* was raised on the flagstaff of the fort, and a salute fired by the men. . . . All in camp were then allowed the free and uncontrolled use of liquor, and, as usual, the consequence was a scene of rioting, noise, and fighting during the whole day. . . . We had gouging, biting, fisticuffing, and stamping in the most scientific perfection. . . ."[3]

Leaving eleven men to take care of the post and initiate trading with the Indians, Wyeth and the remainder of his party moved northwest by way of Godin's River and Malade River, detaching small groups to trap these streams. Appropriately, Antoine Godin, whose father had been killed by Blackfeet near the river bearing his name, was one of them.

On September 2, Wyeth caught up with the Jason Lee party, which had traveled more slowly, at Fort Walla Walla. He noted with puzzlement that the leader and several men of the Hudson's Bay Company brigade were missing.

"Mr. McKay for some reason had remained in the mountains. . . ."

The reason soon became apparent. After seeing Wyeth start building Fort Hall, Thomas McKay decided that the Hudson's Bay Company should have a post in the area, too. Divulging his plans to no one, he and a few men lingered behind the brigade, chose a site on the Boise River ten miles upstream from its juncture with the Snake, and began building a fort whose flagstaff would bear the British banner.

It would be called Fort Boise.

As the crow flew, it was located some two hundred and fifty miles west of Fort Hall—just good "neighboring" distance in this country. But exchanging neighborly visits was not its intended function. In the game of rolling stones into gardens, any number could play, and the Hudson's Bay Company was adept at bowling on the green. . . .

Meantime, Wyeth reached the lower Columbia, and his supply ship, the *May Dacre*, soon was anchored in the stream. The British still were polite, but they still would not trade. The Indians had furs, but not for him. The river was full of fat, gleaming salmon which the Indians caught, cured, stored, and sold to the Britishers in great numbers, but would not catch for him. Work though they would, his own men lacked the equipment and know-how to obtain a substantial number of fish themselves, grew disgusted, and quit him to seek their fortunes in other fields for other employers.

Hearing that trade was going badly at Fort Hall, Wyeth hired thirteen Sandwich Islanders, whom he called "Kanakas," and sent them inland with Captain Joseph Thing and a load of fresh supplies. But the Hawaiians disliked the looks of the interior country, deserting their landlocked commander west of the Blue Mountains and returning to the lower Columbia. Captain Thing continued inland to Fort Hall, spent a brutal, frustrating winter there, competing with the Hudson's Bay Company and fighting Blackfeet, then came back to his employer's fishery just across the river from Fort Vancouver in July, 1835. ". . . emaciated, pale, and apparently seven years older than the season before. . . ."[4]

Reluctantly, Wyeth sent the *May Dacre* back to Boston with half a cargo of salmon and furs. Recognizing the fact he was facing financial ruin, he headed overland to Fort Hall to do what he could there. Again, his best efforts failed, so he returned to Boston and consulted with his backers. They could give him no more help, they said; he must carry on alone.

In a final attempt to salvage what little could be saved, Wyeth made one more trip west to Green River rendezvous in July, 1836. He arranged to sell Fort Hall to the only interested buyer, the Hudson's Bay Company. He learned that the Rocky Mountain Fur Company was now in its death throes; it would be succeeded by Astor's American Fur Company.

Well and good. Now the game would be played to its bitter end by two giant monopolies, one American, the other British, and the most ruthless would win. He would go back to farm managing and ice selling.

By now he should have been immune to surprises, but one sight he observed at the 1836 rendezvous moved him deeply. White women were there, traveling west. Lord in Heaven! Did they really mean to settle and make homes for their husbands in the Snake River Country?

2. Ibid., p. 148.
3. Ibid., p. 151.
4. Ibid., p. 163.

Left:

WALLOWA LAKE

". . . a most beautiful body of water." So wrote the missionary, Henry Spalding, when he first laid eyes on Wallowa Lake, in northeastern Oregon, in 1838. Apparently realizing that he was the first white man to view it, he wrote in his diary that he had named it "Spalding Lake." But it retained its Indian name. In the Nez Perce tongue, the word Wallowa means "Winding Waters."

They certainly did. For these were missionary couples drawn west by the pealing of a distant bell, responding to the New Testament's Great Command:

"Go ye therefore. . . ."

° ° °

5.

At rendezvous, the Flatheads and Nez Perces were overjoyed that at long last their pleas were being answered and white missionaries possessed of Big Medicine were coming to live with them. Marcus Whitman was a doctor, as well as a missionary, and the Indians marveled at his skill as he operated on Jim Bridger's well-muscled back to remove an arrowhead that had lodged in the gristle under the shoulder blade. They marveled, too, over his wife, Narcissa, who was blonde, lovely, cheerful, and gay.

The other missionary couple, Henry and Eliza Spalding, were more somber, less outgoing people, the husband a stern, strait-laced man, the wife feeble and often ill, though somehow she always managed to find strength enough to do what must be done. Though both the Whitmans and the Spaldings tried their best to conceal it, it was apparent that friction existed between them, which would cause them to establish separate missions. Learning their intentions, the Indians were delighted, for now, they thought, each tribe would have a missionary couple of its own.

Thomas McKay, the ubiquitous Hudson's Bay Company factor who was making a career of escorting American missionaries through the Snake River Country, advised the Whitmans and Spaldings to set up shop in the Willamette Valley, as Jason Lee had done. They refused. Yes, they would go to Fort Vancouver with the Hudson's Bay Company brigade, but as soon as the women were safely there, the men would return to the interior, select separate stations, build lodgings, and then bring their wives to them. No argument McKay or Dr. John McLoughlin later would make could alter that firm resolve.

With the breakup of the rendezvous, the missionaries, McKay's brigade, and a large contingent of happy Nez Perces crossed the divide to the Snake River watershed and traveled west—their every act a "first." These were the first white women to cross the continent; theirs would be the first white children born on the Pacific Slope. The light wagon which Spalding had insisted on bringing along would be the first to reach Fort Hall, though by then it would be an infernal nuisance and in such bad shape it would be cut down to a two-wheeled cart. As such, it would reach Fort Boise, be abandoned there, then, a few years later, would be brought on across the Blue Mountains as proof that a wagon trail to Oregon was feasible. And Narcissa Whitman's first and only child would be the first to die in this distant land.

The site chosen by Dr. Whitman for his mission was in Cayuse country south and east of the mouth of the Snake. He chose well, for here the climate was mild, the soil ". . . a delight to run a plough through, . . ." and the trail from East to West nearby. In the Cayuse tongue, the spot was called "*Waiilatpu*," the "Place of the Rye Grass."

Spalding chose a site one hundred and twenty miles east, in the heart of the Nez Perce country, twelve miles above the juncture of the Clearwater and the Snake. This sheltered valley was called "*Lapwai*" by the Nez Perces, which meant "Place of the Butterflies." Since the Whitman Mission was located a few miles outside the Snake River watershed, while Spalding's lay well within it, it will be the latter's tribulations and triumphs we shall consider here.

The ofttimes biased and testy historian, H. H. Bancroft, once wrote: "The greatest favor the missionaries could have done the Indians would have been to leave them alone." Which perhaps is true. But contact between white man and red began when Columbus discovered America, and, when cultures meet, selecting which specific feature of one shall not clash with another is as futile as commanding water not to run downhill.

Henry Spalding was a product of his times: a zealot, a firm believer in the rightness of his cause, a humorless, hard-working, extremely moral man. He did not come to the Nez Perces to understand them; he came to convert them. He did not intend to learn their ways; they must learn his. Since they were heathen, they must abandon their trust in medicine men and superstitious beliefs in pagan gods and learn to worship white man style—which to Spalding meant as strict Presbyterians.

Still, he was practical-minded enough to realize that before the Nez Perces could adopt Christianity they must acquire such civilized arts as tilling the soil, tending domesticated livestock, governing themselves under a code of laws, and learning to read and write. In these fields, his labors were truly prodigious.

Since it was simpler for Spalding and his associates to learn the Nez Perce tongue than for the Indians to master English, the missionaries compiled a dictionary, brought in a printing press from the Sandwich Islands, and began translating the Word into the Indian tongue. Laws were codified and put into writing, patterned after the Ten Commandments.

Dr. Clifford Drury, who has spent a lifetime studying and writing about the early-day missions in the Pacific Northwest, says:

> "Spalding was indefatigable in his physical labors and versatile in his skills. With help, he was able to construct and operate a gristmill, a sawmill, blacksmith shop, and a printing shop. He knew some of the simple practices of medicine. He was able to construct irrigation ditches, build houses, farm, raise his own vegetables and some fruit, care for his ever-increasing herds and flocks, and at the same time learn an Indian language, translate a part of the Bible into that tongue, compose hymns for the natives, teach

school, take long itinerating trips, and faithfully preach to the Indians Sunday after Sunday. . . .[1]

Like most Indian tribes, the Nez Perces recognized no single chief as having authority over the nation as a whole. Each band had its own set of leaders, head men, or elders, among whom one might be recognized as being the chief under certain circumstances. There were something like seventeen distinct bands of Nez Perces; those living east of the Snake River commonly were called "Upper Nez Perces," those living west of the river, "Lower Nez Perces." Whether the object be staging a feast, digging roots, going fishing, making meat in the buffalo country, or going to war against a neighboring tribe, the majority usually agreed to be led by the man most capable of accomplishing the particular aim in mind. If a minority dissented, it could go its own way in its own style under its own leader, with no penalty.[2]

How could a white man deal with such a system? Not very well. Inevitably, he called those Indian leaders willing to cooperate with him "Chiefs," demoting those who opposed him to less important roles.

Most of the Nez Perces were given white names, for their own were tongue twisters. *Ish-hol-hol-hoats-toats,* who was always friendly to the whites, a good linguist, a shrewd bargainer, and a convincing talker, became "Lawyer." *Tu-eka-kas,* chief of the Wallowa band, was baptized, officially married to one of his two wives, and given his Christian name, Joseph, in a single ceremony, with no mention being made of his *other* wife, with whom he continued to live.[3] *Tack-en-su-a-tis,* a chief at first friendly to the missionaries, then cool, remained in English "Rotten Belly." Timothy early became a Christian and a loyal friend, remaining both all his life. James, a chief of the Lapwai band and also a medicine man, soon grew jealous of Spalding, turned hostile, stayed heathen, and usually was referred to contemptuously as "Old James."

For a time, the friendship between Spalding and Joseph was that of blood brothers. In spring, summer, and early fall, Joseph's band of Nez Perces lived in one of the loveliest spots in the West, the green, lush, game-filled Wallowa Valley. In winter, it moved north from the forty-five hundred foot level to lower, milder country in the rolling hills and plains west of Snake River. Now and again Spalding paid Chief Joseph a visit in the Wallowa Valley, noting the profusion of fish, game, birds, and fine horses to be found in the high country.

It is probable that Spalding was the first white man to see Wallowa Lake: ". . . the sight of which paid me for my visit. It is a most beautiful body of water. . . ."

He named it "Spalding Lake" in his diary, but by the time his personal writings came to public view other white men had visited the spot, accepted the mellifluous Indian term "*Wallowa,*" which translates into "Winding Waters," and that particular opportunity for geographical immortality was lost.

To give the missionary his due, he must be credited for supervising the first logging operation and the first river drive down the Clearwater, an industry and colorful practice that endure to this day in stands of the West's finest timber along one of its most scenic rivers. In late December, 1840, Spalding reports going up the Clearwater a few miles with three white men and thirty-two Indians. While one group cut white pine on the south bank, the other crossed to the north bank and cut cedar. Once the trees were down, they were slid into the river and compacted into rafts:

> "(Dec 26th) Three rafts completed, including 28 beautiful logs and 6 or 7 timbers for the sills, plates and beams for the school house. I take the heavy raft with Timothy and Luke. Strike a bar at the foot of the island and wreck most of our couplings but save our timber. After some lifting in the wet, get off. . . ."

As they neared home, the rafts hung up again:

> "Timothy goes off on two logs, which start the whole raft rolling, and with great difficulty, by jumping square up and down, keeps from being drawn between two logs. Joseph sends in a horse on which I reach the shore in safety. . . ."[4]

If Joseph saved Spalding's life, that day, he was only returning a favor the missionary had done him a few months earlier. On August 26, 1840, Spalding notes in his diary that he has just received an express from Joseph stating that the chief is very ill and not expected to live. In following these excerpts, it should be born in mind that Spalding was at Lapwai, twelve miles up the Clearwater, while Joseph lay ill in the high Wallowa Valley, twenty hours of the hardest kind of riding away, the distance being, as the trail wound, in the neighborhood of one hundred miles.

> "About 4 P.M. I jump onto one of the horses the Indians rode up and start to see my dear brother Joseph . . . find the horse very hard. Reach the river (The Snake) and cross, dark. My guides are soon far behind and asleep. Stop 11½ P.M.
>
> "(27th) Start early, eat a bit of dry Buffalo . . . my horse is too weak to ride easy. Suffer much from riding. Reach the spruce plain about 5 P.M. Am in great pain. Find two young men with a spare horse waiting . . . find it extremely easy. Ride 15 miles and arrive about sundown. Find Joseph weak with high fever, pulse 90, no passage for several days. I give

1. *The Diaries and Letters of Henry H. Spalding,* with Introductions and Editorial Notes by Clifford Merrill Drury, Arthur H. Clark Company, Glendale, Calif., 1958, p. 242.

2. Caleb Carter, Lapwai, Idaho, 1955. Much of my information regarding Nez Perce history and traditions has been gathered through informal conversations with the Indians over a period of time. Most of it seems authentic.

3. Again, Joseph the elder.

4. *Spalding Diary,* Drury, p. 305.

him dose of calomel and Jalap[5] and bleed. Mark has reserved a small bit of deer killed yesterday with which I make a good supper. . . .

"(28th) Give Joseph another dose of calomel and Jalap. Soon copious passage. Pulse at eve down to 70. Thank the Lord for his goodness. . . .

"(31st) Joseph speaks again of giving me a horse. I refuse again and tell him I came not for horses but because I loved him . . . finding Joseph grieved, I consented. The horse is large, stout, and tame. . . ."[6]

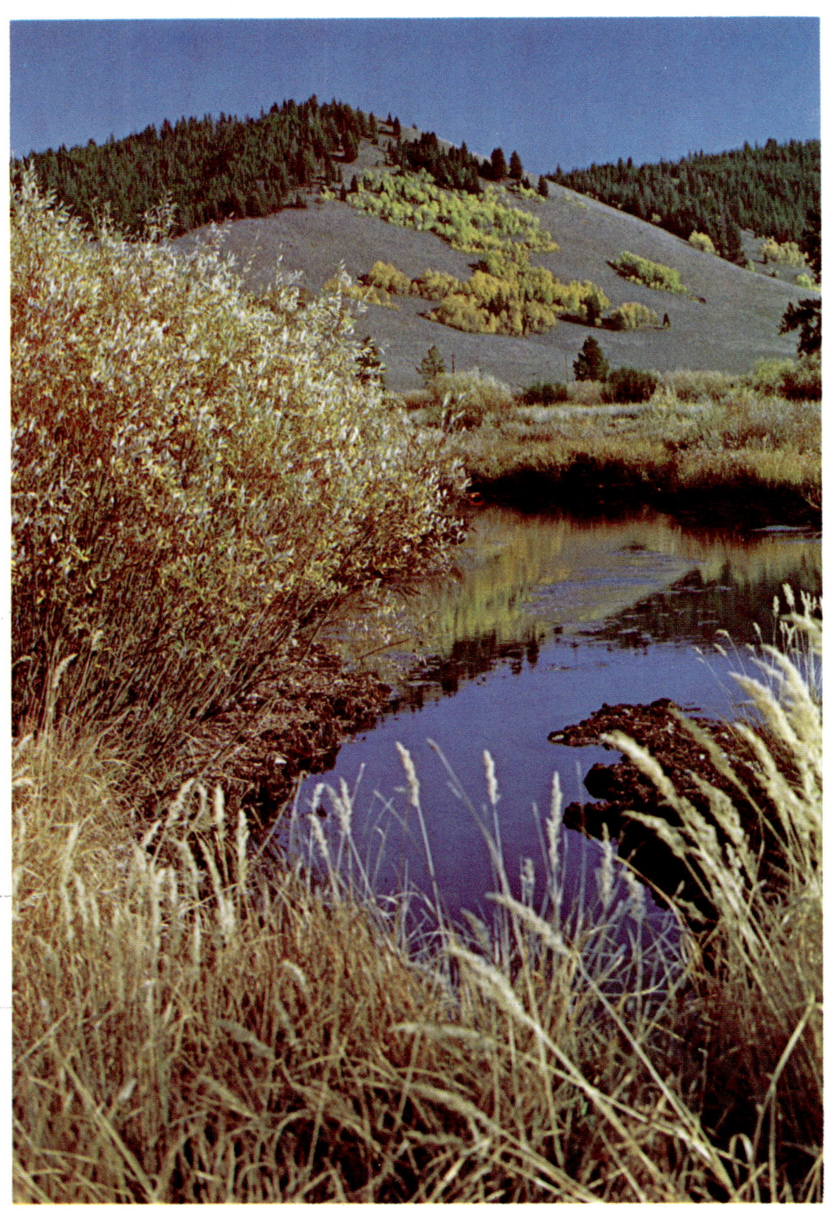

Near Galena Summit, on a tributary to the Salmon

If given time and left alone, it is possible that the missionaries and the Indians of the Snake River Country could have learned to understand one another, work together, and bridge the ages-long cultural gulf separating white and red races. But neither time nor isolation was granted them.

In the world of fashion now, beaver was out, silk in. The day of the trapper was done. Though the two giant monopolies had the field all to themselves, there was nothing left to fight over. Two months before Spalding made his grueling ride to dose Joseph with calomel and Jalap, the American Fur Company held its final big rendezvous, and free trappers like Robert Newell, Joe Meek, and William Craig said their farewells to a way of life they would live no more.

> "Come," said Newell to Meek, "we are done with this life in the mountains—done with wading in beaver dams and freezing or starving alternately—done with Indian trading and Indian fighting. The fur trade is dead in the Rocky Mountains, and it is no place for us now, if ever it was. We are young yet and have life before us. We cannot waste it here. . . ."[7]

At this same rendezvous, the patient Flatheads, who for years had sought missionaries, seen them come, then go on to other localities, received an answer to their prayers. For the Black Robes had sent out a Jesuit priest, Pierre Jean De Smet, who promised to establish a mission in their country.

Learning this, the Flatheads wept with emotion. Father De Smet wrote: "It was like children running to meet their father after a long absence. . . ."[8]

William Craig, unemployed trapper, was redheaded, fiercely independent, and had been a dropout from civilized society ever since he left his Virginia home as a young man twenty-two years earlier. In the Clearwater country a few years ago, he had married a Nez Perce woman, Isobel, who was a member of the Lapwai band. Her father, whom Spalding called Old James, was its chief. When Joe Meek and Robert Newell told Craig that they intended to seek

5. Jalap is a medicinal herb, a Mexican plant with laxative qualities.

6. *Spalding Diary,* Drury, pp. 297-98.

7. *The River of the West,* by Mrs. Frances Fuller Victor, Hartford, Conn., 1870, p. 264.

8. *Black Robe: The Life of Pierre-Jean De Smet, Missionary, Explorer & Pioneer,* by John Upton Terrell, Doubleday, 1964, p. 94.

their fortunes in the Willamette Valley, and invited him to come along, Isobel countered with the suggestion that he go home with her and settle down in the Lapwai Valley.

Well, she *was* his wife. In the Willamette Valley, it rained nine months out of the year. The Nez Perces were friendly people, who enjoyed life, and he'd never cared much for civilized places. Sure, he'd heard that a bunch of self-righteous missionaries had established a station in the Lapwai Valley and were giving his father-in-law all kinds of trouble. But *he* knew how to deal with them. . . .

Such, probably, were Craig's thoughts.

Now, for Henry Spalding, his wife, and the lay brethren assisting them, a time of tribulation began. Never a tolerant man, Spalding regarded the Flathead Mission established by Father De Smet in the Bitter Root Valley to the east as Satan's work. He warned the Nez Perces against Catholicism —which of course whetted the curiosity of the dissidents and encouraged them to exploit the rivalries between the two religions.

Old James, the medicine man, told his son-in-law that the Spaldings should be driven out and that Craig should take over their property. Ex-trapper friends visiting Craig brought along whiskey, cards, and religious disrespect. By their example, they encouraged young Indians to play hooky from school and church, gamble, drink, and race horses.

Spalding found Christianizing ex-trappers more difficult than proselyting Indians. One of Craig's friends, James Conner, did join the church with Timothy and Joseph, but soon backslid and was suspended for: "Sabbath breaking, neglect of duties, fighting, polygamy, sending a challenge to fight a duel, and vending liquor. . . ."[9]

Well, as the aging reprobate commented after hearing a sermon on the Ten Commandments, at least he ". . . never made no graven images. . . ."

Craig told the Indians Spalding was "making dogs and slaves of them . . ." and turning them into "a nation of women. . . ." One day, a group of Nez Perces came into the schoolhouse, where Eliza Spalding was teaching, "naked and painted with the most horrible figures, and continued their indecent gestures until Mrs. S. was obliged to leave. . . ." When she objected, they threatened to tie her up and whip her. They threatened Spalding, too: "I have had a gun cocked and presented to my head for 15 or 20 minutes. . . ."[10]

Spalding's cattle were poisoned; ears and tails were cut off his oxen. One winter night, the Indians built a big bonfire out of his fence rails. "The whole valley rang with their gambling songs and hideous yells. . . ." Donning a heavy buffalo coat, Spalding rushed outside and attempted to rescue his precious fence rails. The Indians "threw me violently to the ground 6 or 7 times, and finally upon the fire. . . ."

His thick coat saved him from serious injury. Doggedly getting up, he pulled his fence rails out of the fire; unable to cope with the stubbornness of the man, the gamblers picked up their belongings and left.

> "I returned to my room to weep with deep regret that such a flood of iniquity had been opened upon this defenseless tribe of babes apparently by the hands of a single white man. . . ."[11]

Competition with the Catholics for heathen souls, intimidation by drunken Indians, and floods of iniquity spread by immoral white men were not the only problems Spalding faced. In addition to his own and Whitman's station, others had been established at Kamiah, sixty miles up the Clearwater, and at Tshimakain, not far from present-day Spokane. Being human, the missionaries often disagreed with one another. Sometimes they put their complaints, accusations, and self-justifications into letters sent East to the American Board of Commissioners for Foreign Missions back in Boston. Inevitably, after six years, the dissension created a crisis.

Meeting in February, 1842, the American Board, whose task it was to fund and supervise the four missions, came to grips with several unpleasant facts. The deficit being incurred to save Indian souls was far out of proportion to the number of converts. Too much time and energy were being wasted by the missionaries in criticizing one another. Even worse, since the trickle of Americans emigrating to Oregon had grown to a sizable stream, the Whitman station seemed more interested in caring for white indigents than it did in caring for the spiritual needs of the Cayuses.

The time had come to consolidate and retrench.

In September, 1842, Dr. Marcus Whitman opened the letter just delivered to Waiilatpu and read:

The Spaldings were being recalled. . . .

Waiilatpu must be closed and sold. . . .

The Whitmans must move to Tshimakain. . . .

Since the seeds of dissension among the missionaries had been sown long before, been nurtured by adversity, frustration, jealously, unrequited love, conceit, and a zeal that at times lapsed into madness, we shall not consider anything here but the bitter harvest. Dr. Whitman called for an assembly of all concerned. After they had arrived, argued, confessed their errors, and devoutly expressed wishes for another chance, he made an astounding proposal.

He would leave for Boston at once, confront the Board, and persuade it to change its collective mind.

Spalding thought the idea preposterous. Narcissa, concerned for her husband's health, felt a winter journey across the continent would be too much for him. Since his lone traveling companion would be a Massachusetts lawyer then visiting Waiilatpu, Asa Lovejoy, who was unaccustomed to the wilderness, the other missionaries felt the trip would be far too dangerous.

Impatiently, he brushed the objections aside. On October 3, Whitman, Lovejoy, and a dog named Trapper, which

9. *First White Women Over the Rockies,* Edited by Clifford M. Drury, Arthur H. Clark Company, Glendale, Calif., 1963. Vol. I, p. 214.

10. Ibid., p. 227.

11. *Spalding Diary,* Drury, p. 325.

had been the pet of the drowned little girl, Alice Clarissa Whitman, left Waiilatpu and headed East.

Ten days later, the trio reached Fort Hall, a distance of five hundred miles. Already the early mountain winter was closing in on the high country; it promised to be a bitter one. Ahead, they were warned by the Hudson's Bay Company factor, Peter Grant, the Sioux and Pawnees were at war, making a crossing of the plains an extremely risky business. Better go back to Waiilatpu and wait for spring.

No, Whitman said, they must go on now. Instead of taking the direct route, they would swing south to Taos and Santa Fe, then back north to Bent's Fort. True, this detour would add a thousand miles to the trip. But he could not wait for spring.

Minus a mule and the family pet, Trapper, both of which had been eaten, Whitman and Lovejoy reached Taos in mid-December. Both men were suffering from exhaustion, frostbite, and starvation. After resting two weeks, they moved on to Bent's Fort, Whitman impatiently leaving Lovejoy behind in his haste to join a party heading for St. Louis.

Still wearing his disreputable, shaggy, smelly buffalo coat that had kept him from freezing in the snow and cold of the high country, Whitman reached Washington, D.C., in early March, 1843. Congress had just adjourned. After a brief stay there, he went on to New York, where a cabman, taking him for a hick from the sticks, fleeced him out of two dollars of his almost exhausted funds. He had a session with Horace Greeley, who admired his courage and principles but thought anybody fool enough to go to Oregon was out of his mind. During a visit to the Methodist Board For Foreign Missions, he learned with concern that it was considering recalling Jason Lee, who seemed to be more interested in real estate and politics than in saving heathen souls.

Broke and shaggy, he reached Boston in early May and presented himself to Secretary David Greene of the American Board. Greene was so shocked by his appearance and smell, he hastily gave him some money and told him to get a bath and some decent clothes.

There is ample evidence that the Board did not approve of Whitman's fantastic journey. But the drama of what the man had done overpowered the committee's conservatism. After due consideration, it granted his two most important requests.

Waiilatpu would be continued. . . .

Spalding would be retained "on trial. . . ."[12]

Thus, the legend that "Marcus Whitman saved Oregon for the United States . . ." began. During the few years of life left him, Dr. Whitman made no such claim himself. In a memorial to Congress, sent through influential friends, he did stress the importance of the Oregon Country and proposed that the military establish a chain of forts along the Oregon Trail to supply and protect emigrants. By coincidence, on his return to Waiilatpu he encountered at Westport the first of the Great Emigrations, that of 1843, and rendered it invaluable assistance on its way West. But he was not the Saviour of Oregon that fanciful writers later painted him.

Like air currents vagrantly stirring on the edges of a gigantic weather front, the winds of change had begun with the journey of the Flatheads and Nez Perces to St. Louis in 1831. Until that time, there appeared to be nothing of value in the Snake River Country but beaver. Wyeth and Bonneville went west to establish commercial ventures, failed, and left the region. Hall Kelley went west to colonize, and failed, too. Then the missionaries went west—and stayed.

Now the air currents no longer were vagrant. Now the winds of change were purposeful and strong. For in the East, the word was spreading that there was fertile, well-watered, limitless land in Oregon.

Land free for the taking.

In the Snake River Country, only the beginnings of settlement existed: Fort Hall and Fort Boise, both Hudson's Bay Company posts; Spalding's Lapwai Mission and the cabins of ex-trapper Craig and his rowdy friends; the mission at Kamiah. But the canvas-covered wagons were beginning to move.

The westering emigrants knew little about the Snake River Country—and cared even less. The maps showed the part crossed by the Oregon Trail as a flat, barren desert—kind of a "passing-through" country, which would take maybe a month's travel time out of the long trek to the lush green paradise of western Oregon.

Well, so long as a river flowed through it, traversing that desert should be no problem.

Time to get rolling. . . .

12. *The Great Command*, by Nard Jones, Little, Brown, 1959. This is a dramatic, readable, yet accurate account of the missionary efforts in the Oregon Country. For Whitman's ride East see pp. 251-62.

Right:

OREGON WILDERNESS STREAM

Bear Creek in early summer, northeastern Oregon. This is one of many streams descending out of the wilderness area of the high Wallowas. All are great fish producers, once you learn their secrets. And learn them personally you must—for the experts never tell.

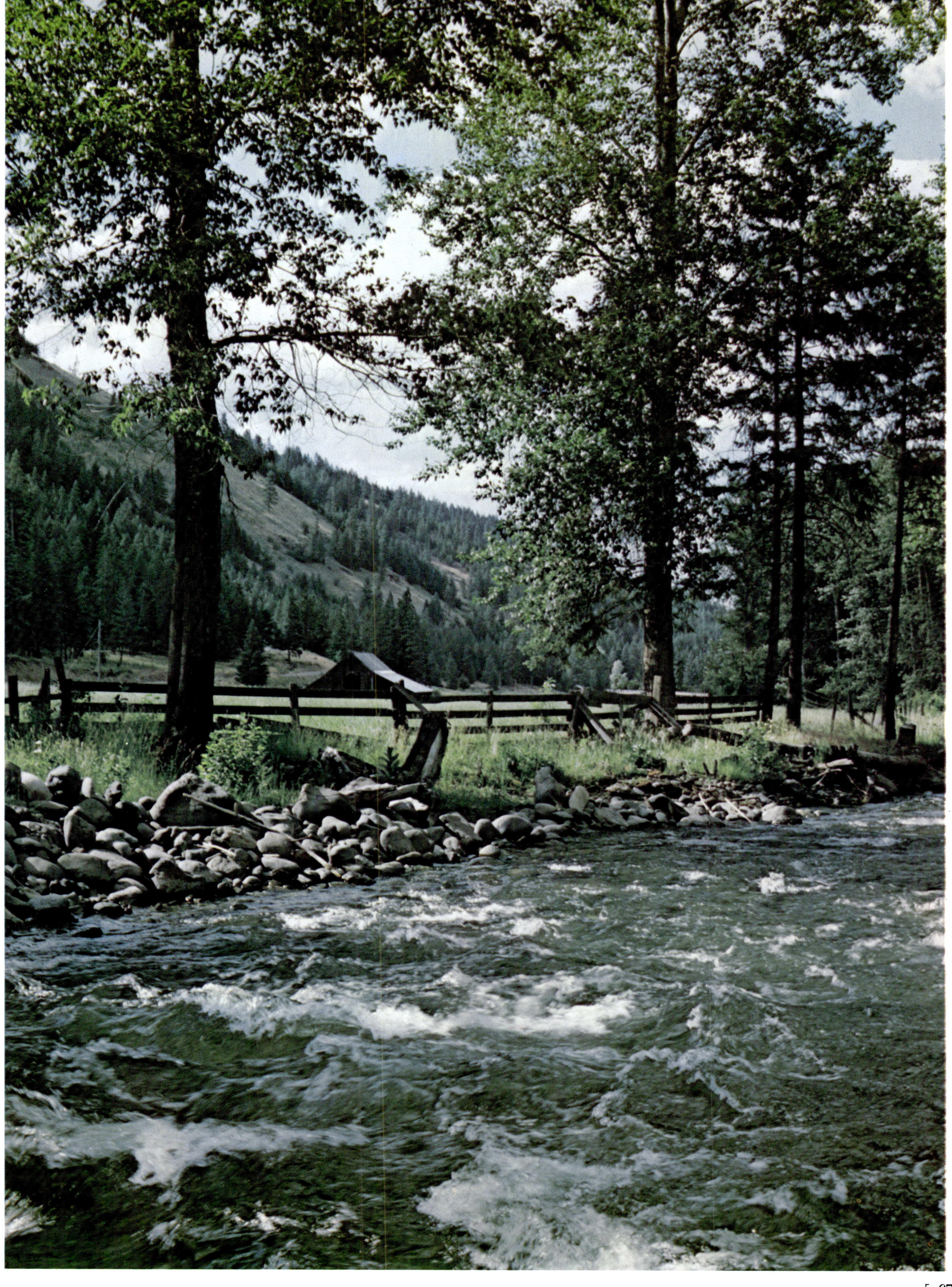

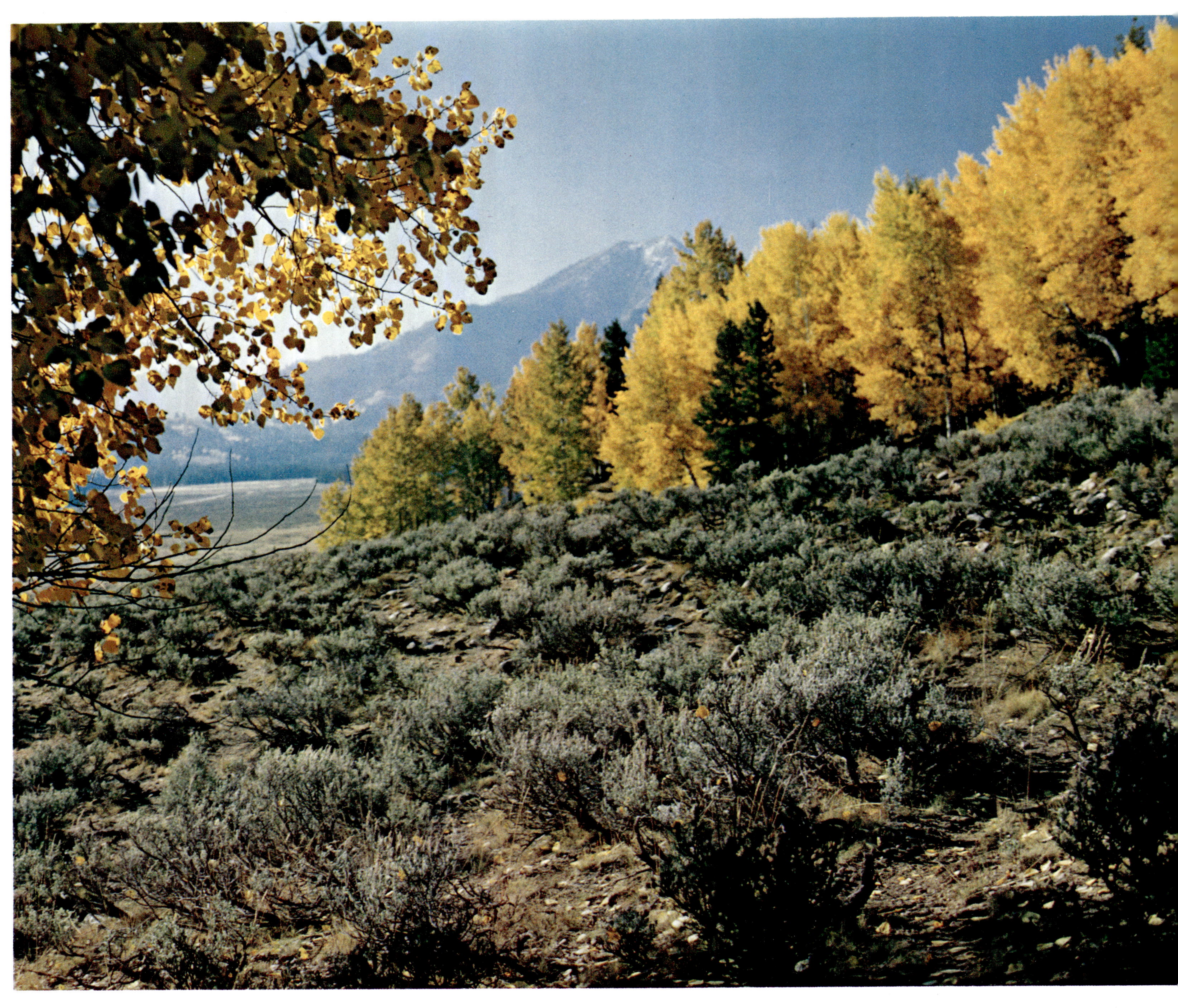

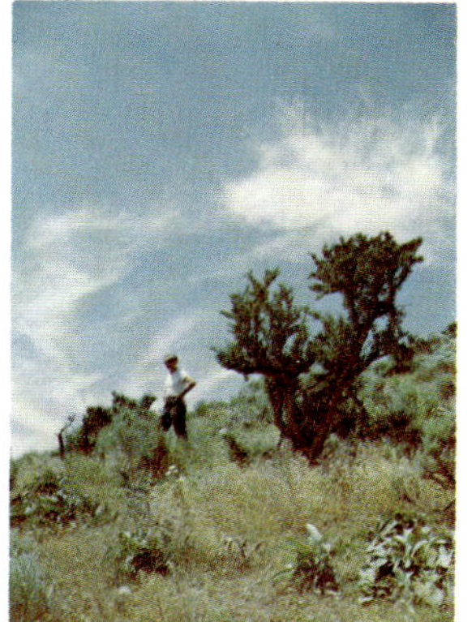

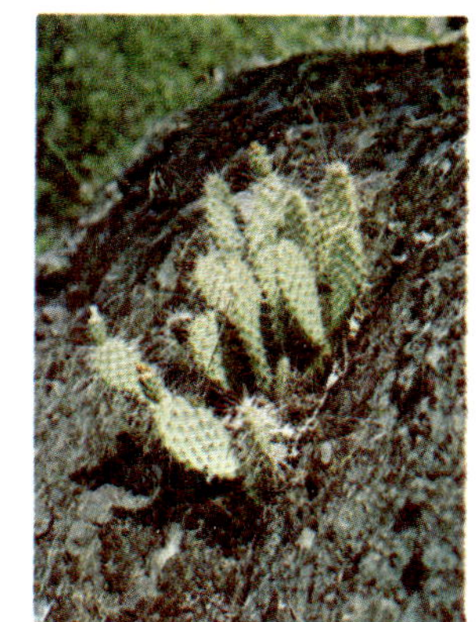

PART FOUR

River of Desert

1843-1860

1.

From the western foot of the Grand Tetons to the eastern base of the Blue Mountains, the Snake River flows in a gently curving arc through a vast basin sixty miles wide and three hundred miles long. Wagon trains bound for Oregon usually struck the Snake near Fort Hall around the first of August. Summer's heat, dust, and drought were at their worst then, and the travelers must spend the better part of a miserable, tedious, energy-depleting month making the crossing.

Rapturous descriptions of scenic vistas, enthusiastic comments on the quality of the soil, and poetic expressions of the thrill of partaking in an epic movement are not to be found in emigrant diaries of that period. This appeared to be barren, worthless country. Why lift up your eyes to the beauties of mountain ranges hazed by dust and heat when they were thirty miles distant to north or south? Why consider the quality of the soil in this land of little rain when it rose like fine powder from hooves and wheels to fill eyes, ears, mouth, and lungs? Why praise the charms of a rapids-filled river when camp five hundred feet from its cooling waters too often meant spending a thirsty night on the plain that vertical distance above it, the dark, sheer, unscalable walls of its gorge making getting down to its moistness an impossibility?

By August most of the game had fled to higher elevations, and time was too precious to send out hunting parties. For meat, one ate buffalo jerky, sand-impregnated dried salmon, or a recently deceased, worn-out oxen as tough and juiceless as its hickory yoke. Grass for the livestock was scarce and tinder dry. Sharp lava rocks slashed the feet of the draft animals, made the wagons torture to ride in, and quickly destroyed boot leather of human pedestrians. Milk cows went dry, or, feeding on bitter sage, gave milk unfit for children to drink. In the dust-filled, searing, low-humidity winds sweeping unimpeded across the plains, lips cracked, sores formed, and fretful babies developed rashes that would not heal.

Usually emigrant women rode in wagons. But Eliza Spalding and Narcissa Whitman, the first white females to cross the continent, rode sidesaddle in long skirts on sometimes fractious horses. Just west of Fort Hall on August 6, 1836, Eliza Spalding records in her diary:

> "Yesterday my horse became unmanageable in consequence of stepping into a hornets nest. I was thrown, and notwithstanding my foot remained a moment in the stirrup, and my body dragged some distance, I received no serious injury. . . ."[1]

On another occasion, this ill, feeble, yet indestructible woman mentions being thrown from her horse without injury, attributing her good fortune to the same source that had improved her health on a diet of dry buffalo meat, though it tasted "very miserable. . . ."

> "The hand of God has been conspicious in preserving my life thus far, on this adventurous journey," she wrote. "Surely the Lord is my Shepherd, and I shall have nothing to fear, if I will but repose my whole trust in Him."

When describing a day's long, hot ride near Fort Hall on August 2, Narcissa Whitman also resorted to paraphrasing an Old Testament verse:

> "The Heavens over us were brass, and the earth iron under our feet."[2]

Left: Aspens and Sagebrush near Stanley, Idaho

1. "Diary," Eliza Spalding. Original at Penrose Library, Whitman College, Walla Walla.

2. "Diary," Narcissa Whitman. Same as above. The Bible quotation is from Deuteronomy 28:23.

The four-wheeled, covered vehicle owned by Spalding, converted by Whitman into a two-wheeled cart at Fort Hall, and finally abandoned at Fort Boise in 1836, was not the big Conestoga prairie schooner of later Oregon Trail days. It was a light vehicle called a Dearborn, whose eventual fate and final resting place are obscure. But the fact that it had made tracks into the Far West gave following travelers the idea that wheeled vehicles *could* get through to the Columbia.

In 1840, a small missionary party led by Harvey Clark appeared at the final American Fur Company rendezvous with three farm wagons. Employing Robert Newell as a guide, the group managed to drive the wagons on to Fort Hall. By then, their horses were exhausted, the wagons badly battered, and the missionaries were ready to accept the advice of Hudson's Bay Company employees that it would be folly to take the wagons any farther. Giving Newell the vehicles in payment for his services, the Clark party traded their jaded horses for fat ones he owned, and proceeded to the Columbia via packtrain, while Newell remained at Fort Hall for a month or so.

> "At the time I took the wagons, I had no idea of undertaking to bring them into this country," Newell later wrote. "(But) the American Fur Company had abandoned the country for good, (so) I concluded to hitch up and try the much dreaded job of bringing a wagon to Oregon. . . ."[3]

Traveling with him were his long-time friends, Joe Meek and William Craig, who also were quitting the trapping game. Details of this first wagon train journey across the Snake River Country are sketchy. But we know that the party reached Fort Boise without incident. And we know that during its brief stop there, Hudson's Bay Company Factor Francis Payette made three mistakes.

First, he invited Robert Newell to be his guest in quarters within the fort, while Meek and Craig were left to camp outside the walls. Second, he sent out a company servant with filets of sturgeon for the two ex-trappers, which, feeling insulted, they rejected with pungent comments. Third, he told the three mountain men that taking wagons across the Blue Mountains was impossible; his considered advice was to leave them behind.

Robert Newell was level-headed; Joe Meek was bullheaded; and William Craig was redheaded. Being Americans, none would take a dare. A man could swallow an insult from a Britisher. But accept considered advice? Never!

Those wagons would cross the Blues if they had to be carried on three broad backs.

Floated across the Snake, tugged and pushed up brushy, rocky Burnt River Canyon, skidded, jolted, and careened across the dividing ridge to the Powder, driven across the lovely, fertile valley of the upper Grande Ronde, then again tugged and pushed, sweated and bullied, cajoled and cursed up steep grades and through thick trees that must be felled to make a road, until the thirty-seven-hundred-foot height to be called Deadman's Pass was crested, and then down through still bigger timber on the slopes of Emigrant Hill until the westward flowing Umatilla was reached—the wagons moved.

Somewhere along the way they lost their beds, but when they pulled to a stop in the yard at the Whitman Mission their wheels and running gear were intact. For the first time, it could be said that wheeled vehicles had crossed the continent to the Columbia River watershed.

Others soon would follow. . . .

* * *

2.

With his twelve-year-old nephew, Perrin, Dr. Marcus Whitman reached Westport May 31, 1843, homeward bound. During previous years, annual migrations to the Far West had been very small, consisting mostly of reinforcements for the missions: fourteen people in 1839; the Clark party of three wagons and six people in 1840; fifty-four people in 1841; one hundred and twelve in 1842—and of these some were bound for California.[1] But this year there was astonishing evidence that a movement unparalleled in the nation's history was under way.

One hundred and twenty wagons, over a thousand men, women, and children, and five thousand oxen, horses, and cattle were preparing to move west, the surprised Dr. Whitman found. To the leaders of the migration, his name and feats were well known, and his appearance at this time and place was regarded as the greatest of good fortune. Eager questions peppered him from every quarter.

Was he returning to his mission station? Could wagons get through to the Columbia? Would he travel with them and give them the benefit of his medical services and advice?

To all questions, he answered yes.

Since many accounts have been published regarding this migration, there is no point in detailing its trials and triumphs here. As already noted, Whitman neither claimed nor should be given credit for directly inspiring it, but his services to it were invaluable.

------

3. Newell to Elwood Evans, quoted by Evans in his *Annual Address, Transactions of the 5th Annual (T.O.P.A.) Re-Union of the Oregon Pioneer Assn. for 1877,* p. 23.

1. *Toward the Setting Sun,* by Miles Cannon, Columbian Press, Portland, Oregon, 1953, p. 89.

Right, above: Snowdrifts, winter gray sagebrush, and the bleak cold of a February day make the desert near Craters of the Moon look barren indeed.

Right, below: A flock of sheep grazes on thinly scattered grass among clumps of sagebrush and lava rock near Palouse Falls, on the lower Snake.

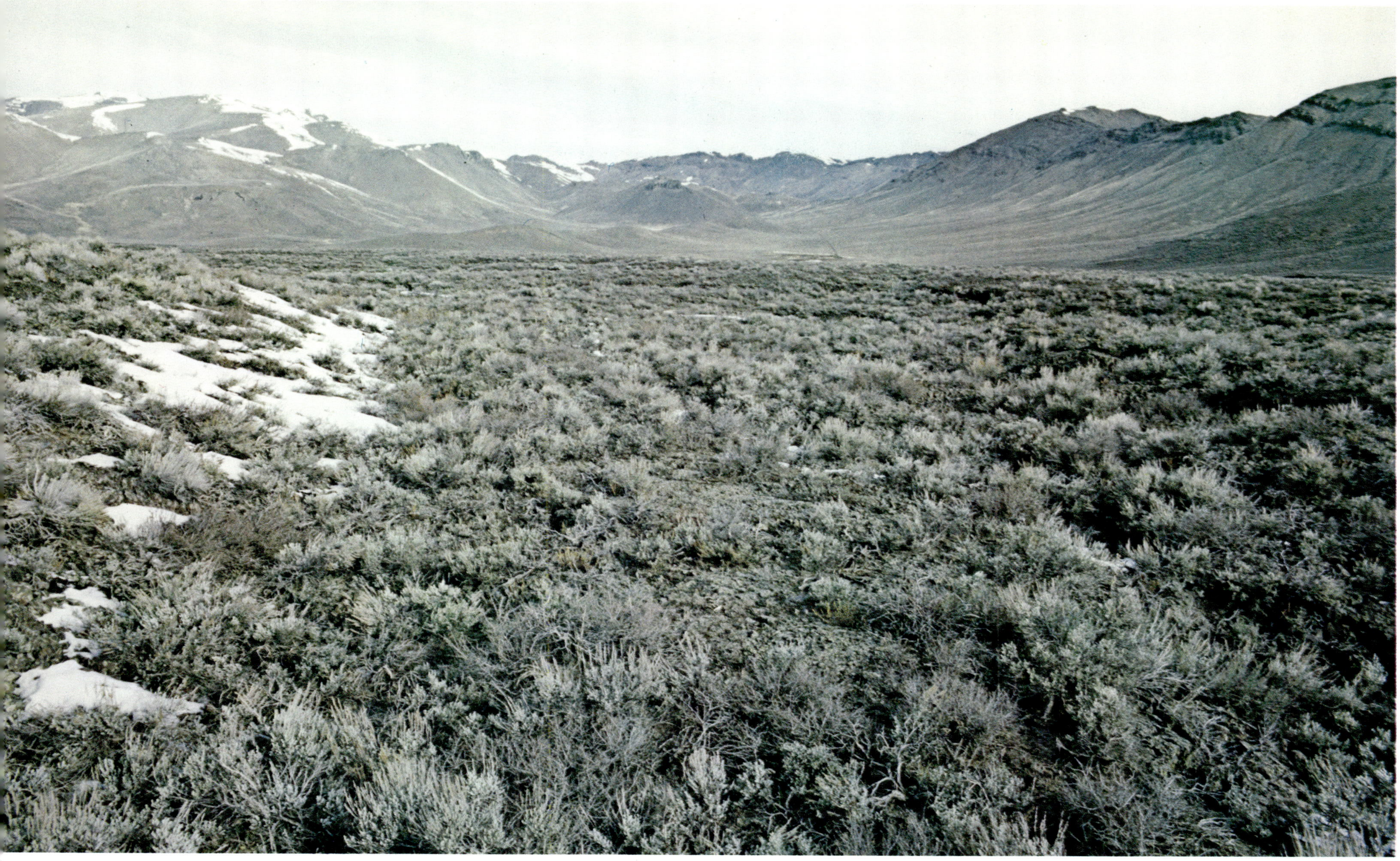

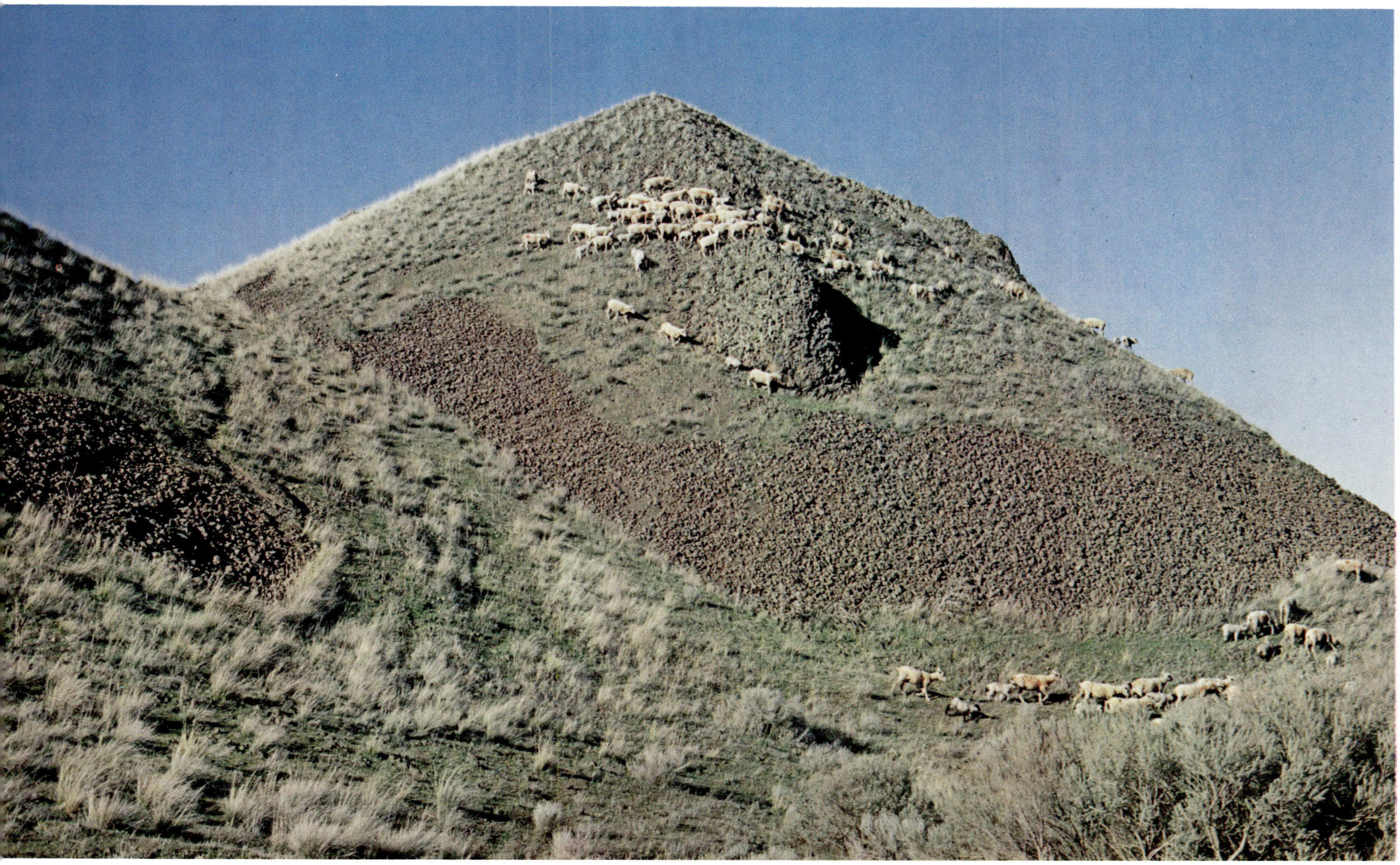

"His constant advice, which we knew was based upon a knowledge of the road before us," Jesse Applegate wrote, "was '*travel, Travel, TRAVEL*—nothing else will take you to the end of your journey; nothing is wise that does not help you along; nothing is good for you that causes a moment's delay. . . .' "[2]

The years of the first wave of emigration to Oregon extended from 1843 through 1859. While completely accurate figures cannot be secured, estimates made of a few sample years are of interest:

1844— 1,475 people
1845— 3,000
1849—25,000
1852—23,000
1853—15,000[3]

So far as the Snake River Country was concerned, the passing through year after year of vast numbers of wagons, people, and livestock brought slow but important changes to the desert region. The Indians, at first curious, friendly, and eager to trade dried salmon for trinkets and cast-off clothing, grew hostile as they saw how wantonly the whites slaughtered game and how ruthlessly draft animals and domesticated livestock destroyed grass customarily saved to nourish their own horses during the winter. In this low-rainfall region, ecological scales were in delicate balance, and the damage done by wheels, hooves, and grazing animals at a time of year when wild game and Indian horses ordinarily let the basin lands rest was incalculable.

Contrary to the expectations of Nathaniel Wyeth and other expansion-minded Americans, the Joint Occupancy Treaty with Great Britain had been renewed in 1838 for another ten years. Though the fur trade was ailing and the Hudson's Bay Company posts of Fort Boise and Fort Hall were currently unprofitable, they continued to be maintained as tokens of occupation and future bargaining points. And the British factors treated the emigrants with the reserved politeness that long had been Company policy.

At both posts, the traveler could buy a blanket or a few pounds of flour at what he regarded as exorbitant prices. In a pinch, he could swap six worn-out oxen for four healthy ones, for the factors knew that a stranded emigrant would have to be given food and shelter all winter. At Fort Hall, he could receive good advice free of charge.

That good advice invariably was to go to California instead of Oregon. Some sixty miles west of Fort Hall, the trail forked, with Oregon-bound trains continuing along the left bank[4] of the Snake, while wagons headed for California turned south and west up the wide, flat valley of Raft River. From it, they must cross to the Humboldt, traverse desert country as bad as or worse than that of the Snake River Plain, then surmount the Sierras by way of Donner Pass.

Being British, factors like Peter Grant minimized the hazards of the California trail, exaggerated those of the road to Oregon, and then pointed out with impeccable logic the inevitability of Mexican-owned California soon becoming American property, just as Oregon was bound to become a part of Great Britain.

Being Americans, a goodly portion of the emigrants regarded the advice as suspect simply because it came from a Britisher. Until the discovery of gold in California, Oregon's green, fertile, well-watered, thick-timbered valleys held far more appeal than a lotus land owned by Spanish-speaking foreigners. Furthermore, since the British were trying to persuade them *not* to go to Oregon, it must be a fine piece of country. So most of the westering wagons stuck to the Snake.

Now that beaver was done, many mountain men had become professional guides. The four dollars a day paid an ex-trapper for his services was the finest insurance against trouble a wagon train could buy. Despite the fact that government-backed "exploring" parties under men such as Captain John Fremont were being sent West "to survey the country" during the 1840s, the Snake River region long had been familiar terrain to white trappers. In fact, the man who later ran for President as the "Great Pathfinder" found no new paths at all, for his every step was guided by ex-mountain men like Kit Carson.

When led by a veteran trapper, a wagon train seldom encountered serious difficulty. He knew every trail, stream, hollow, hill, and landmark. Where the best grass grew, where water could be found, where there was wood for cooking fires, where the nuisances of mosquitoes and flies were abated by cooling evening breezes, where cushioning dust rather than hoof-destroying rocks made the going easier, where canyons and rivers could safely be crossed—all these facts were filed away in his mind in greater detail and with more infallible accuracy than in volumes of official government reports made by Fremont and his ilk. The trapper's very survival attested to the fact that he had graduated from "Rocky Mountain College"[5] with high honors, illiterate though he might be.

The most important service the mountain man rendered the emigrants was his knowledge of Indian tongues, his shrewd judgment of Indian nature, and the respect his pres-

2. *A Day with the Cow Column*, by Jesse Applegate, Caxton Club, Chicago, 1934, p. 18.

3. Cannon, pp. 89, 90

4. Whether traveling upstream or down, the terms "right" or "left" bank always are written by military men as if facing downstream. At least, that is what my personal military expert, Colonel James H. Beddow (Ret.), tells me. He says the usage goes back to Roman days.

5. *Journal of a Trapper*, by Osborne Russell, Syms-York, Boise, 1914; reprint by Oregon Historical Society, 1955. One of the few literate trappers, Russell claimed he learned more in winter camps, which he called "Rocky Mountain College," than he ever did in school.

Right:

DESERT RANGELAND

Located north of Baker, Oregon, this shows the Wallowa Mountains in the distance.

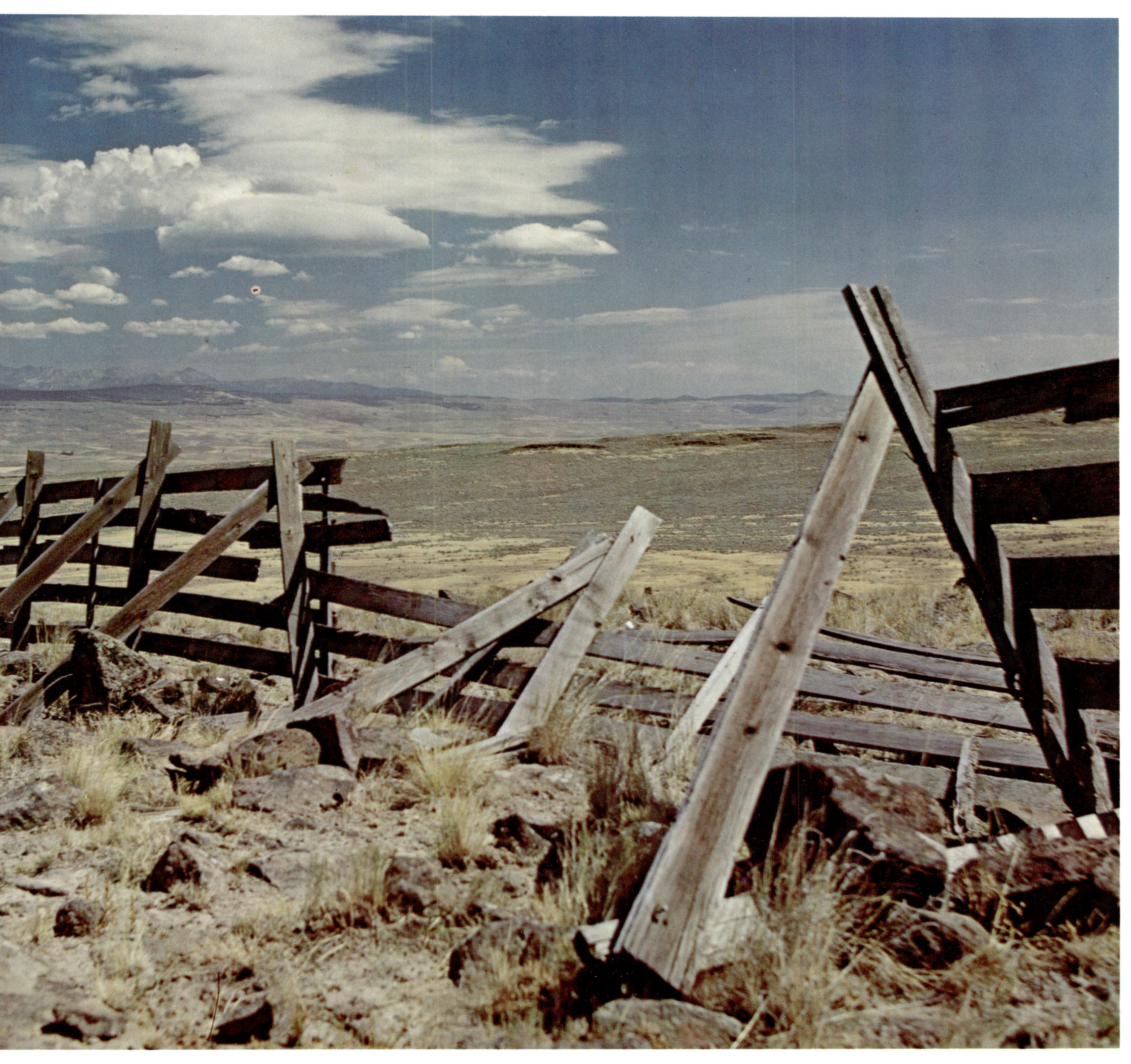

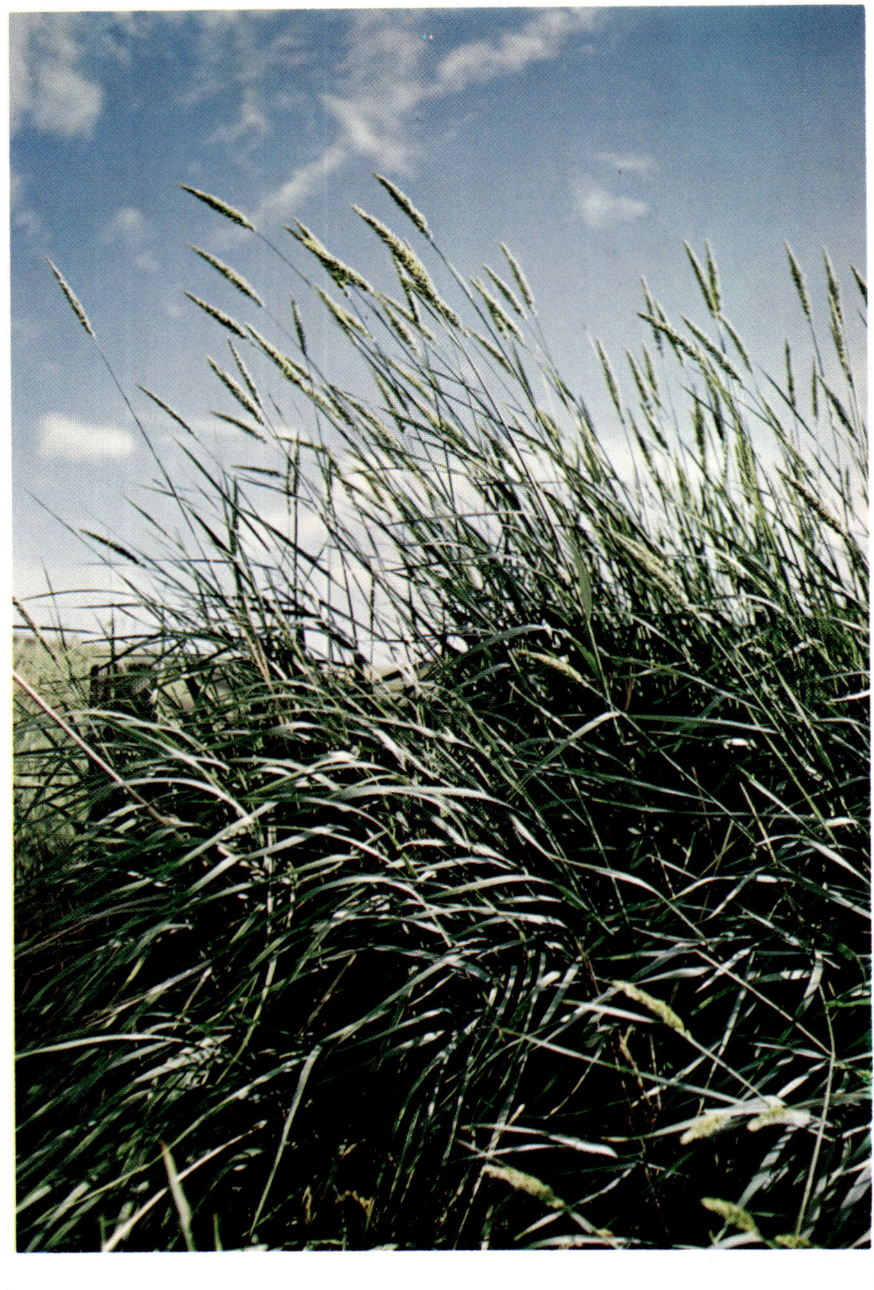

Left:

RYE GRASS

Usually found in marshy lowlands, it gave the Whitman Mission its Indian name. "Wai-i-lat-pu," in the Cayuse tongue, meant "Place of the Rye Grass."

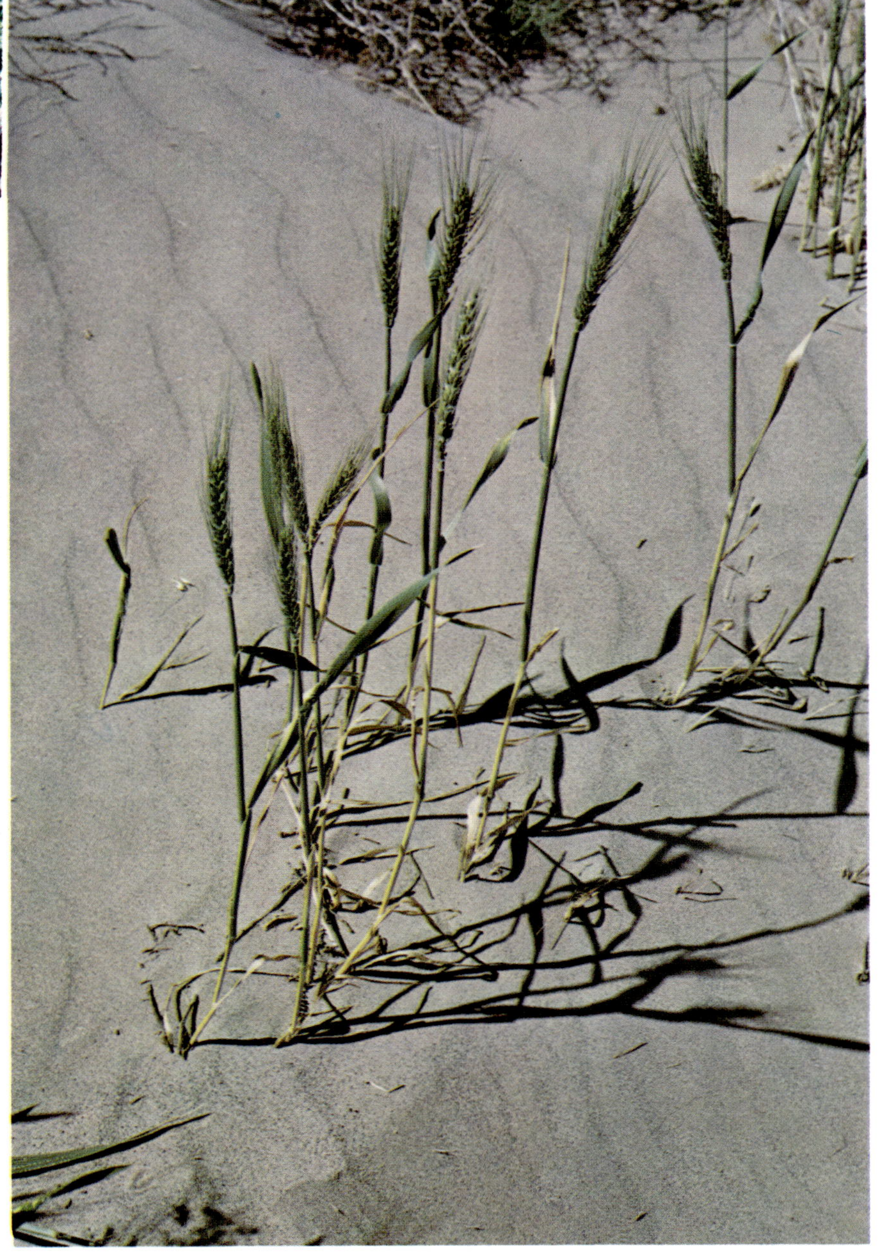

Right:

VOLUNTEER WHEAT

Near the mouth of the Snake blow-sand drifts like snow and nothing but sagebrush grows without irrigation. Still, a kernel can try. . . .

ence with the train engendered among the Indians. Running a bluff, indulging in petty thievery as a game, playing practical jokes, and bullying frightened strangers when they thought they could get away with it, all were part of the savage character, he knew. Since this was their homeland, the Indians were as bold and cocky as the emigrants were nervous and ill at ease. Seeing a horde of savages suddenly top a rise and come galloping toward the wagons with fiendish yells could paralyze women and children, and send panicky husbands and brothers scrambling for their guns. But this was old hat to the ex-trapper, a show-off stunt aimed to draw attention and scare greenhorns. If paid no mind, it would harmlessly end in good-natured laughter, hand-shaking, pipe-smoking, and a useful gabfest. But let a feather-brained pilgrim take it seriously, grab a gun, and fire a shot in anger, there would be hell to pay.

Now and again opinionated emigrants who, before leaving the East, had pored over maps and pamphlets until they considered themselves experts on how to get to Oregon, persuaded their parties to dispense with hiring a guide. Such persons also disregarded vital, common-sense rules of the trail.

Normally, fifty wagons comprised a strong enough train to pass through the Snake River County with no danger from hostiles. But at times smaller groups of only ten, eight, or six wagons attempted to make the journey. Normally, a train must reach Fort Hall early in August if it were to complete its journey before bad weather came, and its livestock should be in good condition before the desert crossing was attempted. But at times poorly equipped, poorly organized, and poorly powered wagon trains came late to the eastern part of the basin, then, against all advice, tried to make up for lost time by pushing exhausted draft animals, and people whose judgment had been seriously impaired by hardship, beyond their strength and endurance.

At Three-Island Crossing near present-day Glenns Ferry, the main branch of the Oregon Trail crossed the Snake, angled northwest across flat, dry, sage-covered plains to the Boise River, then descended that stream to its mouth. Here, the Snake must be crossed a second time. Along this trail, the mileage was shorter, the grass better, the going easier, and the danger from hostile Indians less than along the route which followed the left bank of the Snake. But self-guided trains, after a study of the map, sometimes decided that avoiding the risk of two river crossings was worth a few extra miles, and took the longer way.

Usually, they wished they had not, for the term "Dry Trail" had not been given lightly. Drifted dunes of sand, sheer gorges of incoming streams, and unending miles of glass-sharp lava rock impeded the wheels, wrecked the wagons, and turned the hooves of the oxen into bleeding stumps. There was little grass, less game, and the waters of the Snake often were inaccessible. Worst of all, the Indians in this sector were far less friendly to whites than others in the basin, and, with the rugged, seldom traversed, trackless wilderness of the Owyhee Mountains near at hand, could raid, kill, and vanish with no fear of successful retribution.

During the first wave of emigration across the Snake River Country, two ghastly tragedies wiped out wagon trains—one on the "Dry Trail," the other on the Boise River, to the north. In a sense, both were the end-results of changes in political jurisdiction over a region long claimed and nominally governed by two nations, now claimed only by one —and effectively governed by none.

In order to understand those changes, we must move west to the Willamette Valley. . . .

* * *

3.

When the Irish first began to immigrate to America, there was a popular ethnic joke that went:

> "When two Irishmen meet over here, what's the first thing they do?"
> "Have a drink."
> "Right. The second thing?"
> "Have another drink."
> "Correct. The third thing?"
> "They declare themselves agin the Government."

Change the locale of the story to Oregon, expand the cast of characters to include all Europeans who had migrated first to the New World, then to the Far West, and collectively called themselves "Americans," and the punch line in the 1840s would have been: "They declare themselves a Government." For to Americans of that day, the abhorred vacuum which must be filled was living in the absence of a political entity in which their individual voices could be heard loud and clear.

On the Oregon side of the Columbia across from Fort Vancouver, retired Hudson's Bay Company employees, American missionaries, ex-mountain men, and an ever-increasing number of American merchants and farmers had settled. So far as the French-Canadians were concerned, the Company was all the government they needed or wanted. But the Americans were creating farms, building sawmills, gristmills, and towns; they wanted titles more solid than "squatters' rights" to the properties they were accumulating.

When an ex-trapper named Ewing Young died in 1841, matters came to a head, for he had left neither will nor heir. Disposition of his holdings in land and cattle was a problem to be solved by a probate court, his neighbors felt. Since there was no court, they organized one.

That community effort started them thinking in terms of establishing a local government. After prolonged discussion as to *how* local the government should be, they expanded their concept, took in all the vaguely defined area called Oregon, and, by the slim margin of a single vote, established a Provisional Government in 1843. Two years later they asked Congress that Oregon be organized as a Territory of the United States.[1]

In 1848, their request was granted. All the region south of the forty-ninth parallel was ceded to the United States.

It would be oversimplification to say that the ensuing turmoil and bloodshed in the Snake River Country resulted directly from the Provisional Government proclamation. But news traveled swiftly via the Indian grapevine. Along the Oregon Trail, at Spalding's Lapwai Mission, and particularly at Dr. Whitman's station in the Walla Walla Valley, which had become a major stopping point for the hordes of American emigrants now pouring through the country, the Indians realized that King George men no longer ruled this land and that now they must deal exclusively with the Bostons.

To some, the change in authority was a bitter pill to swallow. The King George men had been trappers and traders, and their numbers had been few. The Bostons were farmers, livestock men, and missionaries, whose ploughs scarred the earth, whose fences blocked off traditional communal grazing lands, and whose unbending religious precepts destroyed the spiritual foundations upon which the Indians from time immemorial had built their societies. Worst of all, the Bostons were bringing in diseases which made them only mildly ill but brought death to the Indians in horrifying numbers.

At both Lapwai and Waiilatpu, the nature and purpose of the missions had changed drastically since Whitman's ride East during the winter of 1842-43. Before that time, the missionaries were torn by dissension among themselves, but were relatively successful in their efforts to convert the Indians, teach them, civilize them, and develop their skills in agriculture and the raising of livestock. Afterwards, the missionaries were at peace with one another, but faced increasing hostility from the natives.[2]

At Lapwai, by the autumn of 1847, Henry Spalding and William Craig had mellowed toward each other; from time to time, they even joined forces to mill timber, sell cattle, and make improvements on their farms. Though Craig did attempt to file on a 640-acre tract that included mission land, when he went down to the Willamette Valley to record the claim and found that he must take oath no one was living on it, he balked at committing perjury. Though Spalding complained that the ex-mountain man continued to exert influence on the "heathen" Nez Perces, he admitted with rare candor:

> "And yet, this man is remarkably friendly and we have daily intercourse. He is one of the most faithful, expeditious workman we can employ, very accommodating as a neighbor. . . ."[3]

As the mission's relations with Craig improved, they deteriorated with the Indians. Chief Joseph recanted and kept his Wallowa band aloof. Timothy stayed loyal as always; Lawyer remained friendly, but would not join the church; while Old James, Rotten Belly, and a growing number of dissidents opposed school and church attendance so bitterly that only scant handfuls of Nez Perces showed up.

Being well away from the route of emigrant travel, the Lapwai band was not visually aware of the number of Americans passing through the country, but the grapevine kept them well informed. And now, to increase their uneasiness and apprehension, came the most deadly poison-spreader of all—an educated Indian from the eastern United States, who could and did relate every atrocity the white man had perpetrated against people of their race.

Tom Hill was a full-blood Delaware who had come West during beaver days, trapped with Kit Carson, married a Nez Perce woman, then moved to Lapwai about the same time William Craig did. One writer describes him as:

> ". . . a striking figure with an intense hatred of whites for reasons well remembered. He could speak eloquently for hours, and seems to have acquired a following of perhaps a thousand among the Nez Perces, including more than half a dozen chiefs. Whitman suspected that Hill was friendly to the Catholic priests, but actually he was a thoroughgoing agnostic where the white man's religion was concerned. . . ."[4]

The message Tom Hill had for the Nez Perces and all the other Indians of the region was stark and simple: *"Kill the whites or they will destroy you."*

One hundred and twenty miles west, at Waiilatpu, his words not only were being listened to, they were being confirmed by a series of tragic events. On a trip to California, the son of a Christianized Cayuse chief had quarreled with a white man over a horse, been shot, and killed. When the chief demanded that the white man be tried and punished under the same code of laws the Indians had agreed to live by, nothing happened. When Indian youngsters persisted in swiping melons out of the mission garden patch, Dr. Whitman tried to teach them a lesson by inserting purgative powders into temptingly convenient melons, the boys stole and ate them, and got sick as poisoned pups. In scolding a Cayuse brave for a minor offense, Whitman inadvertently laid a hand on his shoulder, and that night the In-

-----

1. According to terms of the ten-year extension to the Joint Occupation Treaty of 1838, either nation could terminate it by giving a year's notice. Since the United States had given Great Britain such notice in 1845, it obviously would be only a matter of time before some sort of American government would be set up in Oregon. But the settlers, growing impatient, acted on their own.

2. *The Diaries and Letters of Henry H. Spalding*, with Introductions and Editorial Notes by C. M. Drury, Arthur H. Clark Company, Glendale, Calif., 1958, p. 337.

3. *Henry Harmon Spalding*, by C. M. Drury, Caxton, 1936, p. 324.

4. *Great Command*, by Nard Jones, p. 242. Though Drury says Tom Hill was a half-breed, Jones says he was a full blood. Josephy says Hill was a half blood; Lavender says he was a full blood. In such distinguished company, I shall simply quote and run.

dian got a bite of meat stuck in his throat, and choked to death.

If the Cayuses failed to see ominous significance in these occurrences, Joe Lewis, who had become Tom Hill's principal disciple, was quick to point it out to them. Half French-Canadian and half Indian, Lewis came from Maine, knew what the white man had done to the Iroquois there, and though not as well educated and eloquent as Hill, was his equal in bitterness and advocacy of violence. He had arrived at the Whitman Mission as a wagon driver a short time before, made friends with another half-breed who lived in the Cayuse village, and now devoted his energy to stirring up all the trouble he could.

Since the Whitman station lay directly on the Oregon Trail and was the only place emigrants could get supplies and medical services from a fellow American between the Snake River headwaters and the Willamette Valley, the demands on its resources were becoming increasingly burdensome. Jim Bridger had sent his half-breed daughter, Mary Ann, now twelve years old, here to be schooled and raised like a lady. Joe Meek, on his way to the Willamette, had done the same thing with his half-breed daughter, ten-year-old Helen Mar. A Swiss immigrant, John Sutter, had stopped for a visit on his way to California. Captain Fremont had called while his party camped nearby.

A bachelor too sick to travel with his train had been housed, nursed, and fed until he regained his health. Other indigents had been taken in for short or long periods of time. And what, in God's name, could you do with seven young brothers and sisters, ranging from five months to thirteen years of age, whose parents had died along the way? Well, you could say, as Narcissa Whitman did, that you would take in only the girls. Then, when you saw the looks in the eyes of the parentless children about to be parted, you could change your mind, as Marcus Whitman did, and, in God's name, say gruffly: "We'll take them all."[5]

In November, 1847, there were sixty-nine more or less permanent residents with white blood in their veins living at Waiilatpu. The chief concern of the mission now was not saving Indian souls, but feeding the hungry, clothing the naked, and nursing the ill Americans dropped off by wagon trains moving west. Understandably, the Cayuses resented the neglect of their spiritual needs and the ever-growing white community occupying their lands. But resentment changed to horror when one of the ill Americans, sick with black measles, inadvertently passed on his disease to the Cayuses, who possessed no natural immunity to measles whatsoever. . . .

On November 28, 1847, Henry Spalding, who had ridden down from Lapwai, went with Dr. Whitman to a Umatilla Indian village some twenty-five miles south of Waiilatpu. Spalding knew that the epidemic of measles now locally raging like an out-of-control prairie fire had made several white children at the mission ill. He was deeply concerned, for his own daughter, Eliza, was attending school there.

He knew that the fatality rate among the Indians was extremely high; if the disease itself failed to kill them, their home remedy of a sweat bath followed by a plunge into an icy stream did.[6] He knew that Dr. Whitman, who was doing everything within his power to cope with the epidemic, was running a great risk in ministering to the Indians. By their savage code, when the *tewat* (medicine man) failed to effect a cure, his own life could become forfeit. But as a Christian and a doctor, Whitman could not neglect a person who was ill.

That afternoon, Dr. Whitman said he must return to Waiilatpu, where his services were sorely needed. Was Spalding ready to go? Since he was very tired and suffering from an ailment that made riding most unpleasant, Spalding told Whitman to go on without him—he would rest here, then come to Waiilatpu in a day or two.

So Whitman rode home alone. . . .

At noon, next day, the Cayuses took the course of action Tom Hill, Joe Lewis, and grief for their dead long had urged them to take. By the time they finished their bloody work, Dr. Marcus Whitman, his wife Narcissa, and twelve more white people were dead, fifty-one whites were being held captive, and terror stalked the land.

By a freak of fate, Spalding remained alive and free. But the Cayuses knew where he was—and had sworn to kill him. . . .

* * *

4.

During her eleven years at Lapwai, Mrs. Spalding had borne four children, though her health remained fragile. With her in her husband's absence were Henry, eight; Martha, two; and the baby, Amelia, whose first birthday would be celebrated in just a week. As already noted, ten-year-old Eliza was in school at the Whitman Mission.

The massacre took place on Monday, November 29. In garbled form, word of it reached Lapwai through a loyal Nez Perce the following Sunday morning, December 5. The Indian did not know what had happened to her husband and daughter. But he had heard that a band of dissident Nez Perces was planning to attack the Lapwai Mission and kill all white people here, just as the Cayuses had done at Waiilatpu. William Craig and a few friendly Nez Perces would do what they could to protect her family, he said, but unless she and her children went quickly to Craig's house a few miles up the valley, their lives were in danger.

Very well, she replied. She would take the children to Craig's house tomorrow morning. Tomorrow? Why not to-

-----

5. For the poignant story of the seven Sager children, see *Shallow Grave at Waiilatpu*, by Erwin N. Thompson, Oregon Historical Society, 1969. An extremely well written, as well as authentic, account.

6. Drury estimates that of four hundred members of the Cayuse tribe living in the vicinity, half of them died during this epidemic; the exact figure he states is 197. *Spalding Diaries*, 1958, p. 342.

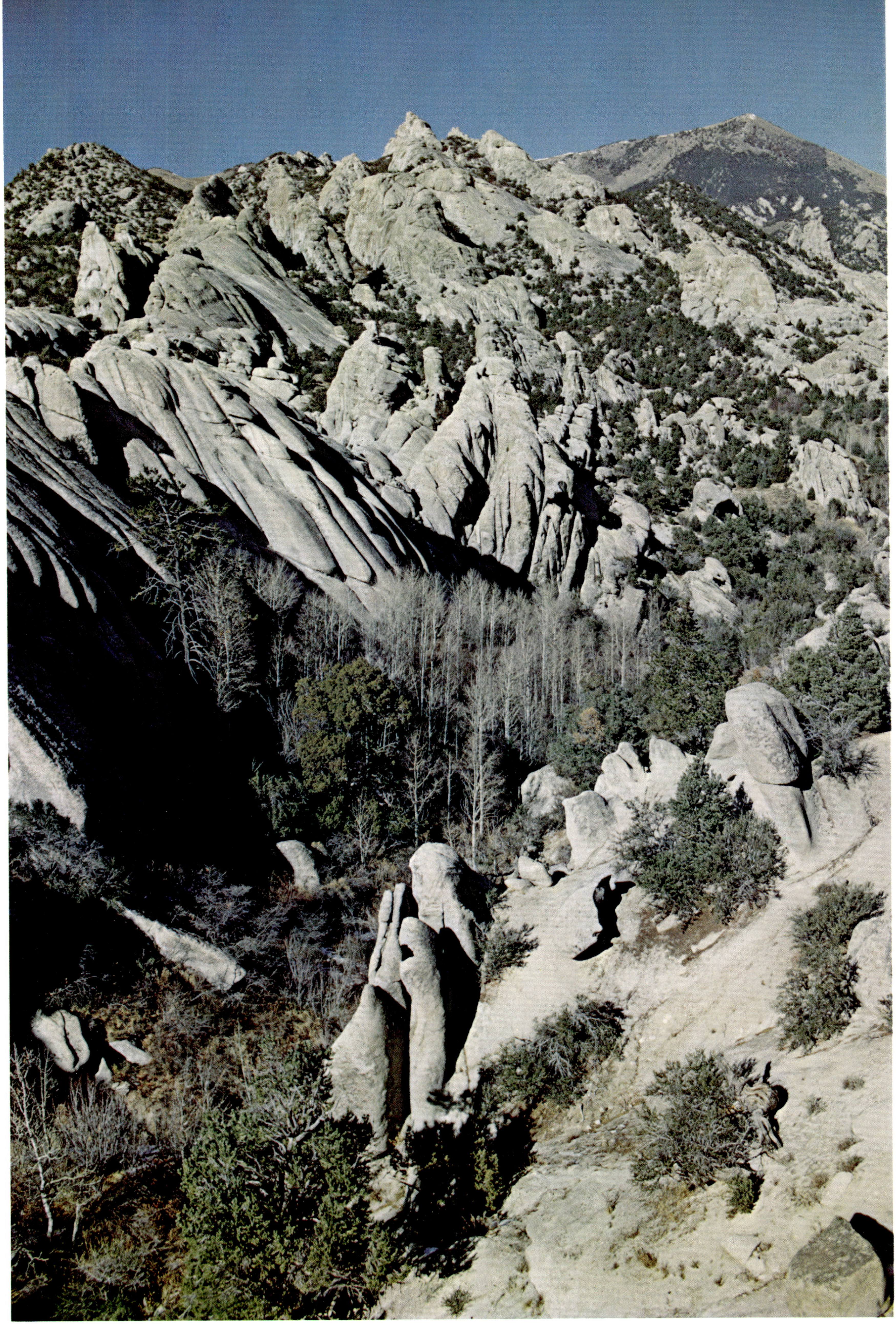

day? Because this was the Sabbath, she said. Even at the risk of death, she would not violate the Lord's Day.

How she passed that long Sunday, how every argument used by Craig and the loyal Nez Perces shattered on the rock of her obstinacy, and whether, when she prayed—as she surely did—she again voiced the phrase written in her diary eleven years before: "*Surely the Lord is my Shepherd, and I shall have nothing to fear, if I will but repose my whole trust in Him* . . ." must remain in the realm of speculation, for no written record has survived. But the Nez Perces never forgot her courage; in memory, they would hold this frail woman's spirit in awe long after her flesh had left their presence.

Monday morning, Mrs. Spalding and her children moved to the safety of William Craig's cabin. Shortly thereafter, a band of "heathen" Nez Perces, led, one writer says, by a "renegade" who had participated in the Whitman Massacre,[1] vandalized the vacant mission buildings. But under Craig's protective wing, Mrs. Spalding and her children were safe.

Now, she could only wait and wonder if her husband and eldest daughter still lived. . . .

Father J. B. A. Brouillet, a Catholic priest, who, with his associates, recently had established a mission near the Umatilla village, chanced to visit Waiilatpu the day after the massacre. As a Black Robe and a King George man, he was for the moment immune to Cayuse wrath, a neutral who would not be harmed so long as he minded his own business. He was horrified by what he saw. Knowing that Spalding was in the area and hearing that the Cayuses intended to kill him, Father Brouillet jeopardized his neutrality and life by hastening south, intercepted Spalding, who was on his way to the mission, and told him what had occurred.

Spalding was stunned. Learning that Eliza was one of the captives and that he and perhaps his wife and other children were marked for death, he headed for Lapwai, half-crazed with dread of what he might find there. Fortunately, the temperature hovered near the freezing point, the air was saturated with moisture, and a veil of icy fog hung over the Walla Walla Valley; thus, the three Cayuse braves detailed to find and kill him narrowly missed meeting him, as the Catholic priest so providentially had done.

After riding forty miles or so, he lay down to rest for a few hours. In his distracted, exhausted state, he neglected to tie up his horse. When he woke, the animal was gone. He walked the last ninety miles to Lapwai, arriving there Monday afternoon. His physical and mental ordeal had so altered his appearance that a Nez Perce woman, who knew him well, did not recognize him until he told her who he was.

Reunited with his wife and three of their children, he concentrated on doing what he could to preserve the lives of young Eliza and the other captives. His immediate fear was that Americans living in the Willamette Valley would raise a force of volunteers and send it upriver to punish the Indians. In a letter to a Catholic missionary, Bishop Blanchet, he wrote:

> "My daughter is yet a captive, I fear, but in the hands of our merciful Heavenly Father. Two Indians have gone for her. . . . We do not wish the Americans to come from below to avenge the wrong. . . . The Nez Perces held a meeting yesterday. They pledged themselves to protect us from the Cayuses, if we would prevent the Americans from coming up to avenge the murders. This we have pledged to do, and for this we beg for the sake of our lives at this place and at Mr. Walker's. By all means keep quiet, and send no war reports; send nothing but proposals for peace."[2]

Ever since the Joint Occupancy Treaty had been terminated and the country south of the forty-ninth parallel ceded to the United States, the Hudson's Bay Company factors had devoted their energies to winding up business affairs. Conflict between Indians and Americans in the region was not their concern. But to their eternal credit, the British reacted to the tragedy with the cool-headedness that long had marked their dealings with Indians.

Soon after word of the massacre reached Fort Walla Walla, twenty-three miles west of Waiilatpu, Factor William McBean dispatched a courier downriver with a secret, urgent message to be delivered to the only man who, in McBean's judgment, was capable of handling such a ticklish situation. Not even Perrin Whitman, now sixteen years old and living at The Dalles, was to be told what had happened. The message must go directly and privately to the factor now in charge at Fort Vancouver, Peter Skene Ogden.

Two decades had passed since the former Prince of Good Fellows and Terror of All Indians had made his gruelling treks across the Snake River Country. And the years had taken their toll. White-haired, pudgy, and full of an old man's aches and pains, Ogden could have said this was not

1. Nard Jones says a "renegade" Nez Perce did take part in the Whitman Massacre; Drury says not; and Josephy points out that the often repeated story that the Nez Perces never shed white blood before 1877 is myth. In view of the frequent intermarriages among Nez Perces, Cayuses, Umatillas and Walla Wallas, all one can do is generalize and say that as a tribe the Nez Perces did not make war on the whites until 1877.

2. *Spalding Diaries*, Drury, 1958, p. 346. Bishop Blanchet passed on the letter to an Oregon newspaper, which published it, embarrassed Spalding, and sowed the seed of a lifetime feud between Spalding and the Catholics, whom he later came to blame for the massacre itself.

Right:

CITY OF ROCKS

This unique area of granitic outcroppings, rising abruptly out of the flat Idaho desert southeast of Burley, is more spectacular than the famed Garden of the Gods, near Colorado Springs. Yet because it is off the beaten tourist path, comparatively few people visit it. A portion of the area is an Idaho State Park.

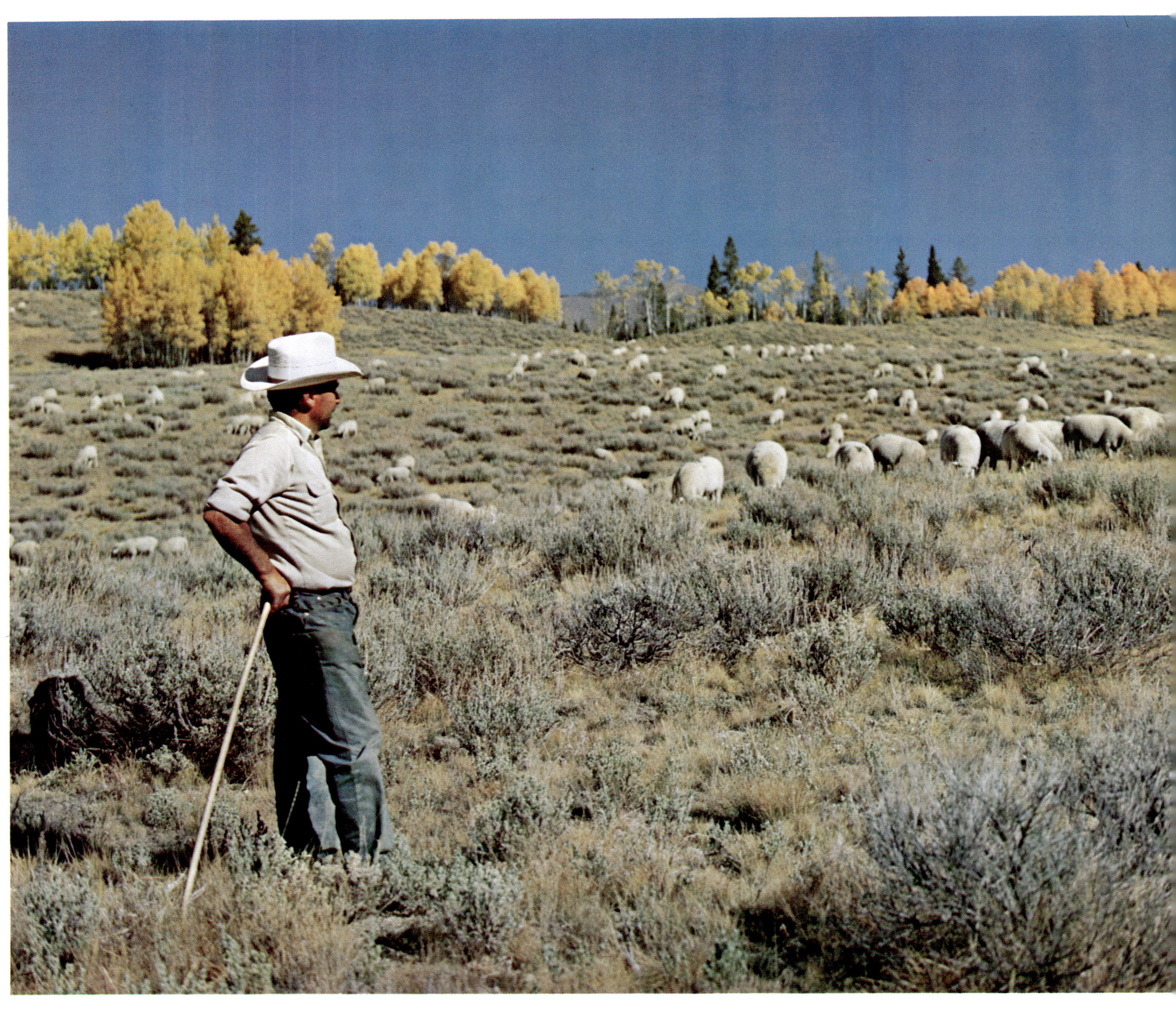

his problem, sent Oregon's Governor Abernethy a sympathetic note, and gone back to his paper work.

Being Peter Skene Ogden, he did no such thing.

Instead, he ordered two bateaux filled with trade goods drawn from Company stores. He sent a brief note to the Governor requesting that he make no move that would jeopardize ransom negotiations. Then he stepped into the lead bateau and headed upriver.

His protective force, if such it could be called, consisted of sixteen French-Canadian paddlers—men notorious for their lack of enthusiasm when it came to fighting Indians—and his well-earned reputation for never making a promise he did not keep.

His mission was successful. While the Willamette Valley settlers raised a volunteer army and prepared for war, he negotiated a ransom price, paid it, and escorted the released captives downriver. These included the Spalding family, which had been brought to Fort Walla Walla under the protection of a band of Nez Perces. The Hudson's Bay Company never billed the Americans for the ransom goods nor did the Americans ever offer payment. Governor Abernethy did write Ogden a note of thanks, but, for the rest of his life, Ogden shrugged off whatever scant showers of gratitude came his way by saying he had done what any other man in his situation would have done.

The force of volunteers marched into the Walla Walla Valley; and for two years a series of desultory, indecisive skirmishes called the Cayuse War spread misery over the land. Deciding at last that the only way to bring peace was to surrender the "murderers," five Cayuse braves gave themselves up, were taken to Oregon City, tried May 22, 1850, found guilty, and sentenced to death. Whether all or any of them actually participated in the massacre was questioned even at the time. Tiloukaikt, when asked why he and the others had surrendered, replied: "Christ died for his people, didn't he? So do we. . . ."

The multiple hanging took place June 3. The officiating officer was U.S. Marshal Joe Meek. In happier days, a trapper friend had loaned Meek the only romantic novel he ever struggled through. Its heroine had been a lovely, ethereal girl named Helen Mar, and he had been so entranced by the fictional character that when his Shoshone woman, Mountain Lamb, bore him a baby daughter, he had a name all ready for her.

Joe and Mountain Lamb long since had parted, and the dirty, vermin-infested, frightened child he had given Narcissa Whitman to raise bore no resemblance to the heroine of a romantic novel. When the Cayuses struck, the child, now ten years old, had been ill. Though the Indians did not harm her, without a doctor and proper care she died ten days later.

It may be Meek was remembering Helen Mar when he gave the execution order. . . .

* * *

5.

What became known as the Ward Massacre took place on the Boise River some twenty-five miles upstream from its juncture with the Snake in late August, 1854. Alexander Ward, his wife, and seven children came from Lexington, Missouri; with Mrs. Ward's sister, her son, and half a dozen strangers whose wagons had joined theirs along the way, they were headed for western Oregon's Umpqua Valley, where their relatives already had settled.

Earlier, the Ward party had been traveling in a train totaling thirty wagons; now the group was reduced to five. Having fallen a day's journey behind the larger party, it had no guide, fire recently had charred the grass, and its livestock were finding little to eat. The Indians in this area were Bannocks, a tribe long troublesome to whites, held in check for the past twenty years by the nearness of the Hudson's Bay Company post, Fort Boise, and the knowledge that bad conduct would be surely and swiftly punished by the King George men.

But the Indians knew that the British no longer ruled this land, and as yet they had seen no evidence of effective American authority. By white standards, they had grown lazy and spoiled. Since Fort Boise had been rebuilt on the eastern bank of the Snake and American emigration had increased, they had worked as ferrymen at eight dollars a wagon, had forced timid travelers into trading horses and cattle to substantial Indian profit, had stolen brazenly, and even had made British factors give them dried salmon from Company stores instead of rustling for themselves.

High water a year ago had washed away part of Fort Boise's adobe walls, making it impossible to defend. White men attempting to kill wolves had put strychnine in carcasses of dead cattle; Indians had eaten the meat and died, and relatives had sworn revenge. Now here, detached from a train too large to be molested, were five wagons, fifty head of livestock, and only twenty people, most of whom were women and children.

The evening before, a group of Bannocks had ridden into the whites' camp, traded several of their horses for those of the Ward party, then afterwards attempted to take back their former property without giving up the horses they had acquired. Thwarted in that effort, they returned next day as the Ward party was breaking camp.

> "My oldest brother, Robert, who was out guarding the stock, came running into camp and said the

Left:

NEAR GALENA SUMMIT

On the headwaters of the Salmon, a Basque sheepherder watches his flock while aspens, turned gold by the first frosts, line the horizon.

Indians had taken one of the horses," wrote William Ward, one of the survivors. "We hitched up as soon as possible and drove out on the road where it was more open. We had hardly reached the road when we were surrounded by Indians, about two hundred in all as we were afterwards told. They immediately attacked us but our men succeeded in keeping them off until nearly sundown when the men were all killed. Then they came to the wagons where the women and children were. My brother Newton and I attempted to escape to the brush but we were both shot down by arrows. I was shot through the left side and lung. The last I remember they were riding their horses over me."[1]

The other survivor, Newton Ward, gives an account that differs only in a few details:

"I think it was Sunday, August 20, in the forenoon, when a party of two white men and three Indians fell in with us and tried to trade for one of the three horses we had. Not being able to make the trade, the three Indians made a sudden rush upon them and drove the horse off. Fearing further trouble, we started corralling the wagons and preparing for an attack.

"I was about thirteen years old at that time and was driving the wagon on which the family rode. Father, Wedin, and William the brothers elder, had hardly gotten the wagons corralled when the Indians made the charge, whooping and yelling like savage demons. The Indians were armed with both guns and bows and arrows. As near as I can tell, there were about 200 of them.

"We held them off for nearly two hours, but they were too much for us. The two Germans that I mentioned before made no resistance at all. They crawled into their wagon and after the other men, of which there were eight, were killed, the Indians dragged those Germans out of the wagons and murdered them. The Indians succeeded in getting the wagon that the women and children were in. They cut it off from the others and ran it into the brush. There was high sagebrush all around. After it seemed that we could make no further resistance, Brother William said to me, 'Let's go into the brush and hide.' "[2]

On the day of the massacre, a party of seven men had set out upriver from Fort Boise in search of a cow that had been stolen. Coming upon the scene while the Indians were still looting the wagons, three of the men charged the savages (while four held back), a young man named Amen was killed, and the group retreated. As the Indians drove the wagons away, the cries of the white women and children could be distinctly heard.

Reinforcements were sent for, but by the time they arrived next day all the captives were dead. Their remains showed evidence of brutal torture and mutilation. Newton Ward, only slightly wounded, was found and taken to Fort Boise. But William Ward, with an arrow driven through his chest, lay unconscious in the sagebrush and was not found. Coming to after the rescue party had left, he broke off both ends of the arrow, then, with a four-inch piece of the shaft still in him, wandered for five days until he found his way to Fort Boise. Miraculously, he recovered.

In all, nineteen men, women, and children died in the Ward tragedy. At about this same time, seventy miles east of Fort Boise, three more white men traveling in a lone wagon across Camas Prairie were attacked and murdered by Indians. In detailing the casualties and attendant horrors, Oregon Indian Agent, R. R. Thompson, wrote:

"From what I can learn, there is a determination on the part of the Snakes to kill and rob all who may fall into their power. They say that the Americans have been continually telling them that unless they cease their depredations, an army would come and destroy them; but no such thing has been done, and that the Americans are afraid of them, and say if we wish to fight them, to come on. . . ."[3]

From coast to coast, newspapers such the *The Oregonian*[4] and the *New York Tribune*[5] told and retold the story in gory, lurid detail, concluding:

"It is that portion of the Snake tribe living between Fort Hall and the Grande Ronde that appear to be the most hostile. They are very well supplied with American rifles and Hudson's Bay Co. guns. They have plenty of ammunition, which they are constantly getting from the H. B. Co.'s posts. And the attempt of the Government to punish these Indians, I fear, will be attended with more expense than any Indian war we have had for years. . . ."

By now, the United States had established a military post at Fort Vancouver, commanded, ironically, by Colonel B. L. E. Bonneville, who two decades before twice had tried and failed to reach it, and another farther up the Columbia at The Dalles. When word of the massacre was received, two companies of soldiers rode into the Snake River Country and attempted to find and punish the Indians, but bad weather closed in, and the soldiers had to withdraw. Next year, 1855, another expedition was mounted under the command of Major Granville O. Haller; despite the slanderous accusa-

-----

1. *Boise, The Peace Valley,* by Annie Laurie Bird, Caxton, 1934, p. 82. William Ward to John Hailey, *Sixth Biennial Report of the State Historical Society.* Quoted from P.F.E. Historical Edition, *Idaho Free Press,* May 6, 1926.

2. Bird, p. 83.

3. House Executive Document, 2nd Sess., 33rd Congress, Part 1, 1854/55, p. 487.

4. *The Oregonian,* Sept. 23, 1854.

5. *New York Tribune,* October 28, 1854.

tions being published in American papers, the Hudson's Bay Company cooperated to the fullest extent of its ability, just as it always had done when the lives of whites were at stake.

> "We had no incidents of any consequence after leaving The Dalles, until we arrived at Fort Boise, where the major held a *wa wa* with the Bannick [*sic*] tribe of Snake Indians," wrote a correspondent to *The Oregonian.* "While holding the confab, four of the Winnass band (which is the tribe by whom the massacre was committed) had the temerity to come into the council, they were known to the interpreter, who signified to the major that they were in camp as spies. The major did not intimate to any person his knowledge of their being there, until the *wa wa* was over, when he had them arrested. They were tried next day by a military commission consisting of three officers, and the first one on being tried confessed all, both the share he himself had in the massacre, and also that of his fellow prisoners, and even went so far as to promise to take the troops to where there were more of the murderers, a promise which he evidently did not intend to fulfil, as circumstances which transpired afterwards proved, for while the sentry over him was being relieved, he made a spring from the tent the court was holding its session in, threw his buffalo robe from his shoulders, and bound with the speed and agility of a deer for the river, which he would have reached in a very few springs, and if he had, his escape was certain, for they are the best swimmers I ever saw. The whole camp was now in an uproar, officers and men running for their guns and revolvers, and hallooing to shoot him. Sergeant Kellehard was sergeant of the guard and was relieving the sentry over the prisoner at the time he jumped from the tent, he drew up his musket and fired, and fortunately (for I consider it only a chance shot for him, although only a few steps off) hit him in the back, he made one spring in the air and fell on his face, and in three or four minutes all was over with him. . . ."[6]

All was soon over with the other three accused Indians, too, for they were found guilty and sentenced to death. Next day, the soldiers took them to the site of the massacre, reburied the remains of the victims, erected gallows directly over the mound, and hanged the convicted Bannocks. Major Haller had been instructed to leave the corpses of any Indians he might execute dangling as examples to other hostiles, the correspondent wrote, ". . . but the officers would not stand it, as being unchristianlike, and barbarous, . . ." so on the following morning the dead Bannocks were buried. However, the gallows themselves were left standing as a symbol of American justice. Twenty years later, they still were there.

Unfortunately for the peace of the Snake River Country, the show of strength by the American military angered the Bannocks more than it impressed them. Since the British had cooperated with the bluecoats, Bannock fury turned against them, too, making their occupation of Fort Boise and Fort Hall as trading posts and emigrant aid stations no longer possible. In 1855, both were abandoned by the Hudson's Bay Company, leaving this section of the Oregon Trail without white settlements or effective authority of any kind.

Meanwhile, Oregon had been organized as a territory in 1849; and in 1853, the region north of the Columbia had become Washington Territory. Since this latter unit's southern boundary extended east along the forty-sixth parallel to the summit of the Rocky Mountains, most of the lands occupied by the Nez Perces along the Clearwater and Salmon River watersheds now were governed by Washington Territory.

Year after year, whites had been pouring into the Pacific Northwest, most of them settling in the green, fertile valleys west of the Cascades. But there were rumors of gold in the Spokane country; a northern route for a transcontinental railroad was being surveyed through that same area; the ranching and farming potential of the interior now was beginning to be appreciated by a few settlers; and pressures were growing to "extinguish" Indian claims to the land.

Energetic, ambitious, highly-charged Isaac Ingalls Stevens, newly appointed governor of Washington Territory, tackled the job with the single-minded purpose of a man who knew exactly what he wanted and intended to get it. After making a number of hasty, outrageously unfair treaties with tribes west of the Cascades, he called an early summer council of five inland tribes, which was held in the Walla Walla Valley six miles east of the former Whitman Mission beginning May 20, 1855. His co-negotiator for the Americans was Joel Palmer, Superintendent of Indian Affairs for Oregon. Present were the Nez Perces, Cayuses, Umatillas, Walla Wallas, and Yakimas—some five thousand Indians in all. At stake was the ownership of an empire-sized piece of country which, in years to come, would prove to possess soil, timber, minerals, and water in more quality and abundance than any other area of comparable size in the entire United States.

The talks, discussions, or whatever one should call the insistence of Stevens and Palmer that the Indians cede lands they had no desire to sell, went on for nineteen days.[7] When

------

6. *Weekly Oregonian,* August 25, 1855.

7. For the way the Indians viewed the Stevens treaties, see *The Nez Perce Indians and the Opening of the Northwest,* by Alvin M. Josephy, Jr., Yale University Press, 1965, pp. 285 to 332. This is the most thorough, accurate work yet written on the Nez Perces. For the white man's side, see *Life of Isaac Ingalls Stevens,* by his son Hazard Stevens, Houghton Mifflin, 1901, Vol. 2, pp. 16 to 65.

In 1955, when descendants of the five Indian tribes signing the treaties agreed to stage an observance of the One Hundredth Anniversary of the event in the Walla Walla Valley, I was given a verbatim transcript of the nineteen days of talks and was asked to write a two-hour pageant based on them. During the six months I worked on the project, I came to know and respect many of the Indians and gained a small glimmer of understanding of what loss of their lands meant to them.

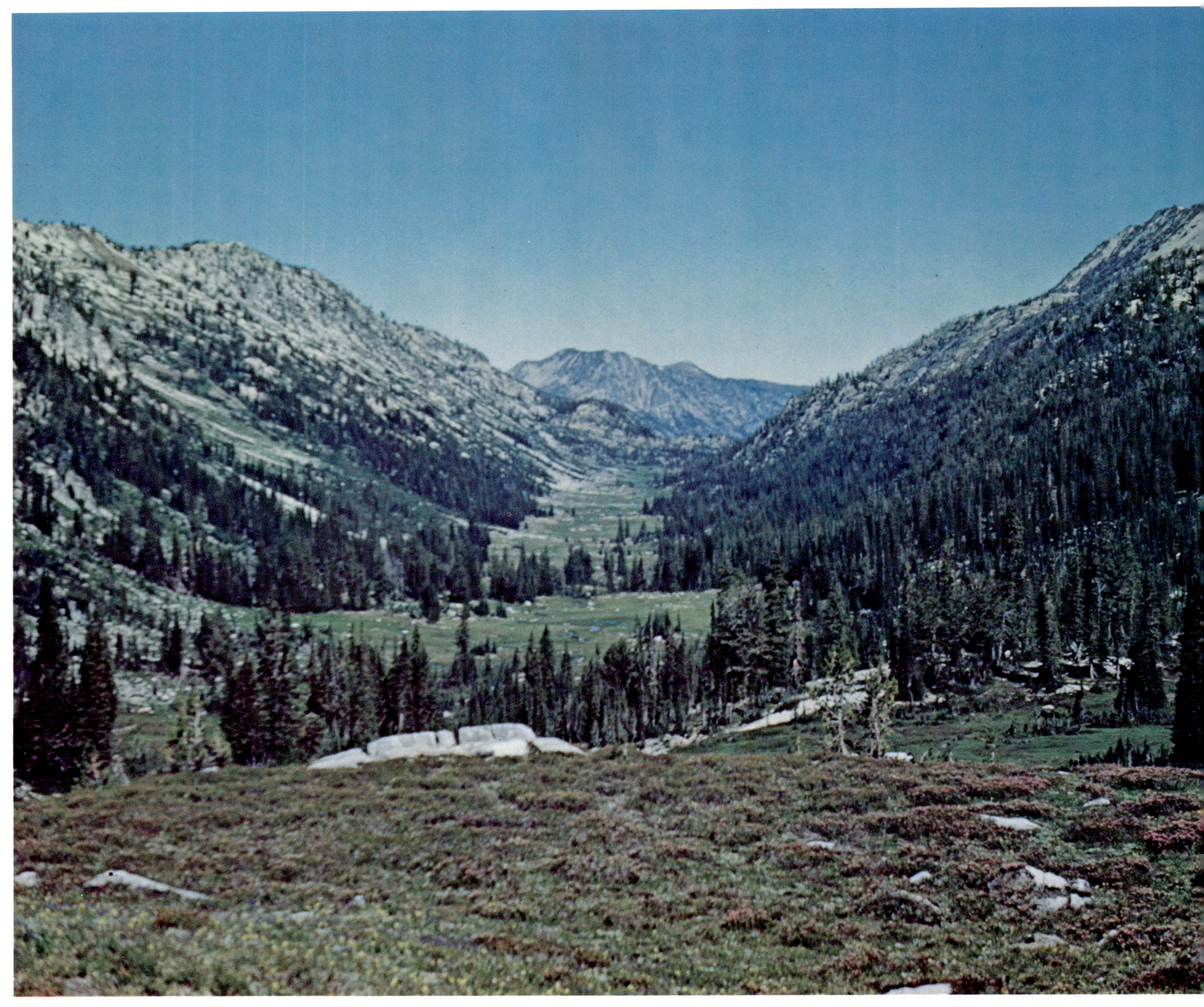

Above: In the High Wallowas, Northeastern Oregon

Right, above: Near Salmon, Idaho

Right, below:

EMPTY LAND

Statistics tell us that in this part of the Snake River Country there are four people per square mile. Here, north of Baker, Oregon, the author and his wife appear to be looking without success for the missing couple.

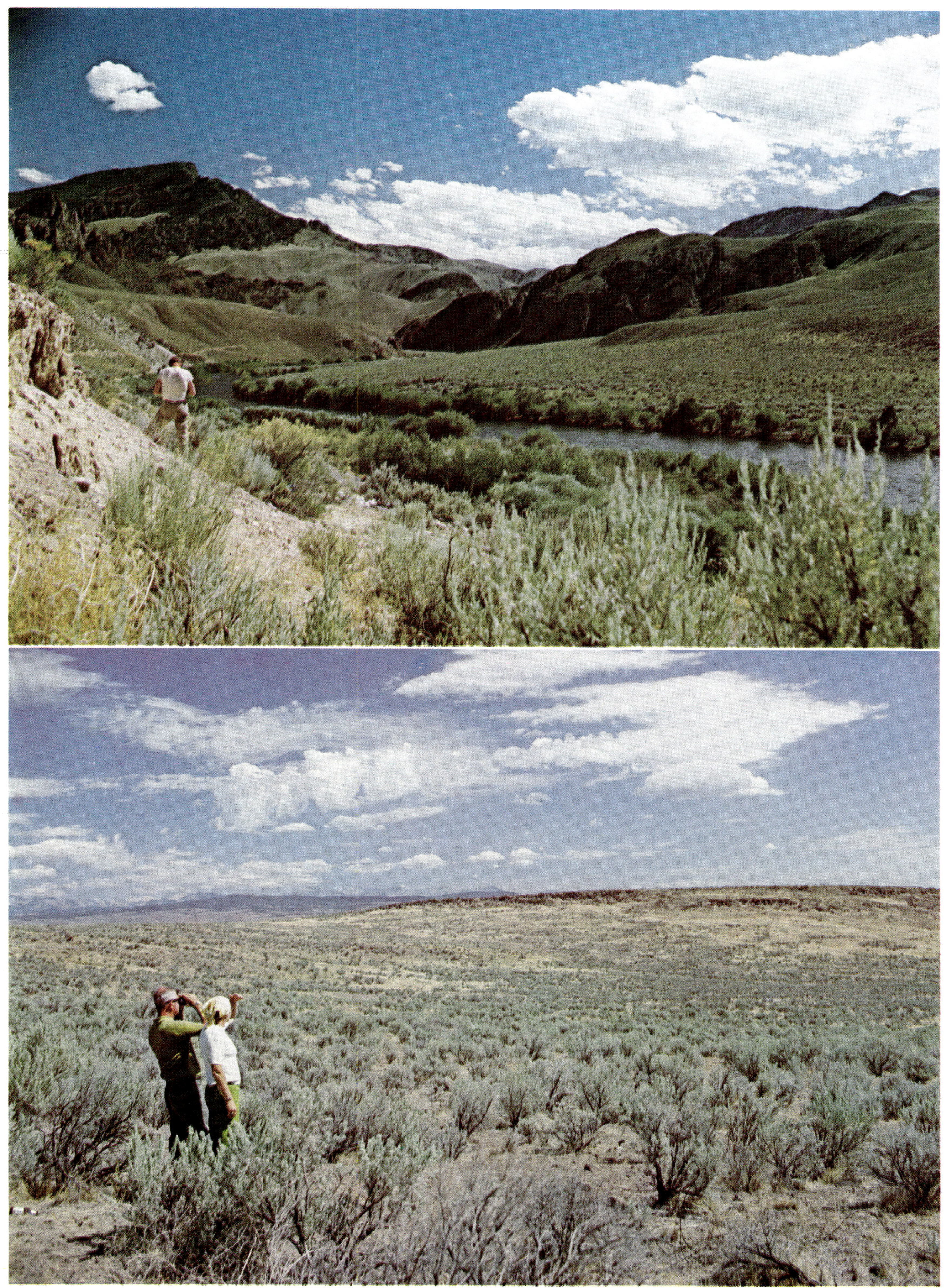

at last the headmen reluctantly touched the tip of the writing stick that was placing an "X" beside their names, three reservations had been set up: one for the Yakimas; a second for the Cayuses, Walla Wallas, and Umatillas; and a third for the Nez Perces.

Compared to the Cayuse-Walla Walla-Umatilla reservation of a meager eight hundred square miles, the Nez Perces fared well, for their five thousand square mile reserve included most of the lands which they traditionally claimed. Lawyer, whom the whites recognized as overall chief, shrewdly had traded friendship for a sizable piece of real estate—and a twenty-year annuity for himself. But few of the other headmen liked the treaties. With the ink barely dry, the entire Pacific Northwest exploded in bitter, bloody warfare.[8]

Since the conflict's extent and consequences are outside the scope of this book, it will be considered here only as it affected the Nez Perces and the tribe commonly called Snakes.

Still true to the pledges their fathers had made to Lewis and Clark fifty years earlier, the Nez Perces refused to take up arms against the white man. Some, like Joseph and his Wallowa band, remained neutral. Some, like Timothy and thirty of his followers, rode with the bluecoats as guides and scouts. In fact, had it not been for Timothy, Lieutenant Colonel Edward Steptoe and one hundred and thirty soldiers under his command very likely would have been "massacred" as were Custer and his men eighteen years later.

After establishing a military post in the Walla Walla Valley and being complimented by having the grogshop owners, storekeepers, and tradespeople name the settlement adjacent to it "Steptoeville," the colonel and his dragoons rode northeast, crossed the Snake, and moved into the country of the Palouse, Spokane, and Coeur d'Alene Indians. His Nez Perce scouts warned him that the Indians were angry and itching for a fight. He disregarded the warning. Confronted by six or seven hundred hostiles, whose chiefs bluntly told him he could not cross their country, he decided to withdraw for the time being and ordered a retrograde march. The Indians attacked and a battle began.

Since his intention had been merely to show the flag and impress the hostiles, his dragoons were lightly armed and short on ammunition. As his men began to fall, the retreat degenerated into panic. By nightfall, the dragoons were out of ammunition, their morale was shattered, and they were completely surrounded by hostiles. Twenty-five men had been killed and it appeared that the rest were doomed.

Whether Timothy's skill as a guide, the failure of the overconfident hostiles to follow up their advantage, or a bit of bribery arranged with the Coeur d'Alenes allowed the dragoons to escape under cover of darkness is a matter still argued by historians. But escape they did, limping back to Steptoeville in such sorry shape that the citizenry soon had second thoughts regarding the name of their metropolis-to-be—and changed it to Walla Walla.

By winning the battle, the Indians doomed themselves to lose the war. Soon a much stronger army force under Colonel George Wright mounted a second campaign; this time with longer-ranged rifles than the Indians possessed, howitzers, and a martinet commander whose terms to the hostiles were total surrender by the fighting men and death by hanging of their leaders. As a final crushing example of what belligerent red men could expect from the bluecoats, after capturing eight hundred Indian horses, Colonel Wright ordered every animal shot.

Thus, the war ended and the interior country, which had been closed by the military to white settlement during hostilities, was reopened. Settlers began moving in.

In the desert section of the Snake River basin, American soldiers now were stationed at Fort Hall, their mission to show the flag and escort emigrant trains through dangerous sectors of the California and Oregon trails. But their numbers were few. And now and then they miscalculated as to where danger lurked.

A train of eight wagons led by Elijah Otter reached Fort Hall August 27, 1860. It consisted of forty-four persons—seventeen men and twenty-seven women and children. When asked for an escort, Colonel H. S. Howe, commandant of the post, said twenty-five soldiers would accompany the emigrants to Raft River, six days travel. But the emigrants need not worry, he said, for they would encounter no trouble beyond that point and there were "soldiers on the road."[9]

Next morning, as the Otter train set out, it was joined by six bluecoats in addition to the promised escort; their enlistments had expired, the men said, they had been discharged and paid, and, since they were headed for western Oregon, they would be happy to accompany the train all the way to its destination. Though none of the six men owned horses or guns, the Otter party was delighted to have them along, for they surely must be experienced fighting men.

What the emigrants did not know was that at least one of the ex-soldiers was a deserter, and four of them were the rankest of cowards.

After parting with the escort at Raft River, the train proceeded along the left bank of the Snake until it reached Three Island Crossing. Here, its leaders weighed the shorter mileage and two river crossings of the Cut-Off route against the longer mileage and hazards of the Dry Trail, then decided in favor of the latter.

Each wagon was pulled by two or three yoke of oxen; the party owned fifty head of loose livestock; and it possessed a number of riding horses, including a big black stallion of exceptional quality. Though not specifically stated in any of the accounts, it may be assumed that the ex-soldiers

8. For two years of war, Oregon and Washington Territories handed Congress a six million dollar bill ". . . for scalping Indians and violating squaws, . . ." as Horace Greeley acidly put it. In Oregon alone, Bancroft estimated, 700 whites were killed before the Indians were put on reservations. He made no estimate of Indian casualties. Bancroft, Vol. 31, pp. 175, 176.

9. Sources for the Otter party story are: *Oregon Argus*, November 24, 1860; *The Idaho Story*, Vol. 2, Ipas, 1968; H.E.D. No. 46, 36th Congress, 2nd Sess., pp. 11-14, Oct., 1860.

retained all or part of their uniforms, which would make them, when mounted and armed, reasonable facsimiles of a military escort. Given saddles, horses, arms, and meals by the emigrants, they rode as flankers and guards.

Near Sinker Creek, in the extreme southwestern corner of what would become Idaho Territory, the emigrants noticed a cloud of dust ahead one morning, saw it was being raised by a large body of approaching Indians, and immediately corralled the wagons. Whether Bannocks, Northern Paiutes, or Western Shoshones, all hostiles in this area were called Snakes; and this band of a hundred or so showed its hostility by attempting to stampede the stock. It did not succeed, for the train had corralled in a favorable position on a hill overlooking the river, though it lacked access to water. A survivor wrote:

> "The Indians, finding they could accomplish nothing, threw down their arms and made friendly signs —came up, and made signs for something to eat. We fed many of them, and they appeared to be satisfied, and made signs for us to go on to the water, that they were friendly. So we started toward the river. After we got out of our strong position they commenced on us, but we expected some kind of treachery, and were on the look-out for them. Before we got corralled and our cattle chained, two of our men were shot down. . . ."[10]

The attack began about ten o'clock in the morning, September 8. All that day, night, and most of the following day the emigrants fought off the Indians from their position on the slope above the river. Two more white men were killed.

> "It was very warm weather, and we were all nearly famished for water, so we hitched up; we left four wagons and considerable things in them, thinking that would satisfy them. . . ."

It did not. After driving off all the loose stock, the Indians ignored the deserted wagons and continued their attack despite heavy casualties.

> "While they had us hemmed up, we killed not less than 25 or 30 of them; it was certain death to an Indian if he showed his head, for we were all pretty good marksmen. . . . The Indians would come right up to the wagons, cut holes in the covers, and shoot their arrows in at the women and children. . . ."

Shortly before sundown, the beleaguered emigrants yoked the oxen, hitched them to their remaining four wagons, and attempted to move to water and grass. The thirsty, hungry cattle were difficult to control. Now the desperate emigrants put their fate in the hands of the ex-soldiers.

10. *Argus,* Nov. 24, 1860. This is apparently a composite story gleaned from the survivors by a reporter.

> "We mounted four men on horses, Murdock, Shamberg, Schneider, and Chaffy—the two Reith boys on foot (these two were members of the Otter party). The object of having these six men ahead was to keep the road open, while we could get our wagons and families along. The Indians pitched in from all sides, and these men (the four who were mounted) instead of staying and helping us, put off as fast as they could go, without firing a shot, and left us. . . ."

Deserted by the four ex-soldiers and cut off from the wagon train, which was being overwhelmed by attacking Indians, Joseph and Jacob Reith (young single men in their teens) fled for their lives on foot. They did not know the country, had no food, and either lost their guns or discarded them as useless because they had exhausted their ammunition. In a vague way, they knew that the nearest white settlement, Walla Walla, was 240 miles to the northwest, but between it and them lay a hostile desert and the towering slopes of the Blue Mountains. Their chances for survival seemed slim indeed.

Behind them, the demoralized emigrants had forsaken the remaining four wagons, given up all efforts at resistance, and sought what scant cover they could find in the sagebrush and clusters of willows flanking the river.

> "When the party abandoned the train, Elizabeth Trimble was carrying in her arms the infant child of her mother, who could not force herself to leave the dead bodies of her husband and daughter, Mary. When Mrs. Otter chose, under stress of excitement, to remain with the dead, three children, Emma, Abby, and Wesley Otter, elected to remain with her. In addition to those already mentioned, the bodies of Lewis Lawson, William Ottley, Charles Kishnell and Judson Creesey—eleven all told—were left within the inclosure."[11]

Of the original forty-four people in the party, twenty-eight still lived—seven men, five women, and sixteen children, several of whom were too small to walk. Now the Indians turned to looting the wagons, taking what they wanted, gorging themselves on food, then setting fire to what was left. For two days and nights, the whites hid, traveled, and managed to survive, moving seven miles down the river. From places of concealment, they watched the savages depart.

> "During the forenoon of the 12th, the Indians left the scene of triumph and proceeded westward along the Snake River in the direction of the ford. It was a remarkable procession that passed in review that September morning. An Indian mounted on the black stallion occupied the place of honor. The line was long—nearly one mile in length—for in addition to

11. *Toward the Setting Sun,* Miles Cannon, p. 136.

about 200 Indian ponies, all the company stock was being driven away."[12]

With the hostiles gone, the problem now facing the emigrants was survival. This was a barren country, devoid of game larger than jackrabbits, and the firearms and ammunition saved were limited. From a "decrepit old Indian" who appeared in camp they obtained fifty pounds of dried salmon in exchange for a gun and several rounds of ammunition. Encumbered by the children, lacking blankets to keep off the night chill, and bewildered by what had happened, they took ten days to travel seventy miles to the mouth of the Owyhee River. Here, they decided they could go no farther without food and assistance. They constructed brush shelters, huddled within them, and waited forlornly for help to come.

Meanwhile, the four ex-soldiers who had left them to fend for themselves were having troubles of their own. Apparently unfamiliar with the country and quarreling among themselves, Murdock, Shamberg, and Schneider went up the Malheur, heading into desert country south of the main branch of the Oregon Trail, while Chaffy, the deserter, turned back toward Snake River, which at this point flows in a northerly direction. While attempting to cross the Blue Mountains near the headwaters of John Day River, Murdock and Shamberg were killed by Indians. After three weeks of aimless wandering, Schneider was found exhausted, destitute, and so incoherent his rescuers could make no sense of his story—which perhaps was just as well.

Running into Chaffy near the mouth of the Malheur, Joseph and Jacob Reith feasted with him on steaks cut off his horse, which he had killed for food, then, when he said he preferred to stay where he was, the two young men headed on across the mountains in search of help.

On October 2, twenty-two days after the massacre, they reached the Umatilla Agency, forty miles south of Fort Walla Walla, and told their terrible story. By the time a military relief party could be organized and sent inland from The Dalles, more time had passed and it was mid-October before:

> "Captain Frederick Dent, 9th infantry, commanding a detachment of troops, left his camp at the foot of the Blue Mountains, about five miles from this agency, on the 14th of the month, en route to the scene of the massacre. . . . I sent Jacob Reith, who is now in my employ, with the expedition. . . ."[13]

Twelve survivors were found. Without going into the morbid details that were published from coast to coast in newspapers of the day, we will note only that the nearly naked, mindless, walking skeletons had eaten snakes, insects, wild rosebuds, grass, and finally their own dead. Chaffy survived, as did Schneider. Two years later, Colonel Patrick Connor, commandant at Fort Douglas near Salt Lake, was advised that in the camp of Bear Hunter, a Bannock, there was a white boy.

> "I at once dispatched Major McGarry with a force to punish the Indians and recapture the boy. Bear Hunter was found in the Cache Valley and Major McGarry ordered his troops to surround them and make a vigorous attack. The soldiers killed three Indians and wounded another, when Bear Hunter surrendered.
>
> "He was at once asked for the Van Orman boy. The chief replied that the white boy had been sent away some days ago. The Major told him to send some of his men out and bring him in and that he should hold the chief and four of his men hostages until the boy returned. Bear Hunter dispatched three of his men and the next day they returned with the lad."[14]

So the list of survivors of the original forty-four members of the Otter party was raised to fifteen. Ten years later, a final footnote closed the tragedy. Jake Reuben, who homesteaded on Sinker Creek near the site of the massacre in 1872, married a Bannock woman and her people frequently were visitors at the Reuben place. He wrote:

> "During one of these visits, an Indian told us he had been in a fight with the whites up there on the trail, and that he had killed a very beautiful girl about ten years of age. He said she had black eyes and black hair and was so beautiful he hated to kill her. He was upbraided by the chief and called a coward. He then shot her through the heart."[15]

In the desert section of the Snake River Country, as 1860 ended, the curtain was descending on the passing-through period and the isolated acts of violence it had engendered. Shadows of war on a larger scale now loomed in the East. To escape involvement in that conflict, people from North and South would initiate a second wave of emigration toward Oregon and Washington Territory. But suddenly this barren land no longer would be just a desert to be crossed.

For in the heart of the Nez Perce country to the north, treasure had been found. . . .

------

12. Ibid., p. 137.

13. G. W. Abbott, Sub-Indian Agent, H.E.D. No. 46, 36th Cong., 2nd Sess., p. 13, Oct. 30, 1860. The Captain Frederick Dent referred to was General Grant's brother-in-law.

14. Cannon, pp. 143-44.

15. Ibid., p. 144.

Right:

NEAR CITY OF ROCKS, SOUTHEASTERN IDAHO
Still a remote, little-traveled area, this was where the Oregon and California trails separated. Someone planted these Lombardy poplars, long ago, and someone built this cabin. But the cabin is empty now—and only the camera can tell its story.

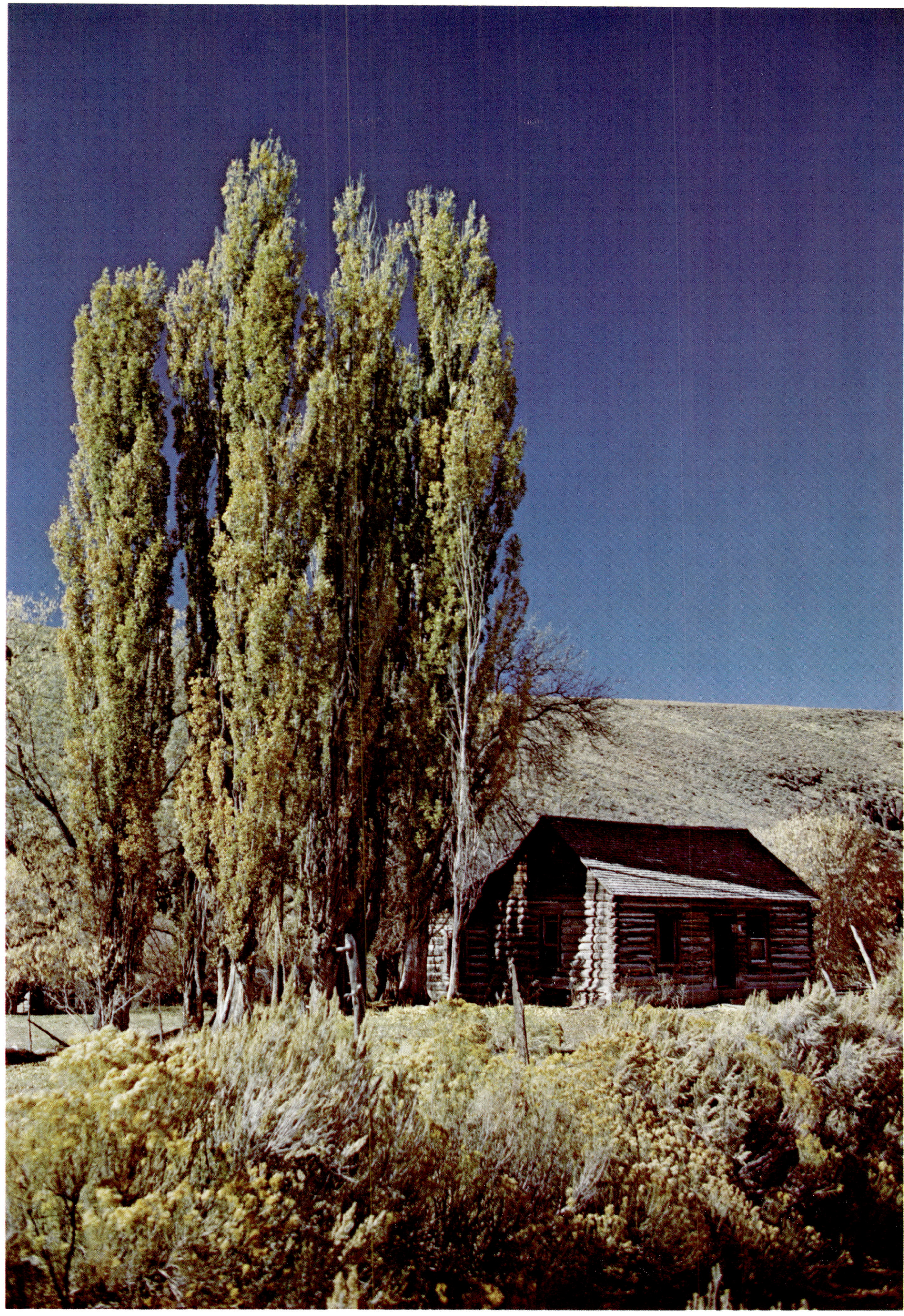

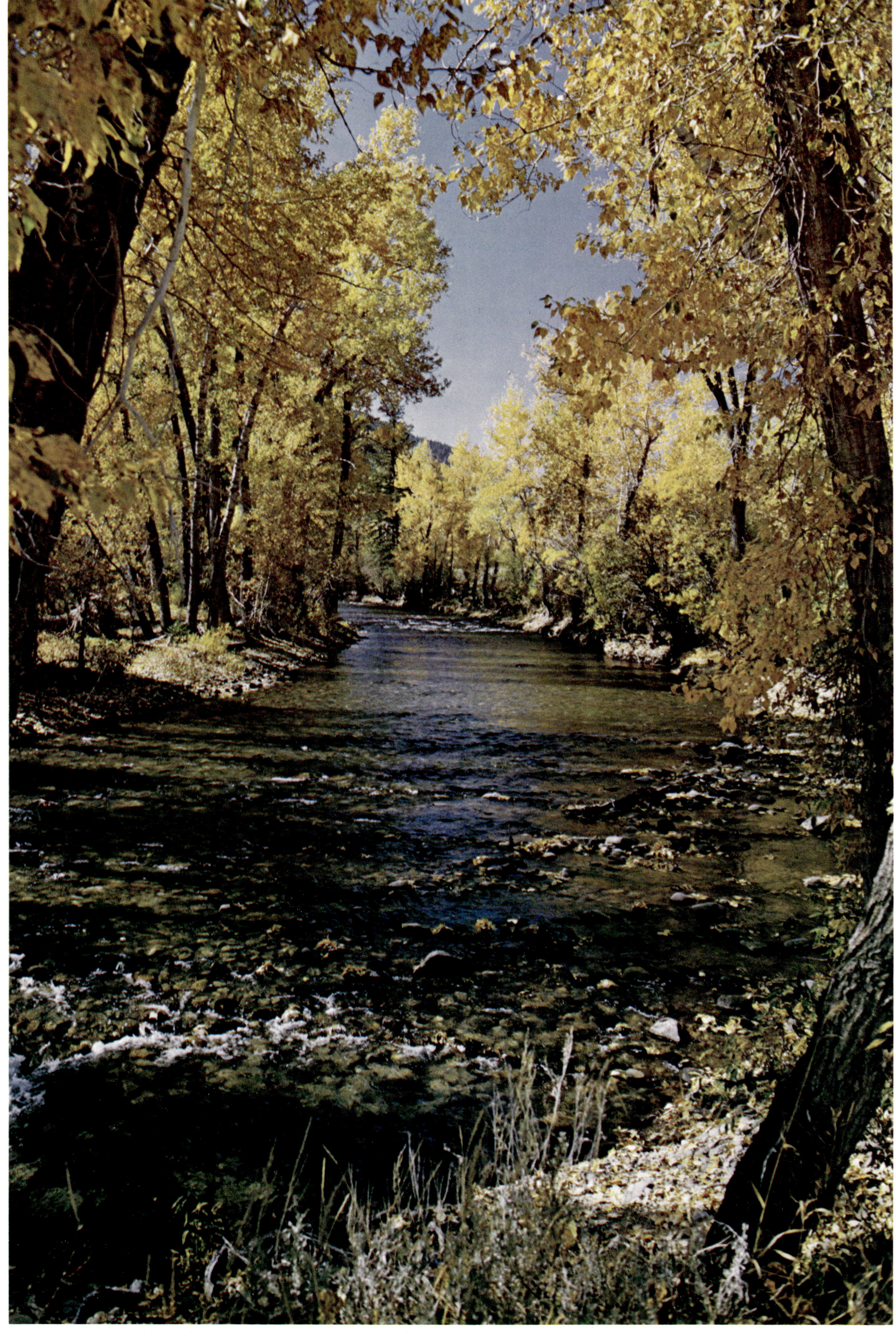

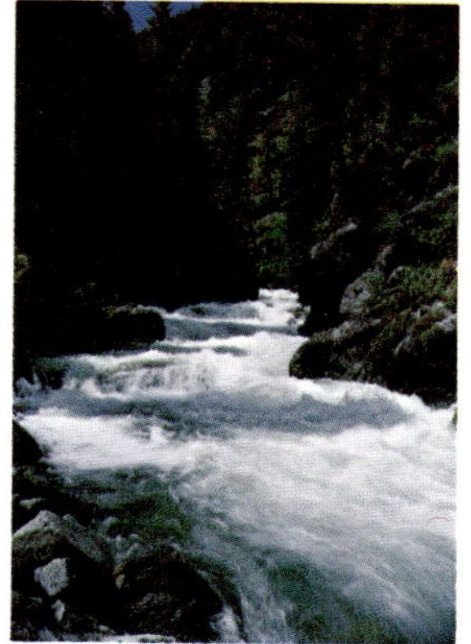

PART FIVE

River of Treasure

1861-1868

1.

Legend claims that the Jesuit priest, Pierre-Jean De Smet, discovered gold in a stream a few miles northeast of the Snake River watershed while visiting the Flatheads in 1840. Because he felt word of its presence would mean ruination to the Indians, he kept it quiet, we are told, took no precious metal for himself, and carried the secret to his grave.[1]

Legend also relates that a member of Isaac Stevens' railroad route survey party found gold to the north of the watershed in 1853, but was ordered to suppress his discovery for the same reason—and did. Historians doubt both tales, pointing out that even though gold later was discovered in Alder Gulch and the Coeur d'Alene country, the legends postdate the finds, so must be folklore.

As already noted, each group of adventurers pushing into the Snake River Country sought a different prize: a Northwest Passage; the River of the West; Beaver; Empire; Heathen Souls To Be Saved; Free Land in Oregon. But whether British, American, French Canadian, or Indian, none was interested in treasure until the California rush of '49 dramatically proved the mineral wealth of the mountains of the Far West.

For hundreds of years, men of Spanish blood had been the New World's experts at extracting precious metal from the earth or from natives who possessed it. But the Americans were quick learners. Furthermore, they were energetic, aggressive, and not averse to doing their own pick and shovel work—a type of backbreaking labor the proud Spaniards abhorred. Soon they were moving north and east from California, into the Snake River Country.

1. *Black Robe: The Life of Pierre-Jean De Smet*, by John Upton Terrell, Doubleday, 1964, p. 177.

Left: Golden Aspen on the Big Wood River near Ketchum, Idaho.

Again legend probably alters fact, but the tale of the Lost Blue Bucket Mine was told in so many versions and was so widely believed at the time that it must be related here. In 1845, while passing through the Snake River Country, a wagon train led by an inept guide attempted to cross the eastern Oregon desert by a new route up the Malheur, came to disaster, and, after many hardships, eventually reached the Willamette Valley.

Somewhere between Fort Hall and the John Day country—a stretch of 350 miles—children playing in a stream found some pretty yellow rocks, tossed them into a blue bucket, and then forgot them. Years later, the rocks were seen by a man who had prospected in California, were identified as gold, and the children were asked when and where they had found them. In a stream, they said, one afternoon along the way. Which stream? Which afternoon? Where along the way?

They did not remember.

Thus, the legend of the Lost Blue Bucket Mine began. That it never was a mine, that it even existed, that it later was found, that it never was found, that it yet may *be* found in all its fabled richness are questions now a part of the region's folklore. What is of interest historically is that the legend did inspire a search, with important consequences, as we shall presently see.[2]

But first, here is one more tale—accepted as truth by at least one early-day historian and some local antiquarians, though doubted by professional scholars because of lack of documentation. This is the believer's account:

> "An Indian from the Nez Perce country found his way into California during the gold excitement in that State, and, chancing one day into a gulch where

2. *And There Were Men*, by Russell Blankenship, Alfred A. Knopf, 1942, p. 276. "The Blue Bucket Mine is the Prester John of Northwest mines," says Blankenship. "There are more versions of the story than a government statistician can enumerate, while the variants of the main theme and the embroidery are limited only by the imaginative horsepower of the narrator."

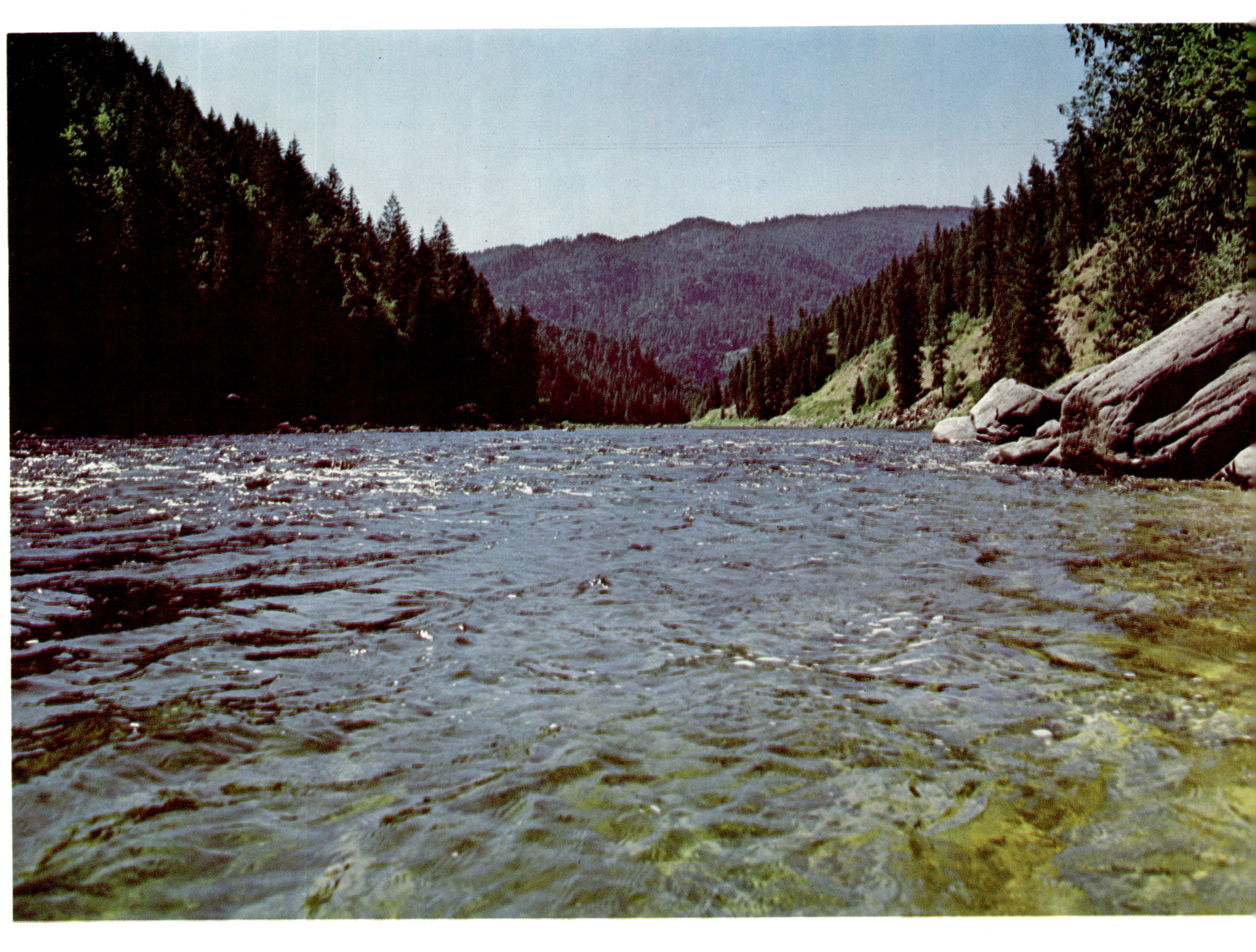

some miners were at work, made himself friendly and useful, and told them in his broken English where he was from and the name of his tribe. He soon made friends.

"Among those miners was one named E. D. Pierce, who was a visionary and susceptible man, liable to be strongly impressed with a romantic tale that possessed points of plausibility. Among his strong characteristics was tenacity, and he was disposed to follow an idea, that might only be a delusion, with a persistence seldom equalled.

"To this man one day the Nez Perce Indian told a strange weird tale of how he, with two companions, had been camping at night in a defile among his native mountains, when suddenly a light like a brilliant star burst forth from among the cliffs. They thought it was the Great Spirit's eye, and watched with superstitious awe until the dawn, when, taking courage with the wakening day, they sought the spot from where the night twinkling had looked down upon them, and found a glittering ball that looked like glass embodied in the solid rock. The Indians believed it was a great medicine, but could not get it from its resting place, and were forced to leave it there.

"This was just the kind of tale to make a strong impression upon Captain Pierce, who believed the Indian had found a diamond more valuable than the famed Kohinoor, and he determined to become its possessor. With that purpose he left California and became a resident of Walla Walla. He scouted through the mountains east of Snake River, and finally induced a party of men to accompany him, they hoping to find gold, he still searching for the mythical diamond. . . ."[3]

Whether Captain Pierce's prospecting trip into the mountains north of the Clearwater was in search of a fist-sized diamond or for gold, this land now was part of the newly approved Nez Perce Indian Reservation. He and his men were halted as trespassers by Agent Andrew J. Cain, refused permission to prospect in the area, and warned that they would be arrested if they returned. For the time being, they obeyed the order; but they had no intention of respecting it for long.

Here, the accounts of what happened differ. One says Pierce had been in the Clearwater country before, knew there was gold in its streams, and was waiting until the Indian troubles simmered down before returning to mine its treasure. When blocked from descending the main branch of the river, he withdrew, circled west, north, and east, and then led his party to its goal through the rugged mountains and thick timber along the North Fork. A more romantic account gives this version:

> "Pierce, however, found a Nez Perce squaw who said she could pilot them through by a route not frequented by her people, and the party then set out under her guidance, spent three days cutting a trail through small cedars over a mountain, and found itself at length in a mountain meadow, where they determined to rest for a while and let their horses recruit. . . ."

Near this same mountain meadow fifty years earlier, Lewis and Clark had left their horses under the watchful eye of Chief Twisted Hair. One wonders how the course of history might have been altered if a member of the exploring party had done what a member of Pierce's group did now.

> "While there, W. F. Bassett went to a stream that ran through the meadow gulch, and tried the soil for gold, finding about three cents in his first panful of dirt. This was the first discovery of that metal in these mountains, and the place where it was found became the noted Oro Fino mines, in what is now Idaho. . . ."[4]

Local tradition has it that the Nez Perce woman who guided the Pierce party onto reservation land by the back way was Jane Silcott, Chief Timothy's daughter, who a year or so before had married a white man who now operated a ferry across Snake River near the mouth of the Clearwater. Building a rough sluice from cedar bark, the party of whites soon recovered eighty dollars in gold dust. Then, being short on supplies, Pierce returned to Walla Walla, spread word of the discovery to a few trusted friends, re-outfitted, and, with a party of fifteen men, returned to the area and dug in for the winter.

It was now November and this was relatively high country where the snows came early and stayed late. Agent Cain and the military knew the white trespassers were there and set out from Lapwai to remove them. But the weather turned stormy, snow closed the trails, and the only thing the authorities could do was go back to Lapwai—and hope that the miners would freeze or starve to death.

Unfortunately for the Indians, the trespassers survived. Building a cluster of five solid log cabins, which they named Pierce City, they continued to pan for gold despite deepening snow. By January, they were so sure they had struck a bonanza that they sent two men to the settlements on snowshoes for more supplies. In March, another member of the party followed, carrying eight hundred dollars in dust to Walla Walla to pay off debts to the merchants. Sent downriver to Portland, the gold and news of the strike "set

3. *Historic Sketches of Walla Walla, Whitman, Columbia and Garfield Counties, Washington Territory*, by Frank T. Gilbert, Portland, 1882, p. 224. The discoverer's full name was Elias Davidson Pierce.

4. Ibid., p. 225.

Left: The Clearwater, above Orofino

off a blaze of excitement. . . ." Within weeks, men by the thousands were moving toward the interior.

This was the spring of 1861. A continent's breadth away, Fort Sumter was under siege; President Lincoln was about to issue a call for 75,000 troops; and the country soon would be rent asunder by the Civil War. But in the Pacific Northwest, there was bigger news.

Gold. . . .

° ° °

2.

So far as its gold-rush days are concerned, poets, historians, and fiction writers have sadly neglected the Snake River Country. As contemporary publicists, California had Bret Harte; Nevada, Mark Twain and Dan DeQuille; the Klondike, Jack London, Rex Beach, and Robert W. Service. All were celebrities known nationwide in their day, who did yeoman work in popularizing the areas they were writing about, and their works have endured even into the present time.

But in the Snake River Country during its bonanza years, despite all the raw material available for drama, only one writer achieved anything like national stature. This was the poet, Joaquin Miller, who lived for a time in the Clearwater country, rode express, let his hair grow long, and was a good friend of ex-mountain man William Craig. Only one of his poems achieved popular acclaim, an ode to the courage of the discoverer of America. In my own boyhood, I once was forced to commit it to memory as a Columbus Day assignment. As I now recall, the lines went something like this:

" 'Oh, what shall we do when hope is gone?'
" 'Sail on!' the Admiral said,
" 'And on . . .
" 'And on. . . .' "

Compared with "The Outcasts of Poker Flat," "The Jumping Frog of Calaveras County," and "The Shooting of Dan McGrew," this is pale stuff, indeed.

In addition to taking second place to the Civil War for national publicity, the gold rush into the Snake River Country suffered an identity problem. First, the area had been jointly occupied by Great Britain and the United States; next, it became a passing-through region nobody was interested in; later, it was attached to but ignored by Oregon Territory and Washington Territory. And when, in 1863, it at last was organized as a territory and given a name, the naming process was offhand.

The word "Idaho" is meaningless, say some historians, borrowed from a place in Colorado called "Idaho Springs" and applied to the newly created territory by an indifferent Congressman. Joaquin Miller, in a demonstration that he could write colorfully when he put his mind to it, disputed this slander with some heat:

"The distinction of naming Idaho certainly belongs to my old friend, Colonel Craig. As for some fellow naming it in Congress—bah! The name was familiar in 5,000 men's mouths as they wallowed through the snow in '61, on their way to the Oro Fino mines. . . .

"Gallop your horse, as I have done hundreds of times, against the rising sun. As you climb the Sweet Water Mountains, you will see a peculiar and beautiful light, a sort of diadem on two grand clusters of mountains that bear away under the clouds, fifty miles distant.

"I called Colonel Craig's attention to this peculiar and beautifully arched light. 'That,' said he, 'is what the Indians call *E-dah-hoe,* which means the light or diadem on the line of mountains.' That was the first time I had ever heard the name.

"On my return to Lewiston I wrote a letter containing a brief account of our trip and of the mines, and it was published in one of the Oregon papers—which one, I have now forgotten. In that account I often mentioned *E-dah-hoe,* but spelled it *I-d-a-h-o.* So that, perhaps, I may have been the first to give it its present spelling; but I certainly did not originate the word."[1]

Despite the thousands of white intruders pouring into their country, the Nez Perces remained peaceful. Short of declaring war against the entire West, there was nothing else they could do. Few Federal soldiers were stationed in the area. Their agent could issue edicts but could not enforce them. Long contact with missionaries had made farmers and livestock raisers of many of the Indians, and, while they disdained grubbing in the earth for gold, they knew its worth. One early-day newspaper correspondent relates

1. *Early History of Idaho,* by William J. McConnell, Caxton, 1913, p. 28. McConnell came to Idaho Territory soon after the first discovery of gold in the Boise Basin, later became Governor and U.S. Senator, and was William Borah's father-in-law.

Right:

OLD ROCK WALL

Upstream from Asotin, Washington, sightseers cruising the Snake into Hell's Canyon view this extensive wall made of hand-hewn lava rocks. Local legend has it that years ago a bachelor homesteader got tired of living alone, wrote to a Chicago matrimonial bureau for a wife, and eventually succeeded in getting a lady to agree to marry him. But she would not come to the Western Wilds until he dug a well, built a comfortable house, and fenced the farm. Working alone, the lonely bachelor labored from dawn till dark for months on end, using the rocks taken out of the hand-dug well to fence the homestead. At long last, all was ready for the bride. But she never came. The bachelor never married. In fact, he never spoke to a woman again for the rest of his life.

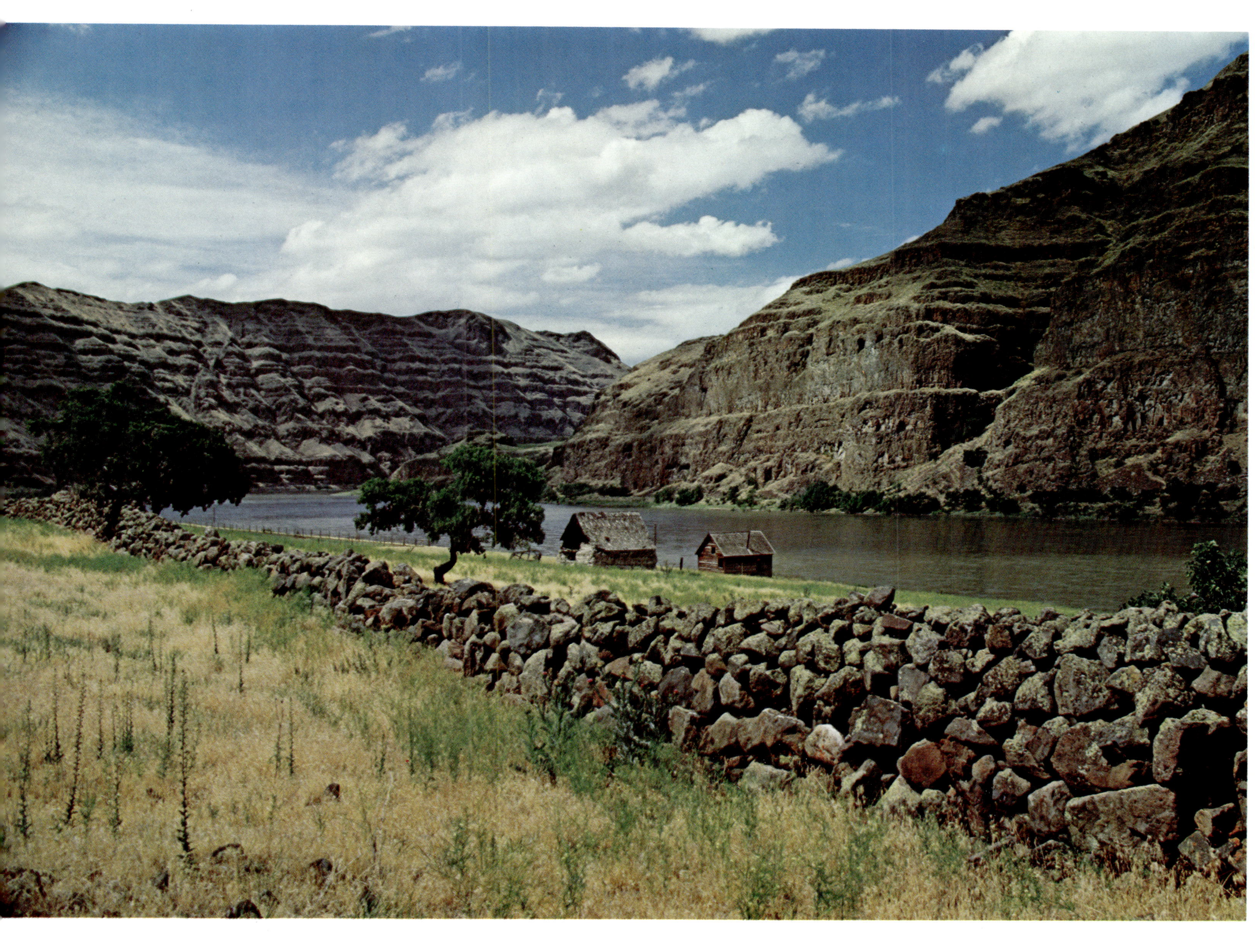

meeting Chief Reuben, a Nez Perce, at what soon would become Lewiston, in June, 1861:

> "He was there urging the other Indians to permit the whites to go to the mines without molestation, telling them that if the white men dug out the gold the Indians could sell horses, cattle, corn and vegetables and get gold in return. He thought it would be much better for the Indians to have the whites in the country and to trade with them than to oppose their coming. . . ."[2]

From time to time as new discoveries were made in other parts of the Nez Perce reservation, its boundaries were redrawn to exclude areas of rich strikes, so that technically the prospectors would not be trespassers. Like the frequently moved little acre dedicated to God by the back-country farmer in Erskine Caldwell's popular novel, principle must not get in the way of the diggers.

The first problem confronting the prospector hoping to make his fortune in the Nez Perce mines was how to get there. This was remote, untracked country, difficult to reach from any direction. From San Francisco, for example, it was three to six days by steamer north to the mouth of the Columbia River over usually stormy seas. Current, wind, tide, and constantly shifting sands made crossing the bar at the six-mile-wide entrance to the river a risky business. At Portland, a hundred miles inland, the traveler must change from ocean to river steamer; and, since water transport was in short supply, his wait would be long, his space aboard minimal, his comforts few. At the Cascades, fifty miles upriver, he must debark from the first steamer, portage himself and his baggage six miles around the unnavigable white water, then board another boat for the traverse of what was called the "middle river."

This took him as far as The Dalles, another fifty miles, where again he must make a portage—this one of fourteen miles—and then board a boat plying the "upper river." If it did not hole its bottom or wreck a paddle wheel on the rocks of the Deschutes, John Day, or Umatilla Rapids, it would reach the mouth of the Snake in a couple of days—providing it did not suffer an engine breakdown, catch fire or burst a boiler.

In early spring breakup, floating ice made the Snake unnavigable; in late spring flood, its current was too strong to be bucked; in early autumn low water, only extremely shallow-draft paddle-wheelers could get to the mouth of the Clearwater; and in any season, the boats were loaded to the rails and charged passengers and freight the limit of what the traffic would bear.

Since we will treat past and present Snake River transport more fully in another section, we will note here only the facts that Lewiston, at the mouth of the Clearwater, became head of navigation, and that the mode of travel sketched above was the *easy* way to get from San Francisco to the Nez Perce mines. Overland travel *really was* tough.

In view of the fact that most of the early prospectors had learned the business in California, it was natural that they should apply Spanish terms to their finds. Along the North Fork of the Clearwater, the first gold panned had been very fine-grained; thus, stream and settlement were named *Orofino.* When a second strike was made along the South Fork of the Clearwater, the grains of gold were large and coarse; thus, the name *Orogrande.* Like the original find by the Pierce party, the second strike was in high, rugged, mountainous country.

Thanks to the courtesy of Dr. Walter Brattain, whose father was involved with mines and miners in the Pacific Northwest for much of his lifetime, we have a unique account of the difficulties encountered in this area and the way they were solved. The following excerpts from his father's unpublished reminiscences[3] are printed with Dr. Brattain's kind permission:

> "So it happened in 1861, when gold was discovered on the South Fork, Bill [Dr. Brattain's grandfather] and Clay Harlow decided to try their luck in the new diggings. From Lewiston, they went over Camas Prairie, down into the South Fork of the Clearwater, thence up the switchback to the Halfway House, then between Pilot Knob and Pilot Mountain, then over Elk Summit and down to Elk City on the edge of the meadows that reach up the Red River, which joins the American River to make the South Fork of the Clearwater. . . ."

The "ups" and "downs" were not matters of a few hundred feet, but of thousands, it should be noted for the benefit of those who never have seen the country being described. Prospecting in this area required strong lungs and legs even to reach the streams where the arm and back work began. The account continues:

> "Bill and Clay located claims on Orogrande Bar where Relief Creek and Crooked River meet. A placer claim could be one hundred feet wide and as long as the pay reached from the stream.
>
> "Orogrande Bar was not large, but rich, and the gold was coarse. Most of the Bar was worked with rockers and the men pitched the gravel into the rock-

-----

2. Lewiston *Teller.* March 31, 1877.

3. After being born and raised in southeastern Washington, near Farmington, Ross R. Brattain graduated from Whitman College in Walla Walla, then served as a teacher in China for several years. There, in Amoy, his son, Walter H. Brattain, was born. Returning to the Pacific Northwest, Ross Brattain remained interested in mining and miners the rest of his life. Dr. Walter Brattain became a physicist, working for Bell Laboratories in the East until his retirement. His research into the properties of semi-conductors resulted in the invention of the transistor, for which he and two fellow scientists were awarded the Nobel Prize in 1956. Dr. Brattain now teaches part time at Whitman College, takes pack trips each summer into the Idaho high country where his grandfather once prospected, and retains friendships with prospectors there who still dream of making new strikes.

er with a shovel and carried the water to wash it in buckets. The rich part of the Bar was about one-half mile long. The claims paid from $18,000 to $25,000 each. All told there was slightly over a million dollars taken out, and it was one of the smaller Bars of the district."

Both Bill Brattain and Clay Harlow were young unmarried men, as were most of the prospectors in the area. As autumn approached, there were five thousand men in the district, supplies were running low, and there would be no more packtrains coming in until late next spring.

> "A miners' meeting was called to discuss the situation. It was decided that each group of five men should appoint one to stay and represent them, while the other four would go out to winter. Not over a thousand should go out at any one time."

Bill and Clay were selected to lead the first thousand-man contingent on the two-day trek from the high country down to the milder weather of the South Fork of the Clearwater. Their friends, Fi Gilbert and Charley Painter, also were going out of the district to winter, leaving behind to represent them on their claims a man whose name they did not record for posterity. Traveling light, they reached the Halfway House the first night. From that point, it was mostly downhill to the Clearwater, which the four young men reached in late afternoon the second day.

Up in the high country, killing frost had come weeks ago; tamarack and aspen had turned to gold; and winter was at hand. But here, as they gathered wood for their campfire and dipped water out of the stream for tea, the air was balmy. In a few days, they would be home—gold in their pockets, exciting tales of adventure to tell their loved ones, and long months ahead in which to talk and dream of the fortunes they surely would make next summer. They built a fire, put tea water on to boil, then. . . .

> "They saw the main body of the long line following them coming around the high point where the switchback began. There were three other points on the steep hill where the trail and the men on it could be seen. As Bill mixed batter for bannocks, Clay Harlow, who was tending the fire, began singing *Annie Laurie*. Bill, Fi, and Charley joined in.
>
> "The long line of men was soon coming into camp, picking out a spot for a fire, dropping their blankets, and preparing their frugal meal. Group by group, they started singing, too. The song spread up the line of moving men like a fire. Soon from the camp to the highest point at the beginning of the switchback the men were singing in one giant chorus about two miles long; all singing *Annie Laurie*.
>
> "Away up on the mountain side, a man would come around one of the points on the switchback singing, and then as he went back into the draw his voice would fade until he would again come out on the next point below, still singing *Annie Laurie*. The singing did not cease until every man was in camp and was wrapped in his blankets, dozing by his fire. Each heart recalled a different name, but all sang *Annie Laurie*. . . ."

Sad to relate, next summer when the four young miners returned to their claims to make their fortunes, they discovered that the unnamed man they had left behind to look after their interests had sold them out, lost the money gambling, and departed the district. The thought of tracking him down and stringing him up when and if caught was discussed—but discarded as a waste of time. The man who had bought Bill Brattain's claim got $18,000 for his summer's work. Bill took a job for wages.

Like other isolated mining camps, Elk City offered little in the way of entertainment when the day's work was done. Bill Brattain's younger brothers, Ank and Cy, who had come back to the district with him, played cards now and then, and did not mind dropping an occasional dollar or two, but after a while a stranger with one bad eye started sitting in on the games. He won so consistently and handled the cards so expertly that Ank and Cy began to suspect they were being cheated. Bill Brattain had a friend named Frank, who had once been a professional gambler, so one day they asked him to play a few hands and see whether the one-eyed man's consistent success was due to skill, luck, or something else.

> "He watched the suspect deal three times, then, the fourth time, Frank laid his Colt on the table and said: 'I don't want to be personal, but if a certain S.O.B. does not quit cheating, I am going to shoot his other eye out.' "

The cockeyed man left the table without cashing in his chips and bothered them no more.

At first, there was an extreme shortage of women in the mining settlements, then an enterprising German whiskey seller and his wife took steps to alleviate the problem. Returning to the old country, the couple found three healthy, sturdy, unattached German girls and made them a proposition:

> "If they would come to Elk City, dance with the men, drink nothing alcoholic, and promise not to marry for one year they would be paid a thousand dollars apiece, be given a commission on all drinks sold, be supplied with clothing and all necessary expenses, and would live with the German and his wife. As a bonus, when their year was up, they were assured that each would have found a respectable man who wished to marry her."

These were the first of the "hurdy-gurdy" girls, a class

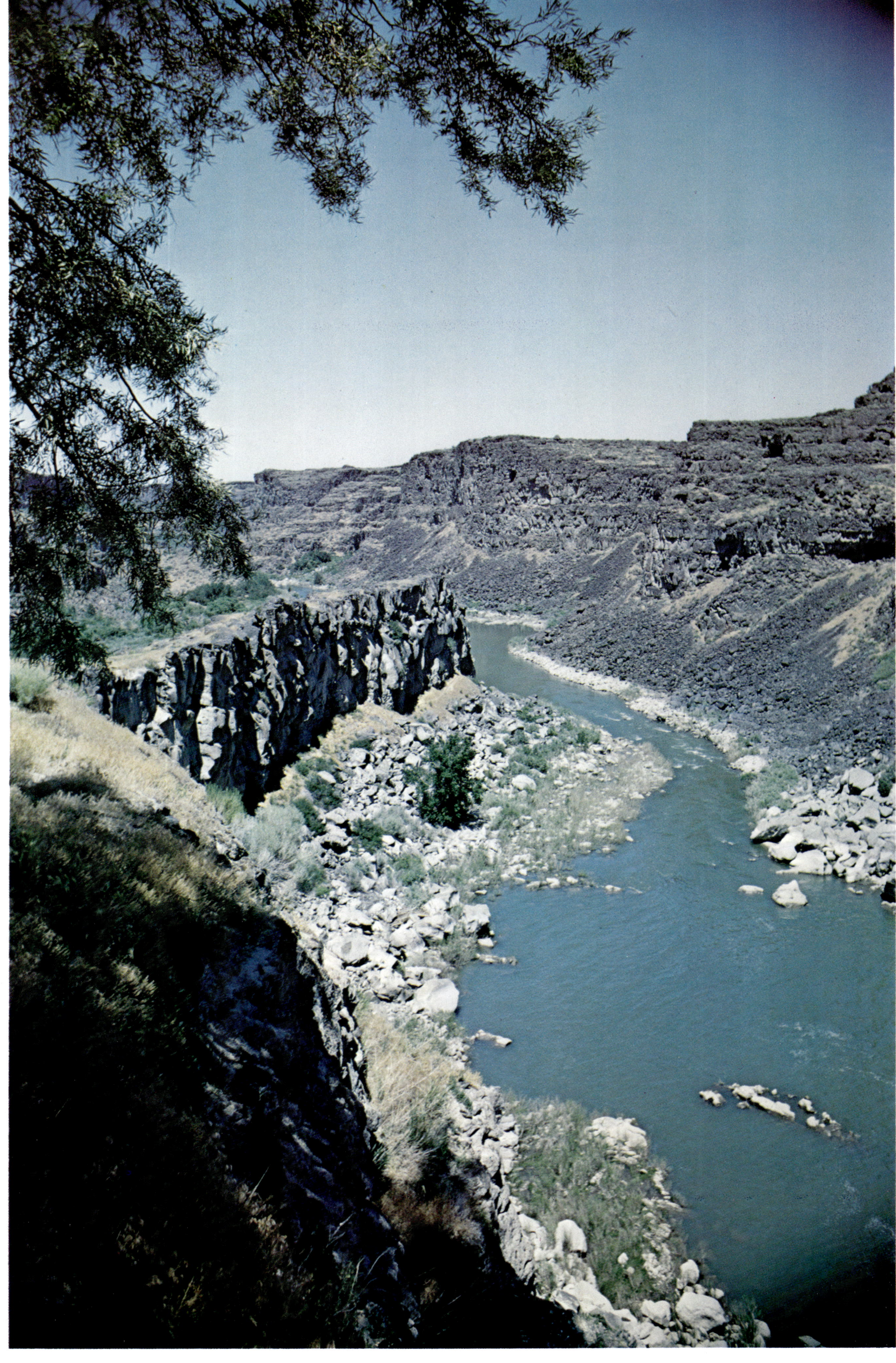

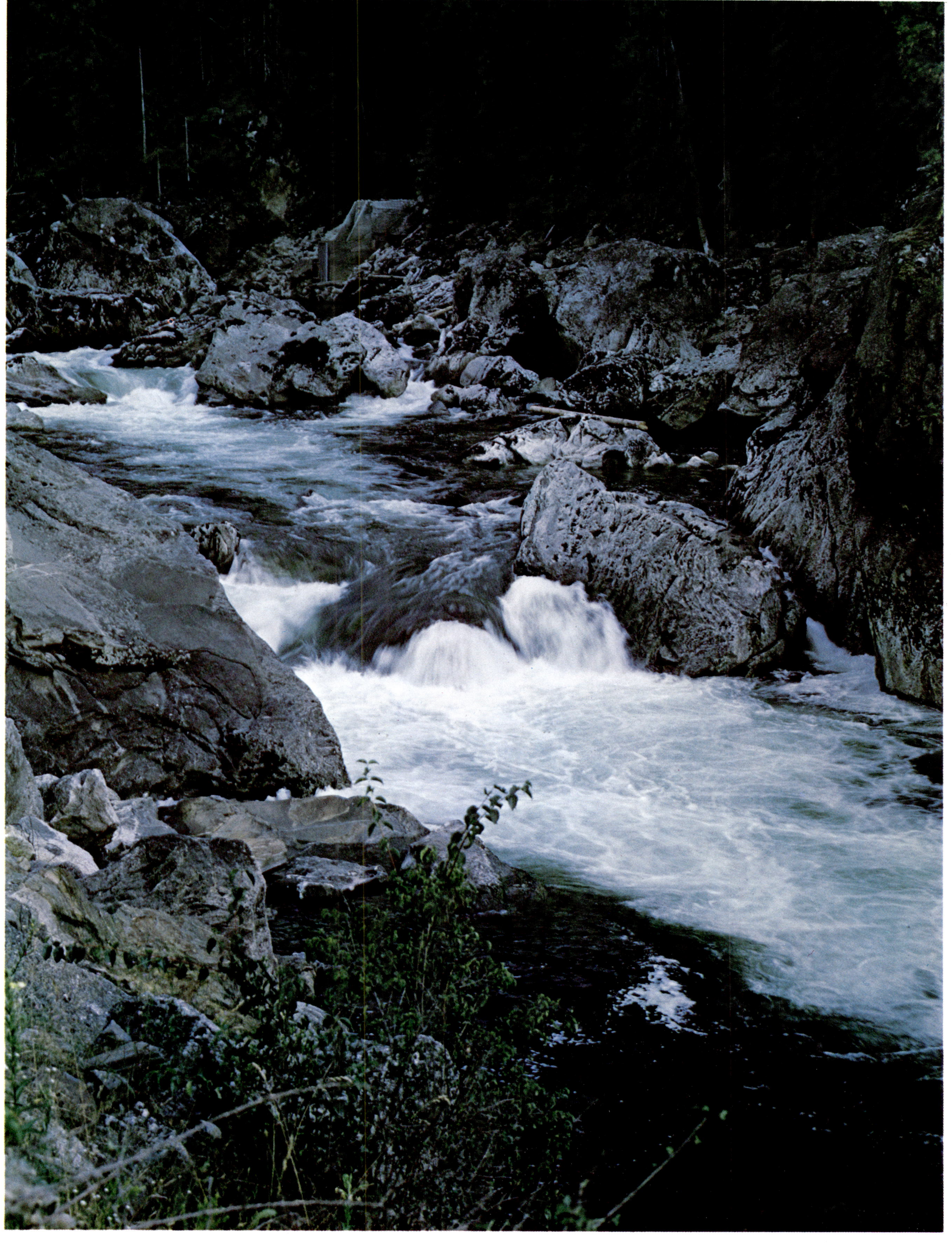

Left: Canyon of the Snake, below Twin Falls

Above:

FALLS ON THE SELWAY RIVER
One of the tributaries that form the Clearwater

of young women soon to be found in all the Idaho gold towns. With few exceptions, they were morally upright young ladies working to earn a dowry and a husband. They were not to be trifled with by look, word, or deed, for if a hefty swing of a husky female arm did not floor the offender, a bung-starter wielded by their patron or his wife most certainly would. As an example of their conduct:

> "Bill had a young friend who danced every Sunday with one of the girls. He was smitten. She told him she couldn't marry him. Later he told Bill he offered her five hundred dollars if she would spend one night with him, but she refused. When their year was up, the German and his wife took the three girls out of Elk City, and, when the couple returned, they said all three were married before they told them good-bye. Whether Bill's friend got one of the girls, we never heard."

In addition to the discoveries along the North and South forks of the Clearwater, gold soon was found on the Salmon. As one camp waned, others boomed. Florence and Warren came into being, and each for a time was "the biggest strike ever." At the mouth of the Clearwater, Lewiston became a major supply point; as agitation grew for territorial status, its merchants, newspaper editors, and politicians enthusiastically promoted it as the logical site for the capital.

But even as Lewiston dreamed of great days to come three hundred miles to the south a party of men set out on yet another search for the Lost Blue Bucket Mine. And in Elk City, a man named Moses Splawn was listening to a Bannock Indian's intriguing tale of a mountain-surrounded basin lying at the headwaters of the Boise River, where he once had seen yellow flakes. . . .

° ° °

3.

Like all prospectors, Moses Splawn was a superstitious man who believed in signs, listened to inner voices, and felt that an ever bigger strike lay over the next range of mountains. In Elk City, in Florence, and again while camped at the mouth of Slate Creek on the Salmon River, he met a friendly Bannock Indian who three times told him a story of a basin far to the south filled with gold. According to frontier folklore, an Indian could lie twice to a white man, but the third time he spoke on the same subject, his religion required he tell the truth.

> "His look was so earnest and his description of the mountains so painstaking, that I not only believed his story, but felt that I should recognize the place he described, if I ever came upon it."[1]

1. *Kamiakin, The Last Hero of the Yakimas,* by A. J. Splawn, Portland, 1917, pp. 186-93.

With a small party of men, next summer, Splawn journeyed into the southwestern corner of Idaho where so many explorers, Sandwich Islanders, trappers, and emigrants had starved, suffered, and died in time past. Here he encountered a man named Tom Turner, who, with fifty settlers from the Willamette Valley, was searching for the lost "Blue Bucket Diggin's."

According to the tale Turner had heard, the name derived from the fact that the emigrants of '45 claimed they could have picked up a blue bucket full of yellow rocks, had they been so minded—the blue bucket being a type of water pail used in those days which would hold about three gallons. Turner's inner voice told him the lost mine lay in the foothills of the Owyhee Mountains, south of Snake River. Though the needle of Splawn's psychic compass inclined in the opposite direction, the two parties agreed to join forces, with the provision that if the search for the lost mine failed south of the Snake, all the men would cross the river and look for Splawn's gold-lined basin there.

After days of diligent search, the lost mine remained lost. Splawn demanded that Turner keep the bargain he had made; Turner replied that he would—after crossing just one more ridge and exploring just one more creek. When that was done and Turner still persisted in continuing the search south of the Snake, Splawn gave up in disgust, invited the men who wished to do so to follow him, enlisted sixteen adherents, and headed north.

As they climbed into the mountains north of Snake River Plain, a heated argument arose as to whether they should ascend the Payette or the Boise River. George Grimes, a family man, favored the former, Splawn the latter. A vote was taken, Grimes won, and, for a time, he was permitted to lead the party up the Payette. Then another argument broke out. Grimes and a man named Westenfelter got off their horses and leveled guns at each other at such close range that the barrels touched.

> "I jumped off my horse, got between them and succeeded in making peace," Splawn wrote. "Both were brave men and we did not have any brave men to spare."

For several days now, a number of Bannocks had been watching the party, and they gave indications of having hostile intentions. When asked why he did not want to cross over the ridge and ascend the Boise to the area Splawn wished to explore, George Grimes answered, "I am afraid of the Indians."

Westenfelter ridiculed his fears. "If we are afraid of the Indians," he said, "we should not have come here at all and had better return home."

Grimes gave in, turning leadership of the group over to Splawn. He said, "I will get behind and bother you no more."

The party crossed the ridge to the watershed of the Boise. There, Splawn's psychic compass and the Indian's thrice-repeated tale of gold were proved to be right. The first panful of dirt, washed by D. G. Fogus, reclaimed fifteen cents worth of gold dust. Soon all the men were working feverishly and the floor of the high mountain valley was pockmarked with prospect holes.

Around them on the timbered, rocky hillsides, Indians in ever-increasing numbers could be seen; as the men dug, they kept their firearms handy. George Grimes still was feeling gloomy. After shaving one day, he took out the picture of his little girl and gazed at it somberly for a long while.

> "He remarked that a fortune teller had told him he would be killed by Indians," Splawn wrote. "Then he said to me: 'Wouldn't that be hell?' "

Next afternoon, while Splawn was taking a nap, he was awakened by the sound of shots. Hostile Bannocks were firing into camp.

> "I got up and saw George Grimes with his shotgun in his hand, close by. Taking my gun, I went to him, and together we made a charge up the hill. As we reached the top, it seemed as if twenty guns were fired in our faces. Grimes fell, his last and only words being: 'Moses, don't let them scalp me.' "

Burying the dead man in one of the prospect holes, the Splawn party retreated and made its way down to the plains of the Snake near the mouth of the Boise River. Here, it encountered an Oregon-bound emigrant train, one of the many now coming West to escape the turmoil of the Civil War. The successful prospectors did not tell the emigrants of their find, saving that piece of good news for the fifty men they would enlist in Walla Walla and bring back to the Boise Basin as forerunners of the horde of whites that soon would invade the interior.

This was in August, 1862.

Now the tide of emigration, which for so many years had moved toward the setting sun, would reverse itself—and this passing-through land would be empty no more.

Like Lewiston in the nothern part of the watershed and Walla Walla near the mouth of the Snake to the northwest, Boise City (as it first was called) came into existence as an outfitting, wintering, entertainment, and general hell-raising center whose main business was separating gold from the men who dug it. Statistics of Snake River Country mineral production are as unreliable as town-booster reports; but from the Boise Basin mines alone the figure of $250 million is often quoted, while, from the Owyhee mines south of the Snake, where both gold and silver were discovered, $100 million is said to have been taken before the boom ended.[2]

As in other frontier mining areas, a "Get-the-gold-and-move-on" philosophy prevailed, and law and order were conspicuous mostly for their absence. But the wild and woolly years of the Snake River Country were heightened even more by three factors not present to the same degree in California, Nevada, the Klondike, and other strikes.

First, there was a war on back East; and though physically the miners had left the conflict behind, emotionally they had brought it with them. Since the mix of Northerners and Southerners was about equal, localized civil wars could and did break out whenever glasses were raised and toasts proposed.

Second, the number of Republicans and Democrats in the area roughly was equal, too; so, once the Territory of Idaho was officially organized in March, 1863, a political squabble of magnificent and sometimes ludicrous proportions was joined for its control.

Third, the Indians of southern Idaho, eastern Oregon, and northern Nevada were not as friendly or tractable as the Nez Perces. For years, the Snakes carried on a warfare against travelers, settlers, and miners so vicious and bloody that—however justified from the savage viewpoint—it made Indian-haters of an entire generation of whites.

The most colorful localized civil war was the Patterson-Pinkham feud and its aftermath. Since none of the first-hand accounts remotely approaches the ideal of objectivity required by scholars, all we shall attempt to do here is tell the tale as legend relates it.

The time was August, 1865. The place, Idaho City, in the heart of the booming Boise Basin.

Ferdinand J. Patterson was a Southerner, a professional gambler, and something of a dandy in his style of dress. A tall, handsome, redheaded man known to be dangerous when drinking, he was reputed to have killed several men in California and Oregon because they had insulted his beloved South. He was also a lady's man. In Portland, he had been haled into court for allegedly scalping a mistress he thought unfaithful to him. He defended himself by saying he only had meant to slice off a lock of her hair as a parting keepsake, but had accidentally taken too deep a divot. When the lady substantiated his story in court, he was acquitted of the charge. With such colorful credentials, he soon became the hero of Idaho City's sporting circle.

In contrast, Sumner S. Pinkham was fat and phlegmatic. He believed in law, order, the Union, and the Republican party. For a time, he had served as sheriff of Boise County, though recently he had been swept out of office with other Republicans by a Democratic election victory.

The South had just lost the war; Lee had surrendered to Grant; and the President of the Confederacy, Jefferson Davis, had been captured while trying to escape, wearing his wife's clothes. Ferd Patterson drank and mourned. Sumner

2. While the rules of foot-noting probably don't allow quoting a work of fiction as authority for a statement of fact, I once spent six years researching and writing a novel dealing with the beginnings of Idaho Territory 1863-68. Some 200,000 words in length, it was called *They Came to a Valley* and was published by Doubleday in 1966, with a paperback edition issued by Popular Library in 1968. My research notes are at Penrose Library, Whitman College, should any historian of the period be interested, along with the microfilm of half a dozen Idaho and Washington Territory newspapers. Where I have not footnoted statements in this section, I am prepared to defend myself as being *generally* correct—and if the historian purist will not accept that, all I can do is wait until *he* writes a novel.

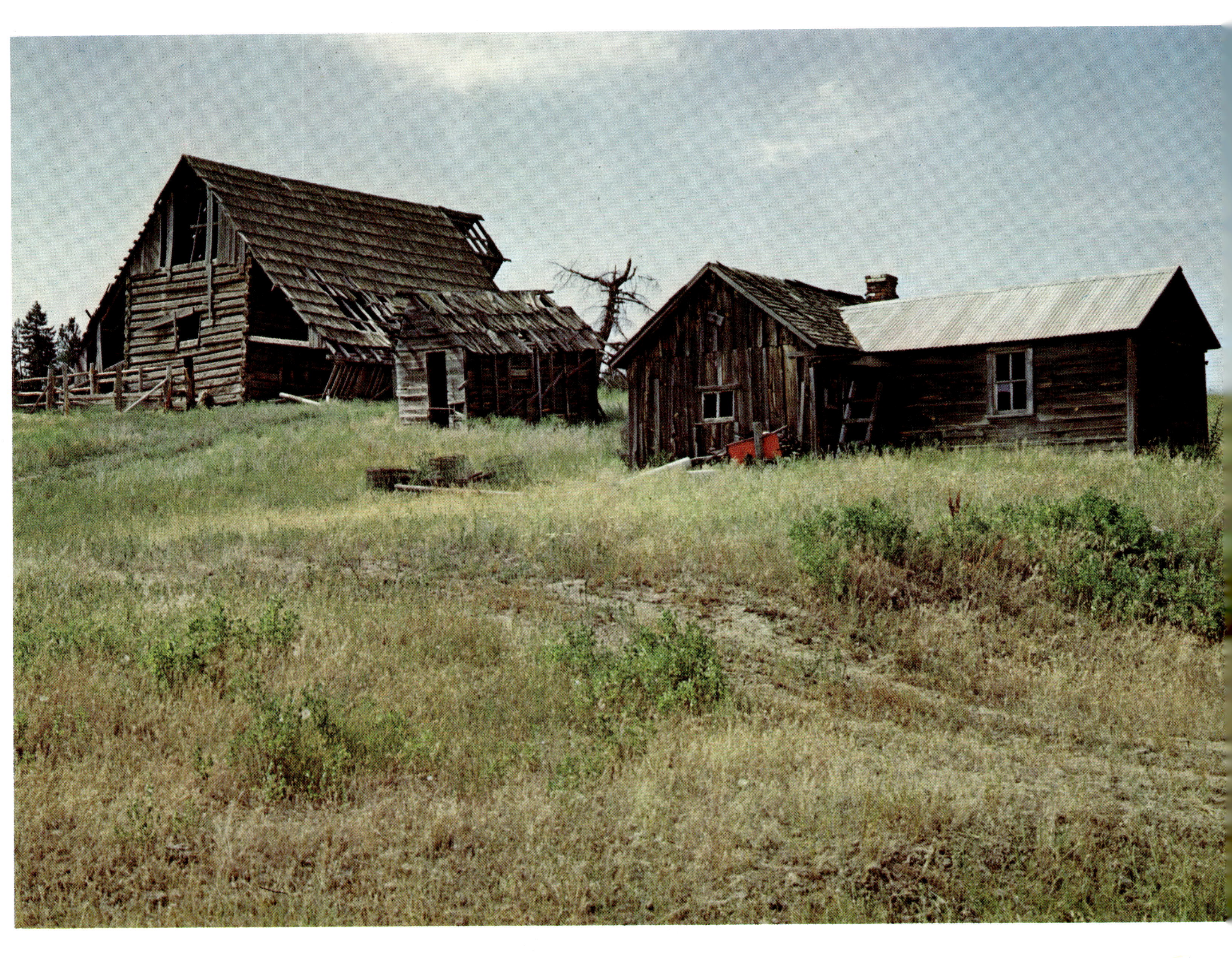

Pinkham drank and gloated. During a patriotic parade organized by Union men to celebrate the great occasion, Pinkham carried Old Glory and lustily sang the popular ditty of the day:

"Oh, we'll hang Jeff Davis
To a sour apple tree;
Yes, we'll hang Jeff Davis. . . ."

Enraged at the affront to the South, Ferd Patterson tore the flag from Pinkham's hands, threw it to the ground, and spat on it. Pinkham, who was unarmed, roared: "If I were heeled, I would kill you for that!"

"Then *be* heeled, next time we meet!" Patterson snapped.

Thus, the die was cast for the shoot-out soon to come.

A mile south of town, there was a spa called Warm Springs, in whose steaming, sulphur-impregnated waters citizens were accustomed to soak out their accumulated poisons on Sundays. One could swim in the outdoor pool, bask in a zinc-lined tub in a private bathroom, and then, when purified, start accumulating next week's poisons in the bar, through which one must pass to reach or leave the private tubs.

This particular Sunday afternoon, Ferd Patterson and Sumner Pinkham both went to the spa and took the waters in one manner or another. An imaginative TV writer of Westerns could create a scene unique to the medium by having the two men emerge from bathrooms at opposite ends of the steam-filled hall at precisely the same moment. Action directions would read: *Neither man wears a gun. In fact, neither man wears anything. They freeze. They reach. . . .*

What *did* happen was that, fully dressed and fully heeled, Patterson and Pinkham met on the veranda, Patterson coming out from the bar, Pinkham leaning against a porch post as he awaited the hack from town. Later testimony reveals that Patterson said:

"Will you draw, you Abolitionist S.O.B. . . . ?"
or
"Oh, you *will* draw (etc.) . . . !"
or
"Draw on *me*, will you (etc.) . . . !"

. . . but opinions differ as to the order and inflection of the words.

A pistol shot sounded. Sumner Pinkham staggered. A second shot sounded, a third—and, some witnesses swear, a fourth, though a later examination of the weapons of the two antagonists made this appear doubtful. At least one of the shots came from Pinkham's pistol, at least two from Patterson's.

Then Sumner Pinkham, ex-sheriff, fervent Unionist, and prominent citizen, slumped to the floor of the veranda, dead.

Aided by Southern friends, Patterson mounted a convenient horse and fled. Aided by Union friends, Rube Robbins, ex-deputy sheriff under Pinkham, pursued and caught him, made a citizen's arrest, and returned him to the Idaho City jail to await trial.

A thousand indignant Unionists prepared to storm the jail and hang Patterson. A thousand righteous Southerners prepared to defend the jail and the accused's right to a fair trial. Pinkham's friends appealed to the military post adjacent to Boise City for the loan of a cannon. The request was curtly turned down.

For several days, battalions of armed men marched and countermarched, spied and counterspied, advanced, withdrew, and performed brilliant flanking maneuvers in and around the town—all of which were reported in great detail by pro and con newspaper writers eager to show off their skills as war correspondents. But since neither side fired the shot required to start the war, it petered out, the troops quit the field, and Ferd Patterson got his day in court.

He was acquitted. The *Idaho World*, whose editor was a Democrat, commented:

"Mr. Patterson has had a fair and impartial trial."[3]

The *Idaho Statesman*, whose editor was a Republican, said acidly:

"Ferd Patterson has been acquitted, as expected. Idaho juries do not inquire whether a crime has been committed. All they ask is: 'Was it a fair fight?' If so, they cry: 'Not guilty! Bully for the boy with the glass eye!' "[4]

But Ferd Patterson did not linger in the Boise Basin to read the reviews of the trial, for he had heard the prophetic words uttered by Sumner Pinkham's friend, William J. McConnell, who had said before the trial began:

"You may give Patterson his trial without hindrance. Since the evidence has been arranged to secure his acquittal, he can go forth into the world. But the world is not big enough to hide him."[5]

Leaving Idaho City, Patterson moved to Walla Walla, where he worked as a professional gambler through the winter. He told a friend he intended to live more quietly. Not so much drinking and carousing. No more violence. Well,

Left:

ONE-HUNDRED-YEAR-OLD BARN

Made of hand-squared logs, it still stands in the Grande Ronde Valley north of Elgin, Oregon. Its present owner, Miles Bates, is a retired serviceman turned rancher.

3. *Idaho World*, November 4, 1865.

4. *Idaho Statesman*, November 7, 1865.

5. *The Idaho Inferno*, deposition made by W. J. McConnell, taken in 1879, microfilm reproduced from original in Bancroft Library, University of California, p. 21 (my copy). I have condensed McConnell's words but have not altered them.

yes, there *was* a certain private policeman employed as a watchman by the local merchants who had bawled him out for being loud and boisterous the other night. That sort of talk he would take from nobody. He had written the man's name, Hugh Donahue, down in his little black book—and told him so. If the so-and-so ever crossed him again. . . .

One February morning, slightly hung over, Patterson went into Richard Bogle's barbershop on the corner of Third and Main. Hanging his hat, coat, gun belt, and tie on a rack at the far side of the room, he stretched out in a chair to be shaved. With a hot towel covering his face, he did not see the night watchman, Hugh Donahue, come into the shop by the same back entrance Patterson himself had used. For a time, Donahue stood warming himself by the potbellied stove, his hands behind his back. One of the hands held a pistol.

His shave finished, Patterson sat up to have his hair dressed. As he did so, Donahue rushed at him and cried: "You must kill me, or I'll kill you!"

With his pistol only a foot or two from Patterson's face, Donahue fired. The shot caught Patterson in the right jaw. He exclaimed: "Oh, my God!" tumbled out of the chair, and sprang for the door. As he ran, Donahue fired twice more, hitting his target with the second ball, missing with the third. Patterson succeeded in getting out of the barbershop and into Welch's Saloon, next door. There, he sank to the floor. Donahue followed, discharging two more bullets into him as he lay helpless. Once sure he was dead, the night watchman gave up his pistol and surrendered to the law.

"He threatened me," was all he would say then and during his subsequent trial. "I was afraid."

Seven of the jurors believed in a broad interpretation of his self-defense plea and voted for acquittal. Five were narrow-minded and voted for conviction. Donahue was remanded to jail to await another trial. Due to a faulty lock, a careless deputy, or a bit of skulduggery by persons unknown, Hugh Donahue found his cell door left ajar one night, walked out, and departed for places unknown.[6]

Some say his pockets were filled with Boise Basin gold. Some say the scalped mistress in Portland grew jealous and hired him to kill her former playmate. Some say the gold—if he had any—came from California friends of men Patterson had slain there.

Whatever the true story was, Ferdinand J. Patterson went to glory like all gunfighters—by meeting a man with a faster draw. The funeral procession to the Walla Walla cemetery, where his remains still lie, was the largest, most impressive of its day.

6. An account of the killing of Ferd Patterson may be found in the Walla Walla *Statesman*, February 16, 1866; trial details April 20; judge's charge to the jury April 27, 1866.

* * *

4.

So far as local government was concerned during the Snake River Country's bonanza years, the same "Get-the-loot-and-move-on" philosophy that existed among the miners prevailed. The miner was king and all property rights were secondary to his desires. Each mining district made its own rules, and invariably those rules favored first-discoverers. A member of a prospecting party finding pay dirt in a new region could file a creek claim, a bar claim, a hill claim, a gulch claim, and, in some cases, another of each for a non-present friend. If a town developed adjacent to a gold-mining district, the prospector could dig test holes big enough to engulf a mule in the center of its main street or undermine its buildings with tunnels to the point of collapse without being liable for damages or responsible for filling up his burrowings when he was done.[1]

Few of the miners took any interest in politics. A week after the organization of Idaho Territory in March, 1863, President Lincoln appointed a governor, a secretary, three judges, and a United States marshal, but months passed before they set foot in their domain. Meantime, a state of virtual anarchy existed, for the laws of Washington Territory and the state of Oregon no longer were in effect, and until a territorial legislature was elected, convened, and passed a code of laws, there would be no laws to be violated. This hiatus lasted for nine months.

In late September, 1863, Governor William H. Wallace at last arrived in Lewiston. His first official act was to decree that on October 31 an election would be held to select a legislature and a territorial delegate to the national congress; his second was to declare himself a candidate for the Territorial Delegate position, which inspired a rash of jokes to the effect that even the governor of Idaho, after one quick look at the Territory, figured the best thing to do was mine whatever political gold he could and then get the hell out.

In establishing residence requirements for voter eligibility, the unique theory was proposed and accepted that residence need not mean actually living on Idaho soil for a specified period. If a man left Ohio in March, say, *intending* to go to Idaho, that made him eligible to vote there, even though he did not arrive until a week before election day. Indians could not vote, of course. But soldiers stationed at distant Fort Laramie could; in fact, it was the weeks-late returns from that area that made Wallace's narrow majority decisive.

If town-booster population figures are to be relied on, there were fifty thousand eligible voters in the Territory. But on election day, less than ten thousand bothered to go to the polls. Immediately following his election as Delegate to Congress, William Wallace resigned as governor and left the Territory. Secretary Daniels, as acting governor, issued a call for the First Legislature to convene in Lewiston in early December, the session to last forty days. The first problem it faced was a real puzzler: how to punish theft and mul-

1. *Across the Continent*, by Samuel Bowles, New York, 1866, p. 423.

tiple murder without a code of laws, proof that a crime had been committed, or corpses.

In August, 1863, a Lewiston merchant named Lloyd Magruder had left town with sixty laden pack mules, crossed the Bitter Root Mountains to the mining camp of Virginia City, sold his goods there for $30,000 in gold dust, and then headed home in early fall. His party totaled nine men.

As the time came and passed when he should have returned to Lewiston, a hotelkeeper friend, Hill Beachey, grew increasingly worried about his safety. In fact, Beachey had a premonition, a vision, or a dream which told him something terrible had happened. Learning presently that four suspicious-acting men had left some mules and saddles at a ranch near Lewiston and then had taken an early stage for Walla Walla, he examined the animals and saddles and recognized them as having belonged to his missing friend. The fact that three of the men in the Magruder party, D. C. Lowry, David Howard, and James Romain, had shady reputations, a fourth, Billy Page, was a witless, weak-spined fellow, and that these four appeared to be the suspicious-acting men, made him positive there had been foul play.

Hill Beachey's premonition was so strong that he went to the Acting Governor and insisted that he be given requisitions on the governors of Oregon, Washington Territory, and California for their assistance in arresting the four suspects. Then he and a man named Tom Pike set out in pursuit of the fugitives. The trail led overland to Walla Walla and Wallula Landing, then downriver by boat to Portland. There, Beachey learned, the four men he wanted had boarded a ship bound for San Francisco.

The nearest point from Portland at which telegraphic communication with San Francisco could be had was Yreka, in northern California. Leaving Tom Pike in Portland to take the next steamer, Beachey rode the stagecoach three days and nights over the worst kind of roads to Yreka, wired a full description of the suspects to the chief of police in San Francisco, and, when their ship made port, they were immediately arrested.

A writ of *habeas corpus* briefly delayed the return of the four men to Lewiston for trial, but the San Francisco court —apparently caring no more for legal nit-picking than Idaho did—denied the writ, and on December 7, the same day the First Legislature convened in Lewiston, Hill Beachey and Tom Pike arrived home with their prisoners.

There were a couple of legal problems to be ironed out. In the first place, there were no bodies with which to prove that murder had been done. This was neatly solved by a confession from Billy Page relating in horrible detail how Magruder and four other men had been slain and their bodies dumped into a canyon deep in the mountains, where they now lay buried under many feet of snow.

Secondly, Idaho Territory had no code of laws. This the Legislature remedied by enacting a Civil and Criminal Code patterned roughly after the Common Law of England. It took effect January 4, 1864. District Court convened in Lewiston January 5, Judge Samuel C. Parks presiding; Howard, Lowry, and Romain were duly tried and convicted. On January 25, Judge Parks sentenced them to be hanged; and on March 4 the sentence was carried out.

Billy Page, who had turned state's evidence, was permitted to depart. The rumor soon floated back that he had been killed—in what manner or by whom no one knew or cared.

Upon the recommendation of Judge Parks, the Legislature passed an appropriation of $6,244 to reimburse Hill Beachey for expenses incurred in the pursuit and capture of the murderers of his friend. When spring at last melted the snows in the high country of the Lolo Trail to the east, Beachey and a party of men journeyed to the canyon into which Billy Page had said the five bodies had been dumped, found the remains exactly where he had said they would be, and gave them a decent burial.

This was early-day Idaho justice—direct, effective, and not subject to appeal.[2]

On the political front, two vexing questions troubled the Territory as the first legislative session came to an end. One was whether Lewiston would remain the capital or whether it would be transferred to Boise City, in whose trading area a majority of the citizens now resided. The other was whether the Territory even *had* a Chief Executive on any given day, and, if so, who he might be.

William Wallace had gone East. Secretary Daniels, the Acting Governor, lingered just long enough to certify the laws passed by the First Session, then departed for San Francisco—ostensibly to have those laws printed—and was heard from no more. Clerk Silas D. Cochrane, elevated by the laws of succession to the Chief Executive position, was a man who allegedly spent more time diminishing the Territory's supply of whiskey than he did running its political affairs. To further complicate matters, Caleb Lyon of Lyonsdale, New York, had been appointed the new governor of Idaho Territory in late February, 1864, but was taking his own sweet time in packing his valise and heading west.

When he finally did arrive in early October, the word soon spread that he took immodest pride in being a gentleman and a scholar, wore a swallow-tailed coat on all formal occasions, bathed frequently, and changed his linen once a week whether it needed it or not—which quickly prejudiced the unwashed majority of the populace against him. And the stupendously sonorous opening sentence of his address to the Second Session, which convened in Lewiston November 16, 1864, made the simple-natured legislators strongly suspect he was not their kind of man:

> "Amid this hour, when clouds of civil war darken the atmosphere—lighted only by the sunbursts of glory that surround the achievements of our heroic army and devoted navy; when a wicked rebellion lies like a writhing serpent;—death-wounded in the last hours of its venomous existence, and over its gory

2. *Boise News*, Bannock (Idaho) City, Nov. 10, 1863; Feb. 13, Feb. 20, March 26, June 25, 1864. See also *Early History of Idaho*, by William J. McConnell, pp. 142-54.

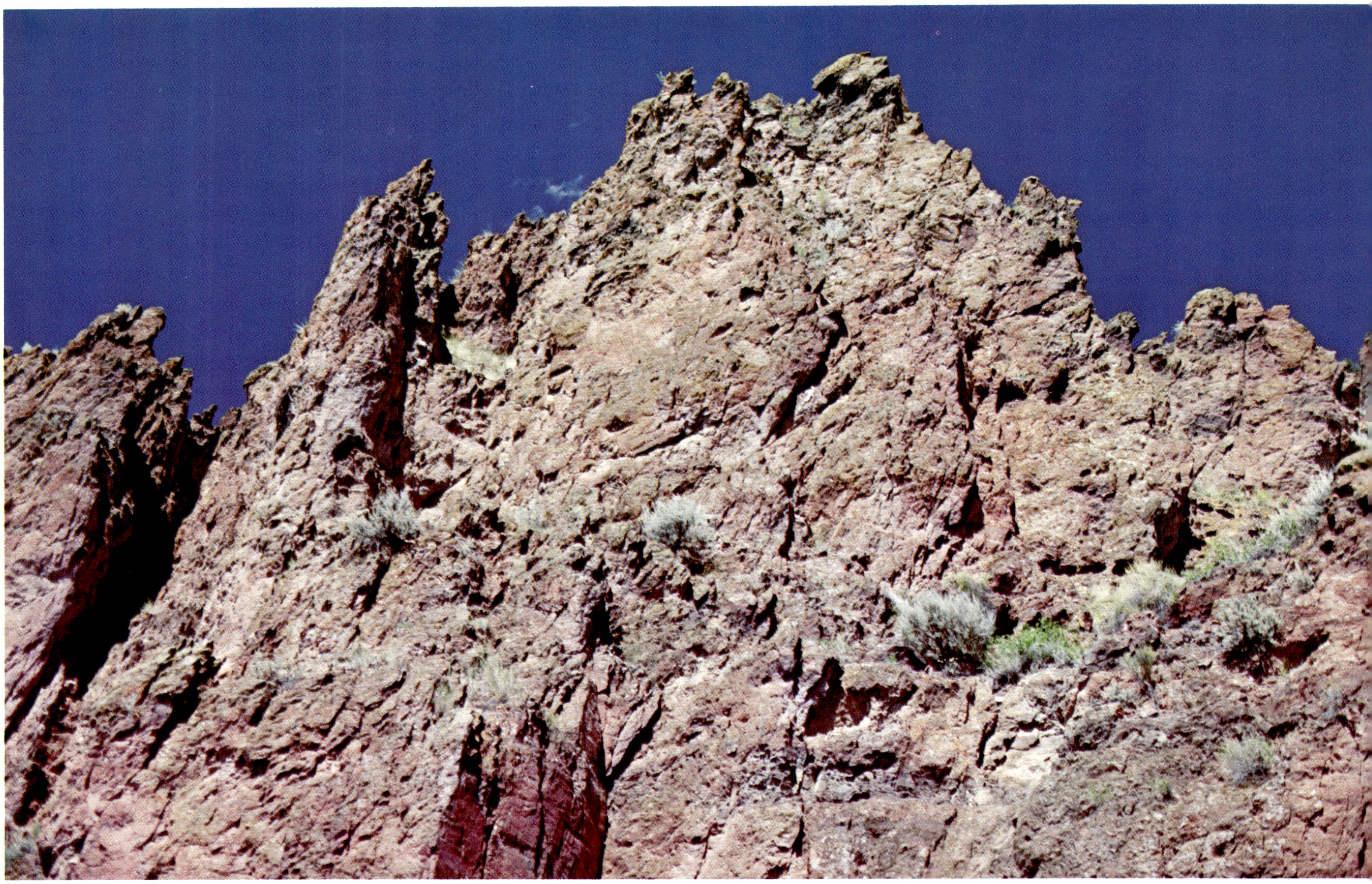

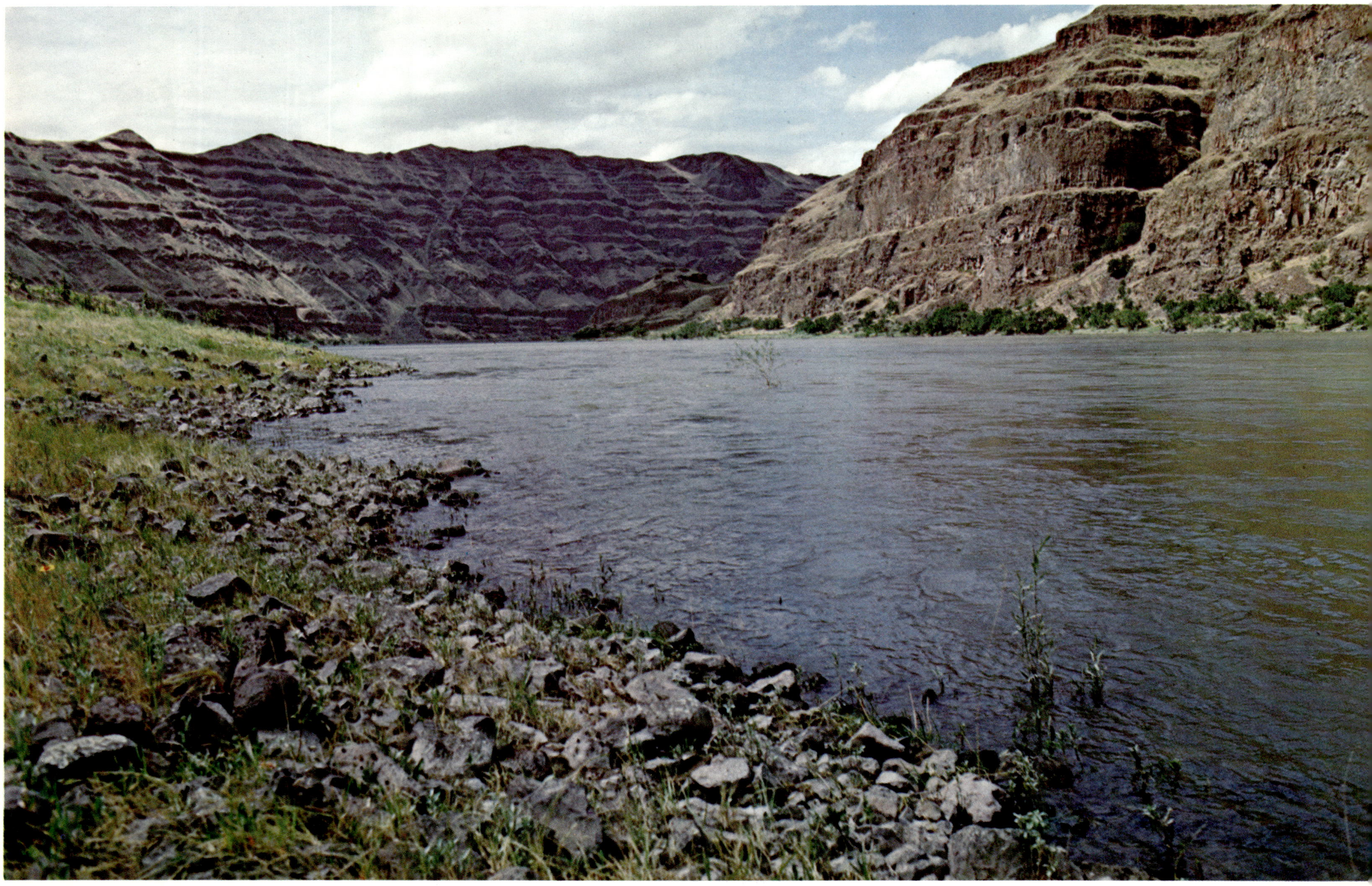

form the shining waters of peace sparkle temptingly, just beyond our lips;—in this hour, when our hearts are still bleeding for the loved ones who have fallen nobly in this great cause for the Union and the Constitution of our fathers, when the tears are undried in the eyes of the widow, and the death-damp still pales the cheeks of the husband;—when the resources and blood and treasure have all gone forth as precious sacrifice upon freedom's holiest altar;—when the rights of self-government are imperiled by this contest, and Emporers and Kings stand ready to cast lots for the parted robe of departing Liberty;—thus you meet, the servants of confiding constituencies, to aid Idaho's advancement toward Statehood, by the patriotism of your purposes, the soundness of your judgment, and the wisdom of your deliberations. . . ."[3]

The patriotic servants of confiding constituencies, after sixty days of bickering, granting divorces, and awarding toll road and ferry franchises, finally passed one major piece of legislation: the transfer of the capital site to Boise City.

Outraged Lewiston residents rose up in arms. Placing the Territorial Seal and Archives under round-the-clock guard, they defied their removal. The legality of the laws passed by the Second Session, the transfer of the capital, and even the validity of Caleb Lyon's appointment as governor were challenged in the local Probate Court. Obligingly, the court issued restraining orders against all concerned. Chaos reigned supreme.

Federal Judge Alex Smith, whose First District Court was loftily ignoring the whole matter, was accused by Boise's *Idaho Statesman* of drunkenness, illiteracy, and of being chief judicial officer not of a Superior Court but of a court ". . . than which none is inferior. . . ." The *Statesman's* editor, Jim Reynolds, was so angered over Lewiston's refusal to accept the capital change, that *he* refused to capitalize the town's name, spelling it "lewiston. . . ," and referring to the editor of its paper, Alonzo Leland, as the "lewiston lelander. . . ."[4]

Caleb Lyon's contribution to the squabble was typically eccentric. He went duck hunting. Admittedly, there was method in his madness, for, like the Territorial Seal and Archives, he was being closely watched lest he take wing or be spirited away to the southern part of the Territory. But since the mid-January weather was cold and the north-south trails were blocked with snow, loyal Lewiston partisans saw no harm in letting the Governor get a bit of exercise and sport on the sandbars adjacent to the town. What they did not know was that a group of southern Idaho solons had arranged to have a rowboat handy. As dusk fell, Governor Lyon was picked up, rowed across the Snake to Washington Territory, and put aboard a stagecoach bound for Walla Walla.

Down in Boise City, southern Idahoans were jubilant. Let "little lewiston" keep the Seal and Archives. "Big Boise" had the Governor! Or soon *would* have him, for from Walla Walla he would turn southeast, cross the Blues by the only stage route passable in winter, come to Boise City, and establish the seat of government where it legally belonged. . . .

As the days passed, bits of news filtering east to Boise City indicated that Caleb Lyon—if he did indeed intend journeying to the new capital—was taking a very roundabout way. On February 7, he was reported to be in The Dalles; a week later he was in Portland; in another week he was said to be on his way to San Francisco, where he had pressing business—perhaps finding Secretary Daniels, the funds he had absconded with, and the missing Code of Laws.

From San Francisco, word eventually drifted back to Idaho that Governor Lyon had told a reporter he had such a great quantity of important matters to be communicated to President Lincoln and the National Congress it would be more economical to make the trip East himself than to go to the expense of telegraphing them. Still later, the New York *Tribune* reported that Governor Lyon was so exhausted by his journey East he had retired to his Lyonsdale home for a rest.

For ten months, the territorial ship of state wallowed through stormy seas without a captain. Then, much to everyone's surprise, Caleb Lyon returned with fanfare, flourish, and flowery rhetoric. When it was learned that he brought with him the authority to make binding treaties with hostile Indians, pledges of substantial federal government assistance to the impoverished territory, and fifty thousand dollars in cash to disburse among the natives, both his long absence and his long-winded speeches were forgiven.[5]

Down in Ruby City and Silver City, the Owyhee mining towns which a year ago had started to take up a collection from the merchants and miners with which to buy Governor Lyon a silver brick as a token of their esteem, then called the project off because of his defection, reactivated the scheme with renewed zeal. In the Rocky Bar district east of Boise City, where hard-rock mining now was beginning to boom, the citizens initiated *their* collection for an esteem-brick to be made of gold. And in other parts of the territory, merchants eager to sell pacified Indians whatever their hearts should desire the moment Governor Lyon paid them their allotments deluged him with invitations to be their guest of honor at champagne and oyster suppers.

But sad to say—like most second honeymoons—expectation exceeded performance. Few of the promises Lyon made the Bruneaus, the Bannocks, the Boises, and the Nez Perces were kept. Schoolhouses remained unbuilt; ploughs,

3. *Idaho Statesman*, November 26, 1864. The speech was made Nov. 16.

4. *Ibid.*, February 17, 1865.

5. Ibid., Nov. 2, 1865.

Left, above: Rose Cliffs, near Salmon, Idaho

Left, below: Snake River, above Asotin, Washington

hoes, and blankets remained undistributed; Indian agency employees remained unpaid except for next-to-worthless script. As complaints from many sources filtered back to Washington City, Senator James Nesmith of Oregon began an investigation. Soon the word reached Idaho that Governor Lyon had been dismissed and summoned East for an accounting of the funds entrusted to him.

As he departed under a cloud, sardonic editorials bade him farewell. This one from the *Owyhee Avalanche* was typical:

> "God in His providence has a way of scourging the people, which is doubtless right. With what pestilence He will next inflict us is uncertain, but can hardly be worse. Cholera, smallpox, yellow fever, diphtheria, and poisonous simoons may be coveted in comparison to such granny governors. These visitations would at least benefit doctors, undertakers, sextons, and probate courts, but the other would be a blight upon the Territory."[6]

Back in the East a few months later, Caleb Lyon complained to the Washington police that he had been robbed of $47,000 in greenbacks.[7] The cash was being carried on his person, he said, in a money belt secured about his waist under his clothes. It was surreptitiously taken from the belt as he slept on the train, though the belt itself had not been disturbed.

When asked if this had been government money, he replied with his usual bold vagueness: "I can account for every dollar I spent in Idaho."

But the boast was empty; his political career was finished. Weary and disheartened, he retired to Lyonsdale, where he grew ill and died. Few of his former confiding constituents noted his passing. And none mourned. . . .

° ° °

5.

South of Snake River, once the green patches of irrigated farm and ranchland are left behind, neither the country nor the winding, rocky, rutted road climbing toward 6,200-foot-high Silver City has changed perceptibly since the first stagecoach passed this way en route from Boise City to Chico, California, in 1865. The sagebrush, the bunchgrass, the canyons filled with tumbled red rocks, the timbered mountains rising ahead, and the brooding emptiness of vast reaches of space make one feel that if ever there were a region ideally suited to an Indian ambush, this is it.

The feeling is soundly based on fact. For years, this was Chief Bigfoot's domain, and though historians have serious doubts that such a fabled monster ever existed, the havoc wrought by the band of savages he supposedly led in their long, bitter war against the whites was brutally real.[1]

As the Owyhee mines boomed and travel increased along the inland routes to California, stage way stations, trading settlements, and cattle, horse, sheep, and hay ranches sprang up every ten miles or so along the long, lonely desert road through southwestern Idaho, eastern Oregon, and northern Nevada. Though the military post of Fort Boise had been established adjacent to the townsite in August, 1863, for the express purpose of protecting travelers, miners, and settlers, its undermanned garrison could do little to prevent or punish raids by hostiles along the road south.

News of an attack on a Reynolds Creek ranch, on a stage station in Jordan Valley, or on a group of unarmed Chinamen traveling afoot across the eastern Oregon desert required from two to four days to reach the military post. Once the decision to send out a punitive force was made, more days were needed to organize, issue rations, and ride; still more to reach the area in which the attack had occurred; and by then the hostiles had vanished like last week's dust.

As one editor sarcastically commented, the Army's mode of going after raiding Indians was "like hunting ducks with a brass band."

Now and again intrepid groups of citizens organized their own bands of volunteers. They would collect money, ammunition, food, and horses from public-spirited townspeople, elect leaders, make elaborate campaign plans, and then sally forth to settle the Indian problem, "once and for all." Since few working merchants, miners, or ranchers could spare the time to go hostile-hunting, these "volunteers" often were loafers, saloon hangers-on, or rowdies looking for excitement. They were the breed of men that loudly recommended killing all Indians, regardless of sex or age, because "nits make lice." Sometimes they even proposed putting a cash bounty upon every Indian scalp taken.[2] But when the action began, their bloodthirstiness usually abated in direct proportion to the number of arrows and bullets fired in their direction.

On one occasion, a Boise City group of hostile-hunters called the "Ada County Volunteers" collected $3,000 in cash and supplies, spent three weeks in the field, sent glowing dispatches detailing their glorious doings to Boise City for publication in the tri-weekly paper, and then returned to bask in accumulated glory. But soon the truth leaked out. Not a single hostile had been sighted nor a single shot fired

---

6. *Owyhee Avalanche,* May 5, 1866.

7. *Idaho Statesman,* Dec. 20, 1866.

1. Actually, there were two "Bigfoots," it now appears, one legendary, the other real; so distinguishing between where one ends and the other begins is a confusing pursuit. The real one was called "Howluck," "Oualuck," or "Oulux." His foot was 14¾" long—whereas, the legendary Chief Bigfoot's moccasin print measured 17½", it was said. For an interesting account of the real and legendary Bigfoot, see Reference Series Number 40 (Revised November, 1970), and *The Origin of the Name Nampa,* prepared by Annie Laurie Bird, Reference Series Number 39 (Revised November, 1970), Idaho Historical Society, Boise.

2. Though proposals to pay a bounty for Indian scalps often were made by such groups and at times written into resolutions, I have found no instances of such a bounty actually having been paid.

in anger. Once south of the Snake, they had stopped to "drill and discipline," laid out a racetrack, set up targets, uncorked bottles, and had themselves a high old time. Understandably, the Boise City merchants underwrote no more Indian hunts.[3]

On another occasion, the "Owyhee Volunteers," organized in Silver City, actually *did* find some Indians who were in a fighting mood. Suffering a stinging defeat, the whites were surrounded in a basin deep in the mountains and very likely would have been "massacred" had not their loyal Indian scout, Bruneau Jim, managed to slip through the lines of the attackers under cover of darkness and make his way on foot fifty miles to Flint, where a relief force was raised to lift the siege.

Ironically, Bruneau Jim was murdered two years later by four white men when he objected to their ravishment of two Indian women who were with him. Among volunteers and newsmen who remembered Bruneau Jim's heroism, sentiment strongly favored hanging the four white men. But sentiment did not prevail. Three of the men were held as material witnesses, while the fourth, John Brady, was tried on the reduced charge of manslaughter. After two hung juries, he was set free.[4]

Chief Bigfoot, the alleged leader of all the hostile Indians in the area, was known by several names. Some years after his alleged demise, he was honored by having the town of Nampa, Idaho, named for him. *"Nam-puh,"* in the Bannock tongue, means "Big-foot." He also was called *"Oulux"* and *"We-ah-we-ha,"* which mean the same thing in other regional Indian dialects. In the tradition of all folklore giants, he was never seen; but whenever a horse or cow was stolen, a stage station or cabin raided, or an atrocity committed, his tracks were found in the vicinity.

Of the dozen or so contemporary references to him, the following account by T. J. Sutton, who accompanied an expedition led by Jeff Standifer against the Bannocks in 1862, is typical:

> "Had cooler heads commanded, we should almost certainly have secured all the horses and probably the thieves as well, including, as I believe, the noted 'Bigfoot' who was their leader and boss horse thief of the plains.
>
> "On looking over the grounds after the skirmish. we discovered the tracks of a band of Indians numbering ten or twelve who had crossed the river at that point two or three days before. We also discovered and measured Bigfoot's track, which was seventeen and a half inches long by six inches wide at the junction of the metatarsus with the toes. At that time we had no knowledge of the man, but the enormous size of his track attracted our attention and so roused our curiosity that careful measurements of its dimensions were made, and no little discussion indulged in as to whether it was a human track.
>
> "A year or two later, the possessor of the abnormally sized foot had become famous because of his connection with and known leadership of gangs of Bannock horse thieves who raided the ranches of settlers whenever opportunity afforded. This continued down to 1868, when Bigfoot was killed in an encounter with a highwayman named Wheeler. . . ."[5]

Before relating the legendary duel in which Bigfoot met his match, we must tell this smaller story, which we know is true. As a result of the raid led by Jeff Standifer:

> "All the Indians were killed with the exception of one squaw and two boys, aged approximately six and twelve years old. The smaller boy was adopted by John Kelly, the violinist. . . ."

Affectionately called "Fiddler John" by his thousands of mining-camp fans in the West, John Kelly was Irish, a bachelor, and one of the most highly paid entertainers in the business. His lively jigs could set clumsy boots to clumping just as quickly as sentimental tunes like "My Mother's Grave" could bring lumps into choked-up throats. He was also a prudent man.

> "The contract under which he played included the installation of a swinging stage, or platform, swung by iron rods from the upper joists, several feet above the heads of those who might stand on the main floor below. This platform was reached by a movable ladder, which, after he ascended, he pulled up out of reach of those below. . . ."

High upon his aerie, Fiddler John was safe from stampedes, panics, and fights—which occurred almost nightly—and above the likely course of bottles and bullets that might damage his person or his precious violin. It was his habit, when bullets began to fly, to turn and face the disturbance, holding his violin behind him, so that the stray slug that shattered it first must pass through his own corpulent body.

Emotionally, he favored the cause of the South. After adopting the Indian boy, whom he named Willie, he had a tailor make the lad

> ". . . a little gray suit, representing a Confederate uniform. When first captured, the child was as wild as a young coyote. With a well knit frame and jet black eyes which fairly sparkled, his looks proclaimed him what he was, a full-blooded aborigine.
>
> "Kelly at once became father and mother to the little waif. He kept him in his presence continually,

---

3. For an account of the exploits of the "Ada Volunteers," see the *Idaho Statesman*, February 21 through April 5, 1866, and the *Owyhee Avalanche*, March 10, 17, 1866.

4. For the adventures of the Owyhee Volunteers, see the *Avalanche* issues between Feb. 17, 1866, and July 28, 1866. Details of the trial of John Brady for the killing of Bruneau Jim are to be found in the *Idaho Statesman*, March 10 to May 7, 1868, and the *Idaho World* March 14, 18, 1868.

5. *History of Idaho*, by John Hailey, Syms-York Co., Boise, 1910, p. 55.

and began at once a course of physical training to fit the boy for the future which he had conceived for him. In a few months he had developed into a contortionist of no mean ability, and nightly occupied a a place with his adopted father, giving occasional exhibitions to vary the performance, thus adding interest to the attraction.

"The boy eventually, either from inherent talent, or from having no other associate than Kelly, developed wonderful skill as a violinist. When eighteen, he equalled his instructor. But while on a visit to Ireland with his inseparable companion, he was taken with a congestive chill and died. Kelly had no children of his own, and while he related to the writer the story of the boy's life and death, his furrowed face was deluged with tears."[6]

Chief Bigfoot's supposed demise marked the end of hostile depredations in the southwestern corner of the Snake River Country. An aprocryphal "eye-witness" account entitled *Bigfoot's Last Fight,* by William T. Anderson, was published serially in the *Idaho Statesman* in November, 1878, ten years after the event.[7] Since its style and authenticity are more Wild West genre than factual history, it is noted here only as a piece of folklore that incorporated many of the tall tales of the day, lightly salted with facts.

John Wheeler, the highwayman, did live for a time in Silver City and was reputed to be a gunman. He once held up a stagecoach in eastern Oregon; and he was killed while attempting the same feat down in Arizona Territory.

The way Anderson tells the story, after lying in wait for three days, Wheeler trapped Bigfoot, challenged him, and the battle was on. The duel took place in what became known as Bigfoot Canyon, a few miles south of Snake River, on the stage road to Silver City. When the shooting ended and the gunsmoke cleared, Bigfoot lay prostrate in the dust, twelve bullets from a Henry rifle in his body. Though both his legs and one of his arms were broken, he still was considered so dangerous that when he asked for a drink of water, Wheeler replied:

> "Hold on till I break the other arm, old rooster; then I'll give you a drink."
>
> "Well, do it quick," Bigfoot said, "and give me a drink and let me die."

According to the eyewitness account, Wheeler drew his pistol, broke the monster's other arm, then went down to the creek, filled a canteen with water, and "placed it in the mouth of the Indian, who drank it all. . . ."

Bigfoot then said he would like some whiskey. Wheeler replied that he had a small bottle of whiskey and ammonia, which he always carried in case of snake bite. Bigfoot said: "Give it to me quick; I'm getting blind." Wheeler handed him the pint flask.

> "The Indian drank it, every drop, and then fell back apparently dead. After a few minutes he revived, and said that he was better. . . ."

That a man with so many bullets in him could even *hold* that much fluid, let alone make the lengthy confession of his lurid life that he now made, shall not be questioned here. This was his story:

He had been born in the Cherokee Nation. His father, a white man named Archer Wilkinson, had been hanged for murder, but his mother, who was part Cherokee and part Negro, had been a good, religious woman. His name was Starr Wilkinson, but he had been called "Bigfoot" as long as he could remember. His height was six feet eight and one-half inches, he weighed more than three hundred pounds, and his chest measured fifty-nine inches.

He had come west with an emigrant train in 1856, driving a wagon for his room and board. He fell in love with a young lady of the company, who thought a good deal of him until a smart, good-looking artist from New York joined the train. From the way the young lady turned cold toward him, Starr Wilkinson suspected that the artist had told her something bad about him. While camped near the Goose Creek Mountains, he and the artist went out to round up the stock one morning, they argued, and the artist admitted having made derogatory references to Wilkinson's parentage.

> "This made me mad, and I told him if he called me that again I would kill him. So he drew his gun on me and repeated it. I was unarmed, but started at him. He shot me in the side but did not hurt me much, so I grabbed him and threw him down, and choked him to death, then threw him into Snake River, took his gun, pistol and knife, and ran off into the hills. . . ."

Thus began Bigfoot's long, bloody career as a renegade leader of the hostiles. For a time, he said, Joe Lewis, instigator of the Whitman Massacre, had been his chief aide. Together, they had planned and carried out as deeds of vengeance the Ward Party Massacre (never mind that it took place two years before Starr Wilkinson started west), the Otter Massacre, the eventual murder of the young lady who had jilted him, and countless other killings.

But now he had reached the end of the trail. Learning that Wheeler had a smattering of Cherokee blood in his veins, Bigfoot broke down and wept. Then he asked Wheeler to grant him two last requests.

The first was that no one be told of his death.

-----

6. *Early History of Idaho,* McConnell, pp. 139, 180, 181.

7. *Heroes and Heroic Deeds of the Pacific Northwest,* by Henry L. Talkington, Caxton, 1929, pp. 145-60.

Right: The Salmon River, below Riggins, Idaho

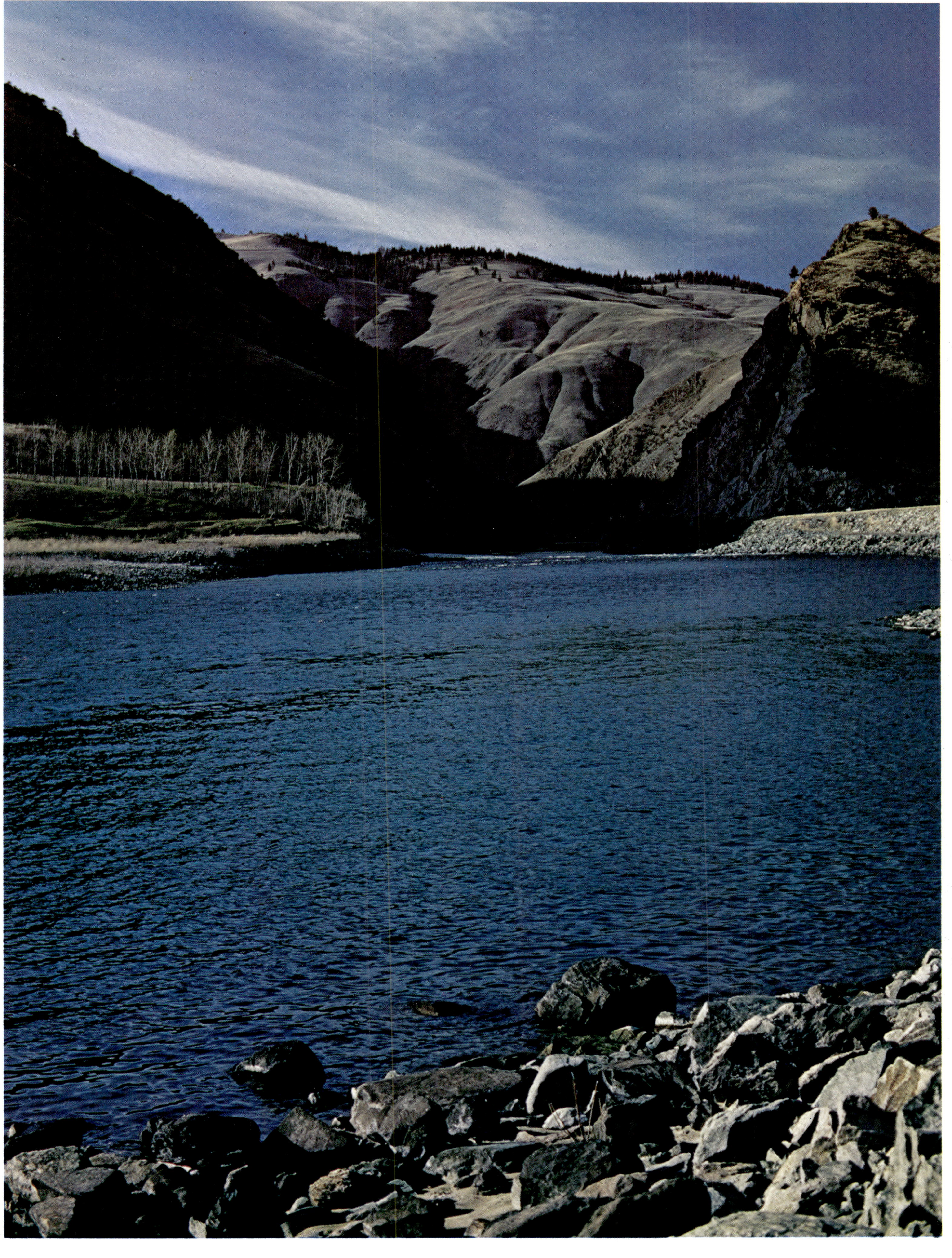

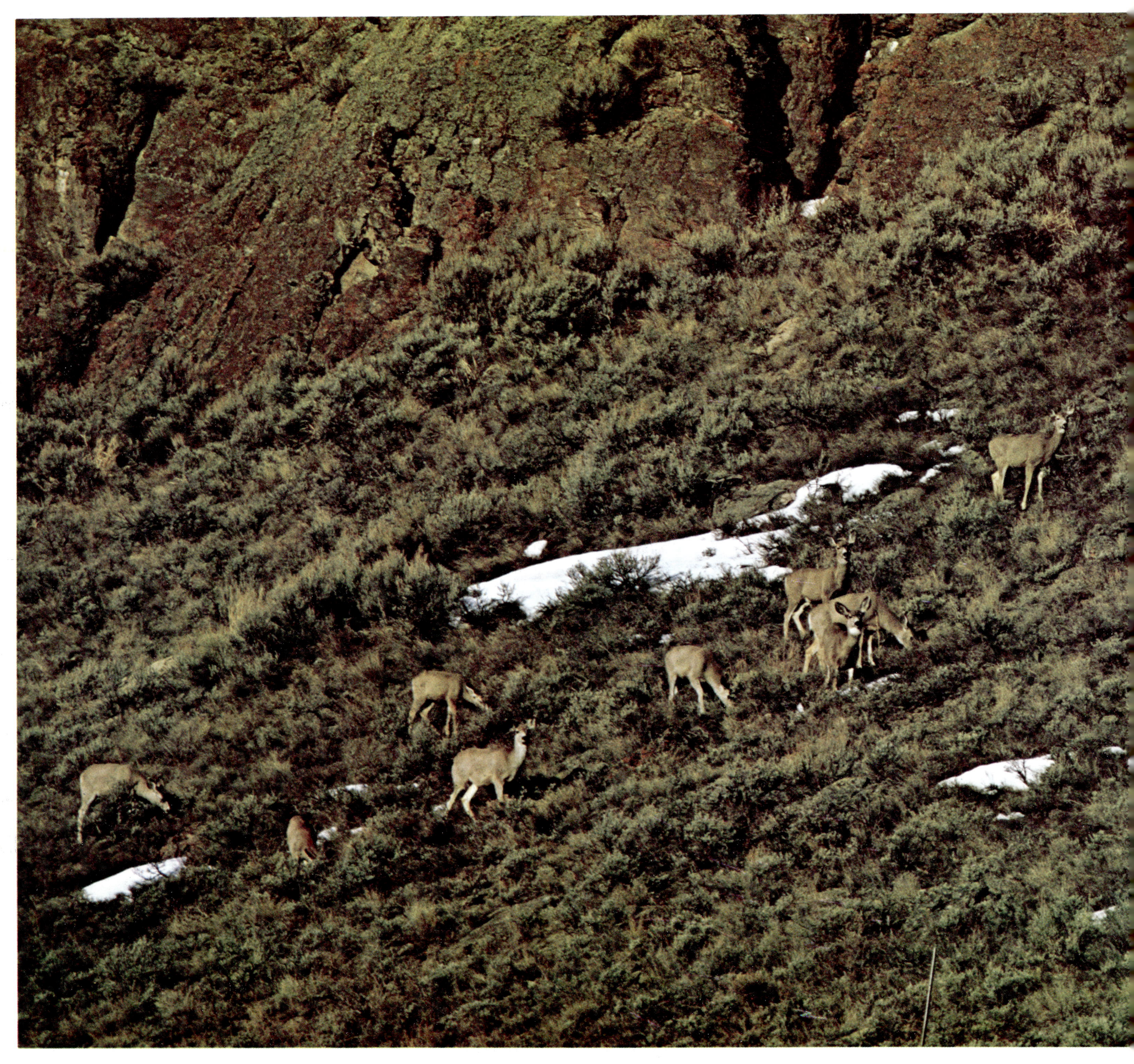

The second was that his body be buried where it could never be found.

John Wheeler agreed.

And Bigfoot died content.

Whether the eyewitness, William T. Anderson, also was in on the pact is not clear in his account. But the fact that he waited ten years to write his story indicates that he was. If so, his dishonorable act in relating a story he had promised not to tell cannot be condoned simply by saying that writers, as a class, are a notoriously untrustworthy lot.

But this *can* be said for the highwayman, John Wheeler: He never told.

And he buried Bigfoot's body so skillfully that its bones have never been found.

Credit for bringing what the white man called peace to this part of the country actually must be given to George S. Crook, who here perfected the skills he later would use against the Apaches in the Southwest. Put in charge of the military district, he arrived in Boise City on December 11, 1866, replacing Colonel L. H. Marshall, who, to put it kindly, was making no headway against the hostiles. In General Crook's own words:

> "Indian affairs could not have been worse. The whole country was in a state of siege. . . ."[8]

One week after his arrival, a band of Indians made a raid near the mouth of the Boise River, twenty miles west of the fort. Crook wrote:

> "So I took Capt. Perry's company of the 1st Cavalry and left with one change of underclothes, toothbrush, etc., and went to investigate matters, intending to be gone a week. But I got interested after the Indians and did not return there again for over two years. . . ."

Persistence was Crook's chief virtue—and the secret of his success. A man who did not drink, smoke, use coffee or tea, he disliked fancy uniforms, spirited horses, and red tape. His usual mount was a mule, his dress that of an outdoorsman. His passion was hunting wild game; his job hunting wild Indians. And for him the hunt did not end until the quarry was in the bag.

Winter and summer, spring and fall, in all extremes of temperature, weather, and terrain across southwestern Idaho, eastern and central Oregon, northern Nevada, and northern California, he stayed "interested after Indians. . . ." for two years. Remaining in the field while supplies were sent out to his forces, he wore the Indians down until the scattered, starving, decimated bands one by one gave up their hopeless resistance. By the time the last pathetic band surrendered in July, 1868, an estimated two-thirds of their people had died. But General Crook had done the job he was being paid to do.

By the autumn of 1868, the days of quick and easy treasure in the Snake River Country were over. Chinamen content to labor for more modest returns now were working the placer claims. In the Rocky Bar district, big-time promoters like Wilson P. Waddingham had departed for greener fields, leaving behind huge piles of debts, lawsuits, and expensive milling equipment, which rusted where it stood or was used as fencing material by lowland farmers where freighters had dumped it when early snows or the bursted bubbles of bonanzas-to-be-that-never-became had caught it along the road.

In the Owyhees, whose silver-lined mountains once had been the marvel of the mining world, the War Eagle, the Poorman, and the Hays and Ray no longer hired gunmen to guard their disputed claims, encouraged employees to fight pitched battles with rifles, pistols, and live steam far underground, or required the sending of troops into the district to prevent the outbreak of mining wars. True, there still was gold in Rocky Bar and silver in Owyhee, but since both lay deep in hardrock, recovering the treasure meant expensive equipment, corporate management, Eastern capital, clever lawyers, and Welsh workingmen willing to labor in the stopes, shafts, and tunnels for day wages, as few independent-minded American prospectors would do.

Pierce City, Elk City, Florence, Warren, Placerville, Pioneerville, Centerville, Idaho City, and Silver City—all were on the wane. Except for the frugal Chinese, most human traffic was outward bound. So far as its treasure was concerned, the Snake River Country seemed to be "played out."

And yet, down in the lowland valleys where no gold or silver ever had been found, Boise City, Lewiston, and the town near the mouth of the Snake whose destiny was so closely tied into the watershed, Walla Walla, lived on and thrived. For in this land of little rain, farmers and ranchers were beginning to appreciate the treasure that fell on 109,000 square miles of land from the sky each winter, preserved itself without man-made regulation until needed, and then filled the creeks and rivers at their feet with the essence of all life and wealth.

Water. . . .

8. *General George Crook, His Autobiography,* edited by Martin F. Schmitt, University of Oklahoma Press, 1946, pp. 142-59.

Left: Mule Deer Feeding, Jackson Hole, Wyoming

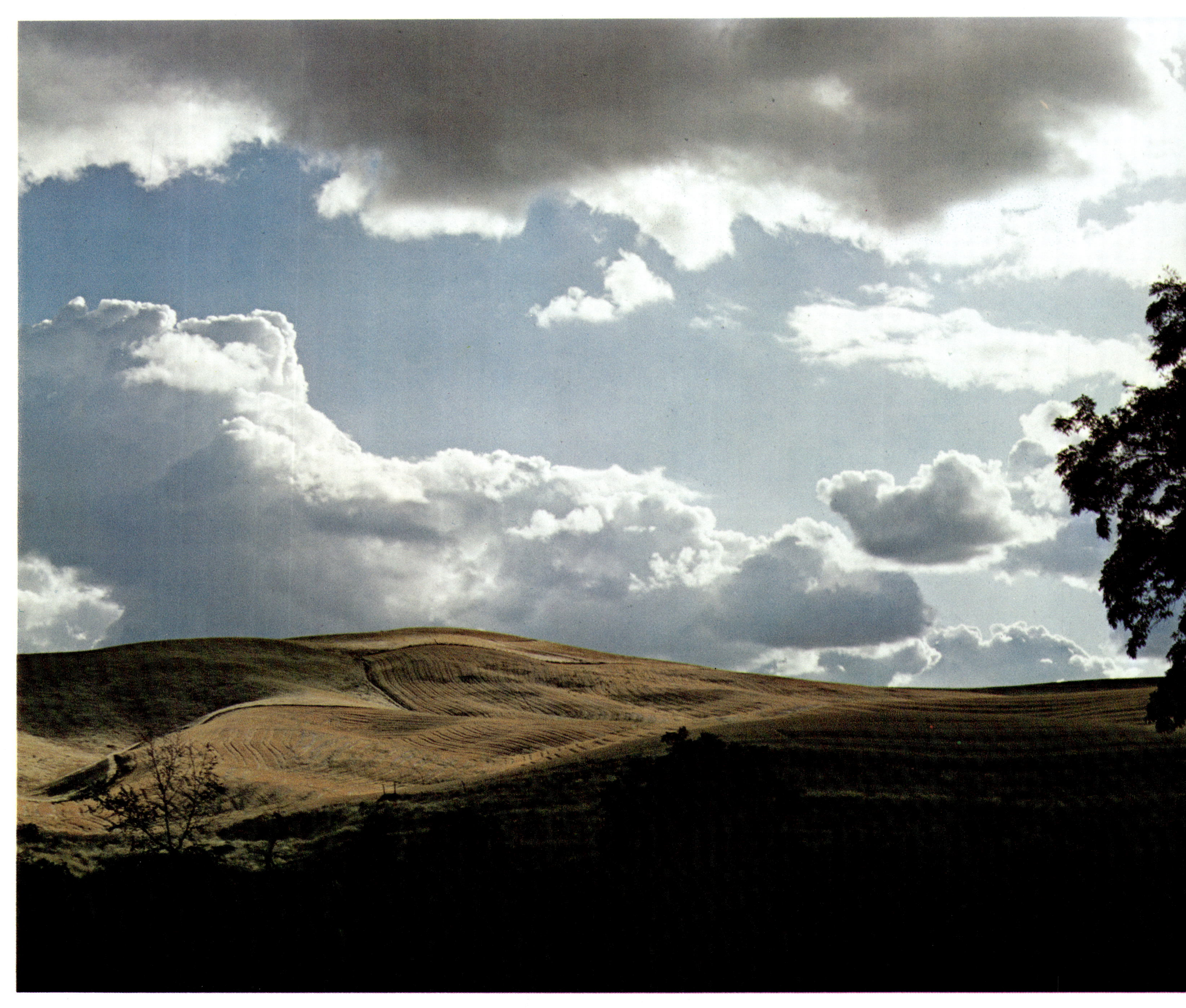

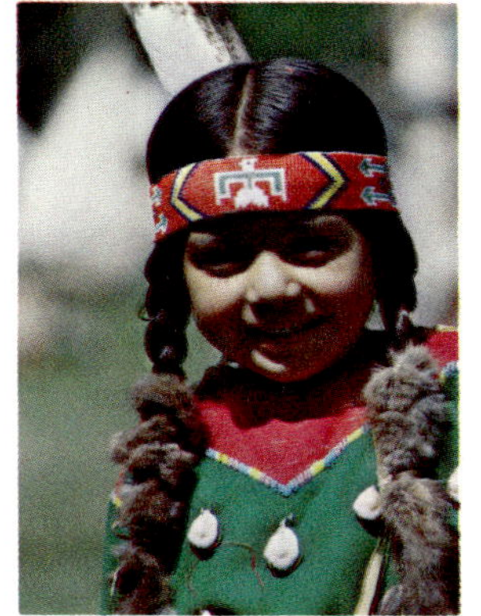

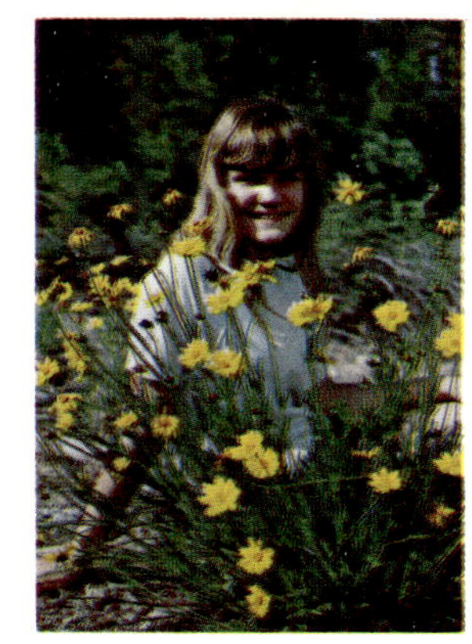

PART SIX

River of Life

1.

Like gold mining, irrigation was a skill that westering Americans had to acquire. In upstate New York, Ohio, or Iowa, the farmer ploughed, planted, and prayed for rain. In the Snake River Country, neither God nor the weather patterns could be depended upon to deliver moisture through the crucial months of the growing season. So the successful farmer used breath saved by not saying rain prayers for the laborious chore of digging ditches.

The Indians of the region were not agriculturists, and, being horse Indians, disdained all exertion that could not be done on horseback. Whether their aversion to tilling the soil really stemmed from their often expressed feeling that "The Earth is our Mother; we cannot slash her breast" or from their justifiable suspicion that farming was hard work, is debatable. In any case, even after Henry Spalding and Marcus Whitman had shown them how prodigiously irrigated garden patches of potatoes and corn would produce, the attitude of the Indian men remained: "If the Great Spirit wants a plant to grow, He will water it. We will fish and hunt buffalo. Let the women tend your gardens."

Digging in the earth was woman's work, of course. Each tribe had its favorite wild camas meadow where, in late June, square miles of delicate bluish-purple blossoms indicated that the tiny bulbs were ready to be harvested. This was always marshy land watered by snowmelt, where mosquitoes rose in swarms. But the women paid the voracious insects no mind, patiently thrusting their digging sticks into the wet earth, lifting the bulb, snapping it off its slender stem, tossing it into a basket. Then they would boil out its poison, mash it into a paste, and store it—to be mixed with the huckleberries, elderberries, and other wild sweets which they would gather in the mountains later in the summer. With dried fish, buffalo, deer, and elk, this was their winter food supply.

Statistics as to how much labor was required to provide sufficient food gathered in this fashion for the average Indian family are not available. But we know that the average Indian family often went to bed hungry when snow covered the land. As a gardener, Mother Nature was a stingy producer of nourishment even for animal wildlife over much of the Snake River watershed. The human family that would reap where it did not sow existed on the perpetual brink of starvation.

As man learned in the Middle East two thousand years before Christ, the paradox of plant growth is that the most nutritious vegetables, grasses, fruits, and grains produce most abundantly in the most arid lands when irrigated. Water for the roots; warm sunlight for the portion above ground—this is the formula that makes the desert yield its gold.

In arable desert land, summer sunshine, and a supply of irrigation water, the Snake River Country is well endowed. Though the motorist who has crossed southern Idaho on a blistering August day or the skier who has been caught in a blizzard on the slopes of the Grand Tetons may raise an eyebrow at this statement, the climate of the region, agriculturally speaking, is benign.

On most of the irrigated lands along the mainstem of the Snake, the growing season ranges from 130 to 200 days a year. The annual rainfall averages ten inches; there are few cloudy days between June and October; and damaging cloudbursts, hailstorms, and tornadoes common to the Plains States are practically unknown. The moderating influence of the Japan Current, which bathes the coast of Oregon, Washington, and British Columbia, reaches inland to eastern Idaho, making the climate of the region much milder than that of similar latitudes along the Eastern seaboard.

Chains of mountain peaks ranging from 9,000 to 13,000 feet enclose the Snake River Plain, where most of the irri-

Left:

ROLLING WHEATLANDS
Near Starbuck, on the Snake, Southeastern Washington

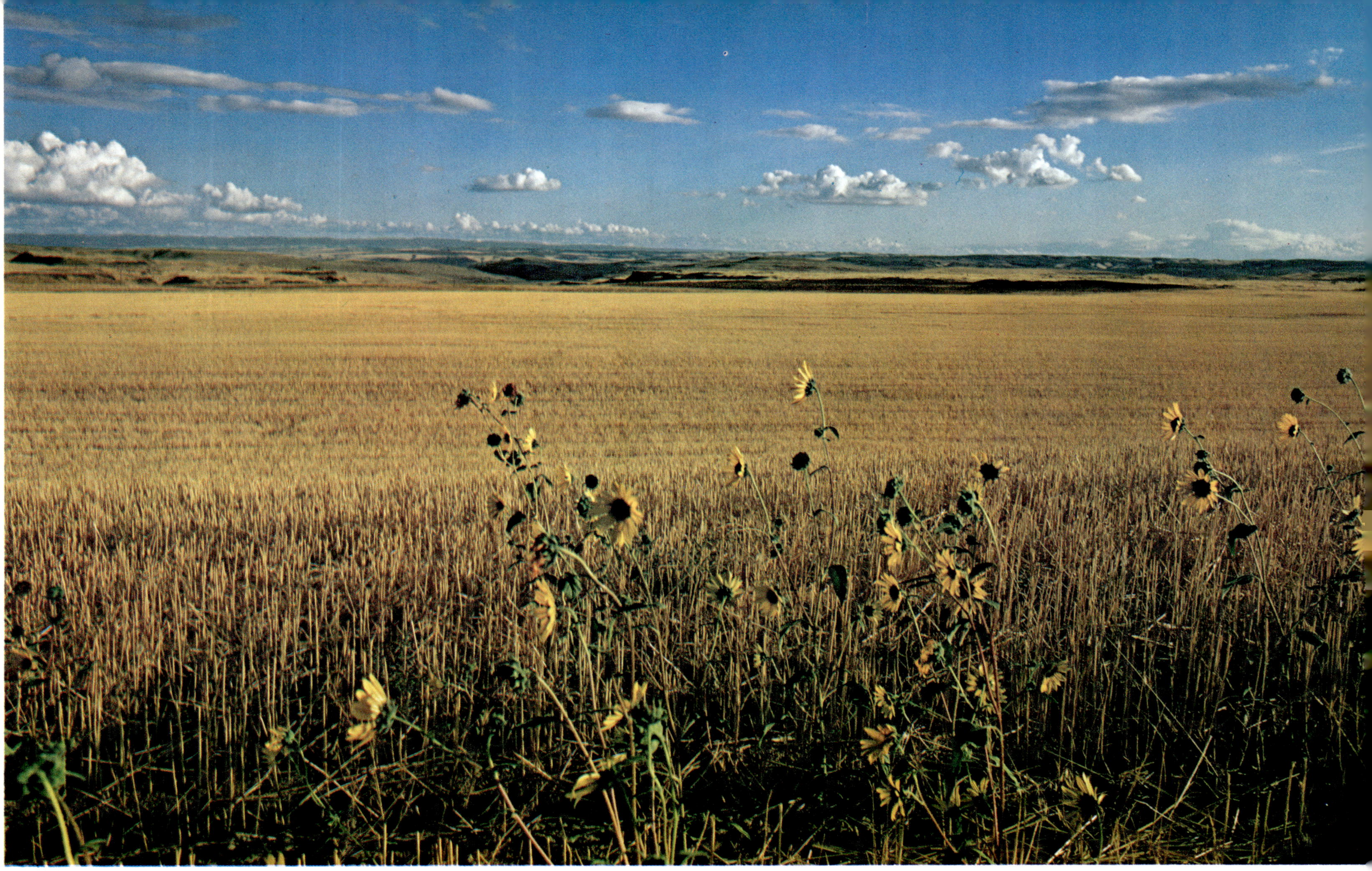

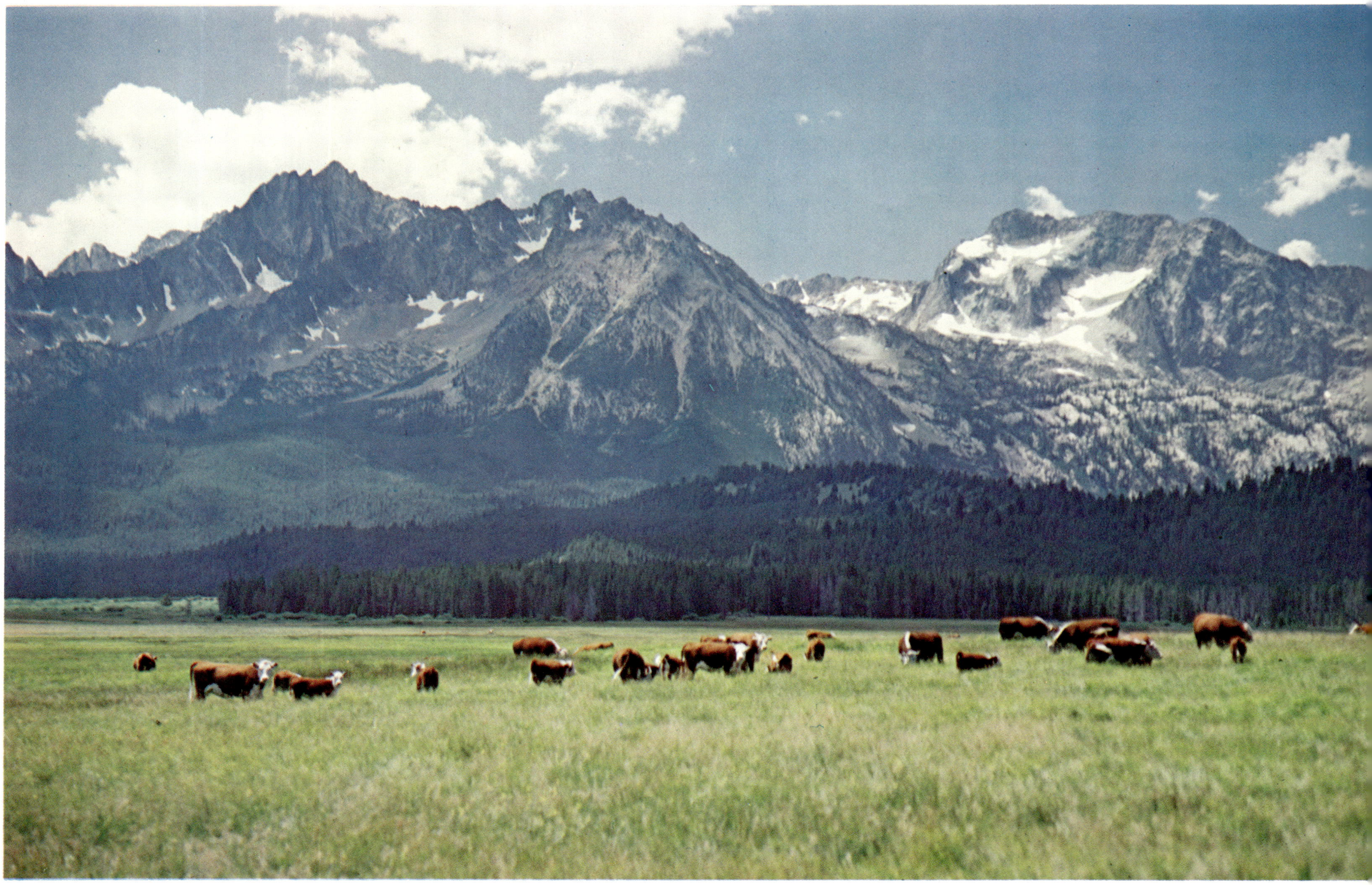

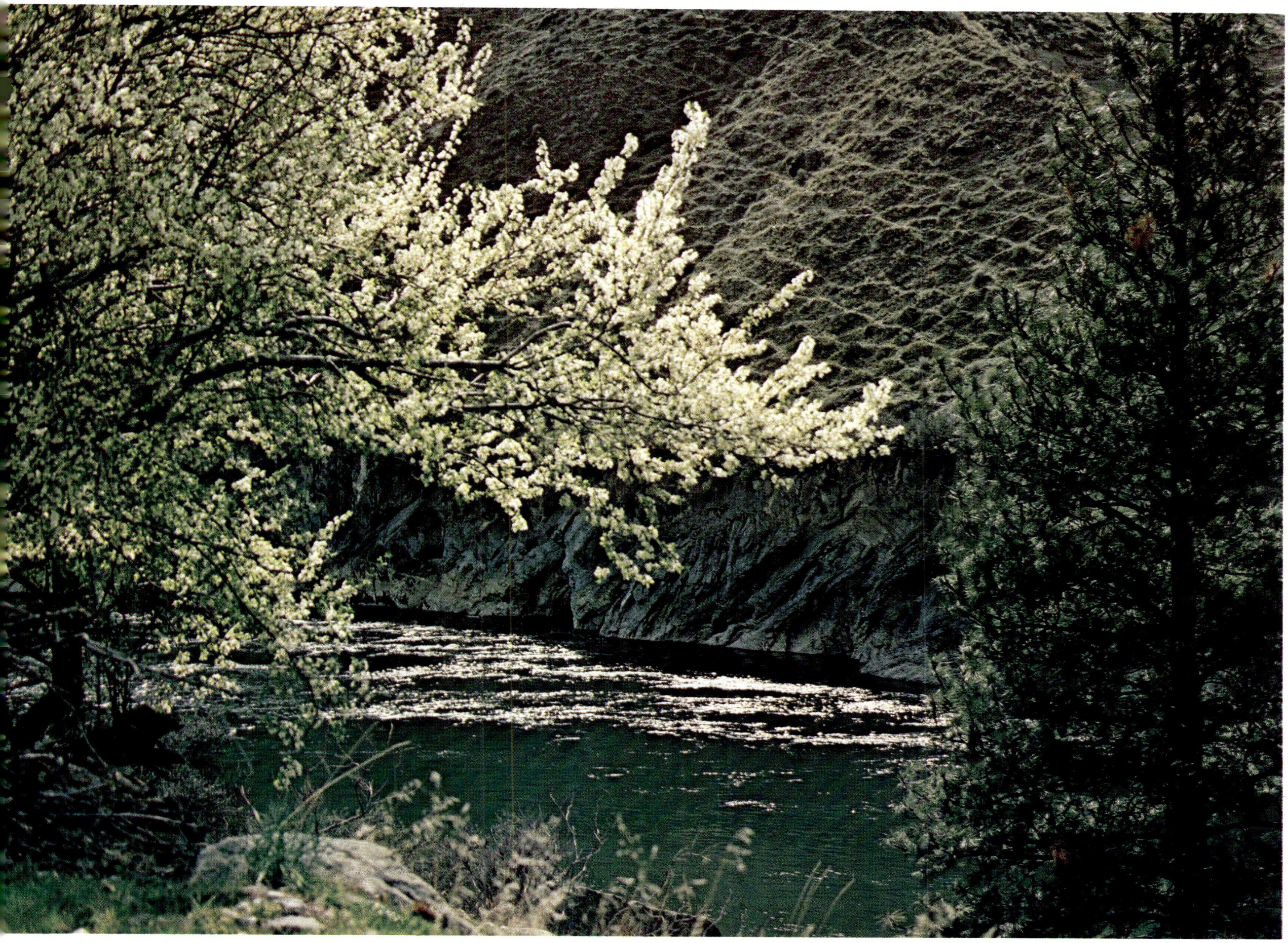

Spring Blossoms, Salmon River

Left, above:
SUNFLOWERS AND WHEAT STUBBLE
North of Snake River, near Washtucna, Washington

Left, below:
Cattle Graze in the Green Lushness of Stanley Basin
The Sawtooth Mountains in the background

gable lands lie, serving the double purpose of storing winter snow for summer use and shielding the area from extremes of weather. To the west rise the Blue Mountains and the Wallowas; to the north, the Bitter Roots and Sawtooths; to the east, the Grand Tetons; to the southeast, the Bear River Mountains; and, to the southwest, the Owyhees. Frigid weather fronts moving south from Canada normally are pushed eastward by the moist, relatively warm fronts moving inland from the Pacific, making it possible for Snake River Valley cities like Lewiston and Clarkston—in the same latitude as Bangor, Maine—to brag about being located in a "banana belt" climate zone.

Vital though irrigation has been to the development of the region, it has inspired very little popular literature, folklore, or romantic tradition. The prospector, the cowboy, the Indian, the logger, and the Basque sheepherder keeping his lonely vigil on the sagebrush plains all have found their place in fiction and legend. But the man in gum boots standing shovel in hand beside an irrigation ditch head gate seems to have fired the imagination of few writers.

Perhaps the reason for this is that bringing water to thirsty land has until recent times been hard, dirty, unglamorous work. And though violence sometimes erupted over the rights to sources of water, charging the villain with six-shooter blazing never dug a foot of ditch or put a gallon of water on the potato patch. That could only be done by taking a firm grip on the shovel handle and bending one's back. If the project were of any size, many shovels and many backs must join in the effort—and cooperative ditch digging is not the sort of activity that makes folk heroes.

Following the aborted missions of the Whitmans and the Spaldings at Waiilatpu and Lapwai, the Mormons came into the eastern part of the Snake River Country in 1855, establishing a settlement ten miles southeast of Salmon, Idaho, called Fort Lemhi. This was Bannock country, and though Brigham Young long had stressed the theory that "It is cheaper to feed an Indian than it is to fight him," the attempts by the Latter-day Saints to live at peace with their red neighbors met a cool response. Cool, too, were the nights in the 5,000-foot-high valley, limiting the crops that could be grown despite the abundance of irrigation water available. And to further discourage the contingent of twenty-seven Saints who had come to this remote spot to spread the faith and show the natives how to live, most of the potatoes, peas, carrots, and grain grown the first two years were devoured by swarms of grasshoppers.

After a visit from Brigham Young the third year, during which he praised the colony's energy but questioned the wisdom of its location so far removed from the Great Salt Lake basin, the plague of grasshoppers ended. But the Bannocks grew increasingly troublesome. Since the Saints insisted they were friends, the Indians felt that *real* friends should share what food they had—and their appetites proved greater than those of the grasshoppers. After a number of quarrels, the Indians killed three of the whites, the settlement appealed to Brigham Young for help, a relief force was sent north, and the community was abandoned to the Indians. Later settlements established closer to Salt Lake—notably Franklin and Malad—prospered in the lower desert.[1]

As the Boise Basin mines boomed, two young men who had come into the country to seek their fortunes decided there was more money in digging irrigation ditches than in grubbing for gold. William J. McConnell and his English-Canadian partner, John Porter, located on a tributary to the Payette River, about four miles above Horse Shoe Bend, in April, 1863, engaged in farming and gardening there for four years, and found a ready market for all the produce they could raise. McConnell wrote:

> ". . . there were not enough men engaged in farming to supply the mining camps, consequently there was always a shortage. When Porter and I began operations we had only about two gallons of onion sets; these we planted, spading up a piece of ground in the bend of the creek. It was a sunny spot, and the soil being a rich loam, the young plants grew rapidly, and four weeks after planting them we pulled them all and tied them in bunches of one dozen each. There were one hundred bunches, which we sold in Placerville as fast as we could pass them out at one dollar a bunch. They were the first green vegetables sold in the Basin. Cucumbers brought two dollars per dozen, green corn the same price."[2]

While taking a packtrain load of ripe watermelons to one of the mining camps, McConnell met a bachelor prospector who was eager to impress two pretty emigrant girls just arrived from Missouri. Without asking the price, the young gallant yelled: "Hey, Cap, bring us a melon!"

McConnell selected the largest one he had, the prospector treated the girls, then asked McConnell how much he owed him.

> "I told him 25 cents per pound, the weight was marked on the rind. Upon examination, it was found to weigh thirty-two pounds, making the price eight dollars."[3]

Among the early settlers who tried their hand at farming, many misconceptions existed and many mistakes were made before they learned to adapt their ways to the peculiarities of the country. For instance, in journal after journal written during Oregon Trail days the soil of the Snake River Basin was dismissed as infertile "alkali powder," unfit for agriculture. Indeed, when dry—as it invariably was during August— the soil was very light in color and texture, rising like smoke from the wheels of the wagons and hoofs of the draft animals, letting one's feet sink to the ankles, moving in choking clouds on the least breath of wind. But when

1. *Early History of Idaho*, by William J. McConnell, Caxton, 1913, pp. 43-54.

2. Ibid., p. 122.

3. Ibid., p. 123.

watered, it turned dark, becoming the "rich loam" which the emigrants did not expect to find until they reached the Willamette Valley.

Another misconception of the early settlers was that the only soil worth cultivating was that in the broad-stream valleys. A farmer accustomed to tilling New England fields wanted a piece of level land, for, as every New England farmer knew, sloping land was hard to work, washed with the first heavy rain, possessed only a thin layer of soil, and, when farmed, soon became nothing but a hillside of exposed rocks.

This was not true in the Snake River Country. Steep and high though the Palouse Hills along the lower Snake were, the soil consisted of rich, windblown loess deposited by eons of erosion; in many places, you could dig forty vertical feet and never find a rock. When rain fell, it came down in fine droplets with little or no wind, often taking a full twenty-four hours to total half an inch. Consequently, most of it sank in, making erosion a minor problem. And, after mid-June, weeks of uninterrupted sunshine ripened the grain and gave the farmer plenty of time to harvest it.

Learning these things, farmers began ploughing and planting grain on the hillsides, utilizing slopes as steep as 20 percent. By the turn of the century, they were bragging that crop failures in the Palouse country were unknown, and that wheat yields as high as one hundred bushels an acre were being achieved.[4]

It was in this region that the teamster's art reached its finest flowering, for it took twenty-four to thirty horses or mules to pull the headers on the steep hills. When runaways or upsets occurred, they were spectacular, old-timers say. As gasoline-powered equipment came into use, the immense gangploughs, discs, harrows, and drills were pulled by huge crawler tractors called "Caterpillars," for wheel tractors could not operate on the slopes. And a peculiar monster called a "self-leveling" combine came into use—a piece of equipment which still is a marvel to Kansas-raised farm boys, for, like the legendary Ozark cow bred to graze on steep-sloping pasturelands, its downhill legs are longer than its uphill.

Today, though wheat farmers in the lower Snake River Country still boast that crop failures are unknown, the one hundred bushel per acre yield of the 1890s no longer stands as a record. Thanks to new strains of wheat, and modern farm technology, which conserves moisture, fertilizes, sprays by plane, and, in a few fields, gives the wheat extra inches of water just when it needs them most, experimental plots yielding 209 bushels to the acre have been harvested.[5] And the ultimate limit is not in sight.

At the present time, almost all of the grain raised in the Palouse Hills is dry-farmed, only 1 percent of the wheat acreage and 3 percent of the barley being irrigated. Since the fields lie one to two thousand feet above the level of the river, high-lift pumps and expensive sprinkling systems are required; thus, irrigation is not economically practical. But future food demands and the availability of water and cheap power may one day alter the picture.[6]

Before discussing present-day uses of and future needs for irrigation water, we should take a brief look at some basic facts related to irrigation.

° ° °

2.

To the city dweller, water is something to drink, bathe in, boat and ski on, swim and fish in, and take pictures of at scenic falls. Statistics regarding it make dry reading to him—which is yet another paradox associated with the subject of water. Here are still others, which must be understood before we can comprehend the problems related to putting water on the land.

As much water exists in the world today as existed at Earth's creation. We can use water. But we cannot use it up.

Water cannot be compressed.

Water is heavy—a cubic foot of it contains 7.5 gallons and weighs 64.5 pounds.

To irrigate fields properly in the Snake River Basin requires not an application of an inch or two of moisture now and then, but four to ten vertical feet of water per year applied to every acre of ground.

The mean annual evaporation rate of water in the Snake River Basin is fifty inches.

Where water is least needed in the Snake River Country, it is available in its largest volume. This area of least need is not in the high, cool country of the headwaters, as we might expect, but in the low, hot country near the river's mouth. As a final paradox, the greatest shortage of water exists in the upper part of the watershed, where one would think it would be needed least.

Now, to the history lesson, which we'll keep as brief as possible. . . .

The American dream of individual freedom and material independence has always been based upon the "little man's" ownership of the land. Even as recently as the 1930s, a book titled *Five Acres and Independence*, which outlined in detail how a family could make a good living on a small truck-farm, was a best-seller. A hundred years earlier, as industrialization displaced workers and built up pockets of poverty in the cities of the East, the magic answer to all economic ills was "Go West," claim, and farm a piece of land.

Both the National Congress and the Far Western legislatures encouraged the movement by passing laws designed to give land to the little people. In Oregon, between 1850-

4. *History of Whitman County* (no author named), W. H. Lever Publ., 1901, p. 116.

5. *Union Bulletin*, Walla Walla, Wash., December 7, 1965.

6. *Irrigation*, Appendix IX, Columbia North Pacific Region Comprehensive Framework Study, January, 1970, Preliminary Report, Pacific Northwest River Basins Commission, Vancouver, Wash., p. 192. Hereafter called *Irrigation*, PNRBC.

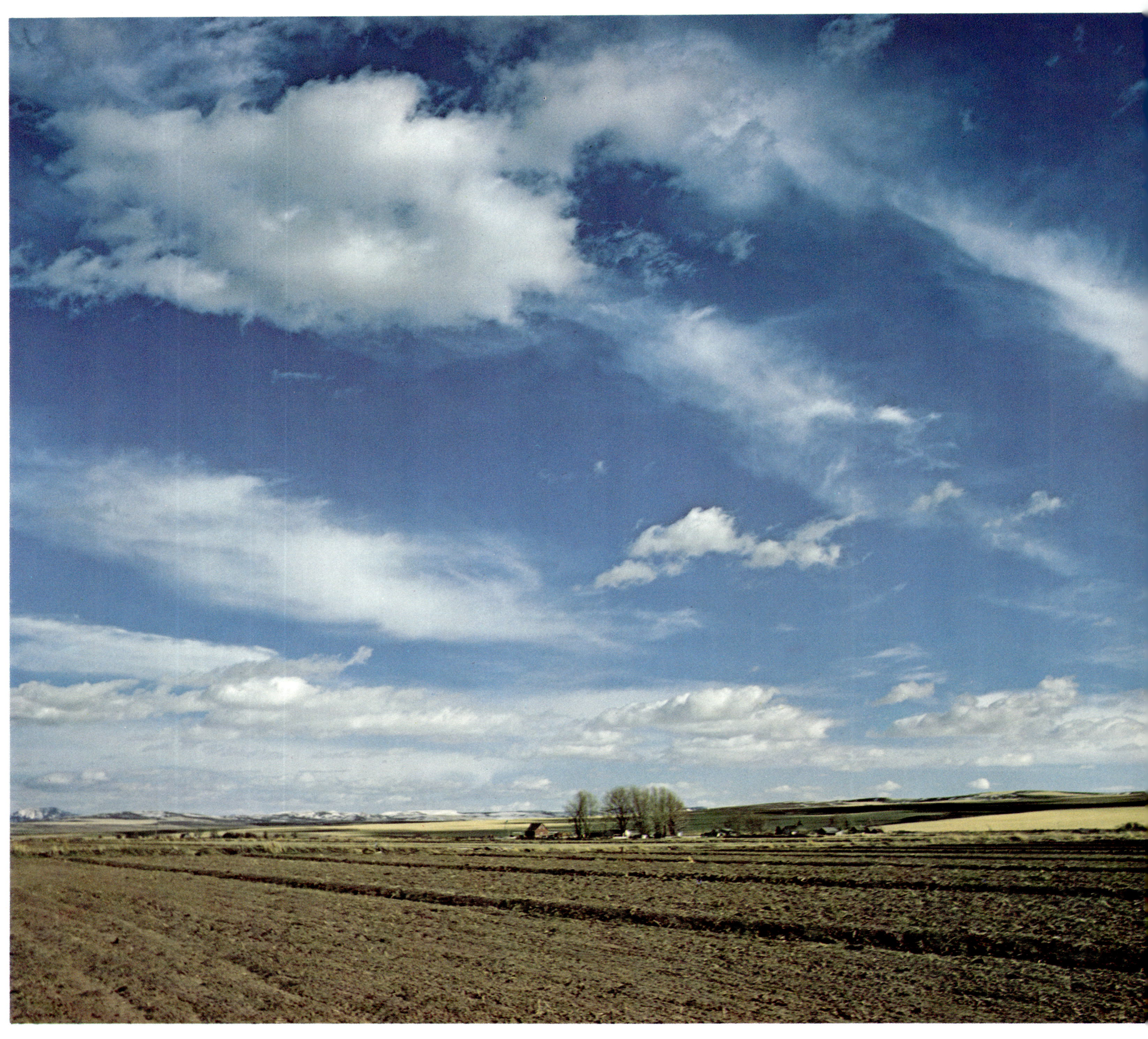

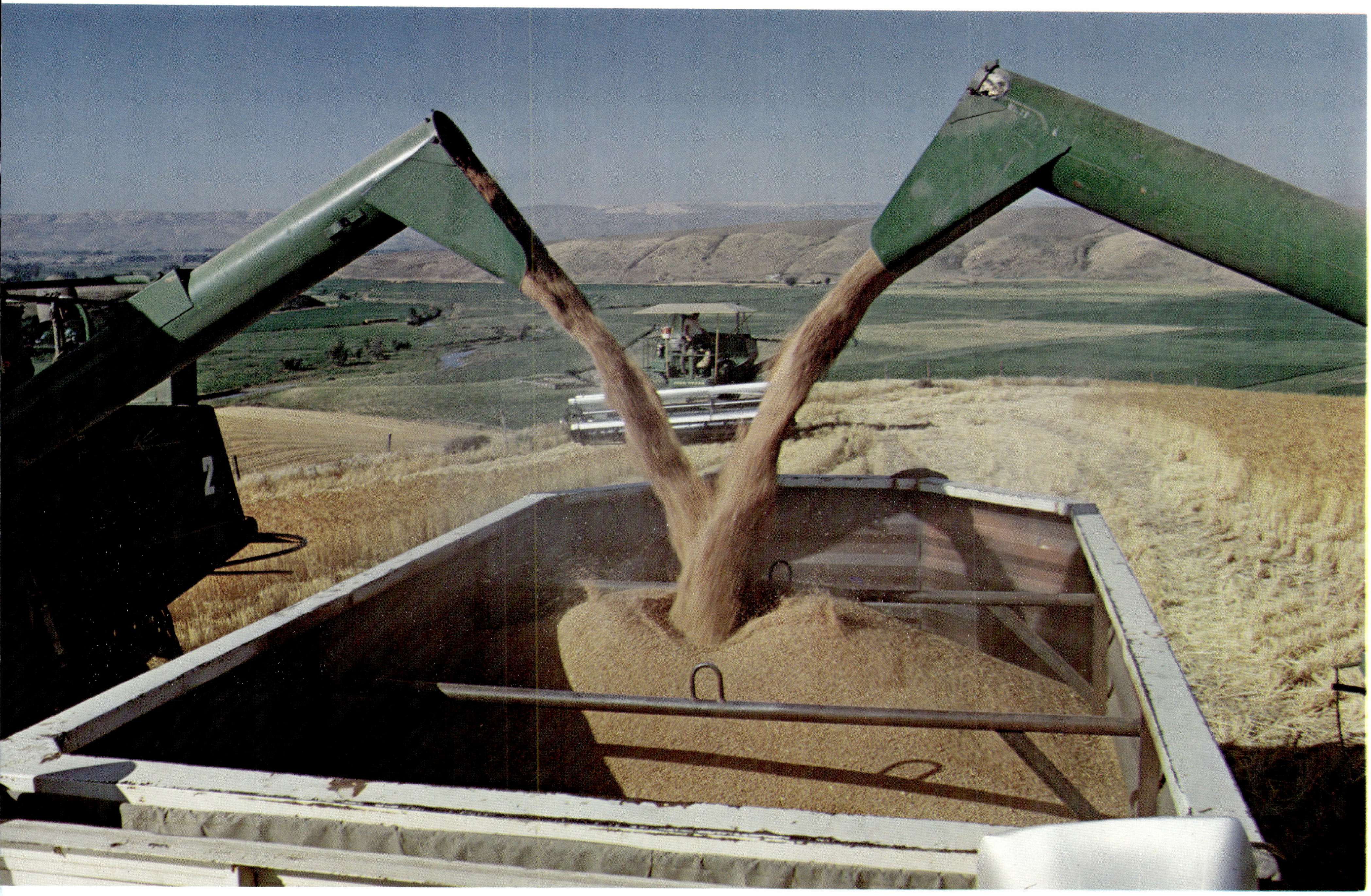

Above: The Golden Grain, Walla Walla County, Lower Snake

Right: Harvest time, Walla Walla County, Washington.

Left: Newly Ploughed Earth and a Spring Sky near Pocatello, Idaho.

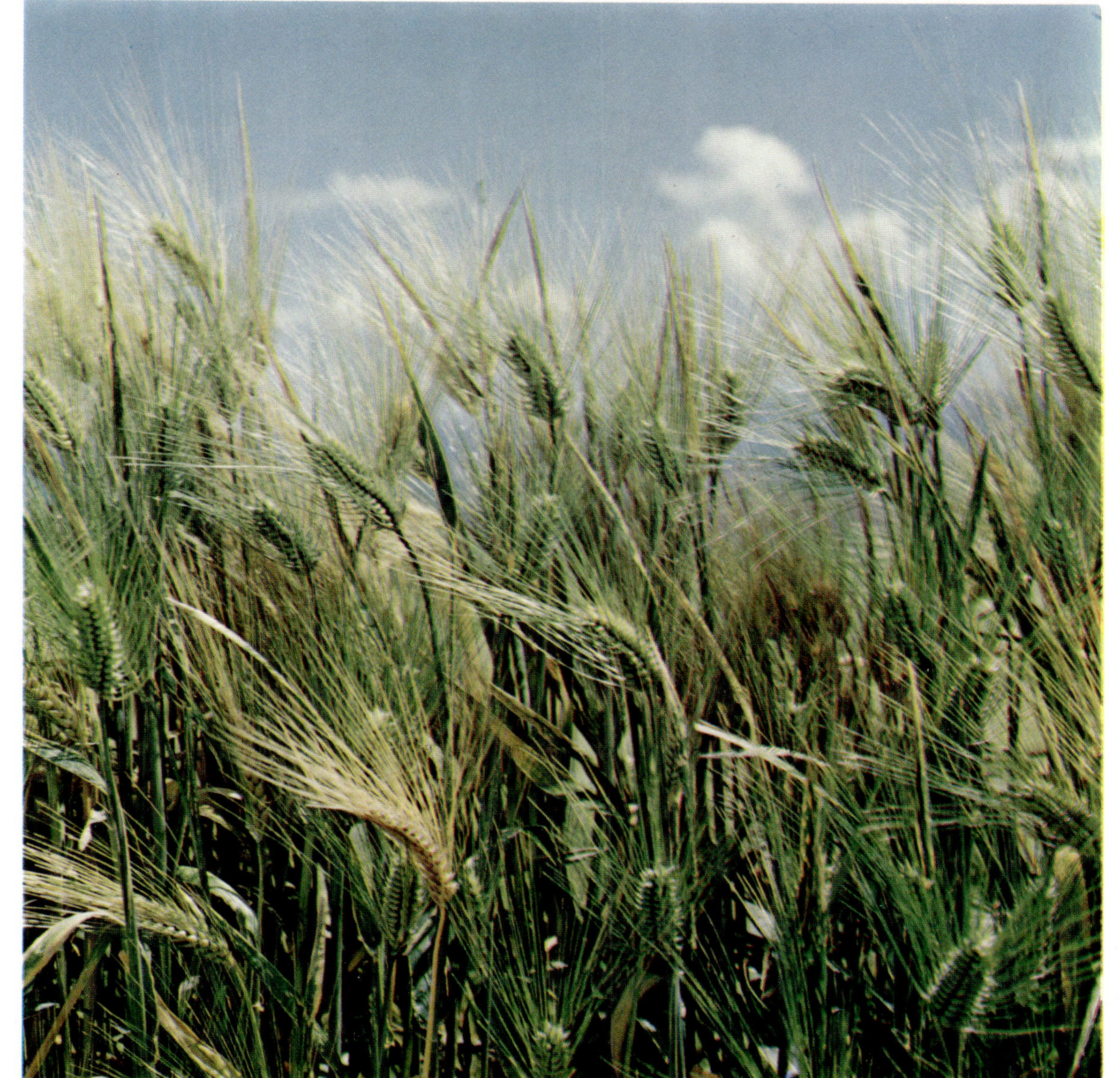

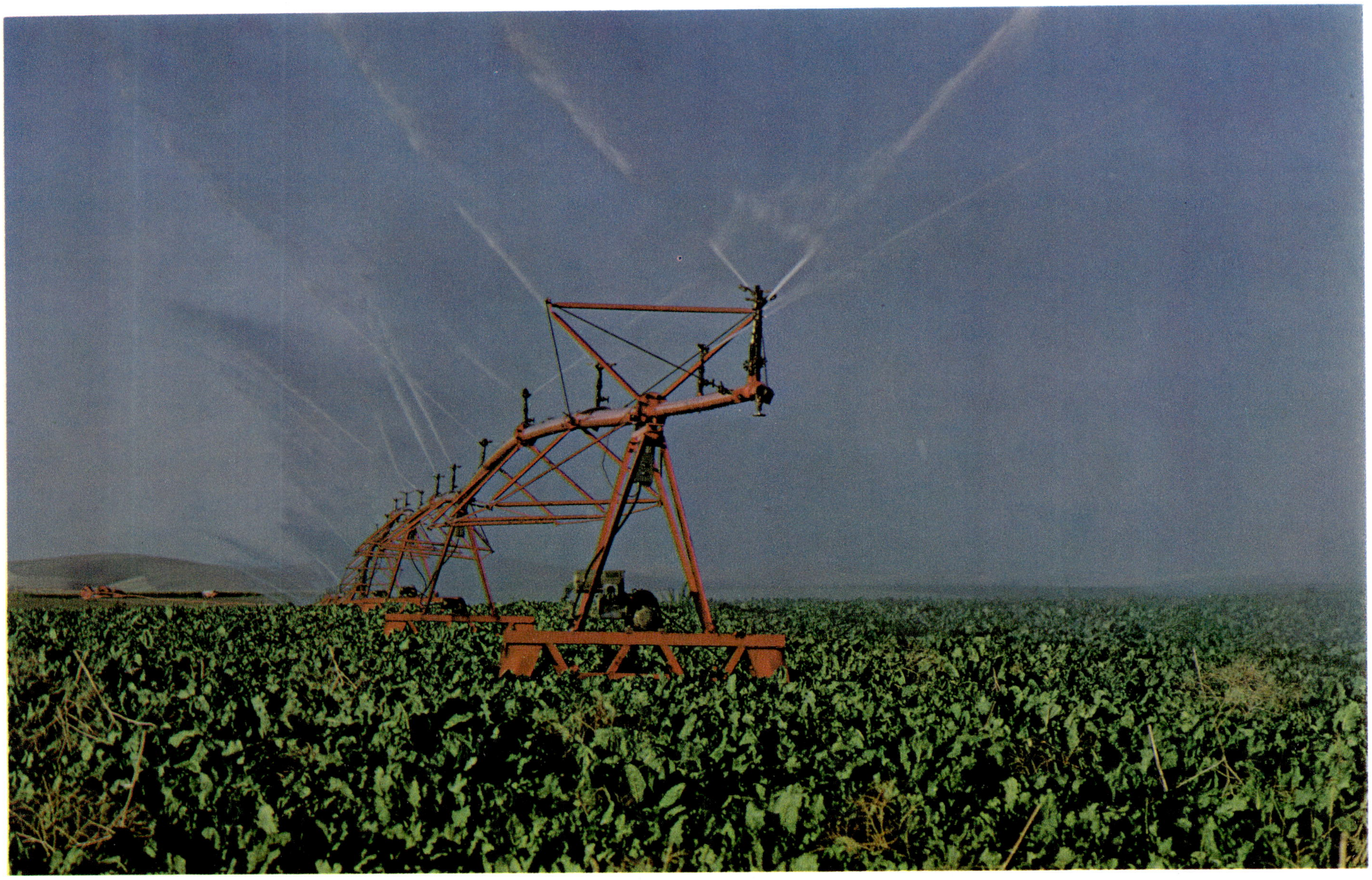

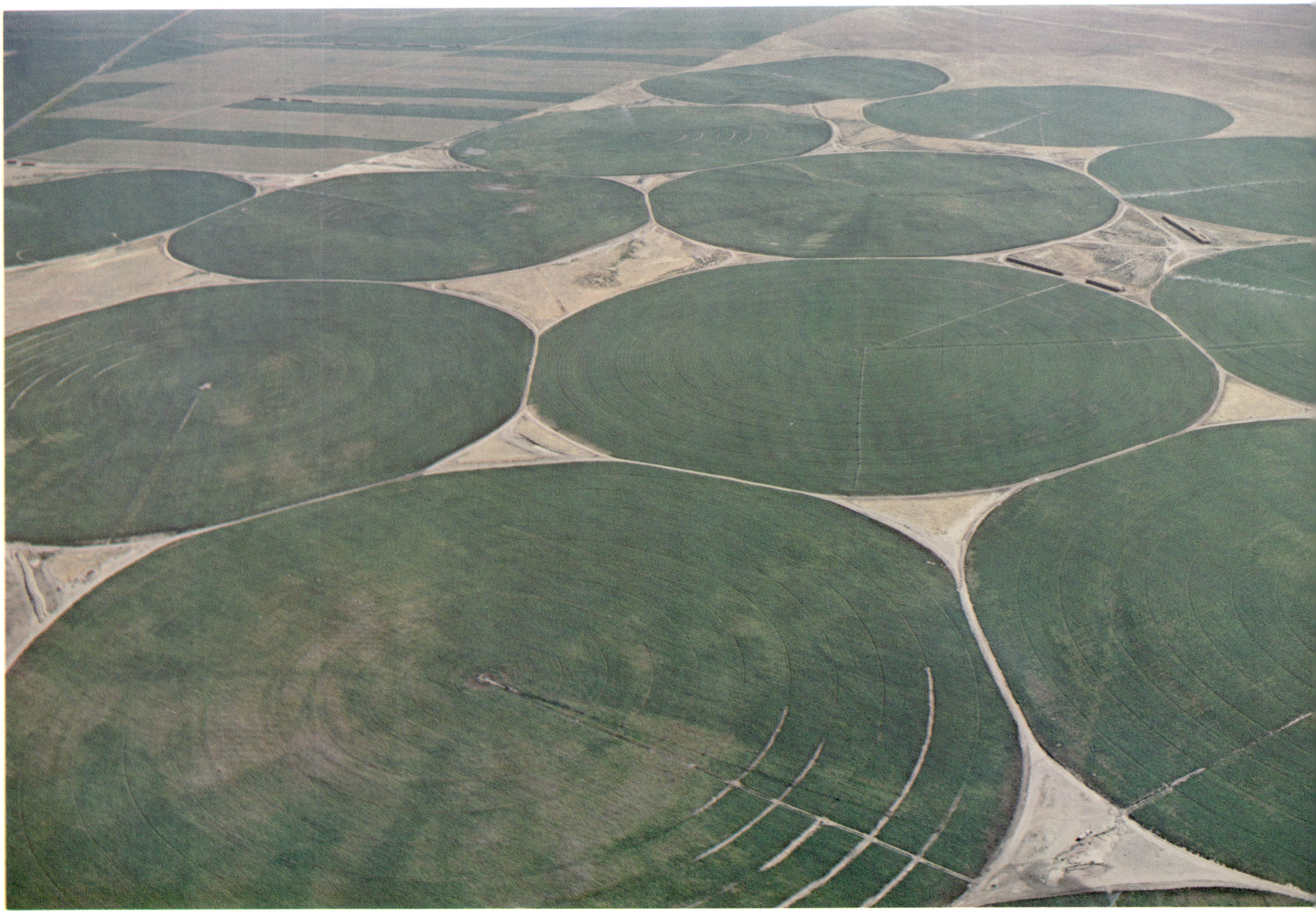

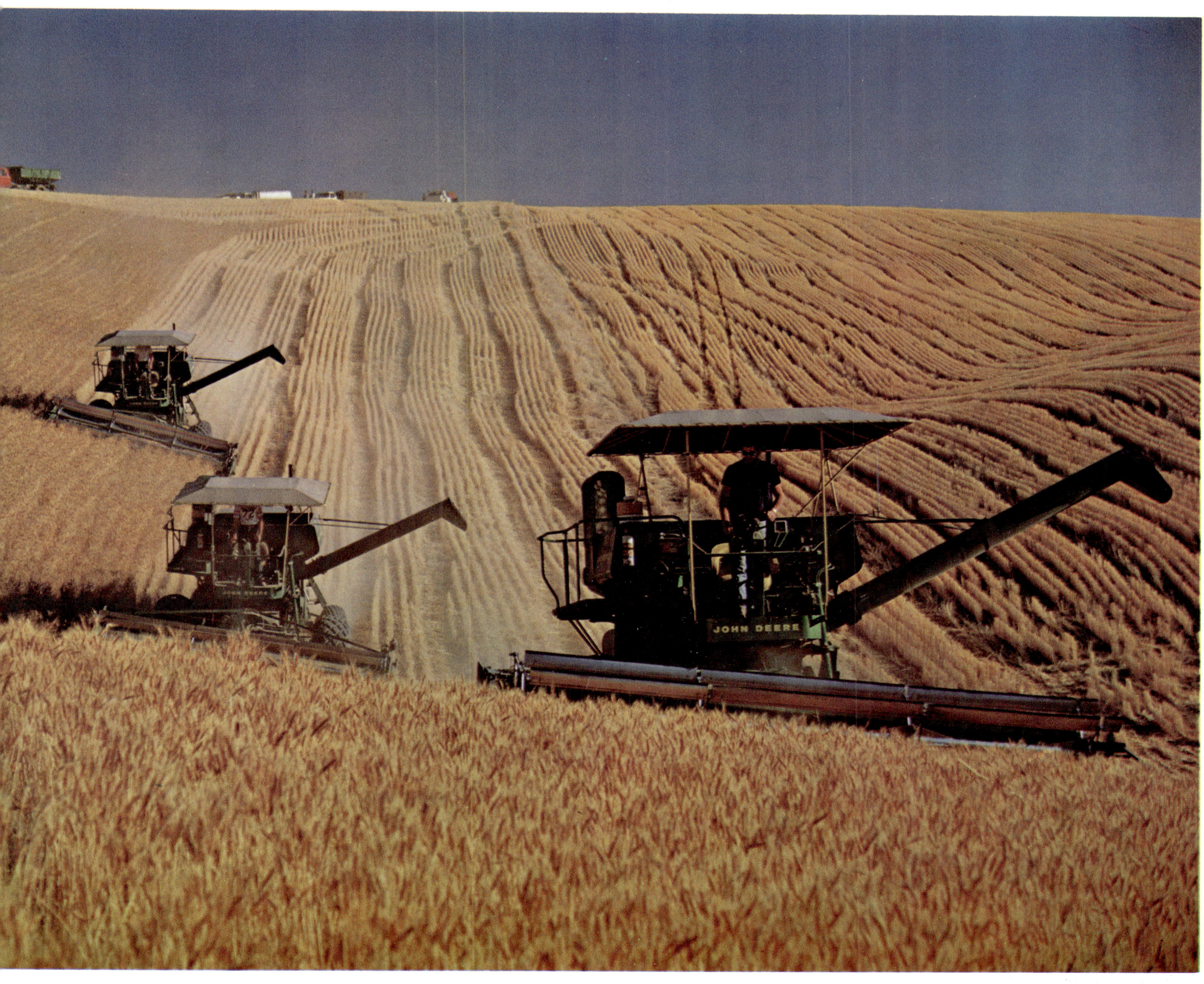

Left, above:

SPRINKLER IRRIGATION, NEAR BURBANK, WASHINGTON

This piece of equipment, operating on a center-pivot and self-propelled, can cover a circular field 138 acres in extent up to twenty times in a 24-hour period Its price tag currently is $22,000.

Left, below:

AUTOMATED IRRIGATION

From a plane a few thousand feet up, these sprinkler-irrigated fields resemble lily pads. Cutting a circle out of a quarter-section of land (160 acres), the self-propelled sprinklers put water on 138 acres. The fields pictured here are near Burbank, Washington, at the mouth of the Snake.

Above: The Palouse Hills

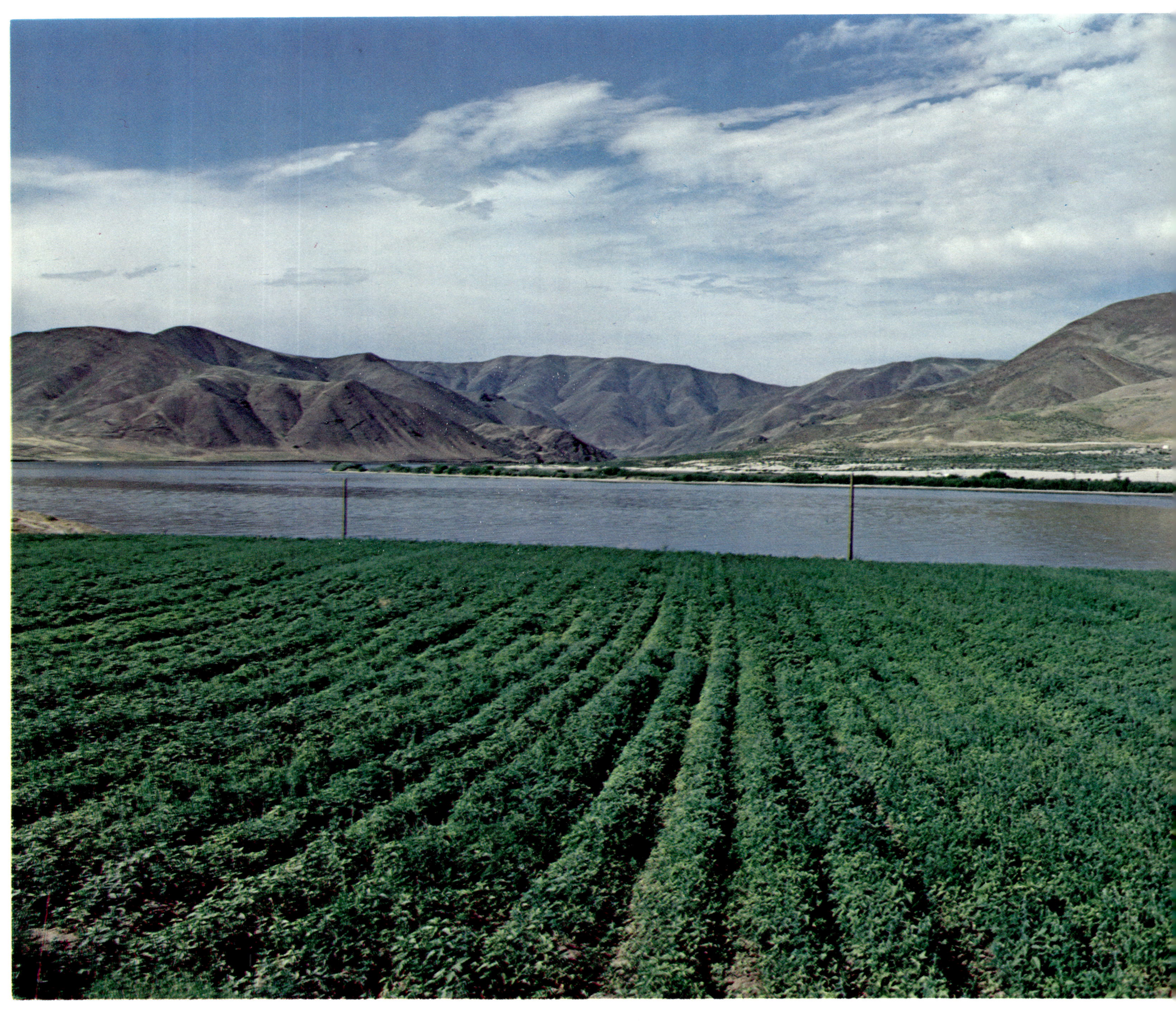

55, the Donation Land Law provided that a man and his wife could acquire from 320 to 640 acres of land simply by settling on them. In 1862, the Federal Homestead Act gave a settler 160 acres if he would cultivate them and make a few improvements. Vast grants of land were given the railroads as inducements to build lines across the country, and they, in turn, mounted promotion schemes to sell land to settlers at modest prices so that they would create the farms, crops, towns, and demand for manufactured products that would generate freight traffic.

By 1866, it had become apparent to the federal government that a piece of land in the West was worthless without water. Having neither the desire nor the means to start irrigation projects itself on desert lands, it encouraged individuals, companies, territories, and states to develop them by surrendering federal control over the use of water in unnavigable streams to regional authority.

From now on, the federal government said, development of irrigation would be left "to local customs, laws, and the decisions of the courts."

In 1877, the Desert Land Act was passed, which provided for the sale of land in 640-acres tracts at a very low price "to anyone who would irrigate it within three years." As a further inducement to the promotion of local irrigation, the Carey Land Act was passed in 1894, encouraging state governments to take the lead in building irrigation projects. By its terms, each western state was given 1,000,000 acres of desert land, which it might distribute to individuals, providing that no one person was awarded more than 160 acres.[1]

None of the foregoing schemes worked very well; in fact, almost all were dismal failures. The basic reason for their failure is not hard to pinpoint:

> "The paradox of irrigation was that while it stimulated individualism and fed upon private speculation, it was actually ill-suited to either one. . . . Reclamation demanded for its success a collective institutional approach. Individualism and capitalism might flourish and prosper once the land was watered, but the task of watering it was one that called for social action. . . ."[2]

Land and town promotion schemes inaugurated by the railroads were seldom the type of "social action" the author quoted above prescribed. In 1877, Jay Gould, of the Union Pacific, hired Robert E. Strahorn to create what was euphemistically called "a literary bureau" extolling the scenic attractions and natural resources of the West. In her intriguing *Fifteen Thousand Miles By Stage,* Carrie Adell Strahorn, his wife, gives an interesting though understandably biased account of the press-agentry, devious dealing, skulduggery, and downright fraud that accompanied the beginnings of towns such as Hailey, Caldwell, and Nampa, Idaho, and Ontario, Baker, and La Grande, Oregon. On at least two occasions, angry citizens proposed lynching Strahorn—once in Boise, which was being bypassed by the railroad, and again in Pocatello, where he was accused of all sorts of crimes against the community.

Though Mrs. Strahorn's credentials as an agronomist may be questioned, her comments on living conditions in the town of Caldwell in 1884-85 give a vivid picture of the times.

> "It didn't rain at Caldwell for a year. This particular lumber couldn't stand the merciless heat and sirocco winds, which shriveled every vulnerable thing. Some said the lumber had simply shrunk to slivers, and others that it had warped itself all over the Snake River desert, because it was well known that an ex-cowboy was kept busy herding the twisting and wriggling boards and timbers inside the limits of Alkali Flat. . . ."[3]

Like the emigrants, Mrs. Strahorn called all light-colored, powdery soil "alkali." After noting the building of irrigation canals in the Caldwell area, she lyrically wrote that the water

> ". . . gave life to the earth's parched lips, that were made to smile in green fields and orchard blooms. Whenever the alkali was drained out, the soil was rich, deep, and fertile. But no one can imagine the trouble that camps on the trail of an irrigating canal. It looks like such a refreshing, innocent joy as it glistens and glides on through the thirsty land, and so it was when it stayed in its bed, but that was a land of badgers, and in a single unguarded night they would dig a hole in the bank and turn the whole stream into someone's house or garden, or flood the wrong territory and empty the ditch. . . ."[4]

On the beginnings of Ontario, Oregon, thirty miles west, she wrote:

> "The Good Book tells us that God made the world out of nothing, but the town of Ontario emerged from sand clouds. There was no other place to compare with it for dust. A shoe or clothes brush hung on many a front door knob as a gentle hint not to carry the dirt inside."[5]

Left:

NEAR HUNTINGTON, OREGON

Farewell Bend, with a greenness Oregon-bound emigrants never saw. The crop is potatoes.

-----

1. *Irrigation,* PNRBC, p. 5.

2. *Empire of the Columbia,* by Dorothy O. Johansen and Charles M. Gates, Harpers, 1957, p. 567.

3. *Fifteen Thousand Miles By Stage,* by Carrie Adell Strahorn, Putnam, 1911, p. 522.

4. Ibid., p. 524.

5. Ibid., p. 545.

The heartbreaks, the failures of private land and water companies, and the tragedies of businesses and towns established with high hopes only to go bankrupt and die because of an inability to put water on the land, would fill a thick volume—with dry reading, in the literal sense of the word. Two examples will suffice here:

> "As larger and larger areas are broken up, the rainfall shows a tendency to increase," a booster wrote regarding a lower Snake River region in 1901. "The prospects seem good that parts of western Whitman County may yet support thrifty and prosperous agricultural populations."[6]

Seventy years later, the annual rainfall in Whitman County has not increased a droplet, and, though a thrifty, prosperous agricultural population is supported by the land, it is supported by dry farming.

In 1890, desperately attempting to reap where it could not afford to sow, the Idaho Legislature passed a law granting farmers "the right" to organize water districts on whatever lands they had settled.

> "But no district could be organized on unsettled land," wrote one early-day resident, "and farmers would not settle without water assured."[7]

Despite the difficulties of bringing water to the land, Idaho was the first of the Western states to use up its allotted 1,000,000-acre grant of desert land. In 1901, it was given a second million acres.

Finally realizing that individuals, private companies, state governments, or any conceivable combination thereof, did not possess the resources capable of overcoming the vast problems of irrigation, the National Congress passed the Reclamation Act in 1902.

> "Briefly, this Act permitted the Secretary of Interior to locate and construct irrigation works. Settlers on a Federal reclamation project were allowed to own up to 160 acres (320 for a man and wife) for the purpose of irrigating crops."[8]

Passage of the act marked the beginning of the modern era of irrigation in the Snake River Country. The Minidoka Project was begun in 1904, from whose American Falls Dam near Pocatello more than a million acres of land that had nourished little but sagebrush eventually would be watered. In 1915, Arrowrock Dam, a few miles northeast of Boise, was completed, being at that time the largest of its kind in the West. Year by year, similar projects followed.

The taming of what its early French-Canadian explorers had called "The Accursed Mad River" was beginning in earnest.

-----

6. *History of Whitman County*, p. 188.

7. *History of Idaho*, by James H. Hawley, S. J. Clarke Co., Chicago, 1920 p. 441.

8. *Irrigation*, PNRBC, p. 5.

3.

When speaking of natural resources, we no longer use the word "unlimited," for we at last have come to realize that all our resources are finite. Where irrigable land and water are concerned in the Snake River Country, we can cautiously say that at present there is quite a bit of both. But both are being measured in a series of comprehensive studies which, when completed, will indicate how they should best be used during the next fifty years, with the specific dates 1980, 2000, and 2020 pinpointed as guideposts.[1]

These studies divide the Snake River watershed into three subregions of approximately equal size: (1) Upper Snake, from its source to King Hill, Idaho, which is forty-five miles west of Twin Falls; (2) Central Snake, from King Hill to just below Oxbow Dam, where the Snake enters Hell's Canyon proper; and (3) Lower Snake, from Oxbow to the river's confluence with the Columbia in southeastern Washington.

Each subregion covers 36,000 square miles, making each equal in size to the state of Indiana. Thus, the watershed as a whole is three times larger than Indiana. For those interested in comparative figures, Indiana contains 5,100,000 people, while the Snake River Country head count is 750,000 souls.

Approximately three-fourths of the irrigated lands in the watershed presently receive water via gravity methods called borders, rills, or wild flooding. Since World War II, when lightweight aluminum pipe, sprinklers, and high-speed pumps capable of lifting water under great pressure were introduced, many of the new lands brought under cultivation have been sprinkler irrigated. Now we are moving into an era of self-propelled, self-regulating, center-pivot systems with which large fields can be given the exact amount of moisture they require at the precise time they need it with very little human exertion.

Gravity irrigation requires huge storage dams, land leveling, an intricate system of feeder and lateral canals, head gates, ditches, and much hand labor. Irrigation by movable pipe and sprinklers requires less labor, is suited to less level land, but demands a large investment in capital equipment. The newest, most exotic systems are the most expensive of all and can be used only on specially laid out fields, but the operating labor costs are relatively low.

At the present time there are forty-six major reservoirs with irrigation as a function on the Snake and its tributaries.[2]

-----

1. *Irrigation*, PNRBC. Pages 129 to 210 cover the Snake River watershed and give many facts, figures, and tables, which I have simplified here because of space limitations.

2. Ibid., p. 18.

Right:

THE WALLOWA VALLEY

Traditional home of Chief Joseph's band of Nez Perces, this is one of the most beautiful regions in the nation.

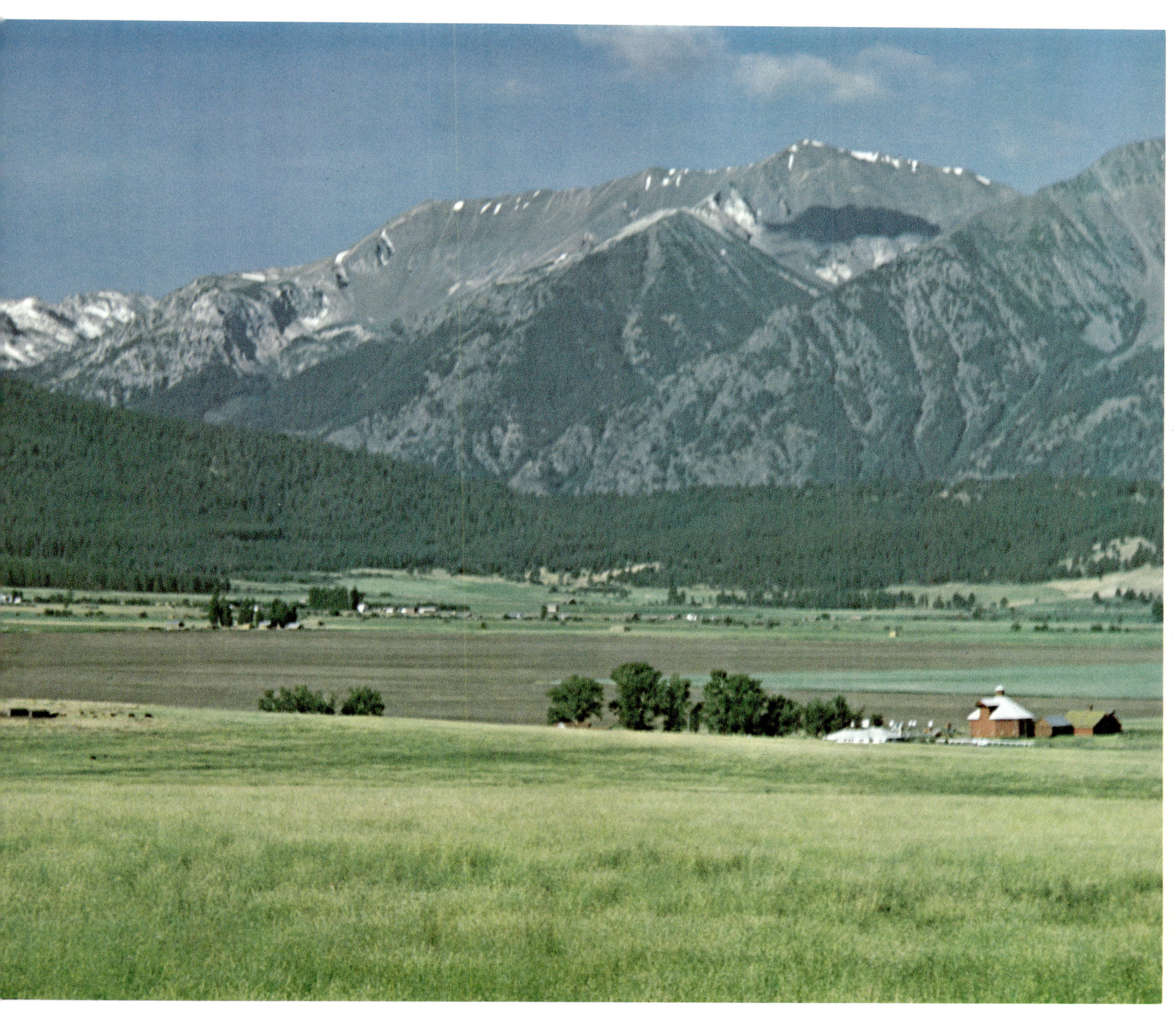

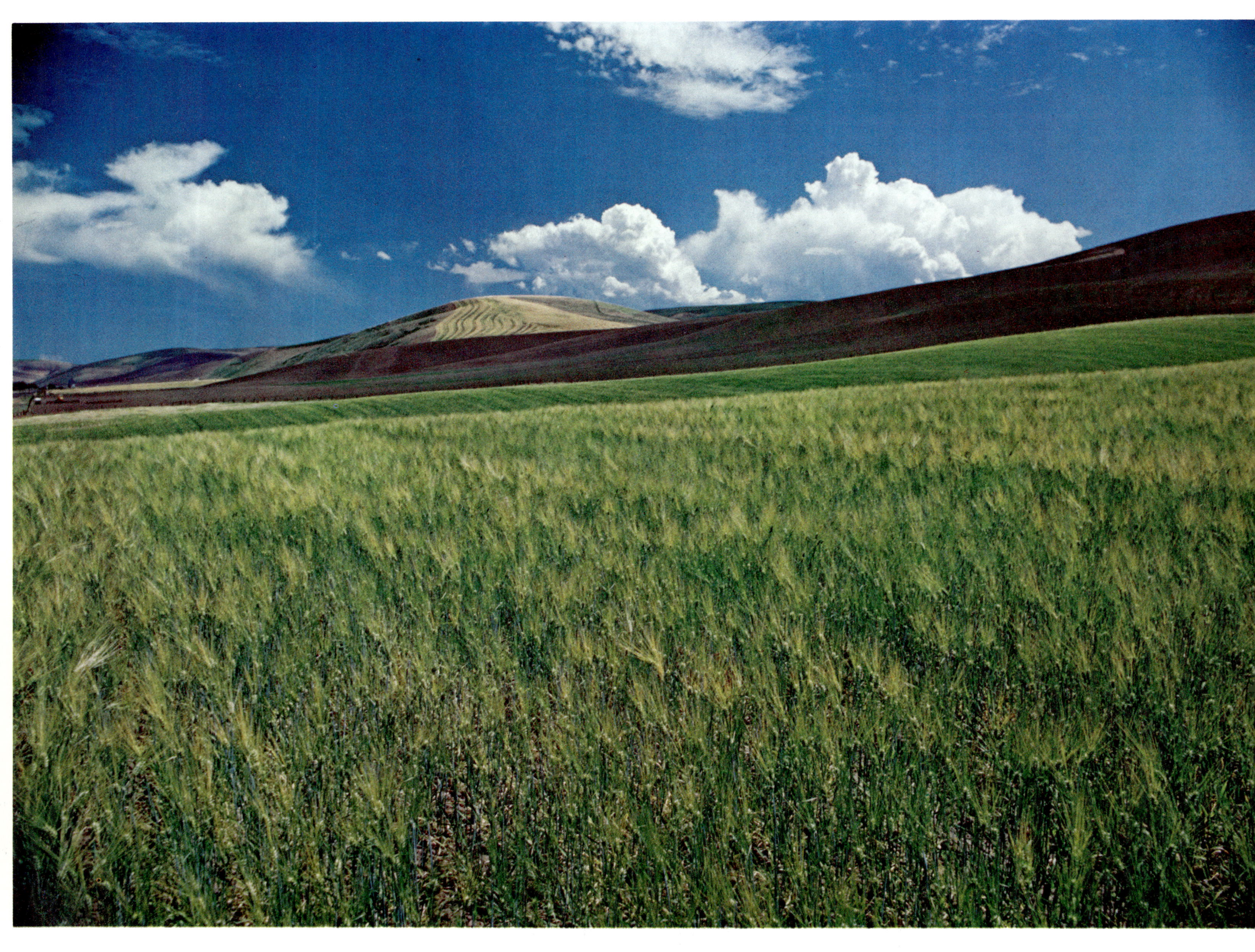

Their total active storage capacity is nine million acre-feet. Over the watershed as a whole, 4.3 million acres now are being irrigated: 2.5 million in the Upper Snake, 1.5 million in the Central Snake, and 276,000 in the Lower Snake.[3]

Each of the three subregions has a low population density and a high percentage of land in public ownership. Upper, Central, and Lower population figures are eight, seven, and four people per square mile, while lands are 70, 75, and 65 percent owned by the government. This means that decisions affecting the bringing of new lands under irrigation inevitably will be influenced more by government policy than by the power of resident voters at the polls.

Each subregion has problems unique to it. For example, although 85 percent of Idaho's nation-leading potato crop is raised in the Upper Snake, the number of irrigated acres devoted to hay, grain, and pasture in the subregion far exceeds that put into potatoes. Specifically, the figures are:

Hay	575,000	acres
Grain	371,000	"
Pasture	290,000	"
Potatoes	209,000	"[4]

Much of the hay, grain, and pasture acreage is located along the higher reaches of the subregion's watershed, where water storage dams are inadequate to late summer needs. Most of the potato acreage is in the lower part of the subregion, where there are ample storage facilities. As a result, ranchers and farmers living upstream flood their fields during spring and early summer high-flow periods with up to ten acre-feet of water to every acre of land in order to build up the water table as much as possible.

A great deal of this water goes back into the stream as return flow, of course. Of the 13.5 million acre-feet annually put on the subregion's croplands, 8.6 million acre-feet return to the river, leaving a net depletion rate of 4.9 million acre-feet. So the problem is not insufficient water; it is timing. In Jackson Hole along the upper Snake and in the country lying along Henry's Fork, ranchers and farmers gladly would trade four feet of May water for one foot of August water; but, since the huge storage reservoirs needed to hold back late-season supplies would flood lands Wyoming and northeastern Idaho deem more valuable for their scenic beauty and recreational use, they cannot be built.

Another peculiarity of the Upper Snake subregion is that a great deal of the water originating within it is inaccessible to gravity flow use. The reason for this is that for 160 miles in an east-west direction along the north side of the Snake no surface waters reach the river. Instead, they sink into what appears to be one of the bleakest, driest expanses of terrain on earth, yet which in reality is one of the world's finest aquifers. It is here that the Little Lost, the Big Lost, and all other streams originating on the south slope of the Sawtooth Mountains sink into the lava flows of an area so forbidding and sterile that a portion of it has been set aside as a national monument called Craters of the Moon.

An aquifer is an underground water carrier. Though a single lava flow is not a good aquifer, the cooling, crinkling, and cracking process that occurs when a number of flows cover an area at different periods of time creates many fissures in which water may percolate, accumulate, and flow. On the surface in this area, there is practically no water at all. But hydrologists estimate that between the depths of 50 and 100 feet, the water table underlying the Snake Plain basalt contains 100 million acre-feet.[5]

Milner Dam, thirty miles east of Twin Falls, is the last major diversion point for irrigation water in the Upper Snake subregion. Of the 13.5 million acre-feet annually available, more than 10 million have been diverted for irrigation use at this point at the height of the growing season, leaving only 1.1 million acre-feet as river outflow. But a few miles downstream, where the sheer north wall of the river's gorge spews forth the phenomenon called Thousand Springs, 6.2 million annual acre-feet once again make the Snake a big river.[6]

Summing up the irrigation problems of the Upper Snake subregion, it is estimated that 510,000 acres of land now in cultivation have inadequate water supplies. The shortages average around 700,000 acre-feet annually. The root of the problem is storage space—of which little potential remains.

So far as the Central Snake subregion is concerned, it uses more irrigation water than originates within its boundaries. Only 10 percent of its water comes from the Snake itself; 90 percent is taken from tributary streams such as the Boise, Payette, Weiser, Owyhee, and Malheur.

> "The source of most of this water is snowmelt from high elevation forest lands. Because the snowpack is normally depleted by the middle of the irrigation season, streamflow becomes inadequate. Therefore, it is necessary to augment late summer supplies with storage water on most tributaries."[7]

Total active storage capacity in the subregion is 4.5 million acre-feet. About 6.4 million acre-feet are diverted annually for irrigation. Since the Snake's inflow at King Hill is over 6 million acre-feet, the natural flow is more than adequate to meet diversion needs for low-lying lands. No reservoirs have as yet been built for irrigation water storage on the mainstem. The reason for this is that through much of the area the Snake flows through a deep canyon, its surface far below most potentially irrigable lands.

It is estimated that 393,000 acres in the subregion now

------

3. Ibid., p. 8.
4. Ibid., p. 135.
5. Ibid., p. 143.
6. Ibid., p. 138.
7. Ibid., p. 167.

Left: Young Wheat, near Pomeroy, Washington

experience water shortages, which total 504,000 acre-feet per year.[8]

The Lower Snake subregion, which includes Hell's Canyon and the deep gorge through which the river flows across southeastern Washington, varies in elevation from 340 to more than 12,000 feet. It is unique in that it possesses more water than it needs or conceivably will need for irrigation in the foreseeable future. Both the Salmon and Clearwater Rivers, which, combined, contribute 40 percent of the water carried by the Snake at its mouth, enter the mainstem within the subregion. Since much of the land is dry farmed, only 5 percent of the runoff is used for irrigation. Where seasonal shortages do occur, they are in the upstream valleys of tributaries such as the Grand Ronde, the Salmon, the Lemhi, and the Pahsimeroi, where the problem is storage.

About 12 million acre-feet of surface water annually enter the subregion, while 34[9] million acre-feet leave it, netting a surplus discharge of 22 million acre-feet per year.

° ° °

4.

Of recent years, the word "surplus" has become emotionally charged, where the Pacific Northwest's water is concerned. At the present time, various regional and national agencies are taking inventory of how much water we have, where it is in short supply, where it exists in excess of needs, and how or whether transfers between have and have-not regions should be made. We will concern ourselves here only with the most recent survey, which has measured arable land and water in the Snake River Country and has projected food and fiber needs to the year 2020.

Now under irrigation in the watershed are 4.3 million acres, some of which suffer seasonal shortages of water. In its survey of lands that could be irrigated in the future, the Bureau of Reclamation divides them into three classes. These are:

> "*Class 1.* Alluvial windblown plains on relatively smooth slopes of less than 4 percent in general gradient. These lands are of excellent quality for irrigated agriculture and in all respects are suitable for sustained production of all climatically adapted crops. The soils are deep, well drained, medium textured, and easily worked. The water-holding capacity is excellent. . . .
>
> "*Class 2.* Lands commonly at higher elevations where soils may be shallower; in windblown areas where a significant amount of coarser material has accumulated; or in low-lying areas which may be subject to moderate drainage or flooding problems . . . of fairly good quality and capable of profitable production but have deficiencies which slightly affect their crop adaptability or yield or increase production costs. . . .
>
> "*Class 3.* Lands of fair to poor quality, having serious deficiencies which limit crop adaptability, restrict yield potential, increase production costs, or require special management to protect against erosion, waterlogging, or other hazards. . . ."

Potentially irrigable lands in the three categories are:

Class 1. 1,351,000 acres.
Class 2. 4,307,900 "
Class 3. 6,069,800 "

Thus, over the watershed as a whole, potentially irrigable lands total 11,728,700 acres.[1]

Since many political, social, and economic factors will influence bringing new lands under cultivation, we will not attempt to do any crystal-ball gazing here. But in talking to food and fiber experts and in studying Bureau of Reclamation reports, we have learned a few things that may be of interest to the reader:

(1) Climate is more important to the raising of food and fiber on irrigated lands than the way the land lies or the quality of the soil. The climate cannot be changed. But land does not have to be level to be irrigated by sprinklers, and soil deficiencies can be remedied to a great degree by chemical means.

(2) By the year 2020, it is estimated that three-fourths of the cultivated lands in the Snake River Country will be sprinkler-irrigated. Today, three fourths of those lands are watered by gravity flow.

(3) Economic projections predict an increased wood fiber demand and a downward trend in the forest land base. This means there is a need for significant increase in wood fiber yields. Irrigation of young trees by sprinklers, along with the application of fertilizers, may be useful for stimulating height and diameter growth during the sapling and pole stage. Foresters are currently experimenting with fertilizers and irrigation, both to test survival and response to these practices.[2]

(4) Farmers, food processors, government and private agronomists, and manufacturers of chemical fertilizers all are "Waiting for a signal" (as one food processor expresses it) to set off an explosion in food growing and processing

-----

8. Ibid., p. 170.
9. Corps of Engineers statistics quoted in Introduction say 36 million acre-feet.
1. *Irrigation,* PNRBC, p. 36, Table 11.
2. Ibid., p. 27.

Right:

FARM MURAL

Pond, farm buildings, and the wide sky of the grain country west of Grangeville, Idaho, combined with perfect light conditions on a February day to give us this picture. Though we drove past this farm many times, we saw it as in this view only once.

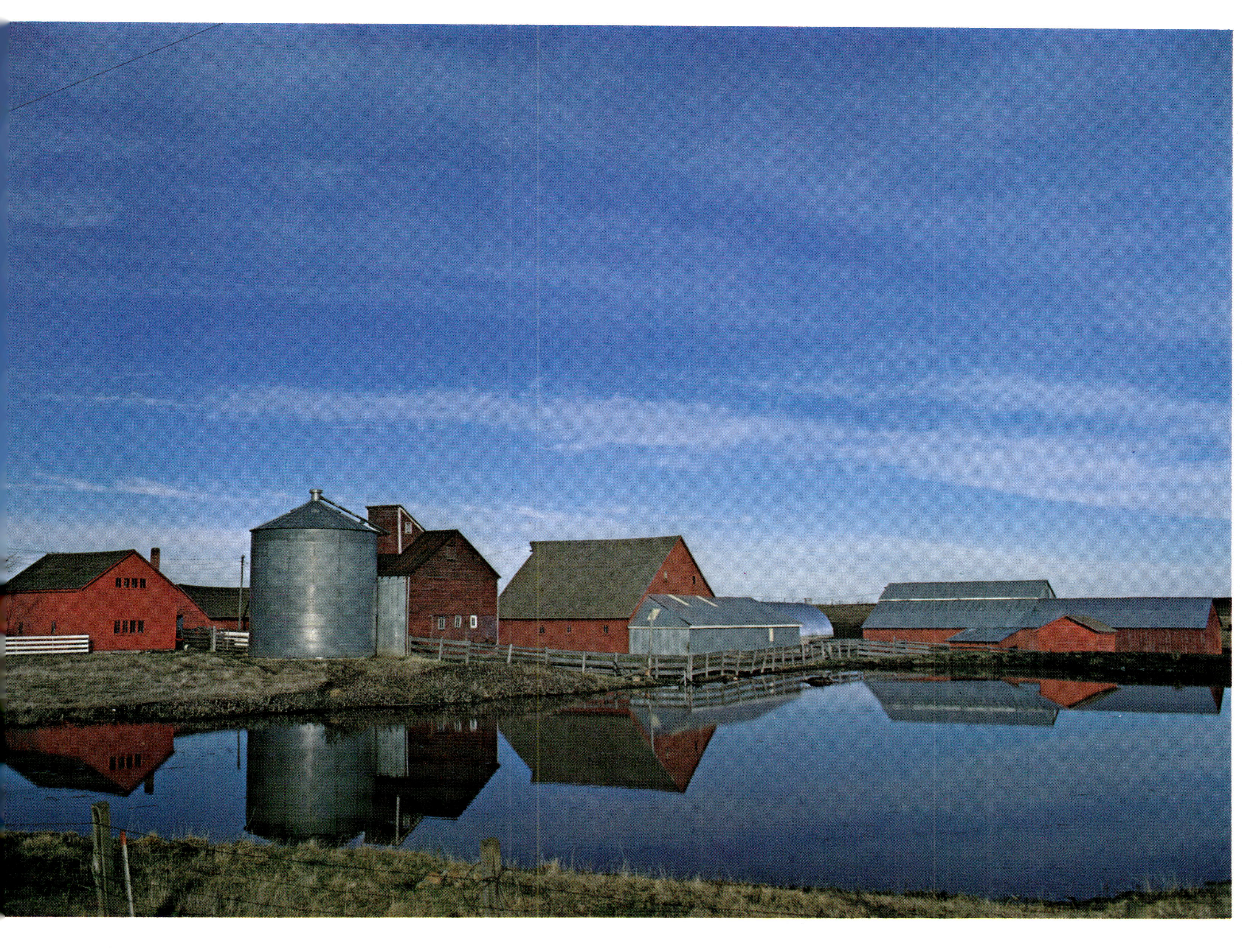

with new strains of seeds and new techniques. Economically, the signal will be the price they can get for their product. Socially, it will relate to how well and by what means this nation attempts to feed its people. Politically, it will tie into the question of whether we can or should feed the world's hungry.

(5) Assuming that the decision is made to give adequate water to all presently irrigated and all potentially irrigable lands in the Snake River Country, no water will out flow the region as surplus in the year 2020.

None? To be precise, less than none.

In the Upper Snake, there will be an annual shortage of 2.6 million acre-feet. In the Central Snake, there will be a shortage of 8.2 million acre-feet. In the Lower Snake, there will be a surplus of 6.2 million acre-feet; but if this water is transferred to the still thirsty lands upriver (as we may reasonably assume Year 2020 farmers will insist it be), the net shortage over the watershed as a whole will be 4.6 million acre-feet per year.[3]

Long range projections can only be based on past performance and present trends, of course. Where heavenly bodies are concerned, all the constants and variables are so well known and so precisely measured that our astronomers can project and predict far into the future with almost total accuracy.

But human bodies, despite all the studies made of them, maintain such erratic orbits individually and in clusters that plotting their collective course fifty years hence is more guesswork than mathematics. For example, at hand as I write this is an article by a historian who claims that the American "population explosion" is a myth. After quoting estimates that the population of the United States will be 375 million in the year 2000 and 939 million in the year 2050, he cites figures showing that the American birth rate has declined from 25.3 per 1,000 in 1957 to a historical low of 17.4 per 1,000 in 1968. He then says:

> "If this 'trend' is extended only 22 years into the future, the birth rate will be down to *zero*. . . ."[4]

Which set of predictions will be proven right in the year 2020 can be judged only by the hundreds of millions of people living in the Snake River Country at that time, or, if the last child is born twenty-two years hence, by the mere thousands of older people who will be tottering around wondering why having babies went out of fashion. But if a novelist who once studied to be a statistician and then gave it up because he could not cope with figures may be allowed to make a prediction of his own, this would be it:

The use of irrigation water and the development of new lands will increase slowly and steadily in the Snake River watershed. And enunciating the word "surplus" will be sure political death to any public figure who lets it fall trippingly off his tongue.

Since time began, great rivers have inspired a kind of romance peculiar to boats moving to and from the sea. Let us now take a nostalgic backward look at the Snake's sternwheeler days, then return to the workaday present for an unromantic whiff of diesel oil.

-----

3. Ibid., p. 48. In this report, the experts attempt to consider such factors as improvement in seed strains, increases in yields, population growth rate, and the amount of new land that may reasonably be expected to be brought under irrigation during the next fifty years. If these factors are kept in balance with projected food and fiber needs, the total acreage of new land irrigated in the year 2020 would be 2,200,000, rather than the 11,728,700 mentioned here. But with 9,500,000 acres of irrigable land still dry, it is doubtful that 2020 farmers would willingly give away their water—and their future.

4. "It's Time to Defuse Population Explosion," by Thomas C. Jermann, *National Observer,* July 27, 1970, p. 10. Dr. Jermann is a professor of history at Rockhurst College, Kansas City, Missouri. This essay originally appeared in the Kansas City *Times.*

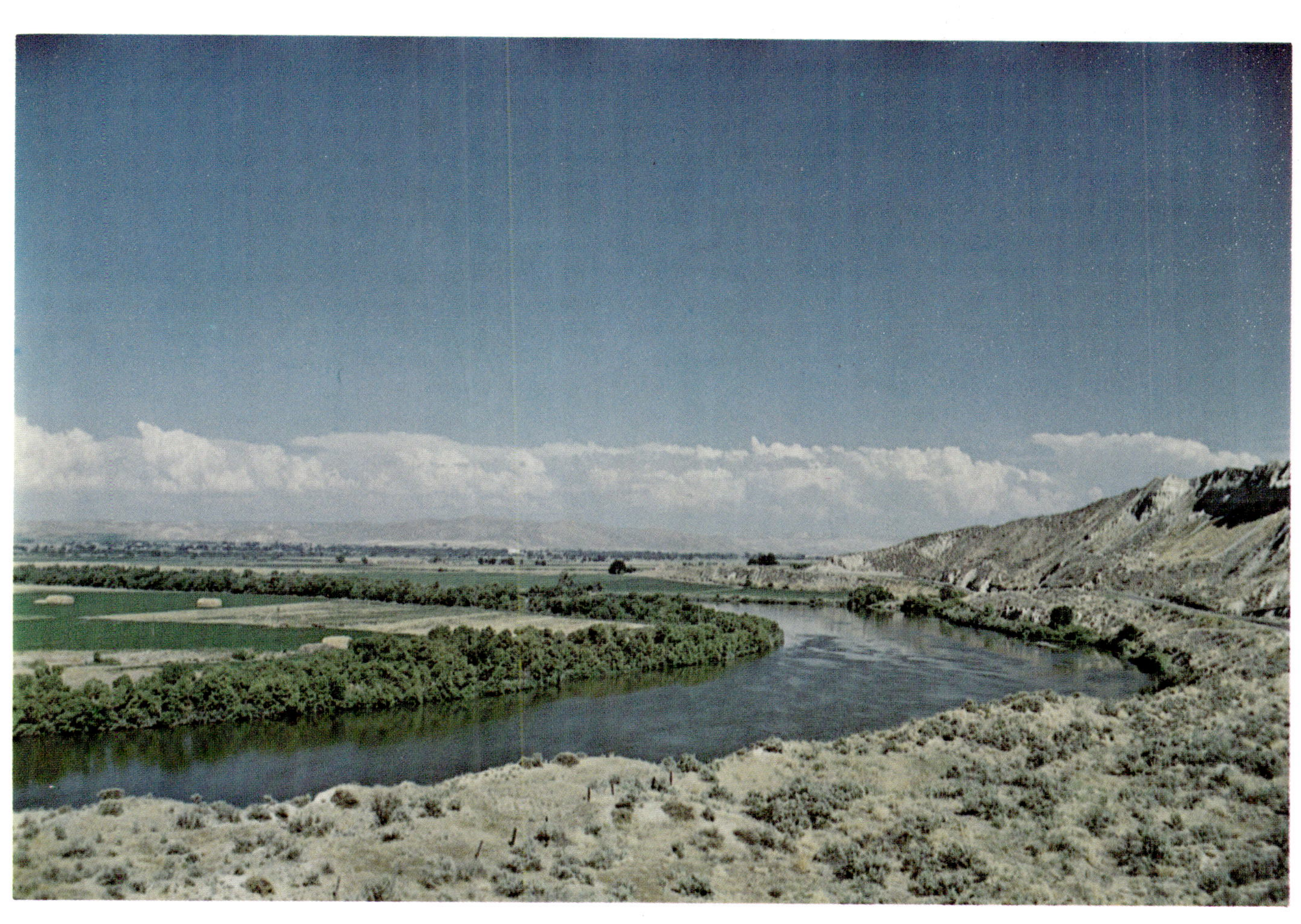

Snake River, near Ontario, Oregon

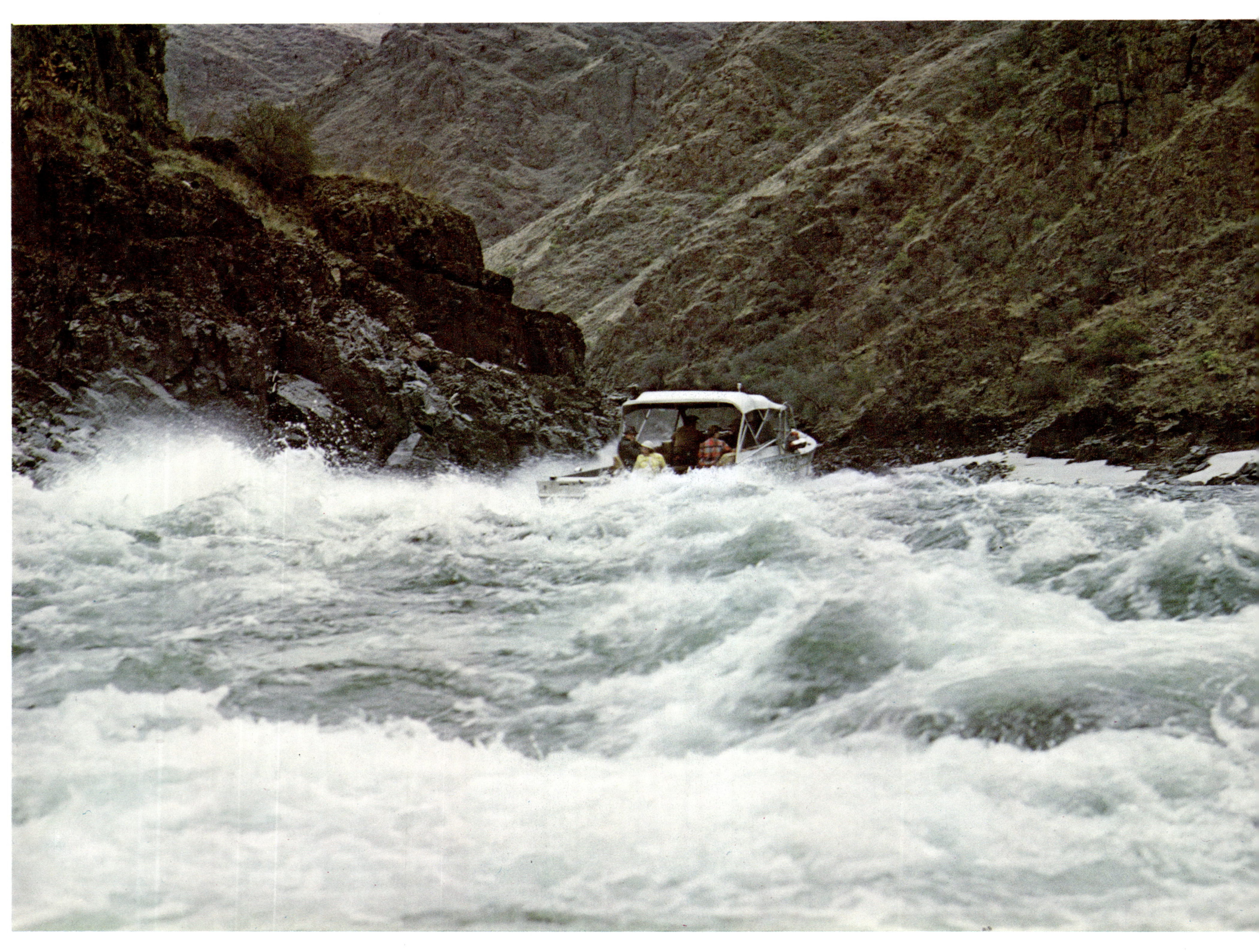

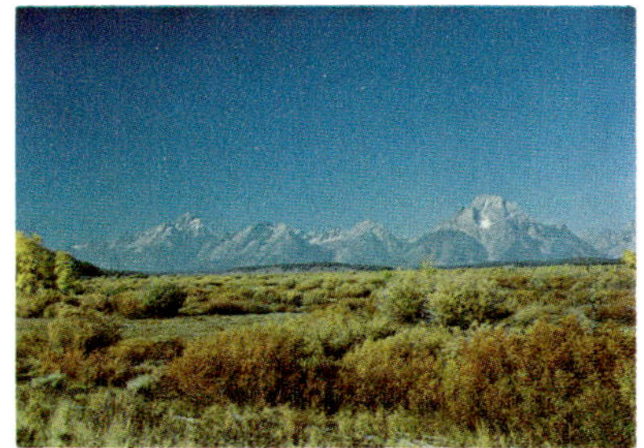

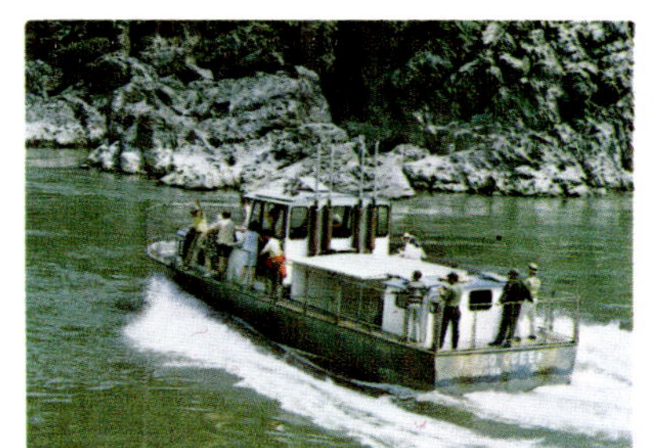

PART SEVEN

River of Transport

1.

The Snake long has been classified as a navigable river by the federal government, but proving it to be one has been left to the nerve, strength, judgment, and skill of a handful of daring men. Lewis and Clark made dugout canoes and floated from the forks of the Clearwater to the mouth of the Snake in 1805. In 1811, the Wilson Price Hunt party attempted to negotiate the middle Snake, came to disaster at Caldron Linn, split into three sections, and, after many hardships, eventually reached Astoria.

Donald McKenzie, who led the party that traveled north through the Salmon River Mountains and made its way to Astoria a full month ahead of the others, was a remarkable man. Redheaded, strong as a bull, and weighing 320 pounds, he literally was big enough to go bear hunting with a switch. More important, his tact in dealing with Indians, his courage, and his talent for leadership were in proportion to his size.

Following the breakup of the Astor enterprise, McKenzie became Chief Factor for the North West Company, in charge of the Snake River Country operations. In the spring of 1819, he and six of his men proved the Hell's Canyon sector of the Snake navigable after a fashion when they rowed, pushed, and pulled a loaded barge from the mouth of the Clearwater upriver to the vicinity of Farewell Bend. Sending four of the men back downriver with the barge, McKenzie wrote with qualified elation:

> "*Point Successful, Head of the Narrows, April 15th, 1819.* The passage by water is now proved to be safe and practicable for loaded boats, without one single carrying place or portage; therefore, the doubtful question is set at rest forever. Yet from the force of the current and the frequency of the rapids it may still be advisable, and perhaps preferable, to continue the land transport. . . .
>
> "We had often recourse to the line. There are two places with bold cut rocks on either side of the river, where the great body of water is compressed within a narrow compass, which may render those parts doubtful during the floods, owing to rocks and whirlpools, but there are only two, and neither of them are long. . . ."[1]

Left: Running the Rapids of the Lower Salmon in a Twin-Jet Boat.

Since the round trip had required two months of superhuman effort, it was not repeated. In fact, fifty years passed before a boat of any size ventured into the treacherous rapids of Hell's Canyon again.

On the lower reaches of the river during the summer of 1861, a unique attempt at commercial navigation was made by a sailboat. It was built by W. H. Gray, a salty, plain-spoken carpenter who had come west in 1836 and been employed by Spalding and Whitman, with both of whom he soon quarreled. Always a man of positive opinions, Gray said of his first son, who was born in 1845:

> "I named him after President Polk. When I named him, the President had taken a strong stand on 54-40 or fight. Polk reversed his attitude on that question and I have been sorry I called my boy after him ever since. Sometimes I have a notion to wring the youngster's neck, I am so disgusted with President Polk. . . ."[2]

Fortunately for Snake River navigation history, young William Polk Gray did not get his neck wrung by his irate

1. *The Fur Hunters of the Far West,* by Alexander Ross, London, Smith, Elder, 1855; reprint edited by Kenneth A. Spaulding, University of Oklahoma Press, 1956, pp. 138, 139.

2. "Reminiscenses of Captain William P. Gray," by Fred Lockley, *Oregon Historical Quarterly,* XIV, No. 4, December, 1913, pp. 321-41. Other quotes from Gray in this chapter have been taken from the same source.

father; instead, he began learning the ways of rivers at the tender age of thirteen. During the ensuing fifty years, he became the most colorful riverman in the Pacific Northwest—and if in his old age he tended to exaggerate his adventures a bit, his license to do so had been honorably earned.

Even though the stern-wheeler *Colonel Wright* had ascended the Snake fifty miles to the mouth of the Palouse River in 1860, and, the following year, had carried passengers and cargo to the forks of the Clearwater, Portland merchants remained so skeptical of the Snake's navigability that the senior William Gray could obtain no freight for his boat. But he was a very stubborn man. Mortgaging everything he owned, he bought a stock of goods for the Idaho mines, shipped them up the Columbia to the mouth of the Deschutes where his sailboat was waiting, and set sail for the interior.

At Wallula, his entire crew deserted, declaring the Snake too dangerous to be navigated. From that point, William Gray, Jr., who was then fifteen years old, tells the story:

> "Father finally secured a new crew of seven men and on September 20, 1861, we left Wallula. It took us three days to reach the mouth of the Snake, a distance of only 11 miles. The prevailing winds were directly across the current, so that it was necessary for us to cordell the boat almost the entire way.
>
> "Another boy and myself took ropes in a skiff up the stream and found a place where the rope could be made fast. We would then come downstream bringing the rope to our boat where the rope was made fast to the capstan and the rope would be slowly wound up. We had a difficult trip to Lewiston and before we got there my comrade and myself in the skiff had demonstrated that there was not a single rapid in the Snake River that could not be swum. . . ."

Below Five Mile Rapids, young Gray told his father that the current was too dangerous to be swum and that it would be impossible to find any place to secure a rope by which the unwieldy boat could be pulled upriver.

> "My son," his father replied, " 'can't' isn't in my dictionary. Anything can be done if you want to do it badly enough. If you are overturned, you and the skiff will both come downstream. You may not come down together, but you will both come down. You will then go back and make another attempt and continue to do so until you have succeeded. . . ."

How many unsuccessful attempts were made to secure the rope around the rapids-surrounded rock and how many times the two boys and the skiff came bouncing downstream separately or together are details young Gray did not record. But he wrote:

> "After that experience there has never been any combination of wood, iron, or water that has ever scared me. . . ."

After forty days of wet, gruelling, dangerous work, the boat reached Lewiston, where the goods it carried were sold at a substantial profit. Now a seasoned riverman, young Gray worked for several years as a captain of sailboats plying the Columbia between Deschutes and Wallula Landing, being paid the princely wage of $150 per month. Carrying twenty-five to twenty-eight tons of freight each trip, he made as many as five round trips a month.

By the summer of 1864, steam had replaced sail on the upper Columbia and the Snake; so young Gray went to work as a cub pilot on the stern-wheeler *Yakima*. While in port at Lewiston one day, he was approached by a millowner from Asotin, a few miles up the Snake on the Washington Territory side. Lumber here was worth only $15 per thousand, the millowner said, while at the booming port of Umatilla Landing on the Columbia, it could be sold at $55. Did young Gray think it possible to take a raft of lumber down the Snake without its being broken up and lost as all previous rafts floated into the rapids had been?

Gray thought it possible ". . . if you will get the right man . . ." and told the sawmill owner who the right man was—himself. Given a leave of absence from his duties as a cub pilot, Gray picked up a raft containing fifty thousand board feet of lumber at the Asotin mill, floated it down to Lewiston, added another ten thousand board feet there, then embarked on the 180-mile journey down the Snake and Columbia. Atwood, the millowner, was aboard, as apprehensive as Gray was confident.

During previous unsuccessful attempts to float lumber rafts down the river, crews had tried to manage them with side sweeps; all Gray used was a steering oar at the rear. When approaching a rapid, his predecessors had made desperate efforts to keep to the edge and avoid the faster water; in the same situation, Gray steered the raft directly toward the center of the rapid, where the current's force gave the clumsy craft such impetus that it quickly shot through into slack water. If worst came to worst, Gray knew that for him all the rapids were swimmable—a piece of information likely of small comfort to Mr. Atwood.

As they barreled down the Snake at a brisk nine miles an hour, Gray cheerfully told his employer that they would get along all right until they came to the Palouse Rapids. There they were going to have a serious time of it, he warned, for the water poured through a narrow chute and emptied into an eddy, which boiled back toward the current from the south shore.

> "When we got to the Palouse Rapids I sent the raft into the center," Gray wrote. "The current was so swift it shot us into the eddy. The forward part of the raft went under water and the current from the chute caught the back end of the raft and sent it under water. We stayed on the raft until the water was up to our knees. The skiff which we had on the raft started to float off, but I caught the painter and we got aboard. We brought the skiff over where the

raft had been and felt down with the oars but we could not touch the raft.

"We floated down with the current. All I attempted to do was keep the skiff on its course. Atwood said, 'I knew you couldn't do it. With such rapids as the Palouse, it was foolish to think you could.'

"I felt pretty serious, for I was afraid the eddy had broken the fastenings on the raft and we would soon run into the wreckage of floating boards. About half a mile below the rapids our skiff was suddenly lifted out of the water by the reappearance of the raft. Both had gone with the current, and, oddly enough, the raft had appeared directly under us.

"You never saw a man more surprised or delighted than Atwood. . . ."

Small wonder that Mr. Atwood was pleased. If Gray's account may be believed, he had brought a raft of lumber worth $900 at Lewiston to Umatilla Landing in two days' time, where it sold for $3,300. Since Gray's wages were ten dollars a day, Mr. Atwood had made a net profit of $2,400 on his $20 investment in the cub pilot's services.

We shall return presently to relate further Snake River adventures of William Polk Gray in his own inimitable words. But now let's go back to the first stern-wheeler to ply the Snake, the *Colonel Wright,* and *its* inimitable pilot, Captain Leonard White, who steered a far truer course through the rocks of white-water rapids than he did through the shoals of the King's English.

° ° °

2.

Though Len White was a master of rivers, he made misspelling a science in the frequent letters he wrote newspapers on matters of navigation. This excerpt is typical:

> "I anticipat that navigashun wil be opened az far as Ujen Siti [Eugene City] the kuming winter, if the good inhabitants will alou us to Bush-hwak abuve Korvalis [Corvallis] . . . the smal timber that groz along the ej wil be ov yus for Bush-hwaking. . . ."[1]

Should the reader be intrigued, as I was, with this odd use of the obviously misspelled word "Bush-whacking," a now obsolete meaning of the word was: "Pulling a boat against the current by grasping bushes along the bank." In the early 1800s, the speaking style of a politician who sawed the air with his hands also was called "Bushwhacking" by country folk.[2]

-----

1. Oregon City *Argus*, May 19, 1855; quoted in "Frontier Humor in Oregon," by Randall V. Mills, *OHQ*, XLIII, No. 4, December, 1942, p. 345.

2. *A Dictionary of Americanisms on Historical Principles*, edited by Mitford M. Matthews, University of Chicago Press, 1951, p. 228.

Following the building of the *Colonel Wright* by Lawrence W. Coe and Robert R. Thompson at the mouth of the Deschutes River in 1859, Captain Len White piloted it on regular runs as far up the Columbia as Wallula Landing. The boat had a mast carrying a huge square sail, which was used when the wind was favorable. Fuel was a problem, for no trees grew along this stretch of river.

In the spring of 1860, an army quartermaster engaged the stern-wheeler to carry supplies to a depot at the mouth of the Palouse. Then the next summer, June, 1861, Seth Slater, a Portland merchant, offered a full cargo of supplies to be taken upriver to the closest landing point feasible near the Idaho mines.

> "After entering the Snake River the captain touched at an island where an enormous tree had lodged from a former high water, and the crew and volunteer passengers were landed with axes to add to the supply of fuel. Upon disturbing the trunk of the tree a nest of rattlesnakes was also disturbed and a vicious war ensued in which a dozen snakes were killed, two of tremendous size."[3]

Near the mouth of the Palouse River, a ferry had been installed across the Snake. The cable to which it was attached barred the steamer's way. Heated words ensued between the ferryman and Len White, it being the ferryman's contention that the Snake was not navigable above this point, while White argued it *would be* if the cable were removed. In attempting to pass over the slacked-off cable, the boat's stern-wheel caught and snapped it—and the ferryman went out of business.

Palouse Rapids, directly upstream, was running in full early summer flood. For two hours, the *Colonel Wright* fought the current, conquered it at long last, and chugged on. At the next white water, which Captain White named "Texas Rapids" (a euphemism for a much drier, hotter place), a line was put out ahead, the sail was raised to catch the strong westerly breeze, the stern-wheeler threshed at full speed ahead, and the boat lurched forward so suddenly that the cable went slack, fouling into the paddle wheel before it could be hauled in. A landing was made and an hour spent cutting it free.

> "A little farther up the river the boat overtook a party of mounted Indians who were engaged in trying to ascertain its speed by first walking their horses, then trotting, then galloping them. Their experiments amused the passengers for some miles until a rocky bluff shut them off from view. . . ."

After tying up for the night, which was whiled away with music and song, the steamer proceeded upriver at dawn next day, reaching the mouth of the Clearwater with no great difficulty. Following a brief stop at Lapwai Creek,

-----

3. "Up Snake River," by L. W. Coe, *Overland Monthly*, August, 1886, Vol. 8, 2nd Series. Coe was one of the owners of the *Colonel Wright*.

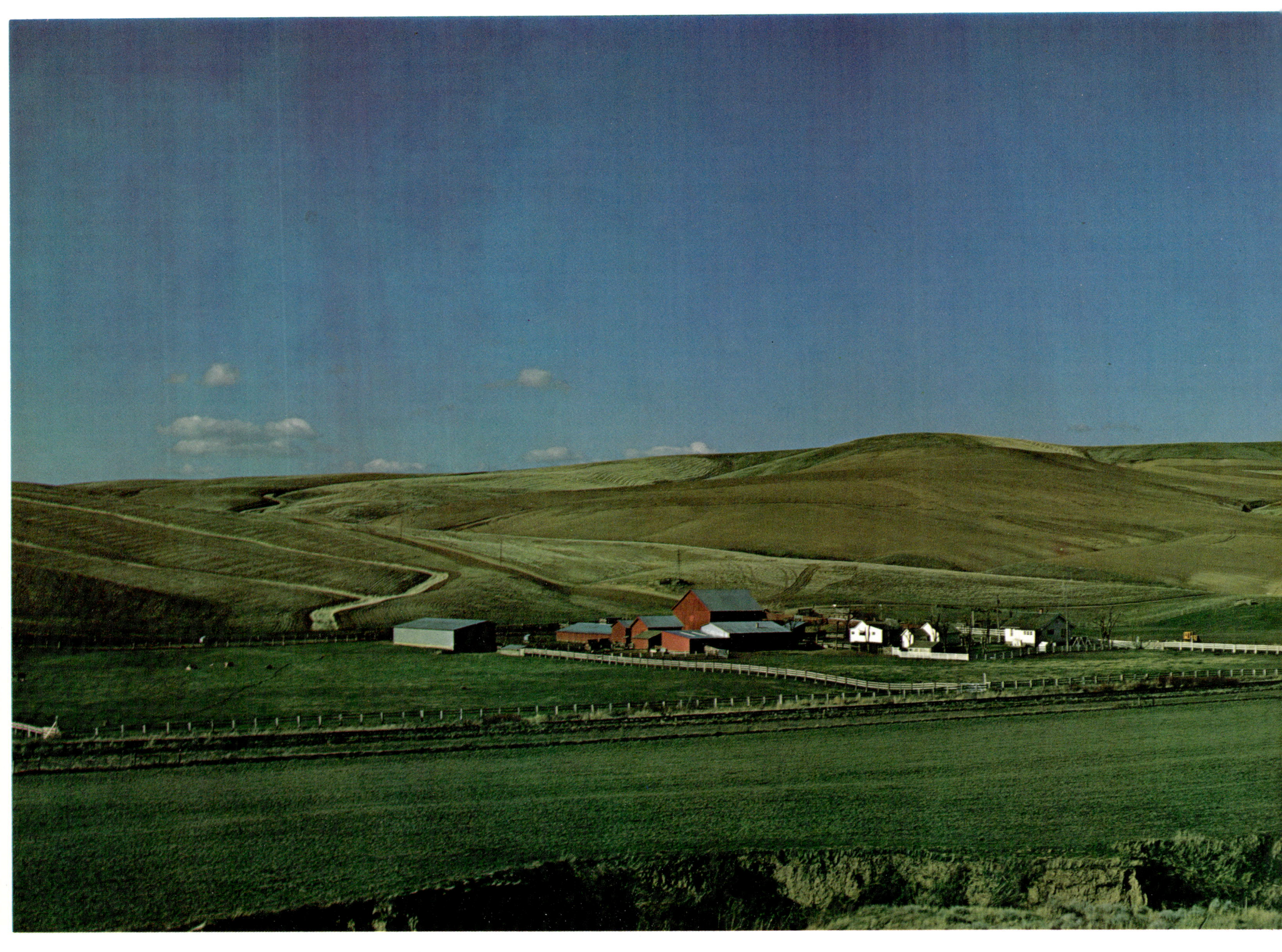

Above: A Typical Wheat Ranch in Southeastern, Washington, near Pomeroy.

Right:

PALOUSE FALLS, LOWER SNAKE

Near here at what is called the Marmes Dig evidence of man dating back 11,000 years has been found. Before the area could be completely explored and its artifacts saved, backwaters from Lower Monumental Dam, whose building schedule could not (or would not) be altered, threatened to flood the site. In a last-minute, poorly planned effort to save the site, a million-dollar dike was thrown around it. It leaked—and the site was flooded anyway.

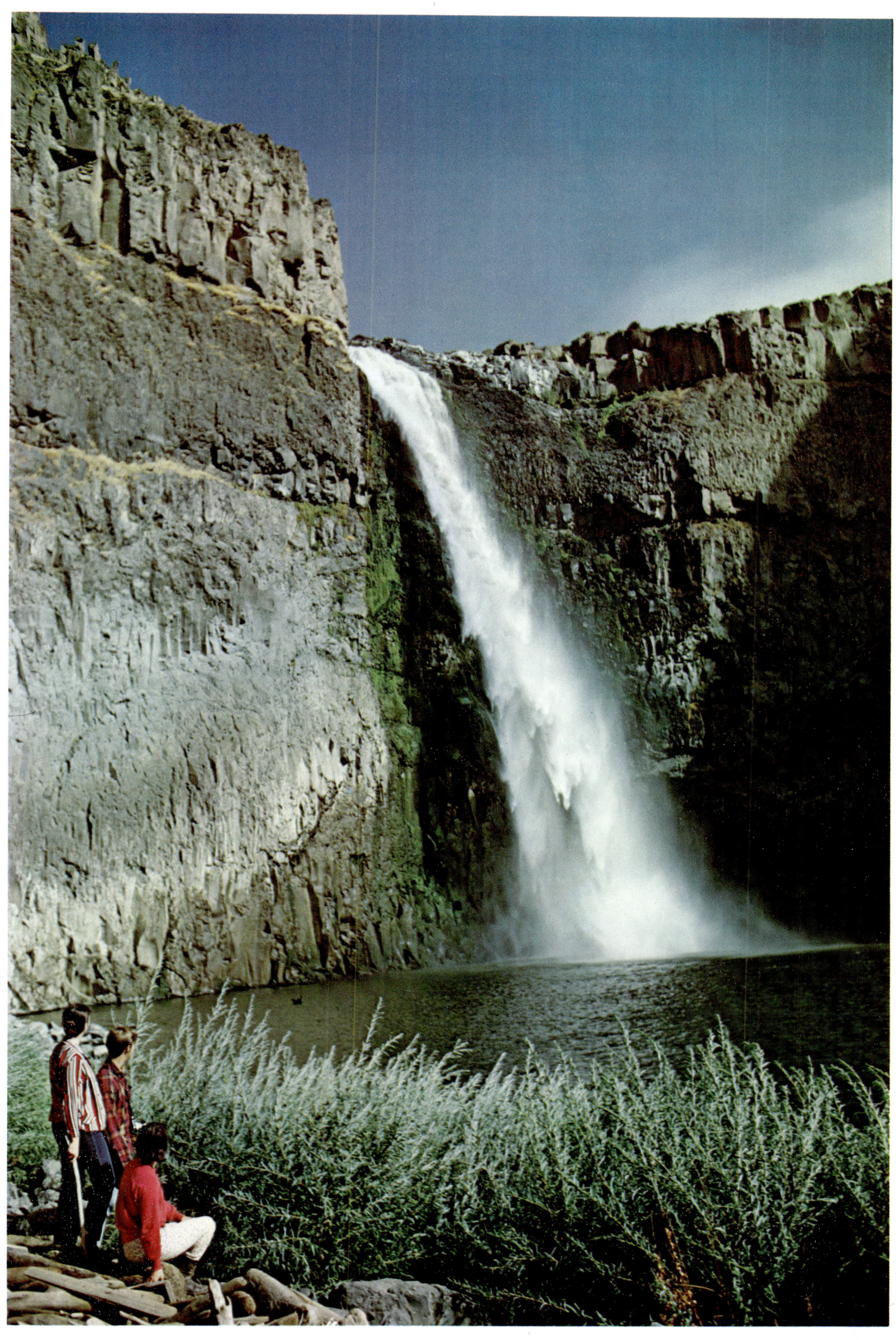

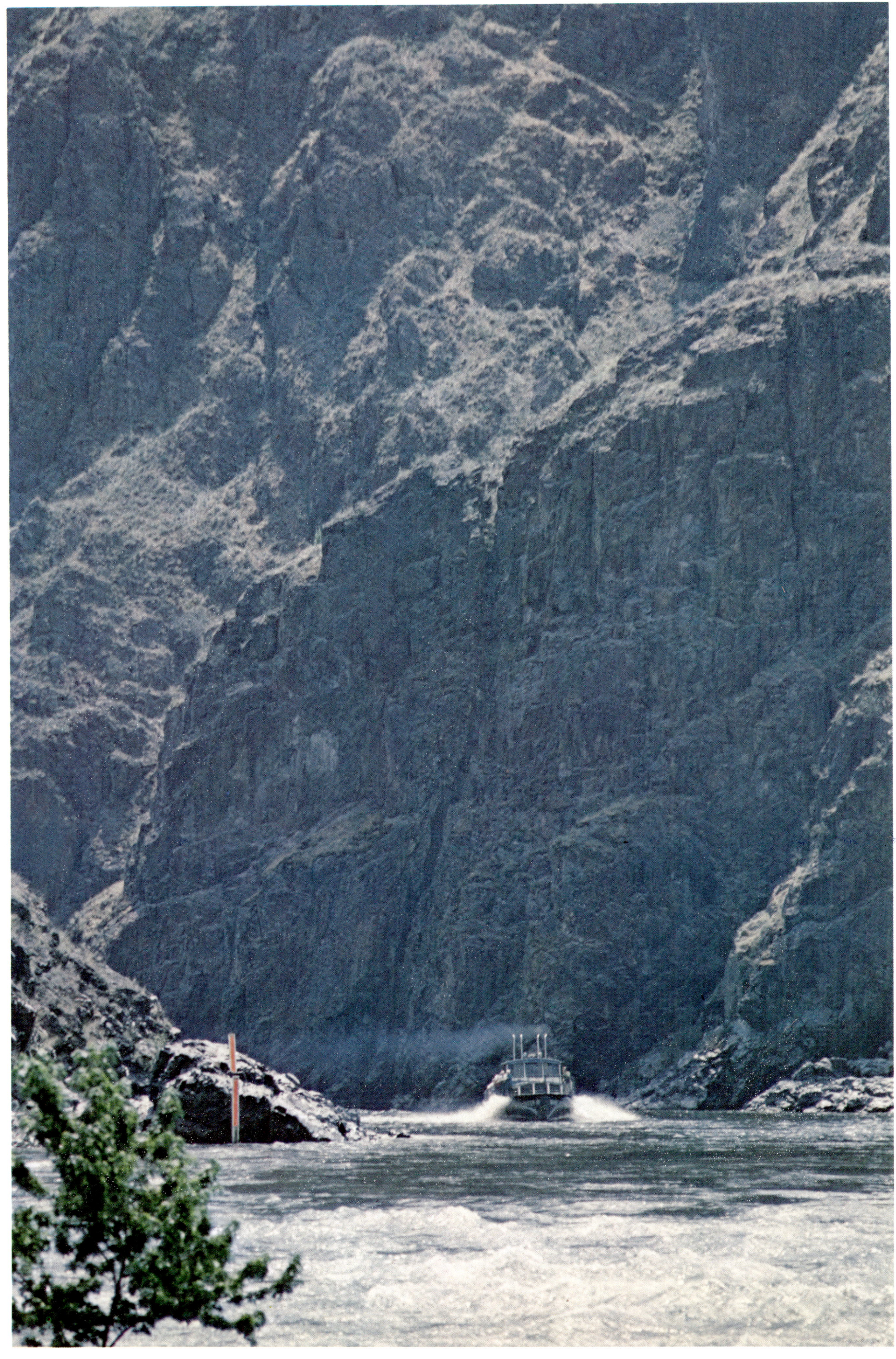

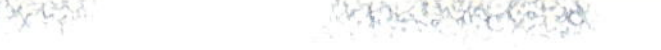

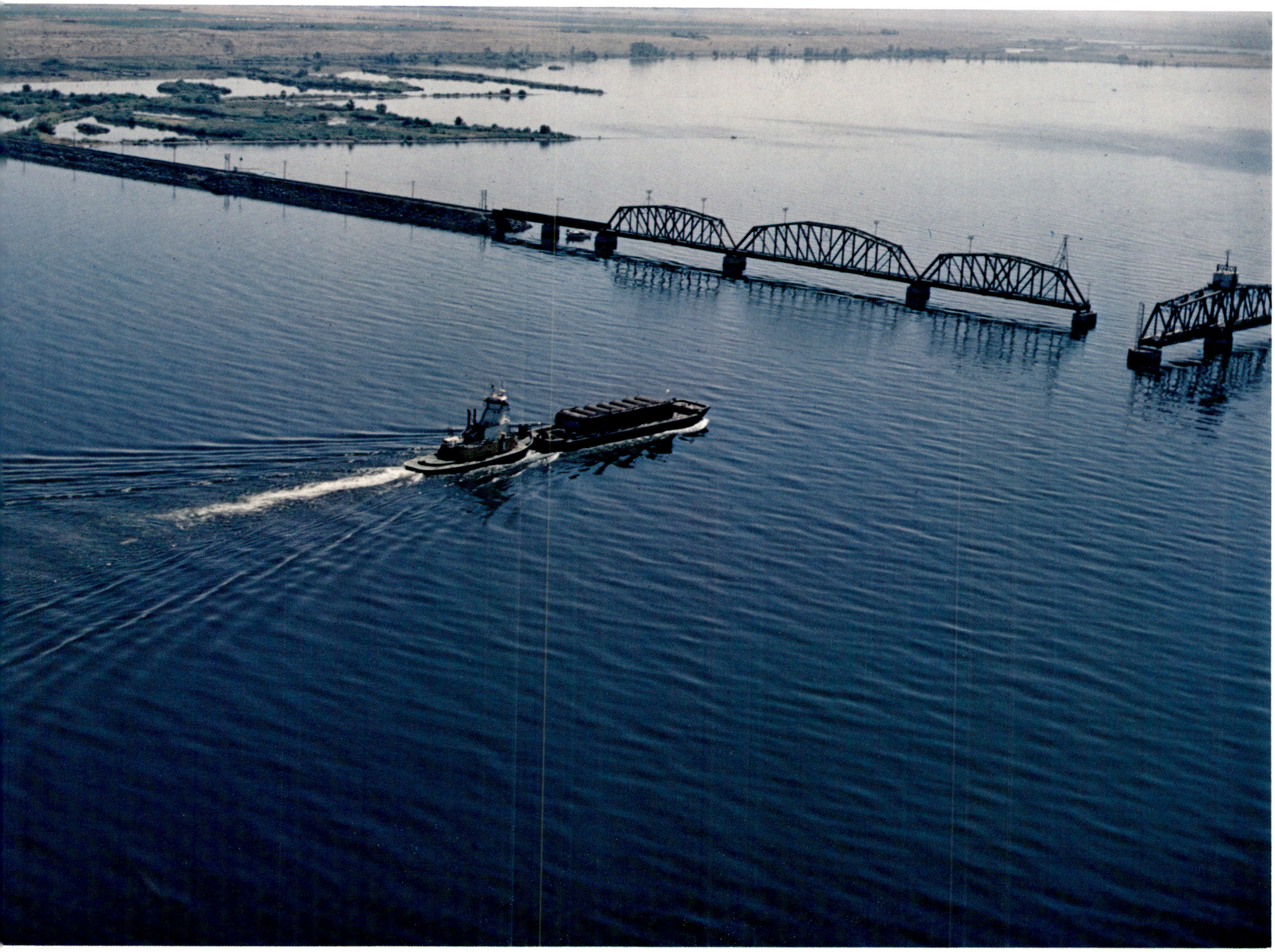

Above:

MOUTH OF THE SNAKE

Tugboat and barge approach a railroad bridge where the Snake and the Columbia blend their waters.

Left:

HELL'S CANYON DELIVERY

Mail, groceries, newspapers, and other necessities are carried to remote spots by the Lewiston based "Idaho Queen," which is operated by the Dick Rivers Navigation Company. Because of increasing traffic and interest in the region, there are now three "Queens." Here, "Idaho Queen I" meets us near the mouth of the Salmon.

where Chief Lawyer cried: "Look! Here comes a water wagon!" the agent and the Nez Perce chief were taken aboard. Twenty-five miles farther upriver, just below the mouth of the North Fork of the Clearwater, Captain White decided that he could go no farther with safety, and Seth Slater's merchandise was landed.

During the next three weeks, the *Colonel Wright* and another steamer, the *Okanagon*, made two more trips up the Clearwater, but as the water level fell it became obvious that the practical head of navigation must be the tongue of land where the Clearwater joined the Snake.

Thus, Lewiston was born. On the opposite shore of the Snake, its twin, Clarkston, came into being.

The trip upriver from Deschutes had taken three and a half days. The return downstream was accomplished in eighteen hours.

As the northern Idaho mines boomed and more sternwheelers began to ply the lower river, Lewiston dreamed of commercial grandeur. Discounting all previous reports of the obstacles to navigation upriver, the town promoters dispatched a scouting expedition in the early autumn of 1862 to determine the "possibility of navigating Snake River with light draught steamers from that point to Fort Boise." The report turned in by the "three reliable men" was highly favorable.

> "The entire distance from Lewiston to Fort Boise is only one hundred and thirty-five miles!" the *Golden Age* declared rapturously. "They found nothing in the river to impede navigation whatever, and pronounced it feasible at any season of the year unless it be by ice. . . .
>
> "A new route will now be opened for steam, the results of which cannot now be foretold. We shall penetrate Nevada and Utah Territories by steam, as it is well known that it is only 90 miles from Fort Boise to Salmon Falls on Snake River. Salmon Falls is within 250 miles of Salt Lake. . . .
>
> "But a few more suns will rise and set before the shrill whistle of the steamer will reverberate along the banks of this noble river, and its echo will be heard for ages yet to come through the ravines, gorges, and canyons, and on the mountain tops of our golden land, as a symbol of ambition, perseverance, and goaheadativeness. . . ."[4]

Unfortunately for the goaheadativeness of the Lewiston promoters, a miscalculation or two had occurred. For one thing, the scouts had underestimated distances by at least a hundred miles. For another, their description of the country they were supposed to have scouted bore little resemblance to reality. So more than a few suns passed before even a reconnaisance by steamer was made up the river of "no impediments." In fact, it was not until two years later that the sturdy stern-wheeler *Colonel Wright* set out upstream.

By then, Captain Len White no longer was in command. He had quit in a huff when the Oregon Steam Navigation Company suggested his five hundred dollar a month salary was excessive. Conning the boat now was Captain Thomas J. Stump. The assistant pilot was William Polk Gray, at eighteen years of age a veteran riverman. Other accounts of this particular venture upriver may be more trustworthy in detail than Gray's, but compared to his they are lukewarm stuff. After listing the names of the crew and passengers, (his father being one of the latter) he wrote:

> "We went up the river to about twenty-five miles above Salmon River. In attempting to make a dangerous eddy at this point, the boat was caught in a bad eddy, thrown into the current and upon a sharp rock reef jutting out from the Idaho shore. It carried away eight feet of her bow, keel and sides to her deck. Things looked desperate for a moment. Captain Stump gave an order from the pilot house to get out a line on shore. You never saw such a universal willingness to get on shore with that line. Every deckhand, the mate, the chief engineer, the fireman and our two passengers, who were standing forward watching the boat, seized the line by both ends, the middle and wherever they could get a hold of it and jumped ashore.
>
> "The only people left on the boat were Captain Stump and myself in the pilothouse, the second engineer, who was below, and old Titus, the cook. Before they could make the line fast the boat was caught by the current and went down the river half a mile. Here Captain Stump succeeded in beaching her. We were here joined by the ambitious line-carriers, who walked down the shore. . . ."[5]

After patchwork repairs were made on her battered hull, the *Colonel Wright* ran back to Lewiston, covering the distance it had taken her four and a half days to ascend in three and a half hours. The point she had reached, 237 miles above the mouth of the Snake, remains today the practical limit of navigation even for jet-powered boats.

Now that it had been established that a steamer could not go through Hell's Canyon, the Oregon Steam Navigation Company considered the possibility of taking a boat around the obstacle. Owned by Portland interests, the company had a profitable monopoly on the freight and passenger traffic ascending the Columbia and Snake to the north Idaho mines. But following the Boise Basin and Owyhee strikes in southern Idaho, passenger traffic from San Francisco began to favor the water route to Sacramento, thence by stage to Red Bluff, California, and northeast across the Nevada desert.

Over this route, the fare from San Francisco to Idaho

-----

4. "Steamboat Down the Snake," by Merle Wells, *Idaho Yesterdays*, Vol. 5, No. 4, Winter, 1961-62.

5. "Reminiscenses," Gray.

City was only $66. By sea to Portland, up the Columbia to Umatilla Landing, then across the Blue Mountains by stage, the ticket price came to $123. Furthermore, since the ocean voyage often was rough and disasters frequent, more and more people bound for the south Idaho mines were bypassing Portland.

> "We must leave 'no stone unturned' to divert all the Boise and Owyhee trade this way," wrote a Portland OSN official. "Hence the building of a steamboat on Snake River to run from Olds Ferry to a point equidistant from Owyhee and Boise City is not a matter of choice but necessity. . . ."[6]

Olds Ferry was located on the Idaho side of the Snake opposite Farewell Bend. By building a steamer that would ply the relatively tranquil 125 miles between the eastern base of the Blue Mountains and the Boise City-Owyhee road, the OSN hoped to divert traffic back to Portland, cut into the revenues of the Oregon-Idaho stage companies, and give the owners of the San Francisco-Red Bluff route something to worry about. If the Snake proved navigable as far upriver as Salmon Falls, a connection might even be made with Salt Lake and the transcontinental railroad hopefully soon to come.

A shipyard was established near the mouth of the Boise River, and in late autumn of 1865 lumber to be used in the steamer began to arrive. Her boilers, engines, and metal parts had to be transported up the Columbia to Umatilla Landing, then freighted across the Blues over often impassable roads. Since the Indian troubles of 1866-68 were beginning at this time, arrows and bullets fired by hostiles now and then made workmen scramble for shelter. But on April 20, 1866, the *Shoshone,* as the steamer built on the western edge of the Idaho desert was named, was launched with enthusiastic ceremony.

On her maiden voyage, the *Shoshone* proved the Snake navigable between Olds Ferry and a point a few miles upstream from the mouth of the Bruneau River. During the summer of 1866, she made several runs from Olds Ferry to Owyhee Ferry, and, though operating at a loss, did have an effect on the rate war. Coal deposits had been discovered along the banks of the Snake in this area, but the coal was of such low grade that it was useless as a fuel. Like most of the country along the middle and lower Snake, the banks were treeless and the supply of firewood soon was exhausted. In August, 1866, John C. Ainsworth of the OSN was forced to report:

> "Our Snake River boat is laid up for want of wood. We do not think of starting her again before next spring, at which time, if we succeed in getting wood and making the proper connections, she will do a fair business. . . ."

———

6. "Steamboat Down the Snake," Wells, p. 25. Other quotes in this chapter are taken from the same source.

But the wood problem could not be solved. For three years the *Shoshone* lay idle at her moorings, then in 1869 the officials of the OSN decided to take a risky gamble. The steamer would be brought downriver through Hell's Canyon.

> "A more perilous and uncertain adventure has never been undertaken in these waters," wrote an editor of the period, "and we shall watch its progress with interest. The canyon between Powder River and the mouth of the Salmon is said to be seventy miles long and supposed to be a continuous succession of rapids the whole way. . . . River men have always considered it an impossibility to navigate the canyon even with a small boat. . . ."

Under the skilled hands of Captain Cy Smith and his crew, the inland-built steamer was brought from Owyhee Landing into the upper reaches of Hell's Canyon by late June, 1869, where low water and desertion by her crew forced her to tie up near a stream still known as Steamboat Creek until the following spring. Then another OSN crew under experienced Captain Sebastian Miller, supplied with plenty of fuel and heavy rope, maneuvered her through the hazardous rocks and rapids of the canyon's depths and brought her badly battered hulk down to Lewiston in late April, 1870.

Eventually, the *Shoshone* was taken through the tamer rapids of the lower Snake, over the Columbia's Celilo Falls, and through the upper and lower Cascades—white water that could be run downstream by a handful of daring pilots when the river was in flood. Later, the still restless steamboat was taken up the Willamette River, hauled around the Oregon City falls, and plied the upper reaches of the river until wrecked near Salem in 1874. Next spring, when high water cast her hulk ashore, a farmer detached her pilothouse and converted it into a chicken coop—the final ignominy for a well-traveled lady who never was really at home in any river.

° ° °

3.

On the Idaho side of Hell's Canyon, the Seven Devils Mountains rise brown and sere from the water's edge to peaks as high as 9,400 feet. Directly west, on the Oregon side, the Wallowa Mountains top or approach 10,000 feet. Catching most of the rain and snowfall brought in from the Pacific by the southwesterly winds, the Wallowas look from a high-flying plane better timbered, better watered, and far more hospitable than the rocky, grim, forbidding Seven Devils, and the Snake itself winds like a smooth silver thread through what appears to be a table contour relief map whose most impressive vistas are horizontal.

But from the deck of a boat borne on the turbulent surface of the water, the view changes dramatically. The pilot stands with feet braced and hands holding onto something solid, aware of towering rock walls to the right, left, behind, ahead, and, most frightening of all, unseen under the foaming rapids through which his craft is being hurtled. In seventy-five miles, which is the extent of the canyon proper, he knows that the water will fall from an elevation of 1,500 to 900 feet. If his is only the third craft in recorded history to descend this stretch of river, we might reasonably expect that even a veteran riverman whom no combination of wood, iron, or water ever had scared would be seriously concerned for the fate of his boat and crew.

Unless he was William Polk Gray, that is, bringing the *Norma* downriver in 1895.

In 1891, there was a flurry of mining excitement called the Seven Devils boom in the upper reaches of Hell's Canyon. Rails had moved into the Snake River Country by then, the Union Pacific having built what was called the Short Line to Portland along the route of the Oregon Trail. Like all mining booms, Seven Devils was to be the "biggest ever." The run of the *Norma,* which was built on the banks of the Snake near Huntington, Oregon, was to be from the railroad connection downriver to Seven Devils Landing, a distance of sixty miles. If traffic warranted, she would also run upriver to Weiser or beyond—providing draws were put into the three bridges which the Union Pacific had built across the Snake without stopping to consider that steamboats might wish to use the river.

The *Norma* was 160 feet long, 32 feet wide, six feet deep in the hold, and drew forty inches of water under her normal load of two hundred tons. Soon after her launching in the spring of 1891, she proved she could run downriver to Seven Devils Landing and back by making a successful trip. But when she attempted to steam upriver, neither pleas, threats, nor lawsuits aimed at the Union Pacific, the War Department, or anyone else the steamer's owners appealed to could remove the inconsiderately built bridges. After several years of unprofitable traffic on a limited stretch of river, the owners decided to do as the OSN had done earlier with the *Shoshone*—bring her downriver.

The man chosen to accomplish the feat was Captain William Polk Gray, now fifty years old, with thirty-seven of those years spent on Pacific Northwest rivers. Though he did not trouble to write a first-hand account of the epic trip of the *Norma* until he reached the age of seventy-five, he did give a verbal report to a newspaper of the day. Despite the time lapse between the two accounts, there are remarkably few discrepancies. Since his own is more colorful, we will let him speak for himself here.[1]

"We left the O.R.&N. Bridge across Snake River near Huntington at 2:00 P.M., May 17, 1895. At Bay Horse Rapids, three miles down, while drifting in a channel improved by Government engineers (a copy of their report was in the pilothouse) we touched on what afterward proved to be a piece of two-inch steel drill which had been broken off and left when the engineers were working there some years before. The drill ripped several holes through the bottom and the boat swung around and damaged the sternwheel badly. Working the boat clear with spars and lines we went down to J. A. Gray's Landing and repaired the wheel and patched the holes in the bottom.

"Left Gray's Landing on the 19th.—no wind. I was steering, my brother, the mate, watching the Government chart. I saw indications of reefs or shoals and remarked: 'It don't look good, what does the chart say?' He replied: 'All clear—there is a black rock marked on the shore.' But I was not satisfied and rung the bell to stop. Almost immediately she struck the starboard knuckel [*sic*?] making a hole forty feet long and four feet wide. I grabbed the chart and flung it out of the window and we touched no reefs or rocks afterwards except at Copper Creek Falls. We had struck the edge of a reef about a foot under the muddy water which the Snake carries while in flood.

"We were drifting while the mate inspected the damages. I knew they were bad but the crew had been a little discouraged at the 'Bay Horse' trouble and I was afraid they would jump the job if we landed above Sturgill Rapids, three miles below us. From where we were the boat could easily steam back to the Bridge. I heard that Sturgill Rapids were very swift and it would be almost impossible to bring the boat back over with our damaged side so I kept on down slowly. The men gathered on the forward deck and one man asked if I was going to land. I made no reply and soon we were below the rapids where we landed. There was some talk and I told them we would repair damages as much as possible. We had plenty of lumber and forty cords of wood in the hull. The boat had bulkheads all through her. We built a bulkhead as close as we could to the hole in her side and pumped out the six bulkheads that had been flooded. The men had understood that we would go back over the rapids to the Bridge and the evening before we were ready to start I had sounded the men as to going on or going back. Every man wanted to go back.

"Approaching the engineer, I said: 'Charlie, this boat is worthless up here, what do you think about going back?' He replied: 'We came up to get her, I

-----

1. In 1920, the Director of the U.S. Geological Survey wrote Captain Gray requesting that he describe the voyage of the *Norma* through Hell's Canyon. On December 2, 1920, Gray replied: "I kept a complete log of the trip but after several days hunt among sixty years relics, cannot find anything but the 'time book' of the crew, and must depend upon my memory for an account of the incidents of the trip."

Gray then wrote the account we quote verbatim here. A copy of his letter ended up in the files of the Idaho Historical Society, was "lost" for a time, then was rediscovered by Archivist Dr. Merle W. Wells, who used it as the core of an article dealing with the building of the *Norma* and her trip down the Snake. See his "She Will Strike About There . . . Steamboating In Hell's Canyon," *Idaho Yesterdays,* Summer, 1957, pp. 2-9.

say go on or put her where they can't find her.' I replied: 'Charlie, you're my man. The boys think I am going to make a short trip down a few miles to test our new bulkhead, but we will forget to come back.'

"We left Sturgill May 21st, and after we had gone downstream about ten miles the boys accepted their fate. About 5:00 P.M. we came around a short point and there was a steel ferry cable across the river and less than eight feet above the water. I stopped and backed the boat instantly. A strong current was carrying us down to certain decapitation of everything above the main deck, but the boat was a good backer and Charlie answered nobly, and I managed to land her, head down, against a rocky cliff and the men wound several ropes around rocks enough to hold her with the engines working.

"I whistled several times for the ferryman to lower the wire but no one moved and I sent the mate and two men across the river to lower the wire. When the mate asked the ferryman (Brownlee) why he delayed lowering the wire Brownlee replied: 'I am doing it to prolong your lives. You have a bullheaded fool running that boat and not a soul will live to go through that canyon. I have been on top of those cliffs and I could jump across the canyon. I saw a drift log a hundred feet long up-end under one cliff and it never came up.'

"The ferryman was slow in lowering the wire and it was dark when we hunted a landing below. I wonder if you can imagine the strain on a pilot on a strange river known to be swift and treacherous, on a dark night, over-shadowing mountains throwing impenetrable gloom over all, and no searchlight.

"About noon the next day we reached the landing above Copper Creek Falls and everyone walked down on the Oregon side to see them. They are more of a pour than a fall. From the brink of a cliff which jutted out to the still water at the foot of the cliff I measured the drop at eighteen feet. For an hour I watched and studied the currents, eddies, and back-lash of the water, and decided that the least damage to the boat would be done by dropping over the fall on the Idaho side and let the back-lash hold me from the cliff as much as possible. The water pours over the fall and the current at about 300 feet below below the summit of the fall. . . .The underside of the point of this cliff has been worn away until the over-hang extends over the water a good many feet and a considerable amount of the current passed under the cliff.

"When I returned to the boat I called the carpenter, who had been foreman on Construction for years with the Oregon Steam Navigation Company and had asked to go with me for the excitement, and putting my foot on the starboard guard about ten feet abaft of the stem said: 'She will strike about here, and I want you to run in a bulkhead six feet back of that to the midship keelson, then have the mate back it up with cordwood in case the water should rush in hard enough to tear away your bulkhead.'

"He examined the falls and replied: 'You ain't intending to go over that place, are you? You will drown us all.' I looked at him a moment and then asked: 'Tom, you never had much notoriety, did you?' 'No, why?' 'They have all our names that are on this boat, and if you should be drowned your name would be in every paper in the United States and Europe.'

"His reply: 'Oh, go to hell' sounded like the decree of fate. I replied: 'Put in the bulkhead, Tom, and we'll chance the other place.' An hour later the sounds of his hammer ceased and I heard a mumbling. Walking softly to the bulkhead hatch I heard: 'Damned old fool, going to be drowned for excitement because a damned fool wants notoriety.' But the bulkhead went in good.

"The next morning I made the only quarterdeck speech of my life. Calling the crew together I said: 'Boys, you have persuaded yourselves that there is danger to your lives in going over those falls but there is not a particle of danger to your lives. This boat is built of wood enough to float her machinery and there is forty cords of wood in the hold. We could knock her bow and side in and while the wreck is floating we have boats enough to carry all of us ashore. There are life preservers enough for three apiece if you want them, but don't get excited and jump overboard. Snake River never gives up her dead. Now get ready to go.'

"When we dropped over the fall we seemed to be facing certain destruction on the cliff below, but I knew my engineer was 'all there' and would answer promptly. We backed slowly and within ten feet of the rocks to starboard her bow passed the mouth of Copper Creek, where an eddy emptying gave her a slight swing out and I backed strong with helm hard to starboard—the bow must take its chances now, the stern must not.

"Almost before one could speak the bow touched the point of the cliff just hard enough to break those guard timbers without touching the hull, and we bounded into the still water below. The carpenter who had stationed himself on the hurricane deck outside of the pilothouse with two life preservers around him stepped out in front of the pilothouse and shouted: 'Hurrah, Cap! You start her for hell and I'll go with you from this on!'

"A little below Copper Creek Falls we entered the canyon and although a bright sun was shining outside, in the canyon it was twilight. I was too busy watching the surface of the river but the men on deck said they saw stars through the gloom. Shortly after coming out of the canyon we passed down a straight cataract that had cut its way through a pla-

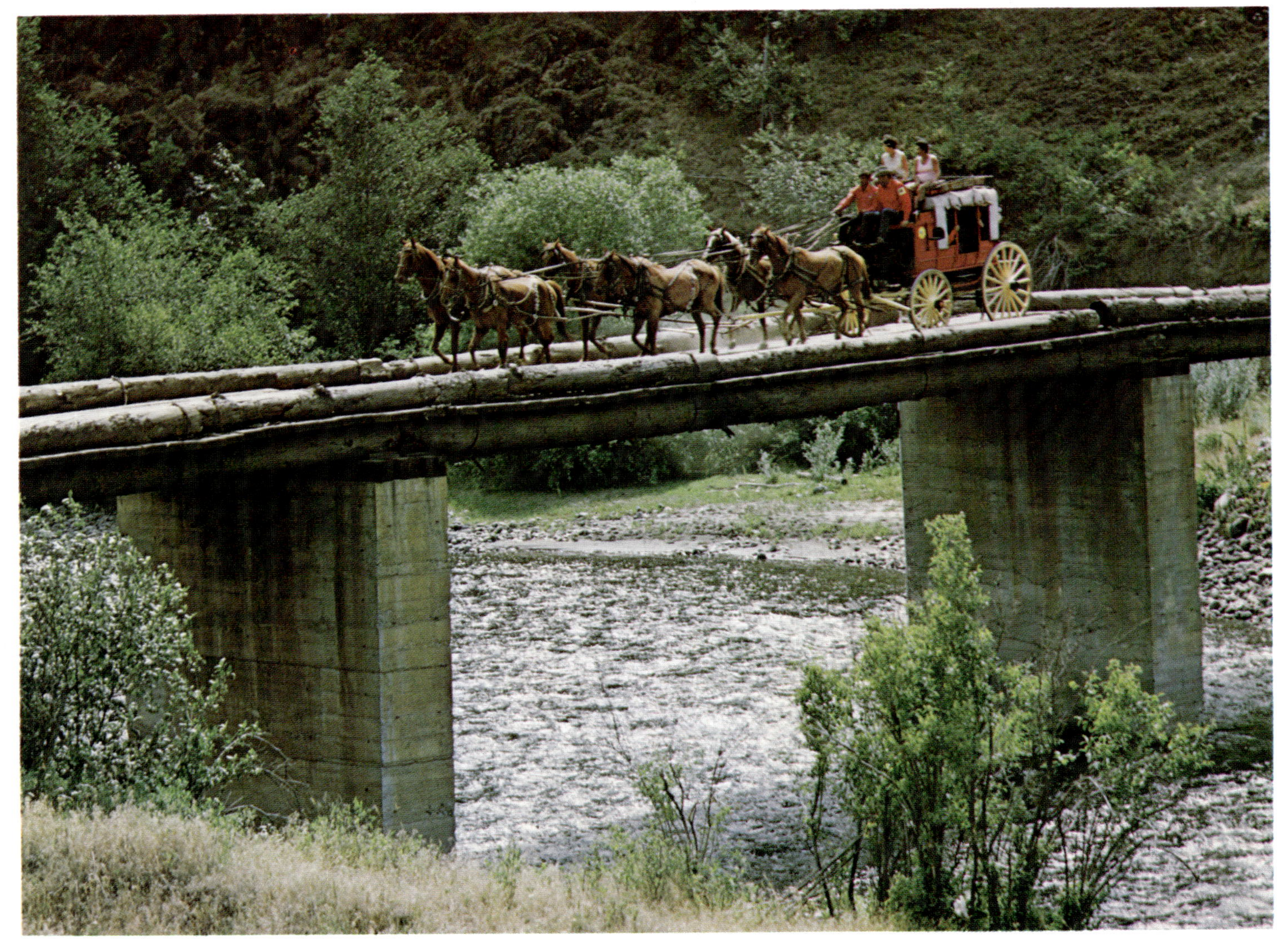

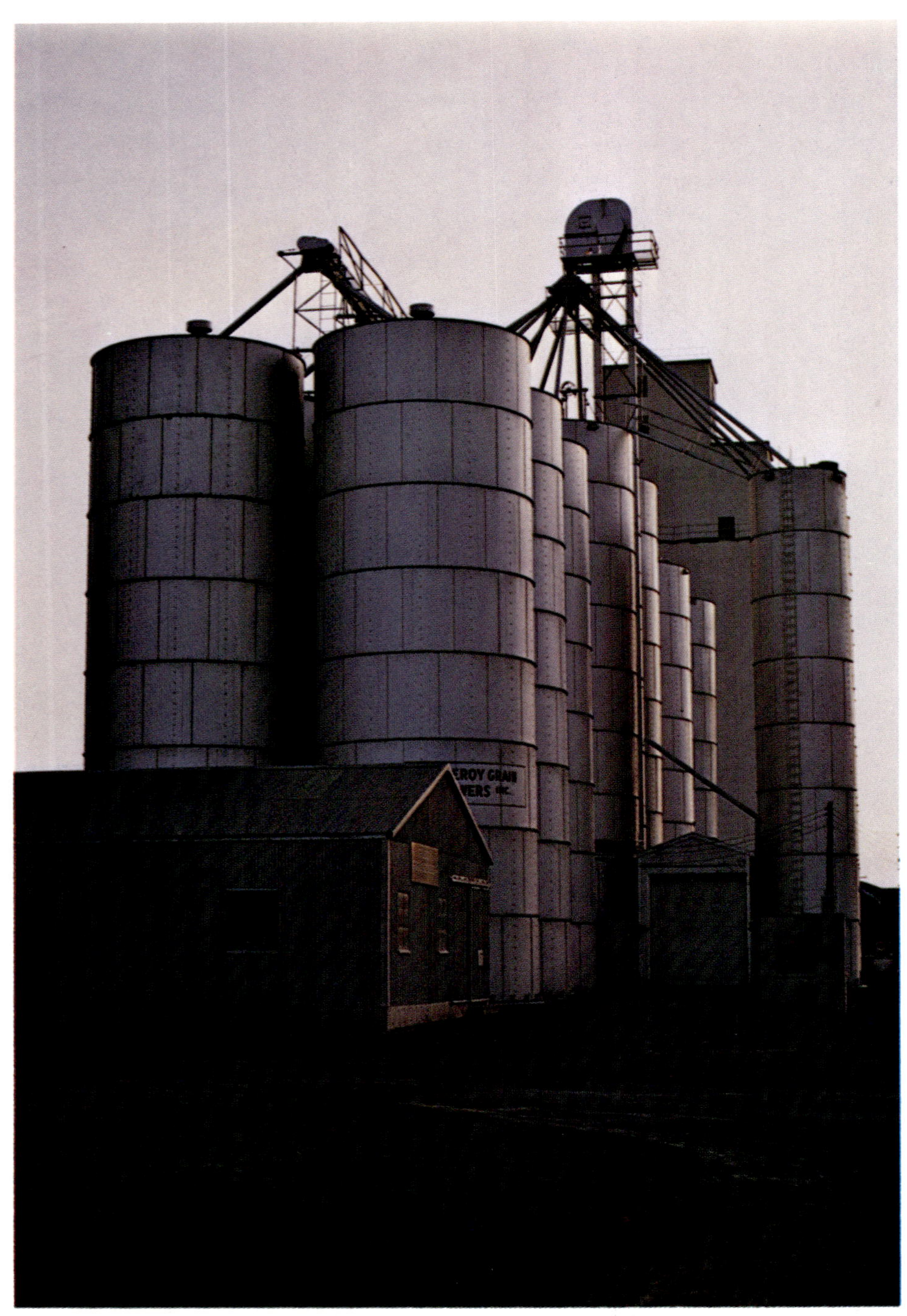

Above:

LAST STAGE FROM WALLA WALLA

This stagecoach actually carried the U.S. mail from Walla Walla to Joseph, Oregon, in July, 1970. Using back roads little changed by progress, the vehicle rebuilt by a group called "The '59ers" made the rugged 120-mile journey in five days.

Left:

HARVEST STORAGE

Grain elevators, near Pomeroy, Washington

teau of Blue Clay and granite boulders. The channel was not over sixty feet wide and a mile or two long with a drop estimated at one hundred feet to the mile. We tied up on account of wind for the rest of the day and all night at Johnson Creek, which is now the head of navigation, and reached Lewiston May 24th. . . ."[2]

For a time during the late 1890s, stern-wheelers carried passengers and freight upriver from Lewiston into the lower part of Hell's Canyon, where mining activity was being carried on. As an aid in ascending white water such as that at the mouth of the Imnaha, a large iron ring was imbedded in the solid rock of the canyon wall above the rapid, a stout wire cable was fastened to the ring, and an empty barrel was secured to the other end of the cable, floating in the water below the rapid. When a stern-wheeler came upstream, it picked up the lower end of the cable, winched itself through the rapid, then returned barrel and cable to the river for the use of the next boat to come along.

Between Lewiston and the mouth of the Snake, as farming developed in the fertile Palouse Hills, a problem unique to the region arose. Through much of this area the Snake lies two thousand feet or more below the surrounding country. Wagon roads down the face of the steep cliffs were expensive to build, difficult to maintain, and dangerous to negotiate. Since the region was thinly populated and could absorb only a small fraction of the grain it raised, the farmers had to ship their wheat, barley, or rye to distant markets. Grain boats on the river offered cheap water transport, but in order to take advantage of it, the farmers first must get their grain a vertical half mile down to the river.

Several ingenious schemes utilizing the law of gravity were tried—with varying degrees of success. One group of farmers built a cable and bucket tramway from plateau to river level, letting the weight of sacked wheat going down pull the empty buckets back to the heights. But cables broke, brake drums burned out, supports collapsed, and on at least one occasion when a reckless workman hitched a ride up in an empty bucket and a braking device failed there was a fatal accident.

Safety measures in those days, old-timers say, consisted of a man with a loud voice who, when something went wrong, yelled: "*Look out!*"

A retired Army officer, Major Sewell Truax, devised a slide consisting of a wooden tube four inches in diameter which would carry loose grain from a hopper on the heights down to the wharf where the boat was loading. On paper, the slide looked great. In practice the moving grain created a vacuum in the tube which made it jam, or, when it did move, slide so rapidly and with so much friction that by the time it reached water level the grain was charred black.

After a bit of tinkering and experimenting, Major Truax put baffles and air vents in his tube, found a way to overcome the heat problem, and was pleased to discover that all dirt and chaff were removed from the sliding grain en route down, so that it arrived at the wharf shining and pure. Eventually, he patented his slide and built five of them along the lower reaches of the river, where they worked successfully for years.[3]

With one unique exception, no rail lines were built in the lower Snake River Country until the late 1890s, so for almost forty years all the grain shipped out of the region went by boat. Every three miles or so along the river there was a wharf where the *Harvest Queen*, the *Annie Faxon*, the *Lewiston*, and other stern-wheelers loaded. Now and again a tragedy occurred, as when a boiler exploded aboard the *Annie Faxon* while she was making a landing at Wade's Bar, forty miles downstream from Lewiston, in 1893, killing eight people and sinking the boat on the spot. More often, the boats were delayed because of extremely low or high water or floes of drifting ice. Ten miles above the mouth of the Snake, a sheltered cove where stern-wheelers waited in early spring for ice jams to pass now has its name perpetuated by a dam called Ice Harbor.

The unique exception in railroads was conceived, financed, and built by Dr. Dorsey Syng Baker, a merchant and banker who had settled in Walla Walla with the beginning of the Idaho gold boom in the early 1860s. Since no other railroads existed in the area when he began building his thirty miles of track from the town of Walla Walla to Wallula Landing on the Columbia in 1872, it could truthfully be said that his line connected Noplace with Nowhere.

All the same, when completed it hauled freight, made money, and was sold at a handsome profit after seven years of operation. Later, an imaginative writer put together all the folklore and legends that had grown up around it in a tall tale called *The Rawhide Railroad*.[4]

Doc Baker had never even *seen* a railroad, the story goes, but feeling that every up-and-coming city should have one, he decided to build one himself. Ordering two locomotives and a hundred pairs of wheels to be shipped from New York around the Horn and up the Columbia, he hired an Irishman who claimed to be a civil engineer to lay out a

2. After relating his adventures with the *Norma* Captain Gray summed up his long, colorful career in these words:

"I have been captain and pilot on steam vessels from outside the Columbia River Bar on all its reaches up and into the Okanogan River, the Willamette from mouth to Harrisburg, the Snake from mouth to Imnaha, the Fraser from mouth to Fort Yale, the Stickine from Fort Wrangel to Telegraph Creek, and took a stern-wheeler steamer from Seattle through the Inland Passage to Icy Strait and across the North Pacific Ocean, up Bering Sea to St. Michaels and on up the Yukon River from St. Michaels to White Horse Rapids.

"I am the only man that ever took a steamboat carrying freight and passengers both up and down over Priest Rapids and Rock Island Rapids on the Columbia where all others that have tried have failed.

"On all these voyages I had no chart or pilot but found my way by reading the character of swift water, which has been my vocation since a boy thirteen years old."

3. *Historic Sketches,* by F. T. Gilbert, Portland, 1882, pp. 290, 291.

4. *The Rawhide Railroad,* by George Estes, of Troutdale, Oregon, was written and published in 1916. For more factual accounts of Dorsey Syng Baker's colorful life, see *Forty Years a Pioneer,* by W. W. Baker, Lowman & Hanford, Seattle, 1934; also *Gold, Rawhide, and Iron,* by Helen Baker Reynolds, Pacific Books, Palo Alto, Calif., 1955.

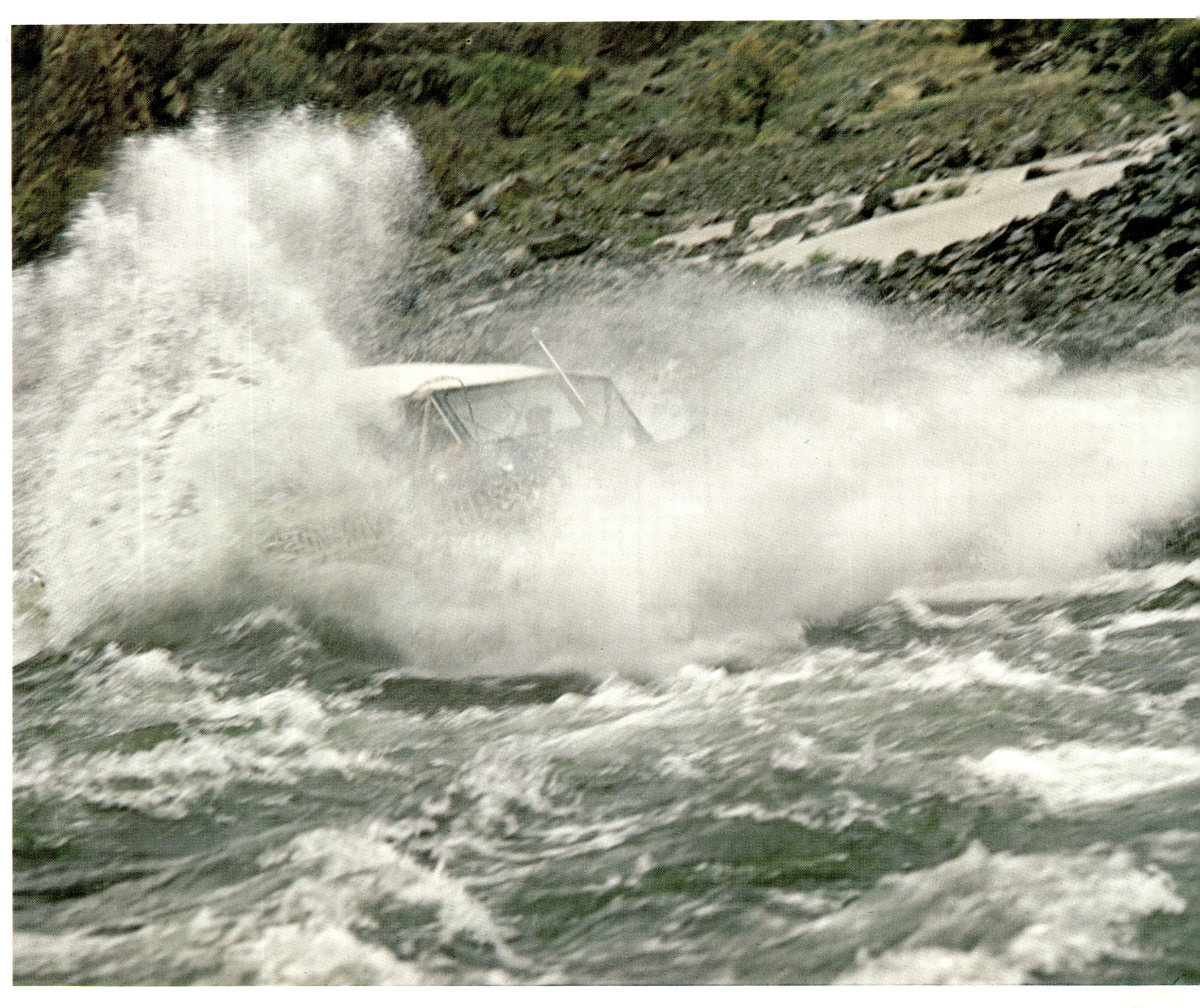

grade. For instruments, the Irishman used a compass and a whiskey bottle half full of water; the grade, we are told, was perfect.

Unable to obtain iron for rails, Doc Baker used wood instead. Since the gauge of the locomotives was not known, only one rail was laid and spiked down until the ship carrying the rolling stock reached Portland. Then the distance between the wheels was carefully measured, marked with a notch on a stick, and a canoe-paddling Indian hurried upriver to deliver the "big medicine" stick to the construction foreman so that the second rail could be put in place.

A manpower problem arose at the Columbia River portages in carrying the locomotives around the rapids. The one thousand Wishram Indians hired to do the job were demanding an exorbitant amount of money. Doc Baker was short on cash. But he had made a good buy in acquiring one thousand black silk plug hats. As every Westerner knows, Indians dote on fancy headpieces. So one thousand Indians wearing black silk plug hats happily carried the locomotives around the portages.

The wooden rails wore out quickly. Since there was no iron available with which to top them, Doc Baker killed and skinned some of his many cattle, covering the rails with rawhide, which wears *like* iron when dry. The expedient worked fine until one bitterly cold winter when starving wolves came down from the hills, ate the rawhide, and put the railroad out of business.

Truth was, the rails were made of 4 by 6 wooden stringers at first. But they were topped by strap-iron instead of rawhide. When the straps worked loose, as they frequently did, they snaked up through the floors of the cars, which tended to make passengers nervous, but since the train traveled slowly no one ever was seriously injured.

And the train traveled *very* slowly, folklore says. On one occasion when a pedestrian found a car derailed and obligingly helped put it back on the track, he was offered a free ride in exchange for his assistance.

"No thanks, I'll walk," he replied. "I'm in a hurry."

* * *

Left:

WHITE WATER

Somewhere in the mist there is a twin-jet powered boat, a diabolical riverman determined to show us how hard water can be, and four slightly green people hanging on for dear life. The photographer is safely ashore, of course, yelling for "more action." The spine-jolting rapid is on the lower Salmon, one of many in that stretch of the river. This one is called "The Sluice Box." Probably because running it shakes the gold fillings out of one's teeth.

4.

The lower Snake River rapids which Captain William Polk Gray found swimmable as a boy are gone now, covered by the still, placid waters backed up from the mouth of the river to Lewiston by Ice Harbor, Lower Monumental, Little Goose, and Lower Granite dams.[1] In the middle Snake, the rapids through which only Captain Miller's *Shoshone* and Captain Gray's *Norma* ever gave steamboat service are buried under the green, quiet pools formed by Brownlee, Oxbow, and Hell's Canyon dams.[2]

Between Lewiston, at Mile 140, and the foot of Hell's Canyon Dam, at Mile 247, the Snake still runs free. It is in this stretch of river that the Imnaha and Grande Ronde enter from the high Wallowas to the west and the Salmon pours in from Idaho's Primitive Area to the east. It was here, at Nez Perce Crossing, that Chief Joseph reluctantly came down with his people and horses from his beloved Wallowa Valley in late spring of 1877, crossed the flood-swollen river, and headed for the Idaho Indian reservation to which he had been ordered by General O. O. Howard—only to find himself embroiled in a tragic, hopeless war.

Between the lower side of Hell's Canyon Dam and Johnson Bar, ten miles downriver, the scenery is stark and awesome in its beauty. From this point, professional rivermen like Jim Zanelli take parties of venturesome tourists downriver by raft to Lewiston on unforgettable float trips, not the least of whose thrills is making a landing in a light plane on the postage-stamp airstrip in the canyon's depths near Oxbow Dam.

Thrice weekly during the summer, and weekly during the remaining months, Dick Rivers or one of his *Idaho Queen* pilots makes the mail, grocery, medicine, or what-do-you-need run from Lewiston to Johnson Bar, going up one day and back the next, servicing sheep camps, hunting camps, and the riverbank mailboxes of permanent residents whose business is nobody's business but their own.

Twin jet-powered boats of light draft and sturdy construction piloted by professionals like Guy Snyder, Everett Spaulding, and Floyd Harvey zoom upriver from Lewiston with fishermen, hunters, and sightseers, sometimes turning east up the Salmon to run spine-jolting rapids like The Eye, The Sluice Box, and The Slide. River-wise amateurs with high-powered prop outboards venture into the white water, too. If they are really river-wise, they carry a spare prop and wear life jackets, for even a good boatman can have an accident—and it is a long walk out to civilization. Too often, amateurs, less river-wise than they think they are, test their skill against the Snake or Salmon—and find themselves overmatched. In the Salmon alone, during a recent year, seven men were drowned in the always dangerous waters.

------

1. These are federal dams built by the Corps of Engineers primarily for power, navigation, and flood control benefits. All have fish passage facilities. Lower Granite is still under construction.

2. These are Idaho Power Company dams, built by the privately owned company primarily for power generation, though they also have flood control benefits and form pools increasingly used for recreation. They have no fish passage facilities.

It is this wilderness stretch of the Snake that has inspired the controversy between the dam builders and the environmentalists. It is here that their final battle will be fought. If the dam builders win and turn the free-flowing river into a quiet pool behind Asotin and High Mountain Sheep dams, then the navigability question, thought set at rest forever by Donald McKenzie in 1819, will be definitely answered—and some bold soul behind a speedboat undoubtedly will make the early adventurers spin in their graves by water-skiing from the mouth of the Snake to Shoshone Falls in south-central Idaho. If the environmentalists win, they undoubtedly will find a way to celebrate their victory in equally spectacular fashion.

So far as present-day navigation is concerned below Lewiston, the Idaho city and its Washington counterpart, Clarkston, soon can truthfully say that they are seaports—even though 470 river miles inland from the sea. One by one during the past 110 years, downriver obstacles such as rapids, falls, portages, rocks, and sandbars, which long made boat traffic between wharfs at the mouth of the Clearwater and the deep-water ports of the world a difficult journey, have been eliminated.

The storm-wracked, shifting bar at the mouth of the Columbia has been tamed and marked; a ship channel deep and wide enough to accommodate all but the latest generation of oceangoing tankers is maintained year round upriver to Portland. Bonneville Dam has eliminated the portage at the Cascades; its lock is 75 feet wide by 500 feet long, with a vertical lift of 70 feet. The Dalles Dam has obliterated Celilo Falls and fourteen miles of unnavigable water; its navigation lock has a maximum lift of 87.5 feet.

Farther up the Columbia, John Day and McNary dams have wiped out the rapids and shoals that troubled Captain Len White and the *Colonel Wright* on her maiden voyage in 1859, creating slackwater on the Columbia and into the Snake as far as the entrance to the Ice Harbor Locks. At Ice Harbor, Lower Monumental, Little Goose, and Lower Granite, on up the Snake, the channel depth is maintained at 14 feet, the lifts average 100 feet, and like all the dams on the Columbia (except Bonneville, whose locks are to be enlarged) the lock facilities are 86 feet wide and 675 feet long.

Theoretically, what this means is that any vessel drawing less than 14 feet may move from sea level to Lewiston's 738 foot elevation with only a very moderate current to breast, making most of the climb via lock. Practically, it means that almost all the water-borne commercial traffic will be barges propelled by unglamorous, highly efficient tugboats, whose operating cost per ton-mile cannot be approached by any other carrier.[3]

What it also means is that for the first time in its history this vast Inland Empire, as it is regionally called, can sell its grains and forest products to Pacific Rim markets on competitive terms, importing the oil, iron, alumina, and other raw products it needs to become a manufacturing area at water-borne freight rates. North Idaho's forests rank with the finest in the world; Japan has a voracious demand for saw-logs and wood chips. Wheat growers in the Palouse Hills are at present running their production machine at idling speed, waiting only for a price-demand signal to open the throttle wide; much of the overseas world is hungry.

Since most of the wheat raised in the Pacific Northwest is soft wheat, little of which is used in the milling of flour for white bread but which makes fine flour for spaghetti or noodles, grower associations are looking to non-white-bread-eating peoples for their market—even to the extent of teaching them to like noodles. They see Japan, southeast Asia, India, the Philippines, and perhaps eventually the hungry masses of Red China as potential customers.

On the lower Columbia, Portland is making long-range plans to outstrip New Orleans as a port for world trade. Following the example of middle Columbia River counties that have voted tax levies to acquire land, build wharfs, and lure industry in need of cheap space, power, and water, every southeastern Washington and northwestern Idaho county bordering Snake River between its mouth and the Lewiston-Clarkston area has organized port districts, acquired land, and started building facilities to load grain and forest products and unload petroleum and chemical fertilizers. With a population of only four people per square mile, there is much empty land available; the climate is mild; 36 million acre-feet of unused water empty into the Columbia each year; and the welcome mat is out to new industry.

Not from everyone, of course. There are still a few obstinate souls who find white water more scenic than a slab of concrete, a sixteen-pound steelhead leaping high in the air at the end of a monofilament line more exciting than a catfish, carp, or squawfish lying like so much lead deep in a silt-filled pool, or a blue, cloudless sky in a canyon devoid of people more inspiring than the eye-stinging plumes from the smokestack of a multi-million-dollar plant manufacturing boxes in which to ship color TV sets on whose screens talk shows discussing the nation's ills may be viewed in detached comfort.

For a long while, this was an unheard minority, few in number, inarticulate when it did speak, and, worst of all, with no identifying name or rallying cry. It has both now—"environmentalist" and "ecology."

Over the long history of the Snake River Country, controversy has played an important role in the exploration, settlement, and development of the region. It still does. So important a role, in fact, that we shall reserve the subject for exclusive treatment in the final section of this book.

But first we must consider one other important product that a great river can generate in addition to controversy.

Electric power. . . .

---

3. According to American Waterways Operators figures, a river towboat can haul eight tons per horsepower compared with the average of one ton per horsepower by a railroad locomotive. A shipper's dollar will move a ton of freight 333 miles by barge compared to 67 miles by rail. Tri-City *Herald*, Braxton B. Carr, president, American Waterway Operators, Inc., September 26, 1968. We will discuss this subject more fully in the final section of this book.

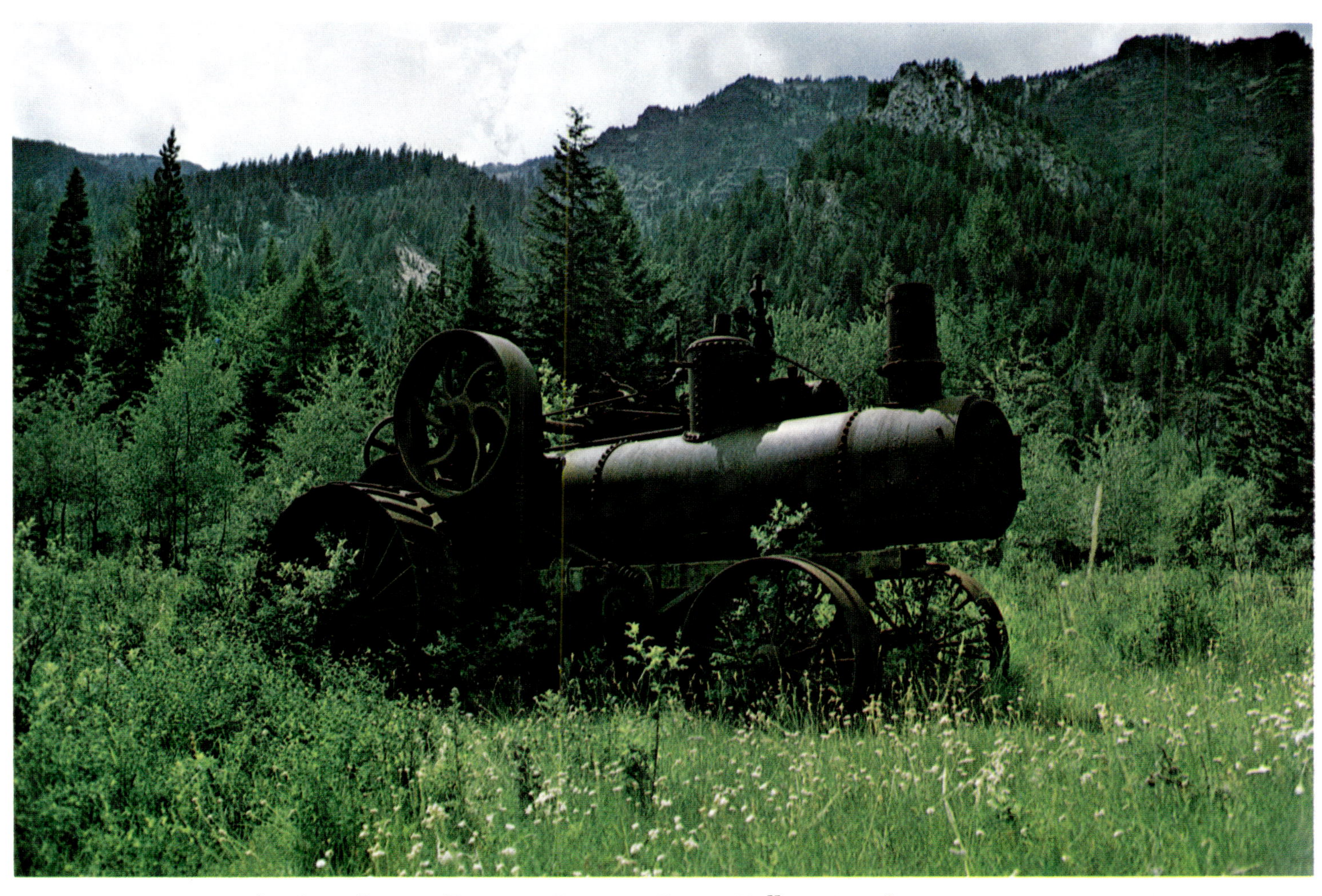

Ancient Steam Tractor, Lostine River Valley, Northeastern Oregon

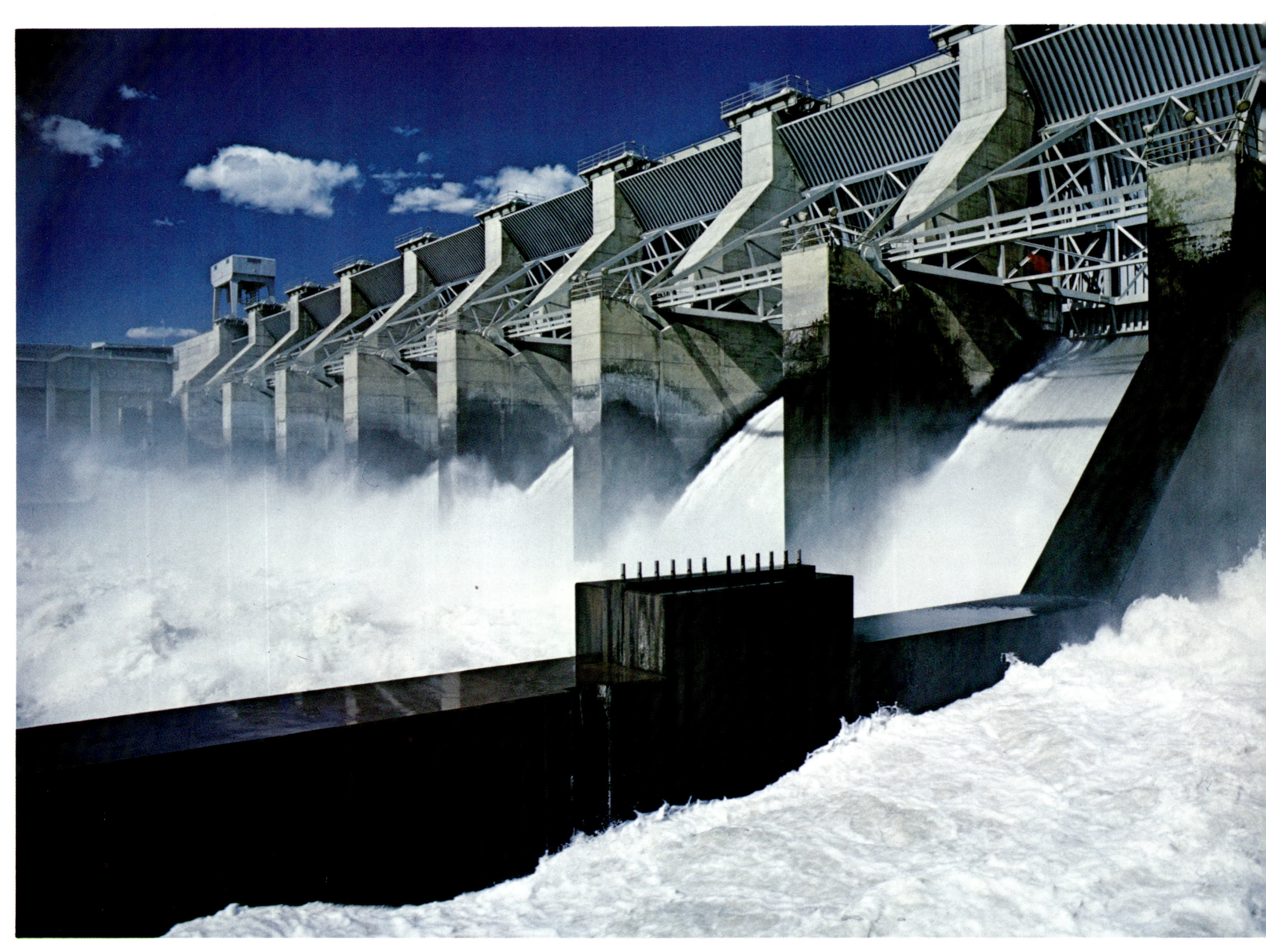

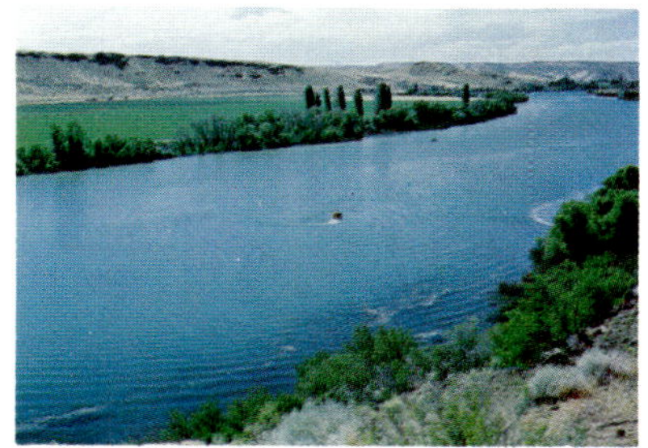

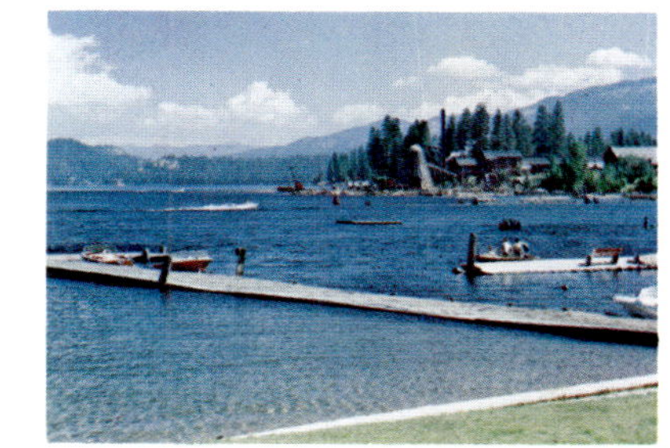

PART EIGHT

River of Power

1.

On a commercial scale, there are only two ways to generate electricity: by heating water into steam that will spin turbines or by using the weight of falling water to accomplish the same purpose. One is called thermal, the other hydro power. If heat is used, a dependable supply of fuel is required—coal, oil, gas, or nuclear—which means that in addition to the capital cost of the plant an annual fuel bill must be met. If the generating force is falling water, natural fall must be utilized or a dam built to create a head—but thereafter the law of gravity does the work and, in theory at least, presents no annual bill for its services.

> "Electricity cannot be stored," one expert points out. "It must be used at the exact instant that it is made. This strange characteristic sets apart the business of generating, transmitting, and using electricity from all others in the field of commerce."[1]

In the Snake River Country as the age of electricity dawned around 1885, the first generating plants were built to serve the mining towns of Hailey and Ketchum.[2] These were steam plants, using cordwood or sawdust to heat their boilers. On July 4, 1887, the first illuminated lamps came on in Boise, lighted by the power from two 15-kilowatt Edison direct-current generators. This was a hydro plant, taking water from an irrigation ditch called Ridenbaugh Canal "into a made reservoir on top of the bench above the city, from which the water dropped 62 feet through the penstock to the turbine wheels."[3]

1. *Electric Power in America,* by Robert McCaig, G. P. Putnam's Sons, N.Y., 1970, p. 12.

2. *Bulletin,* Idaho Power Company, 1966.

3. *Idaho Power Company, A History, 1887-1943,* by R. H. Sessions, p. 7.

Left: Ice Harbor Dam, Lower Snake

As other small thermal and hydro plants were built to serve the mining, lighting, and irrigation water pumping needs of the region, the technological problems of generation and transmission were being solved one by one by the inventive genius of men like Thomas Edison and George Westinghouse, whose quarrels over the merits of direct current versus alternating current, 16⅔-cycle versus 133-cycle electricity, and other engineering matters meant little to the local Idaho plant owner trying to generate and sell kilowatts at a profit.

His first problem was storage of the raw materials required to manufacture electricity: steam pressure or falling water. Then, as now, the demand for power varied widely over a twenty-four-hour period. If his was a thermal plant capable of meeting a certain peak demand, heat expended during under-peak hours was wasted. If a hydro plant, the water must pass the turbines unused or be stored behind a dam. Wasted heat and water were a dead financial loss to the plant owner, of course, and his capital costs went on around the clock.

Some rather ingenious schemes to fit demand to supply were attempted. In Emmett, Idaho, the plant operated by J. H. Forbes in 1904 burned sawdust.

> "The engine was connected to a 75 kilowatt generator, which furnished service to Main Street and a few adjacent residences at a monthly rate of seventy-five cents per lamp of sixteen candle power intensity (about 75 watts). The plant was operated from dusk to midnight, with the exception of Tuesday and Friday each week, when service was also provided from one to four o'clock in the afternoon to accommodate housewives owning electric irons. Collection problems were minimized somewhat by the simple expedient of shutting down the entire plant, and then canvassing each customer with the plea that bills must be paid in order to buy more sawdust to operate the steam engine."[4]

4. Ibid., p. 10.

At Swan Falls on the Snake River south of Boise, the Trade Dollar Consolidated Mining Company built its own 900-kilowatt hydro plant in 1901, then constructed twenty-eight miles of transmission line to carry energy to its operations in the Silver City district. No figures regarding the cost of the installation, maintenance of the plant, and patrolling the line through the deep snows of this mountainous area are available; but the delivered monthly kilowatt hour expense must have been very high.

At Glenns Ferry, Idaho, in 1905, plant operator I. W. Herron tried still another scheme.

> "In order to obtain a fuller use for his investment, the steam engine was used to pump water for local distribution during the day, and then connected to the electric generator in the evening. Lights were turned off at 11 P.M."[5]

Gasoline used to run generators cost thirty-five to forty cents a gallon. Small dams for hydro plants were built on tributaries to the Snake with moderate effort and expense; but when summer came and streamflow lessened, their production of power could not meet demand. In the Thousand Springs area

> "Early developers attempted to force water through a hydraulic ram in an effort to irrigate the mesa above the river. The old pipes, still in place north of the present power plant, indicate that a large sum of money was spent in the experiment, but served only as a warning to subsequent owners, who thereby avoided the unhappy mistakes of their predecessors."[6]

Like Niagara Falls in the East, where a successful hydro plant had gone into production in 1896, Shoshone Falls on the Snake—thirty-three feet higher, though carrying a lesser volume of water—early attracted the attention of private promoters who thought they could parlay falling water, investors' money, and a need for power into a quick fortune. But the combination refused to jell.

The difficulties were many. In 1902, when the project first got under way, the Shoshone Falls site was thirty miles from the nearest railhead, whence all materials must be hauled by team to the rimrock of a canyon half a thousand feet deep. A tunnel several hundred feet long must be driven through solid rock, the engineering problems were formidable, and those two bugaboos of underfinanced, overpromoted private projects—lack of money and litigation—soon reared their ugly heads. At American Falls, farther upstream, where the Bureau of Reclamation was attempting to include enough power facilities in its irrigation project dam to lift water to the land, problems also arose—not the least of which was the necessity to float all construction materials to a mid-river island on rafts in a rapids-filled area where early explorers had come to grief almost a century before.

As in hardrock mining and large-scale irrigation, the lesson was painfully learned that while the end result might benefit the little man, the construction of generating plants and distribution systems was beyond the resources of the small private operator. By 1914, some fifty companies that had come into existence since 1887 had gone bankrupt, failed, or been swallowed up in mergers with the five larger companies that survived—and financially these were in bad shape.

The chaos was resolved by the organization of the Idaho Power Company, which started doing business as a corporate entity in 1916. Representing 7,000 investors and owning $49 million in paper securities, the company took over nine hydro plants, two large undeveloped sites on the Snake, and another on the Malad. Its generating capacity totaled a modest 20,000 kilowatts, roughly 12 percent of the potential of all the sites it had acquired. The first problem it faced was interconnecting the generating plants in its system so that it could provide uniform service to the widely scattered customers of the vast area it planned to serve.

The modern era of electric power generation and distribution in the Snake River Country had begun.

° ° °

2.

So far as electric power is concerned, the Snake River Country—in marked contrast to the rest of the United States—depends 100 percent upon hydro generation. Taken as a whole, it is a power-surplus, power-exporting region—and will continue to be for the next fifty years. Yet oddly enough, the dominant private utility in the watershed—Idaho Power—now has a steam-generating plant under construction in western Wyoming, outside the watershed, whose fuel will be coal and whose electricity will serve customers in the upper reaches of the Snake. Presently we will explain this oddity; but first we must tackle the chore of reducing the monstrous mass of statistics related to hydro power production to understandable terms.

There are two kinds of dams: storage and run-of-the-river. Basically, the purpose of a storage dam is to retain mountain snowmelt and spring rainfall for irrigation use during the months of the growing season when the farming areas of the Snake River Country receive little if any moisture from the sky. Between high and low stage, the water level in a storage dam may vary 150 feet or more. Ideally, storage dams are built on tributaries to the mainstem river

Right:

DWORSHAK DAM

Under construction on the North Fork of the Clearwater

5. Ibid., p. 16.

6. Ibid., p. 79.

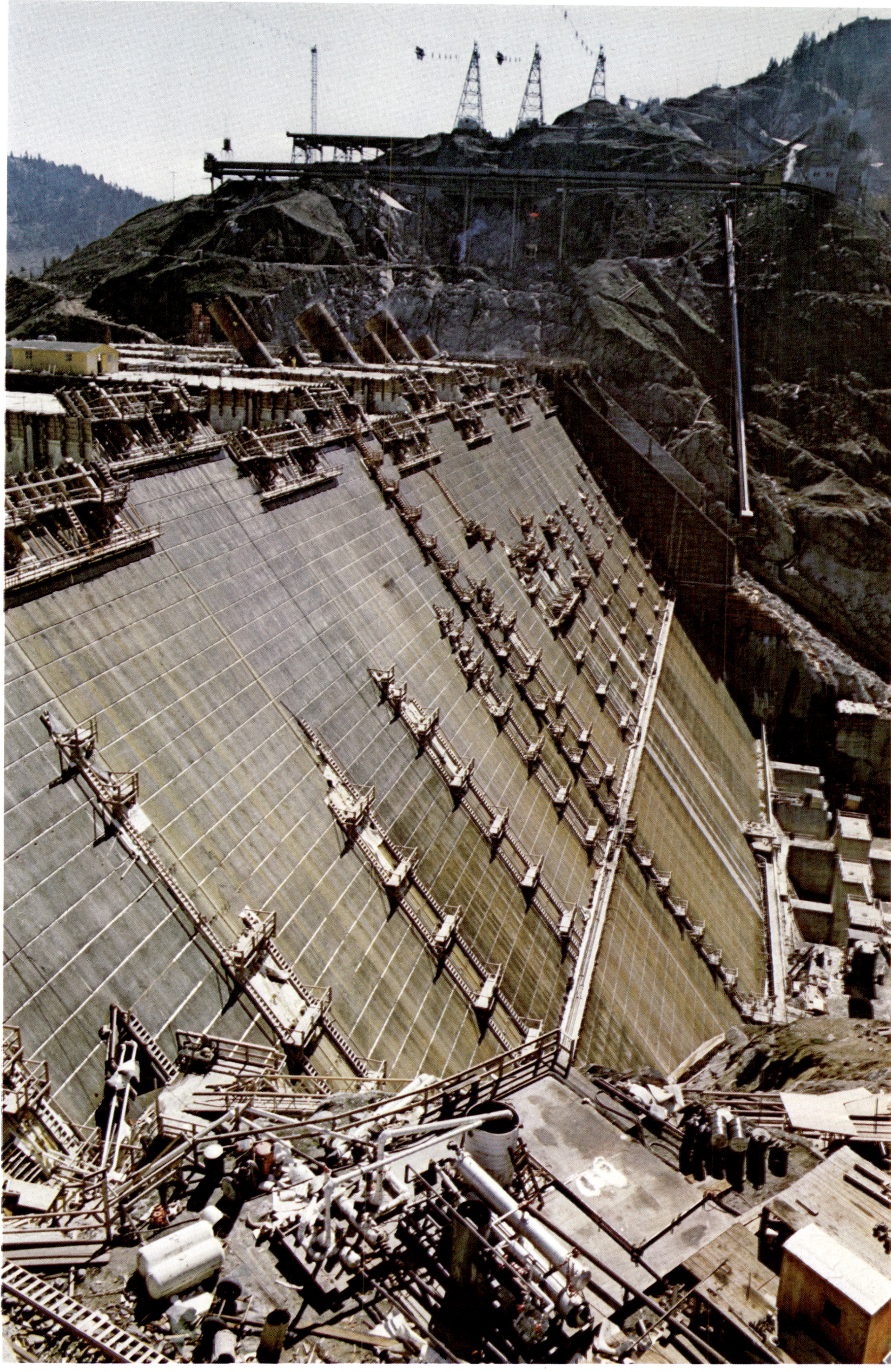

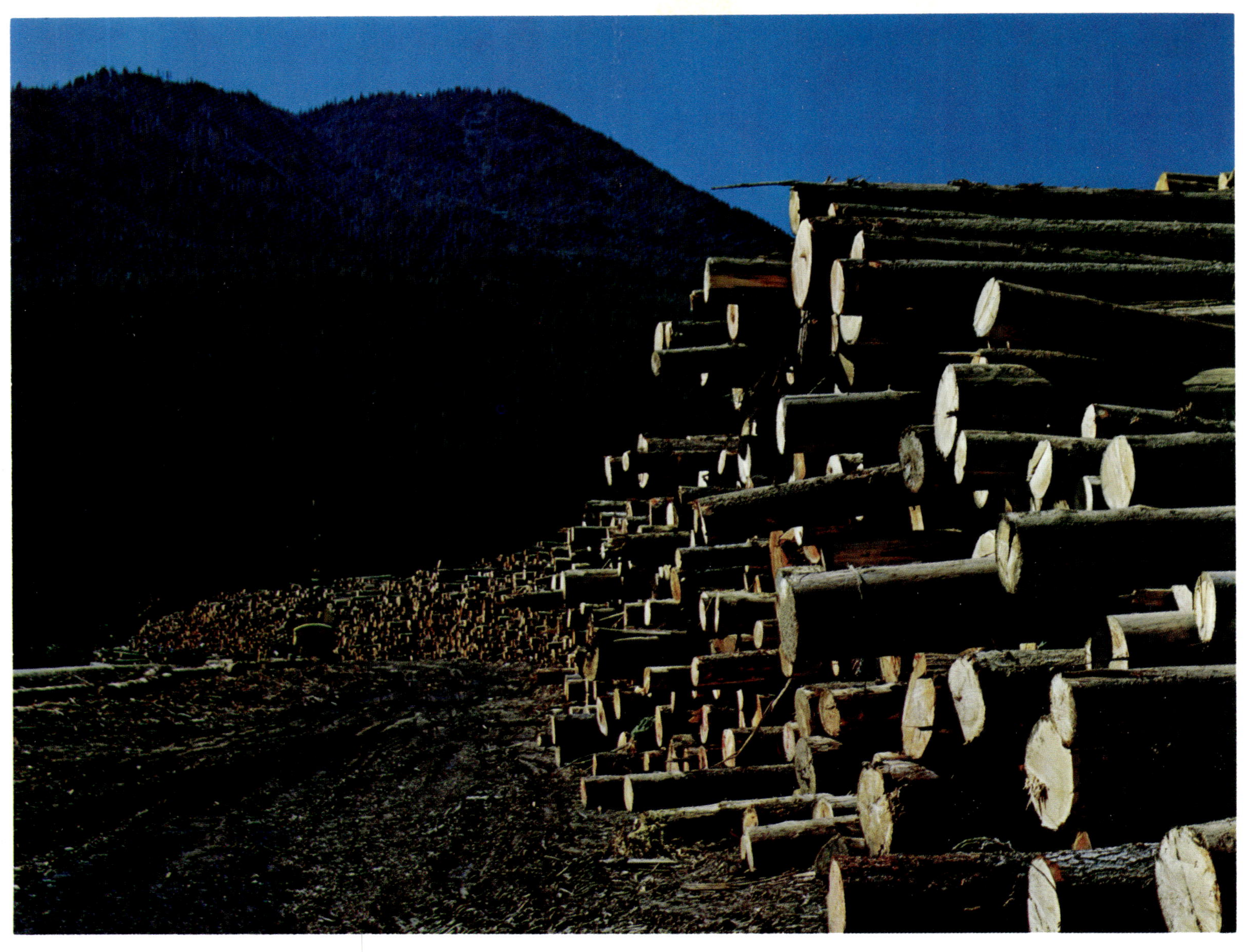

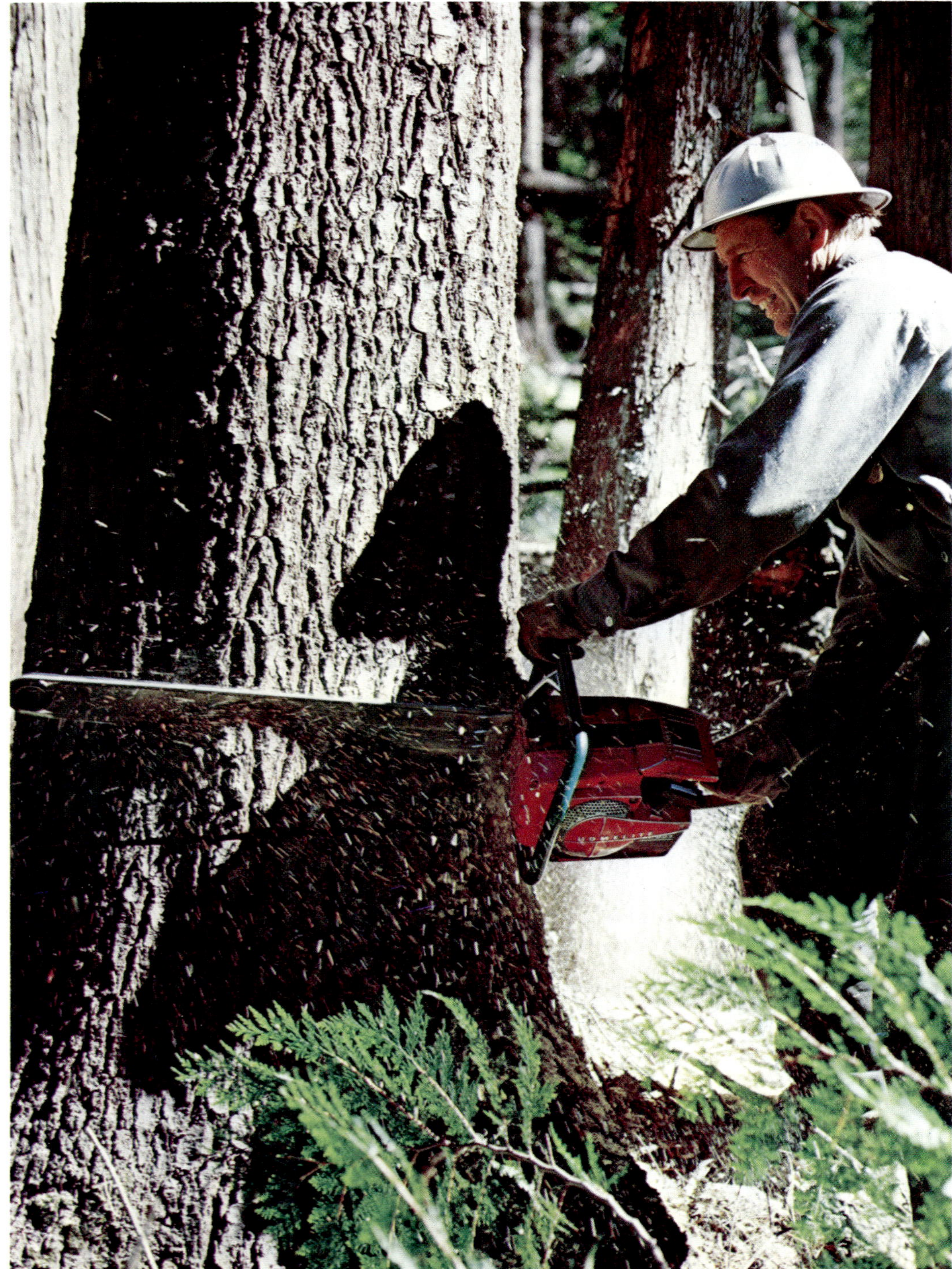

Above:

LAST DRIVE

Logs stacked along the North Fork of the Clearwater. For many years logs such as these were put into the river during times of spring flood and floated down to the Potlatch Forests plant on the mainstem Clearwater east of Lewiston. The building of Dworshak Dam ended that practice. The last drive was made in the spring of 1971.

Left:

A Modern-Day Logger and a Big Tree on the North Fork of the Clearwater, Where Some of the Finest Stands of Timber in the Nation Grow.

Right: Hell's Canyon Dam, Idaho Power Company.

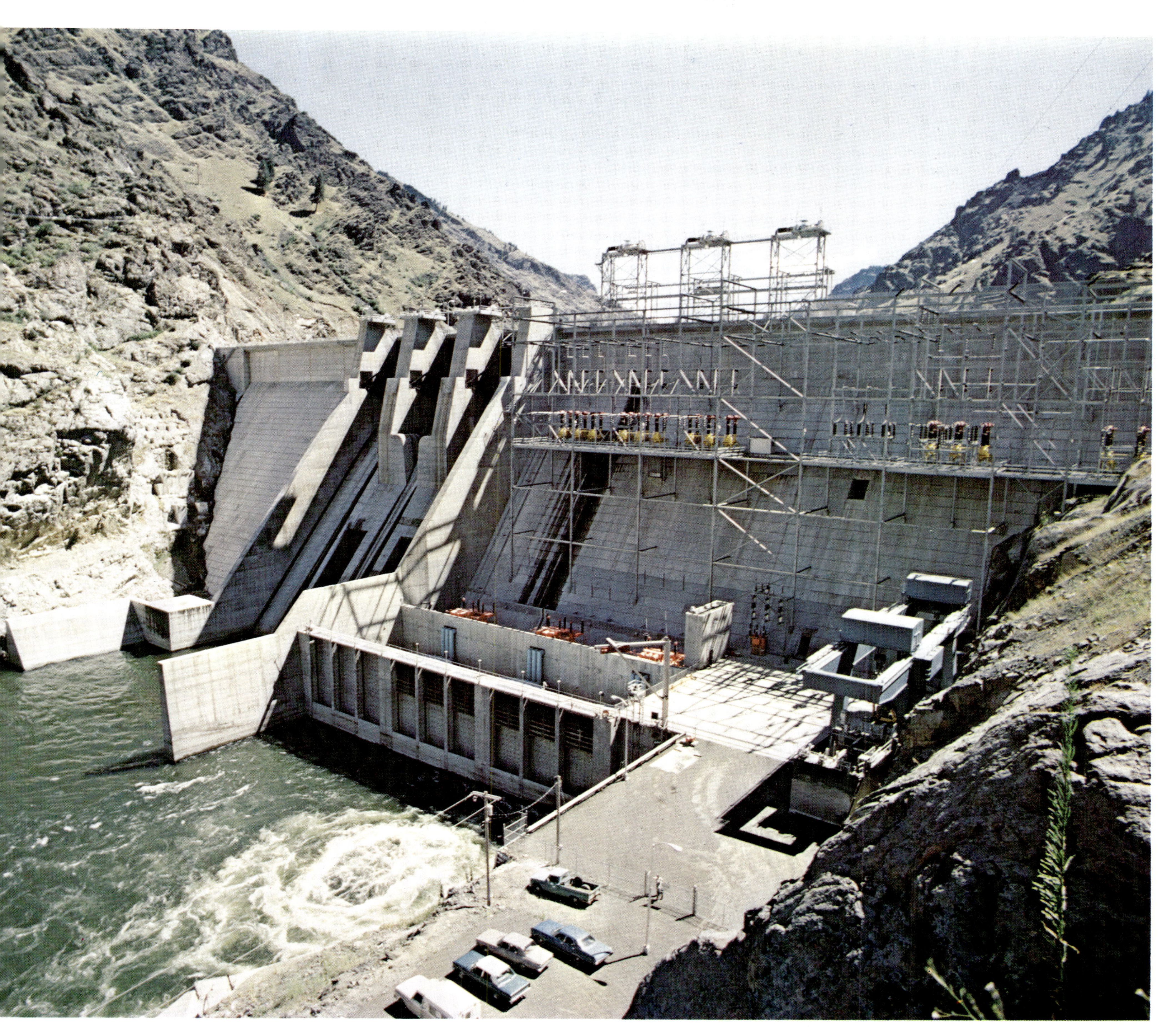

where their waters do not flood good tillable land, are contained in natural canyons, and do not by their seasonal fluctuations impede navigation or offend the esthetic eye with extensive mud flats adjacent to populated areas.

Run-of-the-river dams are built on the mainstem, with the primary aim of producing power with whatever natural flow is available to spin their turbines. By law they are required to release a sufficient quantity of water at all times to meet downstream navigation, fish passage, and irrigation needs, and the rates of fluctuation in the reservoirs behind them are strictly controlled.

Most of the storage dams on the tributaries and upper reaches of the Snake were built by the federal Bureau of Reclamation for irrigation purposes. Though power generation facilities have been included in some, their kilowatt output is small. For example, the six Bureau of Reclamation dams in Idaho and Wyoming have a total installed capacity of only 163,900 kilowatts.

In contrast, the seventeen dams built by the Idaho Power Company on the middle reaches of the Snake and its tributaries have a generating capacity of 1.5 million kilowatts. On the lower river, a relative newcomer to the hydro power generation field, the Corps of Engineers, has completed or currently under construction four large dams on the Snake mainstem and a fifth on the North Fork of the Clearwater whose presently authorized capacity is 2,270,880 kilowatts. When expanded to full capacity—as they no doubt will be eventually—they will generate 4,092,880 kilowatts of electric power.[1]

If we could confine the discussion of electric power generation within the Snake River watershed to the 109,000 square miles of the region itself—as we did the discussion of water in the irrigation section—we could dispense with the subject in one more brief paragraph. This would be it:

According to the most recent studies of current and future power needs of the region, in the years 1980, 2000, and 2020, both the Lower Snake and the Central Snake will produce more power than they require, despite projected growth, and will remain power-exporting areas. In the Upper Snake, that is, from Milner Dam to the headwaters, 600,000 kilowatts of additional capacity will be required by 1980; 600,000 more by 2000; and 1,800,000 by 2020. This will be thermal power, coal at first, then nuclear, and it will be supplied by Idaho Power Company and Utah Power and Light. . . .[2]

But unfortunately for brevity and simplicity, hydroelectric power, once generated, cannot be hoarded. Either the market comes to it or it goes to the market—and since high-voltage electricity can be moved much faster and with far less expense than can factories and cities, no discussion of hydroelectric power produced in the Snake River Country can be complete without a consideration of the Pacific Northwest as a whole, the West Coast, Canada, and, in some measure at least, the rest of the United States.

Just as the fifty small Idaho plants were absorbed by five companies, which in turn became one large company, so has the inexorable tendency toward centralization of authority over the distribution of electricity operated among federal government agencies in the Pacific Northwest. The Corps of Engineers built the first dam on the lower Columbia, Bonneville; the Bureau of Reclamation built the biggest dam, Grand Coulee; and, for a time, the Corps and the Bureau vied with each other for future projects. But neither, President Roosevelt decided, should have anything to do with the distribution of power generated by the dams.

For this purpose, he created a new agency, Bonneville Power Administration. By Executive Order of August 26, 1940, BPA was made the marketing agency for power generated at Grand Coulee Dam, Bonneville Dam, and all future federal dams to be built in the Pacific Northwest. In time, the agency would also take over marketing of power produced by existing Bureau of Reclamation dams in Idaho.

Without delving too deeply into the complex relationships between BPA, private companies, publicly owned companies, farmer-oriented co-ops, city, county, state, and other federal agencies, it may be said that the Bonneville Power Administration has managed to get along rather well with all concerned. As one of its officials recently said to me, "When we catch hell from the manager of a privately owned utility and the executive secretary of a farmer co-op in the same day—as we do—it's a sign we're doing a pretty good job."

Maintaining the most extensive network of transmission lines and controlling the largest bloc of power in the West, Bonneville sells kilowatts to public and private companies, makes contracts to deliver firm or interruptible power to manufacturers, acts as a traffic manager when its lines are used for power exchanges in a practice called "wheeling," does pioneer work in new engineering concepts and techniques, and even ventures into the field of diplomacy to work out treaties with Canada and agreements with southern California.

Truth is, residents of the Pacific Northwest *are* far more amenable to the idea of sharing water and power with their neighbor to the north than with their sister state to the south. But thanks to the patience and tact of former BPA Administrator, Charles Luce, two extremely important agreements have been made with Canada and southern California, which, because of their effect on the present and future power production of the Snake River Country, we shall outline briefly here.

Since the Columbia River's headwaters are in Canada and regulation of its flow would create great downstream power, navigation, and flood control benefits in the United States, this country proposed the following:

-----

1. Ice Harbor is 9.7 miles above the confluence of the Snake with the Columbia, Lower Monumental 41.6 miles, Little Goose 70.3 miles, and Lower Granite 107.5 miles. They are a little over one hundred feet high and are equipped with fish ladders. Dworshak, two miles above the confluence of the North Fork with the mainstem Clearwater, is 717 feet high, making it impractical to install fish ladders. Hoover Dam, on the lower Colorado, at 735 feet is higher—but it is a curved axis dam.

2. *Electric Power*, Appendix XV, Pacific Northwest River Basins Commission, December, 1969 (Preliminary Report), p. 167.

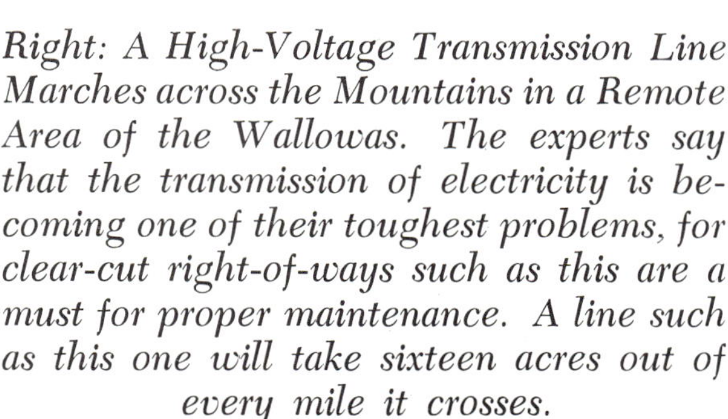

Right: A High-Voltage Transmission Line Marches across the Mountains in a Remote Area of the Wallowas. The experts say that the transmission of electricity is becoming one of their toughest problems, for clear-cut right-of-ways such as this are a must for proper maintenance. A line such as this one will take sixteen acres out of every mile it crosses.

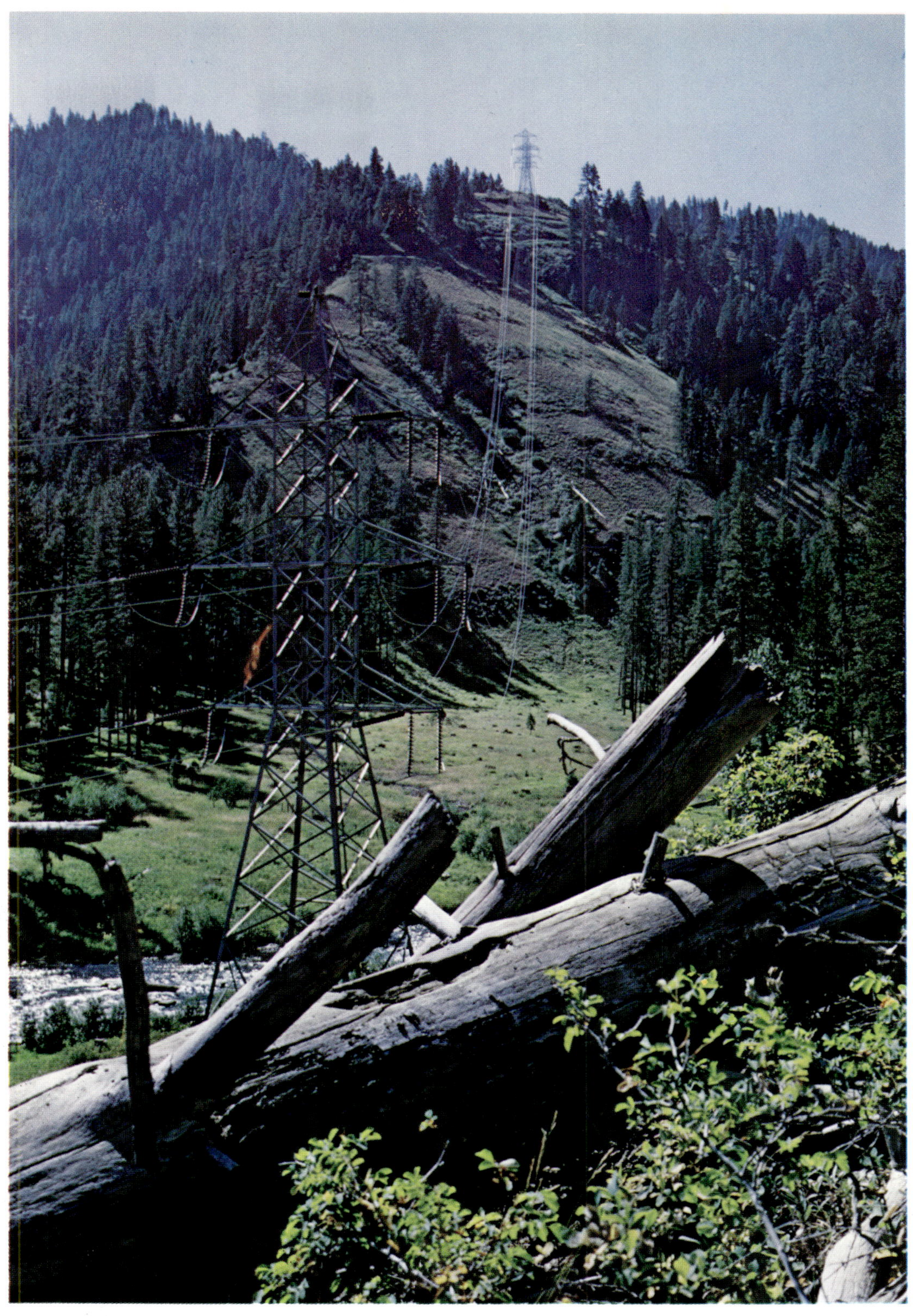

Below: Where the Future Meets Today. This is the Atomic Reactor Testing Station, west of Idaho Falls. Here we are looking at the site of Experimental Breeder Reactor No. II and its associated power plant.

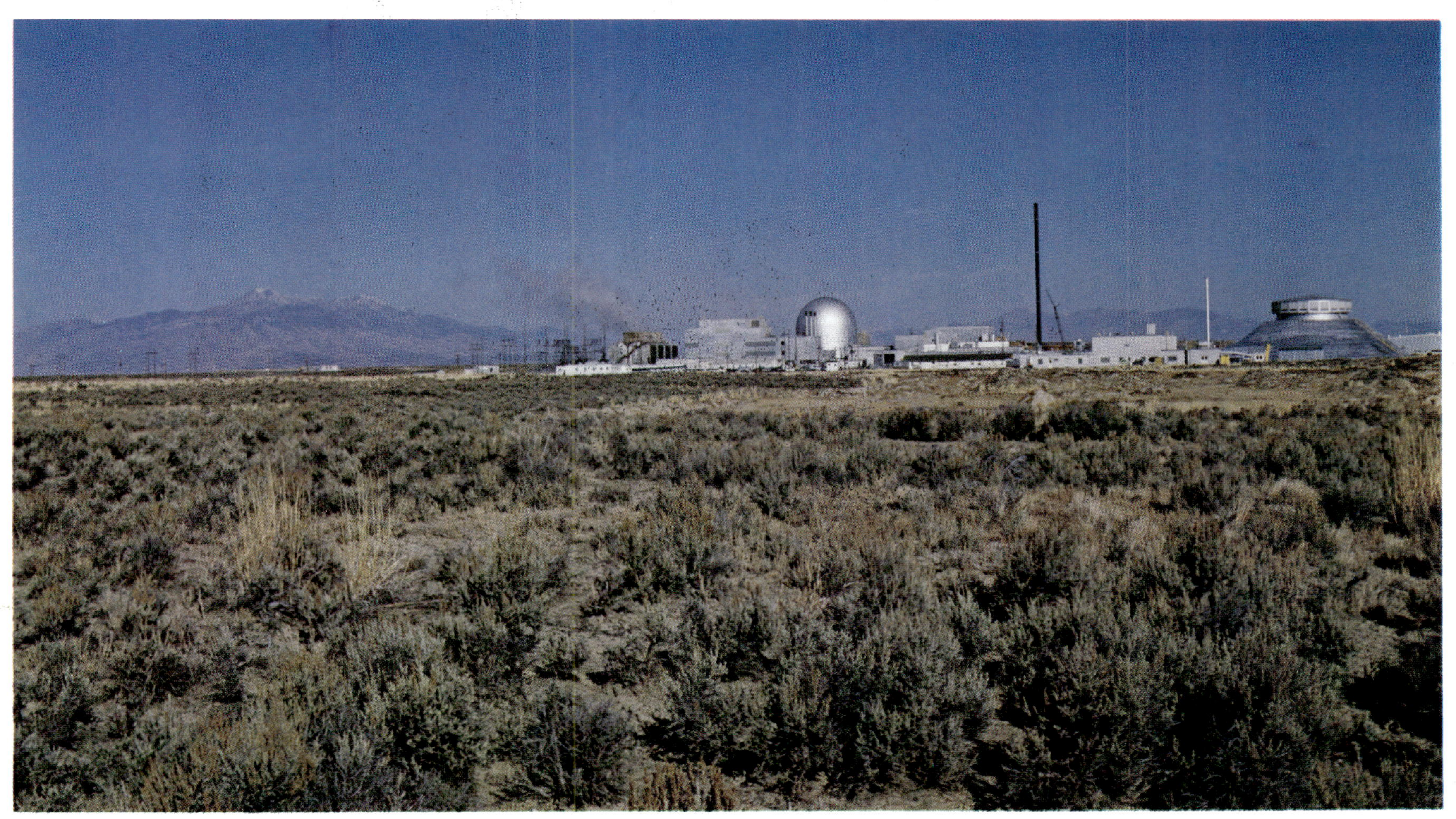

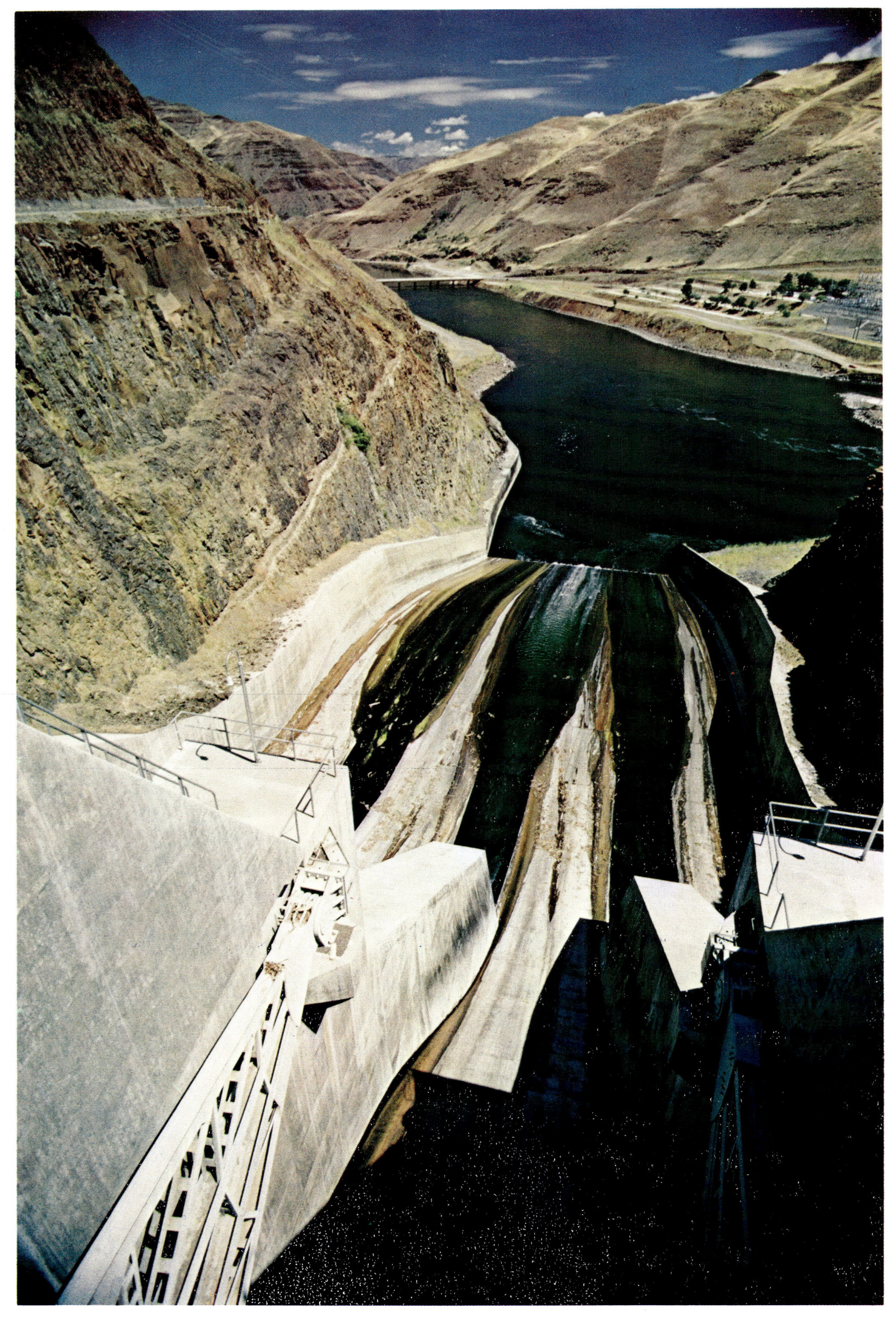

(1) Canada would build three reservoirs—Duncan, Arrow Lakes, and Mica—with a total of 15.5 million acre-feet of storage usable for improving streamflow in the United States.

(2) Construction would be completed within nine years of ratification of the treaty.

(3) The United States would pay Canada $254 million for downstream power and navigation benefits, $64 million for flood control benefits, and would give Canada one-half of the energy gained in the United States by Canadian storage.[3]

In October, 1964, the treaty was signed, the first payment was made, and work was begun to implement the agreement.

More complicated and involving more money, the agreement worked out between the Pacific Northwest and the Pacific Southwest was to tie the two regions together with a network of high-voltage transmission lines. Called "The Intertie," this is the biggest single transmission program ever undertaken in the United States. It is capable of carrying more than 4.5 million kilowatts south or north—roughly enough power to serve the combined needs of Chicago and Philadelphia.

Begun in 1967 and scheduled for completion in 1972, the transmission lines will tie together utilities in eleven western states, from Vancouver, B.C., to the Mexican border. Two of the lines will be extra-high-voltage direct current—a transmission technique imported from Sweden whose chief virtue is low line loss. The total investment in the grid will be $660 million. Of this sum, private utilities will put up $273 million, the Federal government $298 million, and the City of Los Angeles $89 million.[4]

To the natural question asked by residents of the Pacific Northwest: "With all our hydro power, what good will the Intertie do *us*?" the experts give this answer:

(1) Peak loads in the Southwest come in summer when electricity is needed for air conditioning. Normally at this time of year *we* have excess power to sell.

(2) Peak loads in the Northwest come in winter when electricity is needed for heating. Normally at this time of year *they* have excess power to sell.

The word "normally" in relation to power, like the word "surplus" in relation to water, is being used very gingerly by engineers and politicians these days. Like the rest of the nation, the Pacific Northwest is beginning to realize that its electric power resources are finite. But the point to be made here insofar as the Snake River Country is concerned is that as lightly populated and bountifully supplied with hydro generating capacity as it is, its future has been inexorably tied to that of the rest of the West with a skein of wires soaring across desert, plain, and mountain to the centers of population.

Just as the day may come when water requirements of an expanding population demand that a choice be made between raising a carload of Idaho potatoes or filling a swimming pool in a Palm Springs backyard, so may it also become necessary to choose between lighting a theater marquee in Hollywood or starting a fifty-horsepower electric pump to irrigate a field of alfalfa in the Magic Valley, near Twin Falls, Idaho.

That, as the Western movie hero says, *will be the day.*

* * *

3.

Whether hydro, thermal, or a combination of the two, an electric power generation and distribution system works very much like the family car. With 265 horsepower under the hood and a capability to go 120 miles per hour, the car with Mama at the wheel driving to and from the store and chauffeuring the kids around seldom exceeds thirty; Daddy on the freeway cruises at seventy-five; and only on rare occasions does Junior attempt to put the speedometer needle against the peg. But whoever is driving insists that the horsepower and potential for quick acceleration be under his foot.

Today's electric utility company invests nearly half a million dollars in plant for each person it employs.[1] Obviously, it would be financial folly to build an expensive thermal plant capable of carrying the highest conceivable load, then use only 30 to 50 percent of its capacity for twenty hours a day, if some cheaper, more efficient, more flexible means existed to meet peak demand during the other four hours. Whether the fuel be coal, oil, gas, or nuclear, time is required to build up and lower steam pressure, heat and fuel are wasted bringing a generator on and off the line—and this costs money that eventually the consumer must pay.

But water backed up behind a dam is potential energy that can be tapped as easily as turning a faucet on and off. No heat is involved, and the response time is for all practical purposes instantaneous. Whether generating at 30, 50, or 90 percent of capacity, a hydro plant relates the weight of falling water to energy demand so smoothly that, once programmed, computers can operate facilities at one or several sites untended by human hands.

As already noted, power used within the Snake River watershed is today 100 percent hydro. But outside the watershed, where much of it goes, an ever-increasing number of plants are thermal. For economic reasons, they are built

3. Ibid., pp. 7-10.

4. *Building the Pacific Intertie,* BPA Bulletin, August, 1968.

1. *Electric Power in America,* McCaig, p. 83.

Left: Spillways, Brownlee Dam

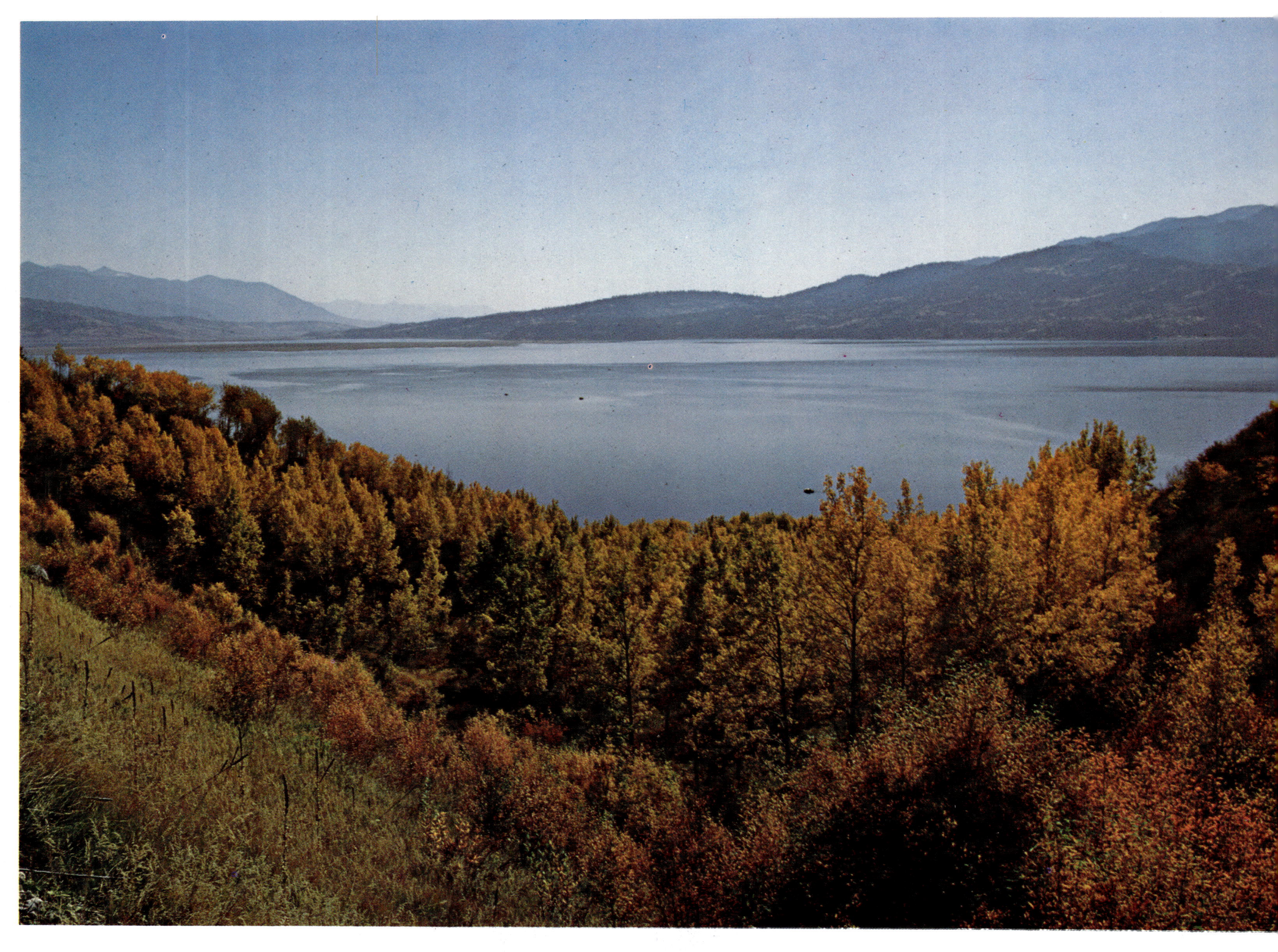

Palisades Reservoir, Upper Snake

to take care of what is called "Base Load." If we put this in terms of the family car analogy, they have the horsepower to cruise efficiently at 60, but when spurts of power are demanded they do not quickly respond to the foot depressing the accelerator.

Two hours each morning and two hours in late afternoon, Daddy takes to the freeway and drives 75; on special occasions, he does 80 or 90; and now and then Junior goes for the peg. And the power must be available—or the family goes shopping for another brand of car.

For these spurts in load, the thermal plants call on hydro facilities for what is termed "Peaking Capacity." It is in this area that the dams in the Snake River Country make their important contribution toward keeping electric rates in the Pacific Northwest the lowest in the nation—and the use of electricity per capita the highest. For those interested in figures, the cost per kilowatt hour over the United States as a whole for residential use is 2.25 cents; in the Pacific Northwest, it is 1.2 cents. Per capita use per year in the United States as a whole is 5,000 kilowatt hours; in the Pacific Northwest, it is 11,000.[2]

So far as big industry is concerned, the electric furnaces producing phosphorus in the Pacific Northwest pay 4 mills per kilowatt hour, while those in Florida pay 7 or 8. Since it requires 13,000 kilowatt hours to obtain a ton of phosphorus, it is not surprising that one-third of the nation's requirements now is produced by the nine plants in the Northwest (seven in Idaho and two in Montana) and that by the year 1985 regional production is expected to take over 45 percent of the market.[3]

Despite our resolve not to fill this brief discussion of power with statistics and tables, the relationship between hydro and thermal generation in the Pacific Northwest can be shown in no other way. Today, 96 percent of the electricity used in the region is hydro-generated. But in the future:

(Year)	*1980*	*2000*	*2020*
Hydro Resources	18 million KW	20 million	20 million
Thermal Resources	4.6 "	39.5 "	129 " [4]

Put in simple prose, these figures mean that the end is in sight, so far as the development of hydroelectric power in the region is concerned. Around 1985, the balance between hydro and thermal power will even out; and from that date on falling water will produce less and less of the region's total electric output. Yet because of its usefulness in the peaking capacity area, it will become ever more valuable.

Working on the theory that if a writer—whose electrical background consists of two youthful years spent as a field clerk with a power company construction crew—could comprehend a complex subject, he might be able to explain it to the layman reader, I have been guilty of simplification in these past three chapters—a crime seldom committed by electrical engineers. Now the time has come to define more complicated principles and terms, which must be grasped if we are to understand the current controversy over the resources of the Snake River Country.

Let's begin with that much-heard phrase: "Multipurpose dam."

* * *

4.

Though the planners of auditoriums, stadiums, and other public facilities seldom admit it, a "multipurpose" *anything* implies compromise and a lessening of value as regards one single purpose. Given a certain amount of money to build an arena that will accommodate intimate theater, ballet, rock 'n' roll concerts, basketball, and hockey games, the architect will come up with a structure in which all can be staged —but he won't really please anybody.

This is the problem faced by the dam builders.

For recreation, the water level behind a dam should remain stable. For irrigation, the reservoir should be filled to the brim during spring flood periods, then drawn down to bare mud flats during summer's drought. For power, water should pour through the turbines in great volume morning and evening to meet peaking needs, then be held back as base load facilities take over. For navigation, a steady flow must be maintained around the clock. For anadromous fish migration, an even flow must be maintained ten months out of the year; too little water means that salmon and steelhead cannot get upstream to spawn, too much creates an excess nitrogen problem, making fish die like decompressed divers with the "bends." And to further complicate the matter, wild animals and birds breed, feed, and lay eggs along shorelines whose water levels should vary (so their instincts tell them) according to the seasons rather than at the dictates of a computer responding to a signal from a load center in far-off Los Angeles.

Past experience has taught distribution engineers in the Pacific Northwest, where many homes are heated by electricity, that a temperature drop of one degree will increase demand by 100,000 kilowatts. Thus, when a cold front rolls in and the temperature drops ten degrees, an additional 1,000,000 kilowatts are required at once—almost half the present capacity of Grand Coulee Dam.[1]

So it was not in jest that the present Bonneville Power Administrator, H. R. Richmond, when speaking of agency plans to meet coming power needs, said that an important element was: "To pray for a mild winter."

In their capacity to generate power, regulate streamflow, and provide quiet pools for boating and water-skiing, all dams are multipurpose to a degree. But the higher the dam and the greater its storage area, the more multipurpose it can be—and the more complicated its operation problems. The best example of this in the Snake River watershed is Dworshak Dam, now nearing completion on the lower reaches of the North Fork of the Clearwater.

Historically, the flow of the North Fork varies from a minimum of 250 cubic feet per second to a maximum of 100,000. Slated to be the highest straight-axis dam in the United States at 717 feet, Dworshak will form a reservoir 53 miles long with a gross capacity of 3.5 million acre-feet. Depth of the water behind the dam will vary 155 feet from minimum to maximum pool, with the maximum level being maintained during the summer recreational period as much as possible. When all the turbines are installed, it will have a generating capacity of over one million kilowatts.[2]

Obviously, a reservoir of this size can hold back a lot of potentially damaging floodwater. Not so obviously (to the

2. *Pacific Northwest Economic Base Study for Power Markets*, Volume I, Summary, BPA, 1970, p. 148.

3. Ibid., p. 70.

4. *Power*, River Basins Comm., p. 147.

1. BPA figures.

2. Corps of Engineer statistics.

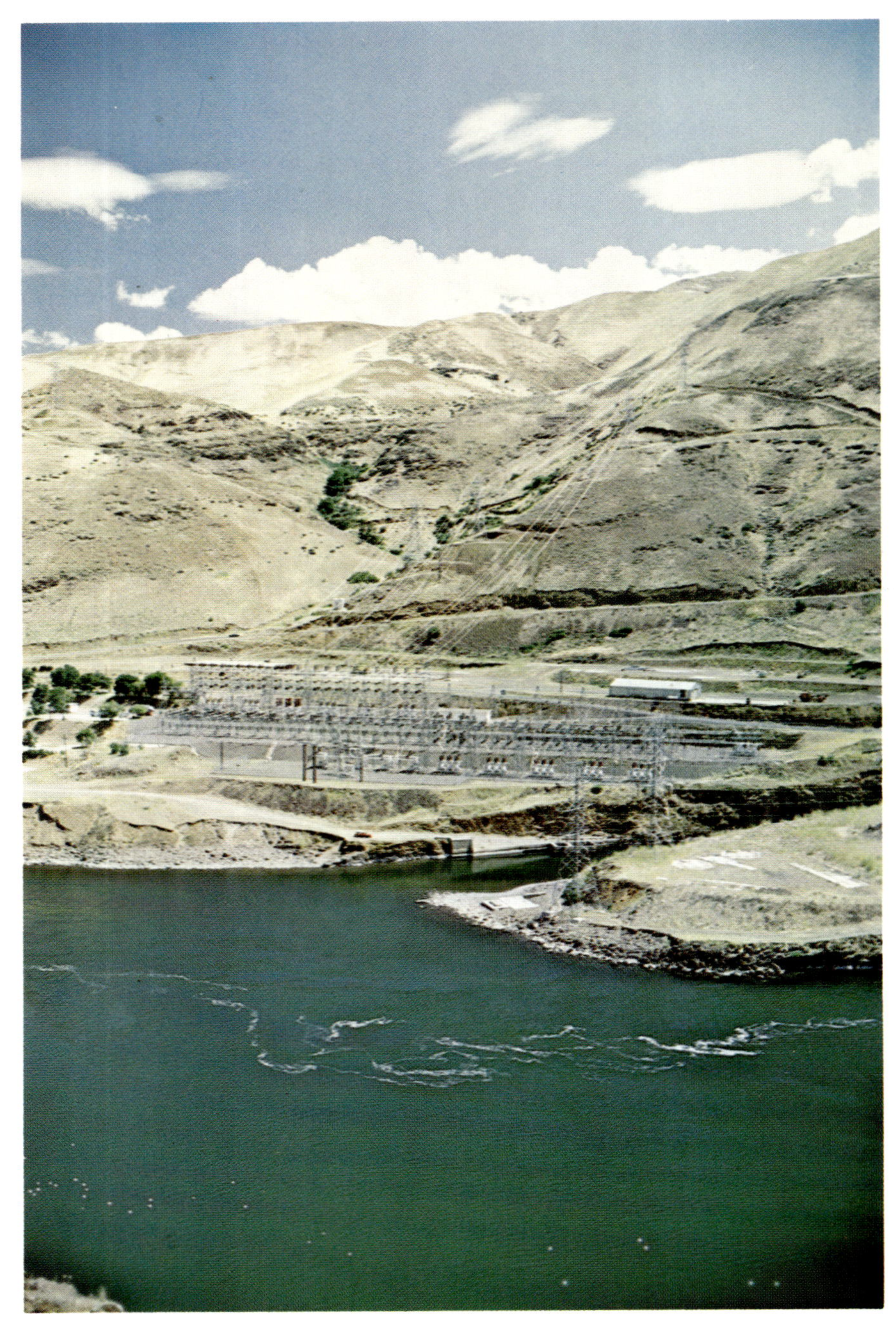

Left: Electric Power Switching Station below Brownlee Dam, Idaho Power Company.

Below: Slack Water behind Lower Monumental Dam, Lower Snake.

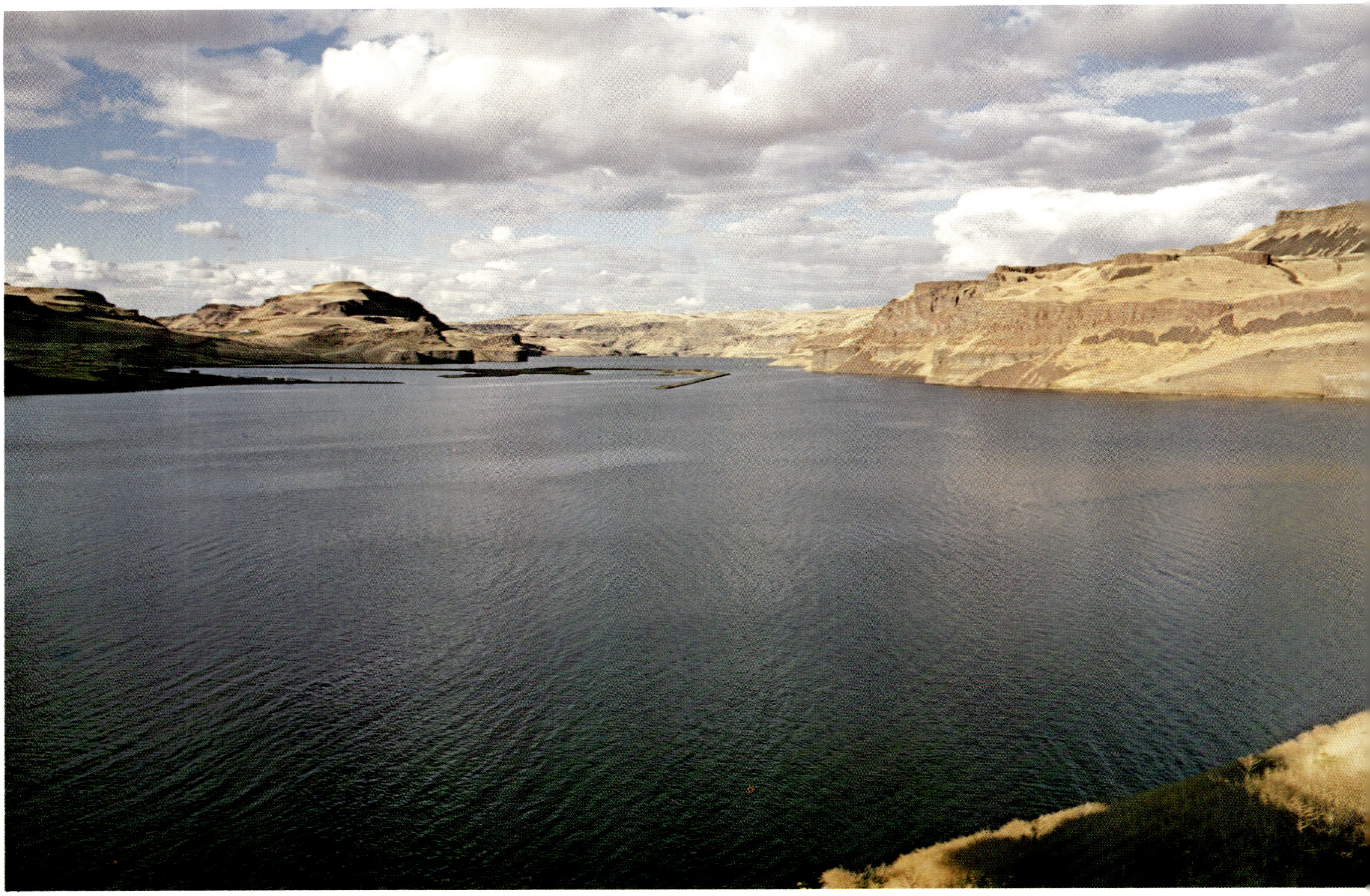

layman, at least), the tremendous amount of water pouring through the turbines when they are spinning at full capacity two hours each morning and again in late afternoon to provide peaking capacity power can cause great fluctuations immediately downstream, making boating and fishing dangerous, if not impossible.

From the viewpoint of the hydro engineer, water for peaking capacity use should pour through the turbines only four or five hours a day, then be held back the other nineteen or twenty hours. Furthermore, he would like to retrieve the peak-release water, if possible, and use it again. And this he can do through a re-regulating dam, reversible turbines, and a practice called "Pumped Storage."

A re-regulating dam is sixty or seventy feet high and is built ten to twenty miles downstream from the main power-generating dam. Its purpose is to contain high-volume releases of water, smooth out river flow, and, when feasible, hold the water in a pool whence it may be pumped back uphill into the main reservoir for later use. The pumping is done during low-demand periods using thermal facilities in the system that would otherwise be idle. Due to transmission losses and inefficiencies in the operation of pump-turbines, approximately one and one-half times as much energy is required for pumping as is obtained in the generating phase. However, this increased energy use is justified by the high value of the peak generation.[3]

In the case of Dworshak, the re-regulating low dam, Lenore, would be located downstream on the mainstem of the Clearwater. Fish passage facilities would be included at Lenore, which would permit the runs of steelhead and salmon to continue their spawning migrations up the Middle and South forks. To replace the loss of the North Fork as a spawning stream, the Corps of Engineers has built the world's largest fish hatchery at Ahsahka (near Orofino), which is operated by the Federal Fish and Wildlife Bureau. Thus, say the Engineers, even with the loss of the North Fork, there will be more fish than ever—and Lenore must be built in order to operate Dworshak at its maximum efficiency.

On the mainstem of the Snake in Hell's Canyon—specifically, the High Mountain Sheep site with a downstream re-regulating dam—the same principle is involved: a high power, flood control, storage dam, and a lower downstream dam to make it work at maximum efficiency. As will presently be shown, the "area of agreement" between the dam builders and the fish advocates is minuscule. But the point to be made here in regard to the generation of hydro power is that obtaining full potential from a high dam does require the construction of a low re-regulating dam downstream.

To the engineer, failing to develop full potential is a capital crime. To those people who view a river as something more than a workhorse to spin turbines, sacrificing kilowatts to retain steady streamflow, fish runs, and a free-running river is a virtue of the highest order.

-----

3. *Power,* River Basins Comm., p. 98.

Thus, the lines of controversy are drawn. But before we follow the contending troops into the field, let us briefly review a matter long debated in the Snake River Country, as in the rest of the United States—private versus public power.

As already noted, a private utility, Idaho Power, has dominated the generation and distribution of electricity in the Upper and Central Snake. Moving gradually downriver into what is sometimes called the Grand Canyon of the Snake, Idaho Power completed Brownlee Dam in 1959; Oxbow in 1961; and Hell's Canyon in 1968. Since the Snake is a navigable river flowing through several states, dams built on it must be licensed by the Federal Power Commission. Until recently, the question put to the FPC was not whether a dam should be built but who should build it—a private or public agency.

On the Lower Snake, the Corps of Engineers completed Ice Harbor in 1961; Lower Monumental in 1969; Little Goose in 1970; is currently at work on Dworshak, which is scheduled to put power on the line in 1972; has begun work on Lower Granite, whose completion will provide slack water for navigation upstream to the Lewiston-Clarkston area; and has an authorization to build Asotin Dam, six miles upstream from Lewiston on the Snake.

This will leave approximately one hundred miles of the river still running free—and it is in this area that the current controversy has reached its peak. With private power moving down and public power moving up the Snake, it appeared for many years that the confrontation would be between these two adversaries. But even as they prepared for their Armageddon in the depths of Hell's Canyon, a third party entered the contest.

The environmentalist.

He had been around for a long while in many guises: the Indian inarticulately protesting the flooding of his traditional fishing grounds; the bird watcher concerned over the loss of nesting areas for migratory waterfowl; the sports fisherman worried about the future of steelhead and salmon; the Sierra Club member in love with wilderness areas; the white-water boatman bent on preserving a few challenging rapids; the naturalist, the antiquarian, the maiden lady in tennis shoes, and other assorted "little" people who for obscure reasons insisted on throwing their fragile bodies down before the juggernaut of Progress.

The question was not *who* should build the next dam, they quietly insisted, but whether *any* dam should be built. For a long while, private power advocates, public power boosters, the Federal Power Commission, and the courts, which were being called upon to referee the frequent quarrels, paid them little heed.

But the mouse had roared.

In the final section of this book, we shall attempt to explain what the ensuing and presently raging sound and fury are all about.

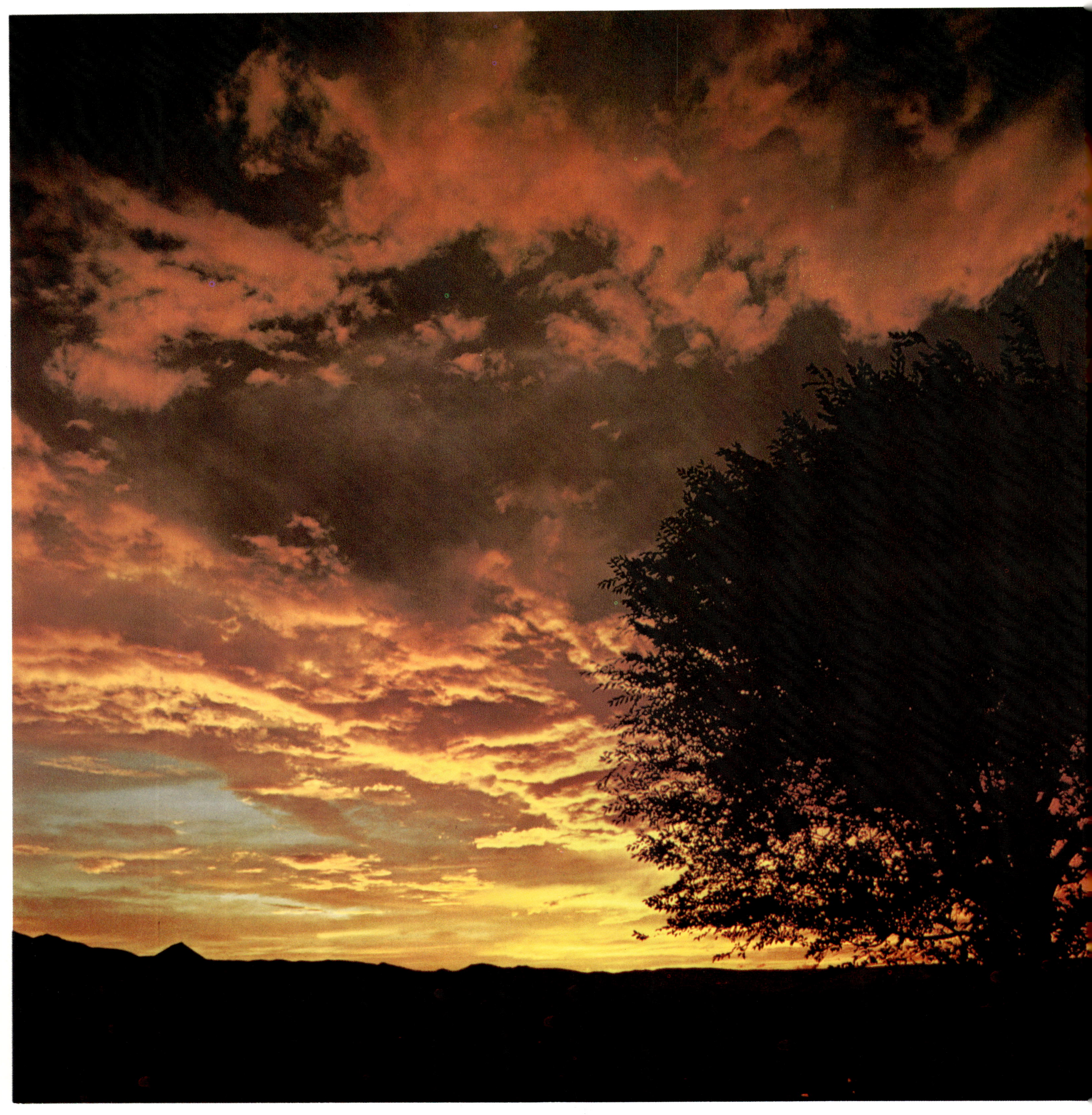

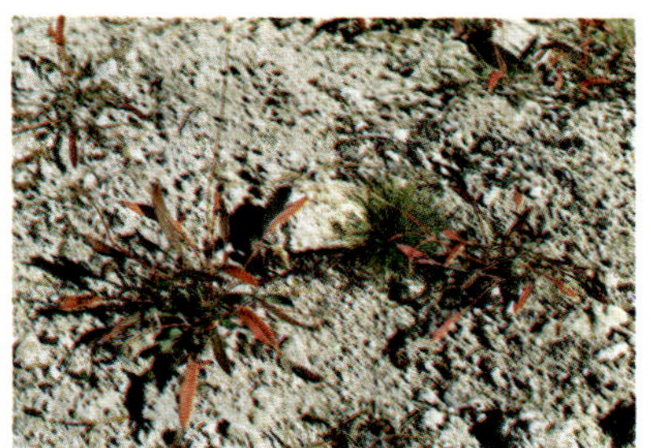

"Anyone who can solve the problem of water will be worthy of two Nobel prizes—one for science and one for peace."
JOHN F. KENNEDY

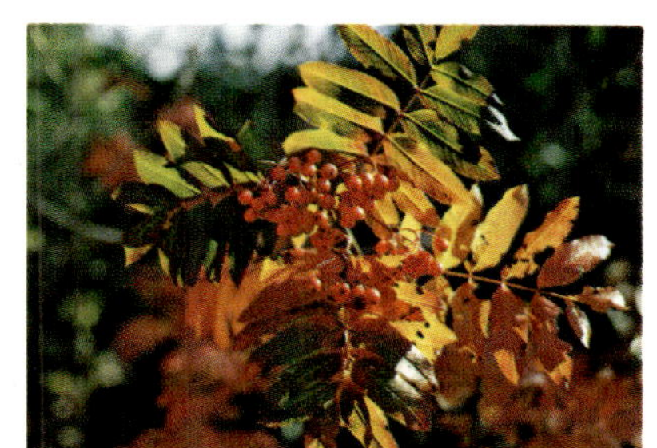

PART NINE

River of Controversy

1.

In the early West, Bret Harte once wrote, more men were killed in disputes over water than in quarrels over gold, women, livestock, and land combined. During modern times in the Snake River Country, water still inspires more vocal violence, legal controversy, editorial polemics, and political rhetoric than any other subject.

Whether we be an engineer, a wilderness lover, a farmer, or a city dweller, we tend to regard rivers as living beings possessed of human, royal, or godlike traits. We call the Hudson majestic, the Mississippi mighty, the Rio Grande sleepy, and the Colorado awesome. When we commit a crime against a river—such as turning the Hudson into a sewer—a few of us suffer the same guilt feelings we would suffer if we contributed to the degradation of a lovely lady. When a river commits a crime against us—such as the Mississippi flooding lands and destroying homes and lives—we put Old Man River on trial, convict him, and pronounce an engineering sentence restricting his antisocial activities.

Geologically speaking, the Snake is a young river through most of its length; certainly, until dams disciplined its brawling, heedless strength, its behavior was that of a juvenile delinquent. Following the time-tested frontier theory that hard work is the surest cure for wildness in horses and teen-agers, the Snake has been forced to labor and mature. In the 1,036-mile length of the mainstem, eighteen dams between Jackson Hole and its confluence with the Columbia have so altered the appearance of "The Accursed Mad River" that the early explorers, should they return to view the child they christened, would recognize it only in two limited stretches.

One of these is in western Wyoming, where for twenty-five miles or so from the mouth of the Hoback to the Idaho border the Snake still tumbles beautiful and free through "a fearsome gorge" in which members of the Wilson Price Hunt party felt no boat could live. But even here the exuberantly youthful river may be forced to grow up, for this area contains the last and best site for a large multipurpose dam.[1] Downstream Idaho farmers in need of more late season summer irrigation water view the proposed Bureau of Reclamation dam three miles upstream from Alpine, Wyoming, as eminently practical and sensible. Wyoming recreation and tourist promoters view it otherwise. But for the time being, at least, the Snake in these few miles still romps and plays.

The other stretch of river that would be recognized by the returning shades of Donald McKenzie, Captain Bonneville, and the daring pilots of the *Shoshone* and the *Norma* is that between the downstream face of Hell's Canyon dam and Lewiston, Idaho—roughly one hundred miles. But here the Snake currently faces the most serious trial of its life. As always, the forces determined to tame it once and for all are formidable. But for the first time in its long history of juvenile delinquency hearings, it has staunch, able defenders sitting at its table in court.

No writer in his right mind would dream of attempting to resolve the complexities of the conflict now approaching a climax in Hell's Canyon within the few pages that can be allotted to them in this book. The transcript from the most recent U.S. Senate Hearing, for example, runs 323 pages of very small print. This same transcript lists no less than 140 *other* hearings in various courts, commissions, and decision-making bodies between 1954 and 1970, many of which were

Left: Sunset, near La Grande, Oregon

---

1. Alpine Dam would be located three miles upstream from the Idaho-Wyoming border. It would be 440 feet high, its pool would provide 1,078,000 acre-feet of storage space, and its generating capacity would be 270,000 kilowatts. Engineers say: "The addition of Alpine to the system would allow greater flexibility in operation of Jackson Lake and thereby enhance its use for recreational purposes." River Basins Commission Report, Preliminary, 1970, *Power,* p. 75. Needless to say, free-running river advocates feel that a dam which will turn 25 miles of beautiful river into a slack-water pool will enhance nothing.

as lengthy and wordy. But since this is fact and not fiction, we are obliged to take a deep breath and wade in.

Between 1945 and 1955, the issue in the stretch of river called the Middle Snake was private versus public power. Coupled with it was the question of whether a single high dam or three low dams should be built. After prolonged and heated controversy, the Federal Power Commission ruled in favor of private enterprise and the three low dams concept, issuing a license on August 4, 1955, to the Idaho Power Company to build Brownlee, Oxbow, and Hell's Canyon dams.

Brownlee, 395 feet high, with a nameplate power generating capacity of 450,000 kilowatts, was completed in 1959. Oxbow, 12.5 miles downstream, 205 feet high, with a capacity of 220,000 kilowatts, was finished in 1961. Hell's Canyon, 23 miles downriver, 270 feet high, with a capacity of 450,000 kilowatts, began putting power on the line in 1968.

Meanwhile, on the Lower Snake, Ice Harbor, Lower Monumental, and Little Goose were built, and preliminary work got under way on Lower Granite. All were Corps of Engineers projects whose completion would provide slack water for navigation upstream to the Lewiston-Clarkston area. Six miles above Lewiston, still another dam, Asotin, was authorized by the Federal Power Commission, which would back up water another thirty miles or so—leaving a little over seventy miles of the Snake in this sector still running free.

The Clearwater and the Salmon, which drain western Idaho's magnificent wilderness area, together contribute 40 percent of the river's flow. Combined with the smaller Grande Ronde and Imnaha rivers, which enter the Middle Snake from the west, they provide one of the most important spawning grounds in the Pacific Northwest for Chinook salmon, steelhead, and other varieties classed under the general head "anadromous" fish. Also native to the Snake in this region is the white sturgeon, which in time past reached lengths of twelve feet or more and weighed up to 1,500 pounds.

None of these fish will spawn in still water, and attempting to catch them on hook and line in pools behind dams is an exercise in futility. Prior to the dam-building era, anadromous fish of one variety or another migrated ten months out of the year as far up the Snake as Shoshone Falls, and up the Columbia into Canada. As was proven at the relatively low dam, Bonneville, it is feasible to provide ladders —that is, a series of stair-step concrete pools through which a current of water flows—up which the fish will climb in their return to the place of their birth, providing the dam is no more than one or two hundred feet high. Above that height, fish passage facilities are impractical.

On the upper Columbia, Grand Coulee Dam, which is 550 feet high, was constructed without any attempt being made to preserve upstream fish runs. In reference to that piece of environmental mayhem, Idaho Senator Len B. Jordan commented during a recent hearing:

> "You mentioned the Grand Coulee Dam and that has raised recollections in my mind. I know when Grand Coulee was built in the 1930s, without consultation with the Canadians we went forward with the project that destroyed a thousand miles of the finest spawning beds in the world, most of them in Canadian waters. The Canadians have never quite forgiven us for that."[2]

In the 1930s, of course, jobs and what was at that time considered to be the most grandiose "make-work" project ever conceived seemed far more important than fish. Northwestern rivers were full of salmon; spawning streams seemed inexhaustible; and, except to a few visionaries, Grand Coulee appeared to be the biggest scheme President Roosevelt had yet devised to waste the taxpayers' money. But as time passed and more dams were proposed and built, the problem of fish preservation came to be taken more seriously. In August, 1962, Idaho Power Company stated:

> "Completion of Hell's Canyon Dam also will put the finishing touches on another broad phase of the company's development—fish conservation.
>
> "Acting on the recommendation of federal and state fishery agencies, Idaho Power already has invested more than $8.6 million in a system of fish facilities that is the only one on the Snake and Columbia rivers providing passage in both directions for migrating salmon and steelhead. The two-way system, which costs $1.1 million annually for fixed costs, operation, and maintenance, includes a net-skimmer facility in the Brownlee reservoir for ocean-bound fingerlings which is the first of its kind ever built.
>
> "At Oxbow, the company is operating a conventional fish ladder to handle adult migrants heading upstream to spawn, as well as a facility for research on artificial propagation of salmon."[3]

But the expensive fish-passage facilities did not work; runs above Hell's Canyon dam were extinguished; and all that could be done with the spawners reaching the dam's lower face was to trap and transport them to artificial propagation facilities. Their eggs were planted in the Salmon, where, it was hoped, runs could be built up to replace those lost upriver.

As dams proliferated on the Columbia and Lower Snake, the Corps of Engineers, too, encountered fish-passage problems. If the dissolved oxygen content goes beneath a certain level in a slack-water pool behind a dam, fish sicken and die—and anadromous fish succumb more quickly than carp, squawfish, and suckers. When a great deal of water tumbles unused over dam spillways, the nitrogen level rises,

-----

2. Middle Snake River Moratorium Hearing, Ninety-First Congress, Second Session on S. 940, A Bill to Prohibit the Licensing of Hydroelectric Projects on the Middle Snake River Below Hell's Canyon for a Period of 10 Years, February 16, 1970, p. 48.

3. *Bulletin,* Idaho Power Company, August, 1962.

causing serious fish kills downstream. When water drops through the penstocks to spin the turbines, descending fish may be chopped to bits by the blades; however, this danger has been remedied to a large degree by the installation of slower spinning turbines, with larger gaps between the blades.

At each dam, a certain number of upstream-bound spawners fail to unravel the confusion of attraction water, ladder steps, and the altered river pathway, thus die without spawning.[4] So the more dams that block their way, the higher the total mortality. Artificial propagation and release can mitigate this loss, of course, but such facilities cost money to build and maintain. Oil spills from river traffic and pollution from industry, food-processing plants, municipalities, and farms, as well as the newest form of pollution—waste heat from nuclear reactors at the Hanford complex on the Columbia above the mouth of the Snake—also take their toll.

Ten years ago, when sportsmen, conservationists, and clean-river advocates first began criticizing the polluters, it was not uncommon to hear a public official or private promoter of progress dismiss the complaints with the comment: "If it's a choice between fish and jobs, the fish will have to go." Such comments are rarely heard today. For the realization has finally dawned on all but the most dinosaur-minded public officials and private promoters of progress that in the Snake River Country fish *are* jobs.

According to figures compiled by the U.S. Fish and Wildlife Service Bureau of Commercial Fisheries, the Middle Snake makes a very large contribution to commercial and sports fisheries from Alaska to California. Annually from fish spawned in the area, commercial fisheries harvest 7,925,000 pounds of Chinook Salmon, 12,000 pounds of Sockeye Salmon, and 276,000 pounds of Steelhead Trout.

Sports fishermen, whose efforts are measured in terms of Angler Days rather than pounds of fish caught, spend 1,942,600 days fishing for Chinook Salmon and 766,700 days fishing for Steelhead Trout.

In money terms, the Bureau sets a value of $0.56 per pound on commercially-caught Chinook and $0.30 per pound on Sockeye and Steelhead. In the Sports Fisheries category, the Bureau sets a value of $6.00 per Angler Day on both Chinook and Steelhead.

A bit of elementary arithmetic indicates that the annual value of the anadromous fish spawned in the Middle Snake is just a shade under $21 million. Which in any area means a lot of jobs.[5]

To Idaho, fishing as a sport is far more important than salmon in a can, for the state's fourth largest and fastest growing industry is tourism. For novice or expert, there are few fishing thrills that can equal hooking a big steelhead in a free-flowing stream or a monster Chinook in a deep pool below a riffle. Theoretically, both fish stop eating when they head upriver to spawn; thus, they strike lure, fly, egg-cluster, plastic golf tee, or gob of worms only in irritation or anger. But whatever their motivation, a ten- to fifty-pound fish on the end of a monofilament line in a fast-running wilderness stream is an experience not soon forgotten.

Considerable animosity between Idaho, eastern Washington, and the downriver area of Oregon exists regarding what the Fish and Wildlife Bureau calls the "Steelhead Trout." Most Snake River Country sportsmen call it a steelhead and let it go at that. It looks like (and is) a rainbow trout, but unlike the inland rainbow—which spends its entire life in fresh water—it goes to sea, matures there for two to four years, then returns to spawn in the waters of its birth. Unlike the salmon, which inevitably dies after spawning, it can survive, go back to sea, and return to fresh water to spawn again. However, because of the obstacles now placed in its way, this seldom happens.[6]

Idaho and Washington classify it as a sports fish. But Oregon permits it to be netted by commercial fishermen on the lower Columbia. Since anadromous fish runs are cyclic, Idaho grows quite angry when forced to curtail its fishing season during light-run years, as occasionally happens, while downstream Oregon gill-netters continue to take Idaho-born steelhead attempting to return and spawn in Idaho waters. To date, all attempts to resolve the controversy have failed as abysmally as the efforts of Alaskans to stop the Russians from poaching in American waters.

With the importance of the fish runs in mind, we now can discuss the battle over power and dams in the Middle Snake.

Following the Federal Power Commission's decision to let private enterprise build three low dams in the upper reaches of Hell's Canyon, public power agencies regrouped their forces. In the seventy-five miles of river still uncommitted, several attractive sites for high multipurpose dams still existed. The one with the greatest potential was Nez Perce, located at River Mile 187, one mile downstream from the mouth of the Salmon, and five miles downstream from the mouth of the Imnaha. Eighteen public utility districts, collectively called the Washington Public Power Supply System, filed application with the FPC in 1960 for a license to build the dam.

The reaction from conservationists was violent. Nez Perce promised to be one of the most destructive dams ever built, they said, for it would: (1) Flood the Lower Salmon; (2) Flood the Lower Imnaha, and (3) Form a slack-water pool over the remaining free-flowing length of the Middle Snake itself. Federal and state fish experts unanimously agreed that a high dam at the Nez Perce site would not simply deplete the anadromous fish runs of the area, it would extinguish the runs forever.

Faced with such strong opposition, the association of public utilities then amended its Nez Perce license applica-

4. Fish experts estimate that 10 to 15 percent of the spawners reaching the base of a given dam fail to negotiate the fish ladders.

5. *Middle Snake Resources Studies, Memorandum,* April 29, 1968, Table 3, p. 8, U.S. Dept. of the Interior, Fish and Wildlife Service, Bureau of Commercial Fisheries.

6. Both rainbow and steelhead are classified as *Salmo Gairdneri* by the Washington State Game and Fish Dept.

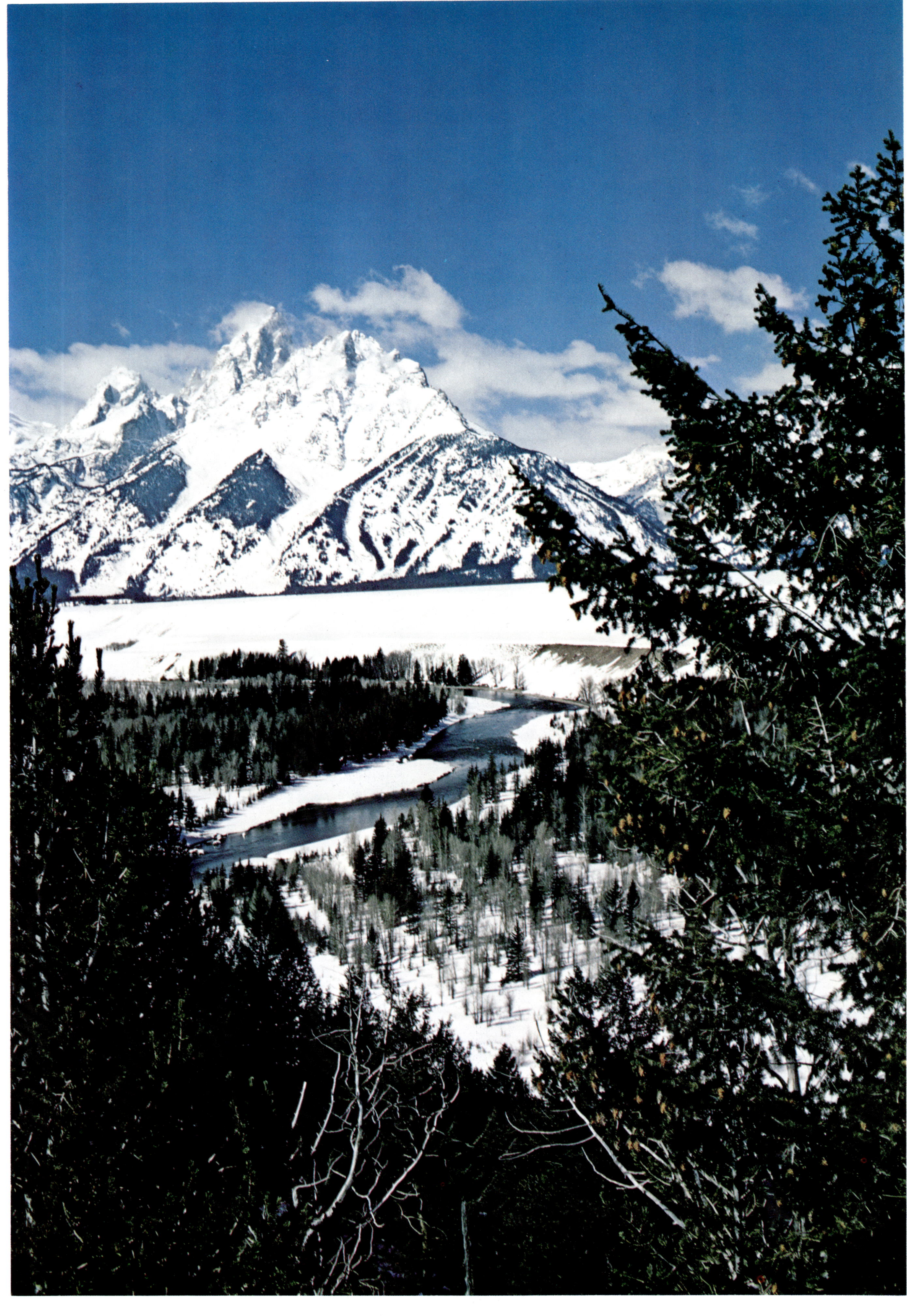

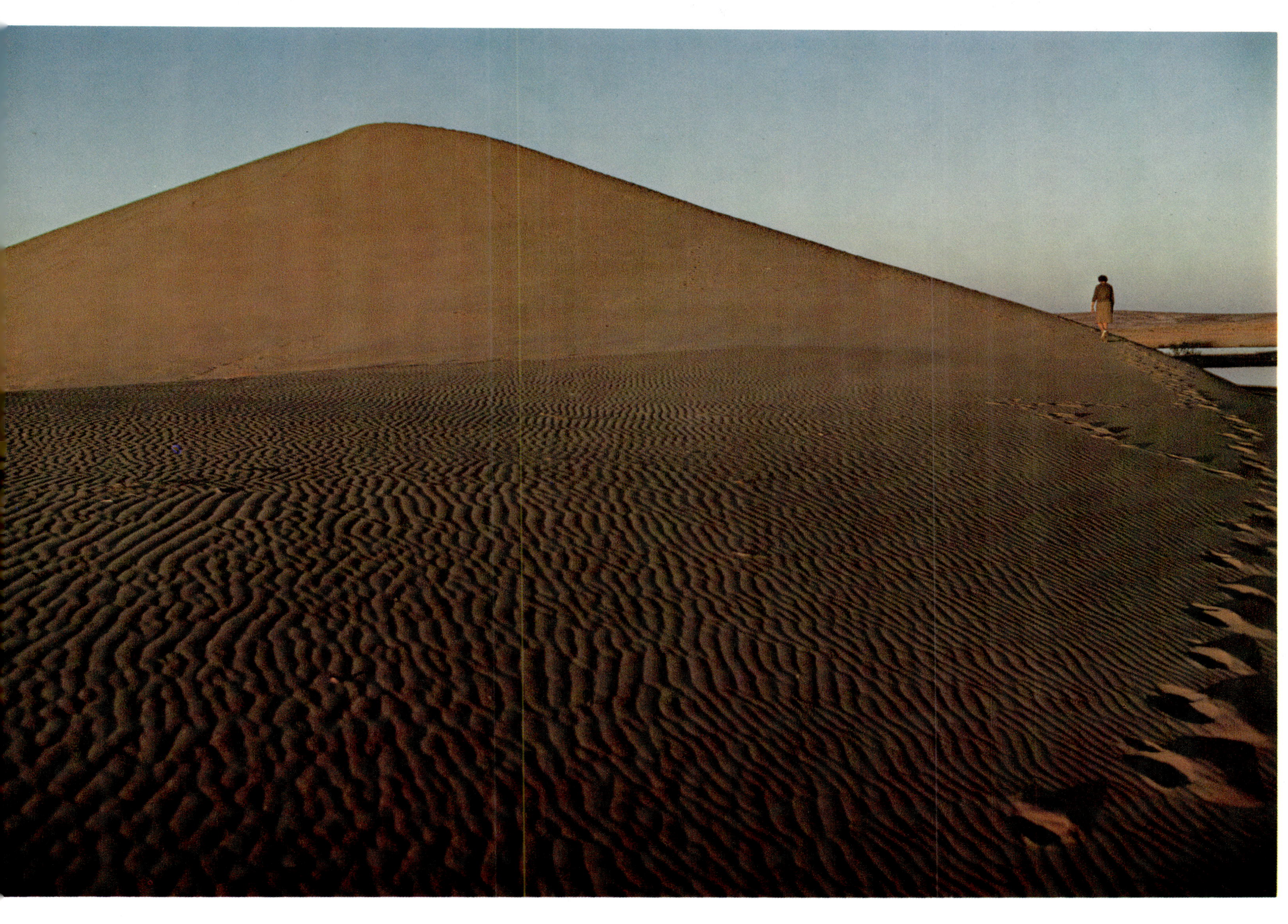

Above:

THE BRUNEAU SAND DUNES

Located south of the Snake, near Bliss, Idaho, and now in the Idaho State Park System, these are the highest sand dunes in North America.

Left: The Snake near Its Birthplace, with the Grand Tetons as a Backdrop.

tion to include a site farther upriver. This was known as the High Mountain Sheep site, located at River Mile 189, a mile upstream from the mouth of the Salmon, two and a half miles downstream from the mouth of the Imnaha. In order to make its power-generating facilities operate at maximum efficiency, a re-regulating low dam—China Gardens—would be required below the mouth of the Salmon at River Mile 172.

Complications arose immediately. Agencies from three states—Washington, Oregon, and Idaho—were involved, as was the federal government. Previously, a corporation consisting of four private companies—Pacific Power and Light, Portland General Electric, Montana Power, and Washington Water Power—had filed an application for a license to build a dam at the same site. And, belatedly, Department of the Interior Secretary Stewart Udall asked to intervene in the Middle Snake River case in favor of federal construction of the High Mountain Sheep Dam. Standing in the wings off-stage waiting for their cue to supply facts and figures pro and con were experts employed by the Corps of Engineers, the Bureau of Reclamation, construction contractors and unions, Forest Service, Fish, Wildlife, and Commercial Fisheries interests, conservationists, and others.

After many hearings, the FPC ruled in favor of Pacific Northwest Power—the combine of four private utilities—and on February 5, 1964, issued this corporation a 50-year license to construct and operate High Mountain Sheep Dam.

But the battle had just begun. All three losers—the association of public utilities, the Department of the Interior, and combined conservation groups as diverse as the Washington State Sportsmen's Council, the Oregon Wildlife Federation, the Alaska Fishermen's Union, and the Makah Indian tribe—petitioned the FPC and the courts to strike the ruling and reconsider the license.

Eventually, the complicated dispute reached the United States Supreme Court, which was asked to rule on a two-part question:

> (1) Should the FPC reconsider its order licensing Pacific Northwest Power to build the dam?
> (2) Did the association of public utilities have a preference claim on the site?

The Court ruled on neither question. Instead, in a 6-2 decision dated June 5, 1967, with Justice William O. Douglas writing the majority opinion, it decreed:

> "The test is whether the project will be in the public interest. And that determination can be made only after an exploration of all issues relevant. . . ."

One highly relevant issue, the opinion stated, was "the public interest in preserving reaches of rivers and wilderness areas, the preservation of anadromous fish for commercial and recreational purposes, and the protection of wildlife. . . ."

In a dissenting opinion, Justice John M. Harlan wrote:

> "I had thought it indisputable . . . that a court may not overturn a determination made by an administrative agency upon a question committed to the agency's judgment. . . . In its haste to give force to its own findings of fact on the breeding requirements of anadromous fish and on the likelihood that solar and nuclear power will shortly be alternative sources of supply, [the court has] submitted its own preferences for the discretion given by Congress to the Federal Power Commission."[7]

As so often happens when the highest court in the land makes a ruling, it was not clear who had gained or lost yardage. But to all the players involved in the contest, one thing was evident:

> "We've got a whole new ball game. . . ."[8]

° ° °

2.

When the opening whistle blew for the second half of the game—a Federal Power Commission pre-hearing conference in Portland, Oregon, September 28, 1967—there were significant changes in the lineups of the starting teams. Taking heart from what they regarded as a score for their side, conservation groups, steelheader clubs, Fish and Wildlife agencies, the Sierra Club, and others now were prepared to fight the Middle Snake dam proposals as a question of national, rather than regional, interest.

On the dam-builder's side, Public Power and Private Power had joined forces, announcing agreement:

> ". . . to undertake as a joint venture the development of the High Mountain Sheep reach of the Snake River . . . to prevent possible delays in the project's construction and to minimize financial and other risks resulting from the prosecution of competing license application by the parties. . . ."[1]

Furthermore, "The agreement recognizes the interests of Idaho and Oregon. The parties also invite Interior to join in whatever extent possible."

In other words, all the past quarrels—which long had delayed the project—had been patched up. But ensuing events soon proved that the repair job was far from watertight. For one thing, Secretary of the Interior Udall, who was beginning to have second thoughts, sent the message "Interior is unable at this time to state its position beyond *Tabula Rasa* ('empty table')." Before taking a position, Interior wanted a year in which to evaluate studies of High Mountain Sheep and alternate sites recently proposed. Secretary Udall did not get a full year; but he did get seven months.

Now that the Nez Perce site had been abandoned, the

-----

7. *Moratorium Hearing*, S. 940, p. 167.

8. *Idaho Statesman*, Boise, June 24, 1970, editorial quoting Corps of Engineers spokesman.

1. *Moratorium Hearing*, S. 940, p. 168.

three next-best sites were High Mountain Sheep, Appaloosa, and Pleasant Valley, respectively located at River Miles 189, 197, and 213. At 670 feet, High Mountain Sheep would be the world's second-highest arch dam, would create a pool extending 58.5 miles to the foot of Hell's Canyon Dam, and would form a storage reservoir with a total capacity of 3,600,000 acre-feet. Initially, its generating capacity would be 1,470,000 kilowatts; ultimately, 3,430,000. Its initial cost, including transmission, would be in the neighborhood of $260,000,000.

Relatively speaking, Appaloosa would have roughly two-thirds of the generating and storage capacity of High Mountain Sheep, while Pleasant Valley would have about half. In the many hearings held before the FPC during the next two years, these attitudes of the contending interests emerged:

> *Power.* The High Mountain Sheep Dam site was by far the best; but it would settle for Appaloosa.
>
> *Interior.* The FPC should recommend to Congress Federal construction of Appaloosa.
>
> *Conservationists.* No dams should be built in the Middle Snake—period.

It was a new ball game, all right. But with three teams on the field, the referee was having trouble finding out who had the pigskin, let alone calling the fouls. And even as the FPC attempted to untangle the pileups, a totally new element was introduced by two veteran Idaho Senators, Frank Church and Len Jordan. They proposed:

> *A ten-year moratorium on any further dam building between the Hell's Canyon project and the Asotin site, in order to keep Idaho's water options open pending further study on use.*

Because the United States Senate hearing held in Washington in late February, 1970, is the most recent and important action so far taken regarding the fate of the Middle Snake, we must attempt to summarize it here. As Senator Church pointed out, one Congress cannot bind a succeeding Congress to a policy. The intent of the Moratorium was to prohibit the FPC from licensing a hydroelectric project in the area for a period of ten years. If the Act were passed, then only Congress could repeal it.[2]

The hearing was held before the Senate Subcommittee on Water and Power Resources, Senator Clinton P. Anderson (N. Mex.) presiding. A Department of Agriculture spokesman testified in favor of the bill, saying:

> "We believe that the value of the Middle Snake Canyon itself, along with its recreation, wildlife, commercial fishery and sports fishery values, far outweighs any presently demonstrated need for hydroelectric projects. We view with increasing optimism the prospect that this nation will find a way to meet water and power needs without serious environmental consequences and without sacrificing existing values of the Middle Snake. . . ."[3]

The Department of the Interior also recommended that the bill be enacted, pointing out that on May 15, 1968, it had warned against the High Mountain Sheep site "because it threatened extinction of the anadromous fish runs . . ." and that on August 12, 1969, Secretary Walter Hickel had filed a statement with the FPC saying: "It is in the public interest to oppose any construction of such a project at this time. . . ."

Interior further stated:

> "Moreover, under the planning program of the Bonneville Power Administration, it is not anticipated that a Middle Snake hydroelectric project will be required to meet the power requirements of the Pacific Northwest before 1986. Until then, alternative feasible means of generation will be developed under the hydrothermal program. . . ."[4]

As the hearing progressed, other points related to conservation emerged. Following the passage of the National Wild and Scenic Rivers Act in 1968, several sections of streams tributary to the Middle Snake have been set aside ". . . in free-flowing condition for the benefit and enjoyment of present and future generations. . . ."[5] These include the Clearwater above Kooskia, Idaho; the Selway; the Lochsa; and the Middle Fork of the Salmon. Many witnesses urged placing the Middle Snake in this category, or, better yet, enlarging the classification into that of a National River or National Park.

Senator Frank Church brought out a hitherto unstressed angle, which may point toward serious controversy in the future:

> "I am presently persuaded that the construction of a hydroelectric dam on the Middle Snake would not contribute greatly to the development of Idaho. The power would be sold almost entirely outside the state to large urban centers. . . . Congressional appropriations for water development projects are limited and it is very important to arrange our priorities in such a way that multipurpose projects, which include irrigation, navigation, and flood control benefits, as well as electric power—and which contribute most to the general growth of our economy—are built ahead of those projects which contribute the least. . . ."[6]

-----

2. As testimony during the hearing amply demonstrated, attitudes of elected representatives and appointed department heads can change drastically in a few years.

3. Testimony of J. Phil Campbell, Under Secretary of Agriculture, S. 940, p. 2.

4. Testimony of James R. Smith, Asst. Secretary of Interior, S. 940, p. 3.

5. Public Law 90-542, known as the National Wild and Scenic Rivers Act, is quoted in full, S. 940, pp. 12-23.

6. S. 940, p. 24.

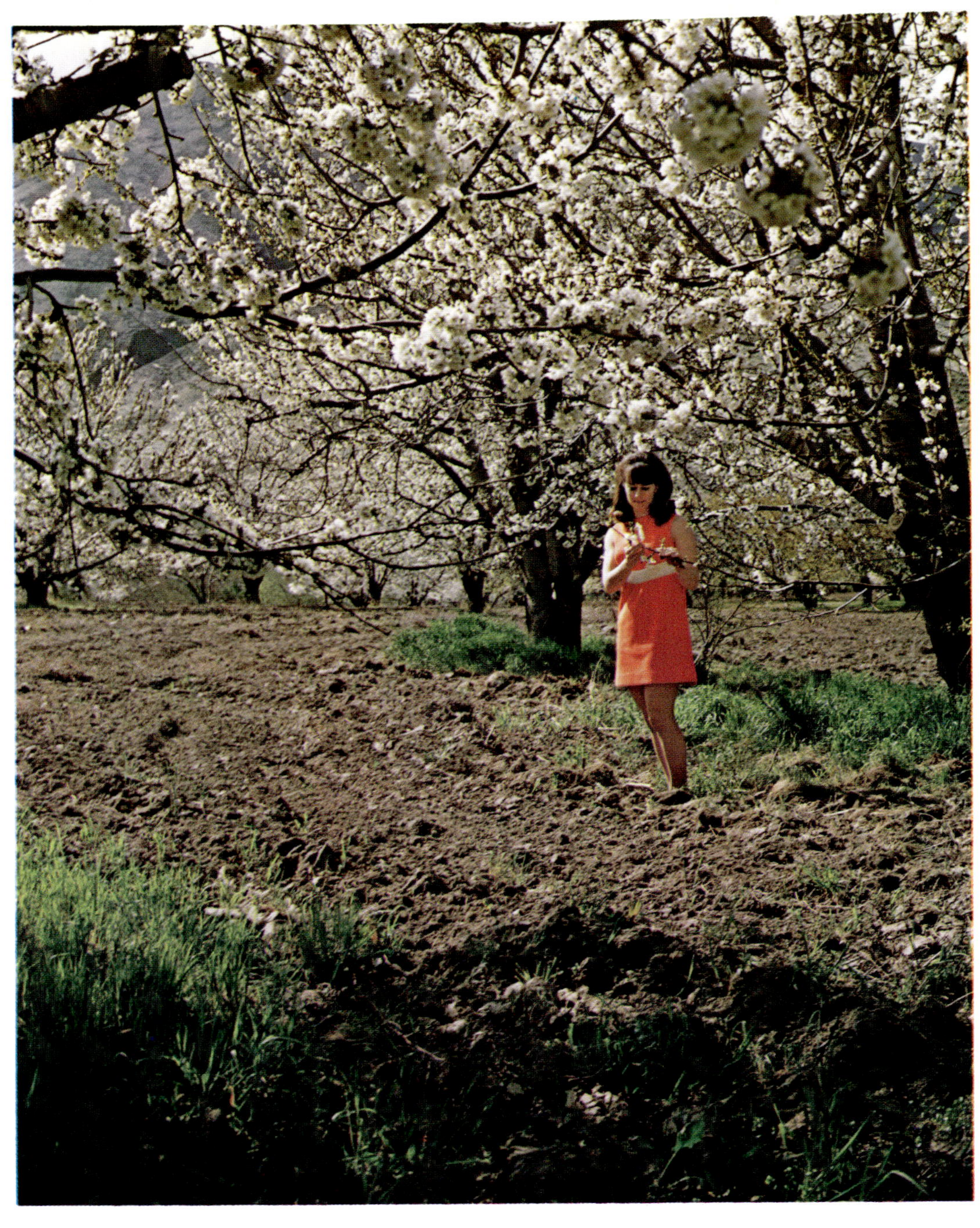

Left: Cherry Orchards in Bloom, near Clarkston, Washington. The model is the photographer's daughter, Millie.

Below: Aspen, Upper Salmon

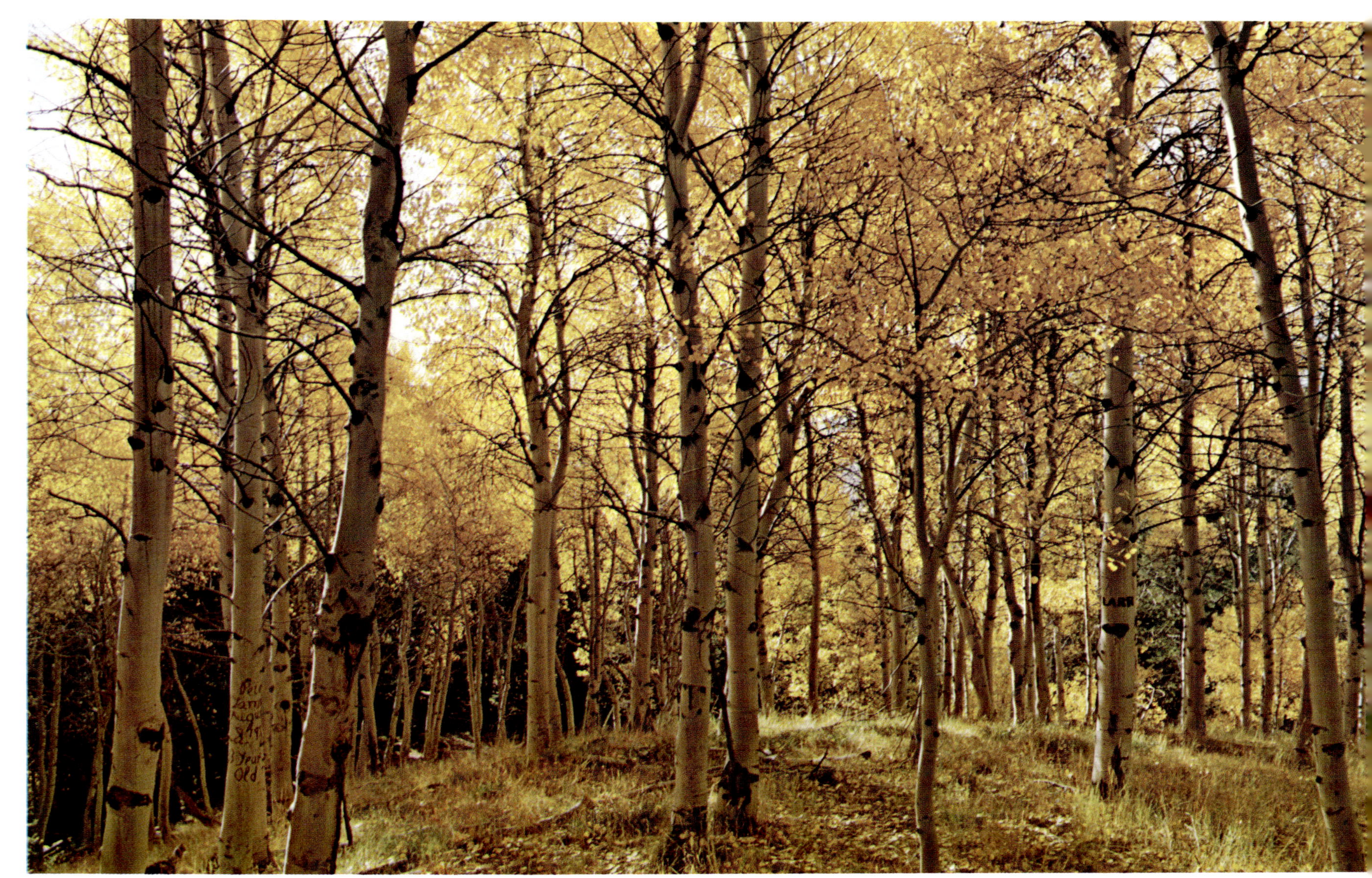

Senator Len Jordan, a former governor of Idaho who for eleven years lived with his wife and children on a ranch in the depths of Hell's Canyon, said:

"There is a time and season for all things. This is a time for study of the Middle Snake River, not for premature development nor for committing it to a natural-river state."

He then put forth his arguments in favor of the Moratorium:

(1) Multipurpose studies of the River Basins Commission established under the Water Resources Planning Act are just getting under way.

(2) The National Water Commission, assigned by Congress to study national water problems, has just published its first annual report and has four years to complete its study.

(3) The State of Idaho's resource planning efforts are barely started.

(4) Federal Wild and Scenic River studies and Wilderness Act studies are just getting off the ground.

(5) This bill merely provides a ten-year delay to glean information before important, perhaps irreversible decisions are made.

"The Snake River and its tributaries represent the only major surface-water resource remaining to meet future water requirements in a tremendous arid and semiarid area in Idaho and in the arid eastern half of our neighboring State of Oregon," Senator Jordan said. "I can see only one available course . . . to keep the options open for an adequate future water supply and a properly managed river resource. . . ."[7]

In comments and questions put to witnesses, the two Idaho senators made it clear that their chief concern was the export of their state's most valuable resource—water. In the broader sense, they pointed out, this includes the loss of power it produces, the loss of recreational facilities which dam construction would entail, the loss of future agricultural and industrial growth, and, most important of all, the loss of opportunity for young people who would be forced to leave the state and go to coastal urban centers to find employment.

Despite its long history of legal controversy, water and its uses in the Snake River Country still are vaguely defined in the ownership area. By law, for example, 95 percent of the water originating in Wyoming is committed to irrigation use downriver from that state's borders. Does it follow, then, that if Idaho farmers in the Upper Snake need more late season irrigation water Wyoming must permit a huge dam to block a stretch of its most scenic river to store water it cannot legally use? Because a flood on the lower Columbia once wreaked havoc in Portland, must 53 miles of Idaho's finest steelhead stream, the North Fork of the Clearwater, be lost to the state's recreation and tourist industry forever to hold back potentially damaging flood water? If so, how is Idaho recompensed?

What about navigation and power needs? Since the dams on the lower Snake will create slack water to Lewiston and bring that part of the state the benefits of low freight rates, Idaho can see the necessity of releasing enough water from its storage dams to augment natural river flow and keep the tugs and barges moving. But if a dam is built in the Middle Snake and power commitments are made to industry in Portland and Seattle, must water pour through the turbines of that dam in ever-increasing quantities, regardless of the growing need for irrigation water on Idaho's thirsty farmlands? What if a power-hungry industry wants to locate *in* Idaho, taking advantage of the state's low-priced space, clean air, and low taxes? Can Idaho promise it a constant supply of power to be used only fifty miles away from the dam that produces it? Or must that power go to coastal cities?

All the above questions were asked or implied during the hearing. The association of public and private utilities, joined together under the name Pacific Northwest Power, did its best to answer them. In a tentative agreement worked out with Robert R. Lee, director of the recently established Idaho Water Resource Board, it promised that:

(1) Idaho would share in the economic benefits of the multipurpose hydroelectric development.

(2) Power rights would be subordinated to upstream consumption use.

(3) Postamortization benefits would be available to assist basin development.

(4) Access roads would be provided to enhance recreational potential of the area.

(5) Idaho and Oregon each could tax one-half of the facilities.

(6) The project would not be an obstacle to but would assist future irrigation development.

"Approximately $2.5 million per year would accrue to the State in taxes from the contemplated development," Lee testified. "Furthermore, Pacific Power has agreed to share 10 percent of its power revenue, a net return of $1.5 million per year."[8]

Saying that the testimony of the Director of the Idaho Water Resource Board came as something of an eleventh-hour surprise, Senator Church asked:

"Has the Board made a study to determine what contribution this dam will make to our power supply in Idaho?"

Lee. "At least 10 percent."

Church. "And 90 percent would go to the urban areas of Oregon and Washington?"

Lee. "That is right."

7. S. 940, pp. 25-27. *Home Below Hell's Canyon,* by Grace E. Jordan, the senator's wife, Crowell, 1954, is an excellent, true account of ranch life in this remote area.

8. S. 940, pp. 55-56.

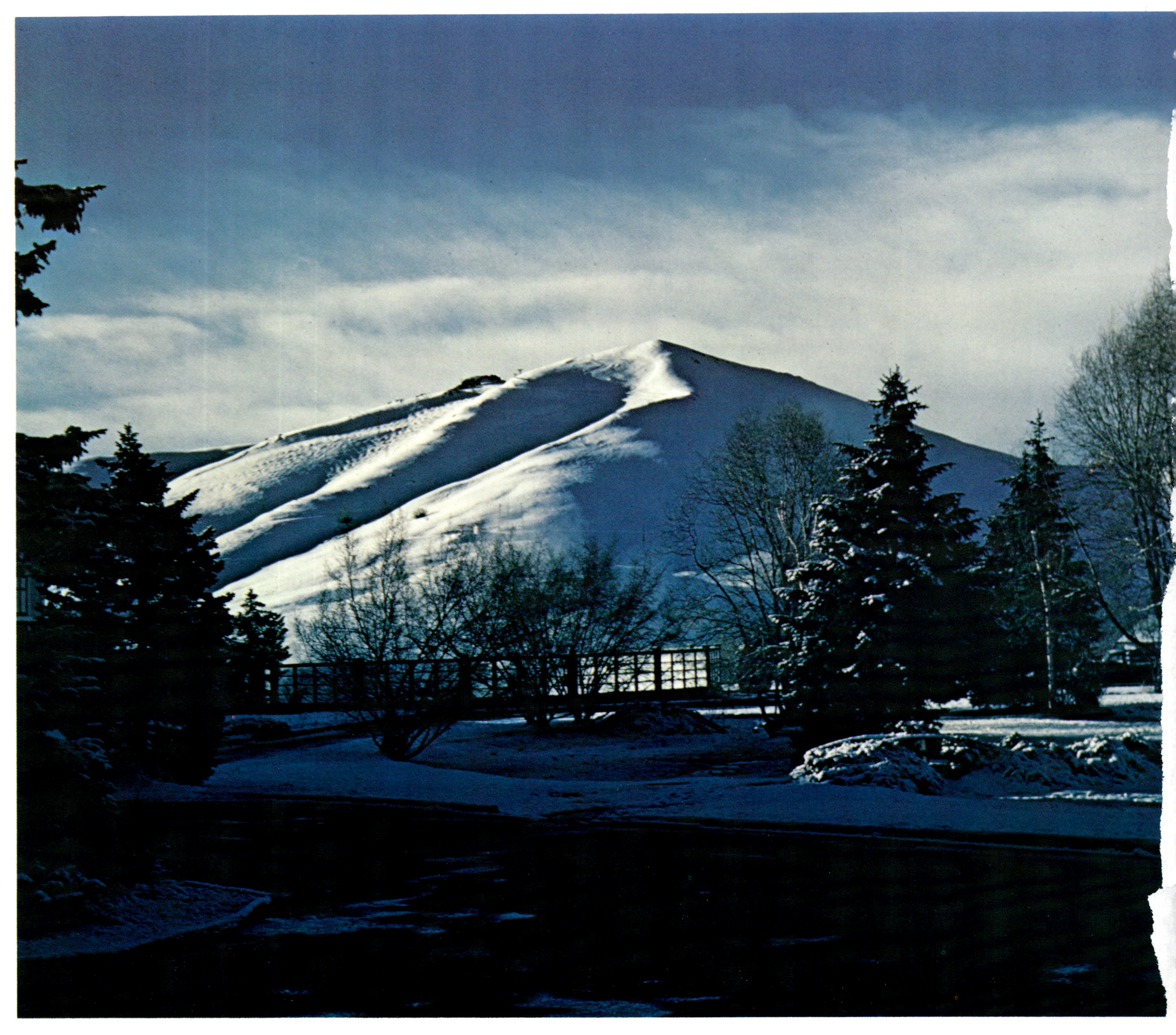

Above: Upper Snake River, near Jackson Hole, Wyoming

Right: Wallowa Lake Scene, Eastern Oregon

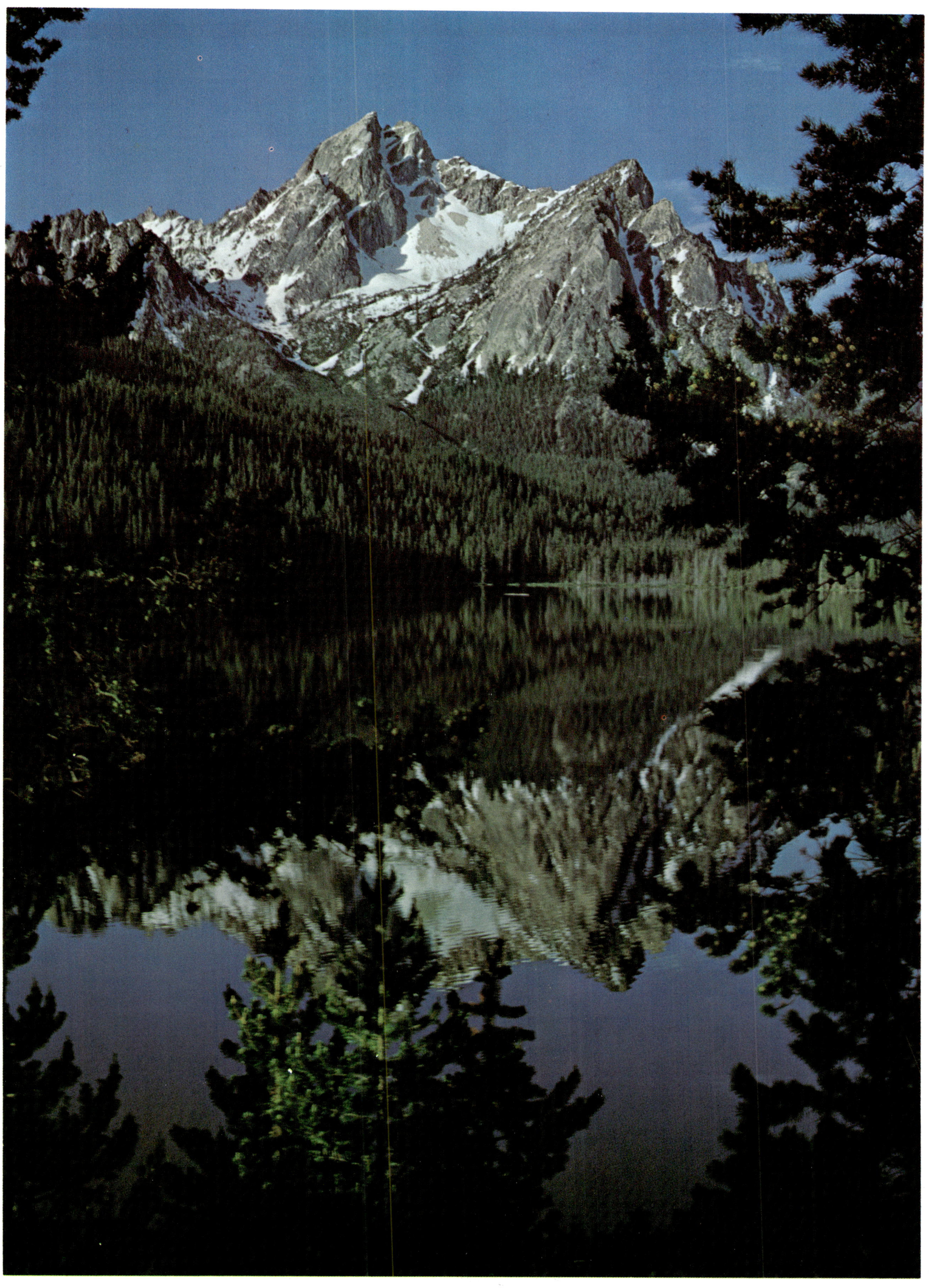

Church. "You make several references in your statement to recreational uses and couple those references with assertions that such uses limit economic development. I find that hard to follow in view of the fact that the recreational and tourist industry has become the fastest growing industry in the State and, therefore, has become a great money earner for the people of Idaho. . . ."[9]

On the question of comparative recreational values on a stretch of free-flowing river in the Middle Snake and on slack-water pools behind existing dams, expert testimony and statistics were in total disagreement. Ratios as high as 10 to 1 were quoted in favor of each. Brought in to reinforce the slack-water pool side were use-figures of Oregon's Farewell Bend State Park, which is well above the area in dispute and conveniently adjacent as a rest-stop to tourists traversing Interstate 80; while the free-flowing river advocates testified that in their section of the Snake bank fishermen often stood shoulder to shoulder and that the river was used by thousands of sightseers and private boatmen.

Testimony from a number of highly respected biologists, naturalists, and other experts who favored preserving the Middle Snake was entered into the hearing record. Dr. Luna Leopold, who has attempted the well-nigh impossible task of "Quantitizing esthetic values," called Hell's Canyon second in worth only to the Grand Canyon. Wildlife biologist Dr. Frank Craighead said:

"It is especially desirable to have an ecological benchmark in the Hells Canyon area because it contains aquatic, terrestrial, and atmospheric habitats that are biologically unique. Nowhere else in the Nation are all these species found together in such collective abundance."[10]

Oregon Senator Mark Hatfield, though not opposing the Moratorium, raised a question of great concern to his constituents: the increasing need for power in western Oregon and the growing opposition of environmentalists to the construction of nuclear and fossil fuel plants. Following the testimony of Sierra Club representative Lloyd Tupling, who favored full protection of the Middle Snake as a National Park, the Oregon senator attempted to do some horse trading.

Hatfield. "I don't think the people of the Northwest are going back to the bonfire. . . . What I want to know is, if we support this moratorium program and move into the thermal, will groups like yours say, 'No, we don't want thermal either.'?"

The Sierra Club spokesman replied that his organization would support the thermal program, providing there were proper pollution controls. However, he felt such measures as birth control and limiting the promotion of excess consumption also should be undertaken. When asked to be specific in regard to the matter of excess consumption, Tupling said:

"I think we have twice as many lights in the room as we need for the purpose of this hearing."

"Would you think that you could get the ophthalmologists to agree with you?"

"I don't know whether I could or not."[11]

The questions of birth control and excess use of energy triggered one of the few moments of humor during the hearing. After listening to Senator Hatfield comment on the population explosion and its relation to the need for electric energy, Senator Church smiled.

Church. "Senator, a little less energy might mean fewer people."

Hatfield. "No. Just the opposite is true. During the blackout on the eastern seaboard, if you recall, nine months later there were more babies born in those hospitals than any time in recent years. The more power we have, and the more television sets, the less population explosion we have."

Church. "The Senator misunderstood me. I was not referring to electrical energy."

Hatfield. "We need to keep the lights on."[12]

In pressing for a project in the Middle Snake, the dam advocates brought forth two relatively new points in relation to anadromous fish: water temperature and oxygen content control. Slack water behind a dam tends to stratify; that is, its temperature and oxygen content vary at different levels. By installing outlets at several levels in the dam, engineers said, the temperature downstream could be controlled; and cold water releases at the proper time could eliminate the thermal blocks that now and then occur downstream during late summer months. By constructing a nine-mile tunnel, which would take cold, oxygen-rich water from the Salmon and transport it into the pool above the proposed Middle Snake dam, the environment for fish downstream could be enhanced.[13] Free-running river advocates disagreed.

"The concept is unproven, and a number of biologists doubt that it would be effective. Besides, they argue, why not modify one of the existing dams, such as Hell's Canyon, to try it out? Building another dam on the Snake-Columbia system to help the fish is like taking another drink of whiskey to sober up."[14]

Though the dam builders expressed willingness to adopt

9. S. 940, pp. 63-66.

10. S. 940, pp. 83-84.

11. S. 940, pp. 149-150.

12. S. 940, p. 49.

13. S. 940, p. 60.

14. S. 940, p. 92.

almost any scheme that would preserve the fish runs, the fish experts rejected as unsatisfactory any combination of a high dam and a re-regulating dam downstream from the mouth of the Imnaha and Salmon. In the pool behind the re-regulating dam, the waters of the two spawning streams would mix, they said, confusing the fish, so that year by year the runs would diminish and eventually cease altogether.

On the question of future irrigation water needs—which was his chief concern—Senator Jordan said:

> "The Columbia River Basin states are a full generation behind the Colorado River Basin states in water resources planning. We expect to make good use of this 10-year period."[15]

The Colorado, he pointed out, is "a fully plumbed river" in that it has a reservoir storage capacity four times greater than its annual flow. In contrast, the Snake has only a 25 percent headwater storage capacity.[16] He was also highly dubious of building a dam in the Middle Snake with a storage capacity in excess of 3.5 million acre-feet, for during the period 1929-48 it could have been filled only four times during the permissible storage season, April 15 to August 15.[17]

Finding a quiet, thoughtful, moderate expression of opinion among the pros and cons attending the hearing comes as something of a surprise to a person reading the transcript. But just such an expression was made by W. D. Hall, Editorial Page Editor for the Lewiston *Tribune*, a newspaper located within a few miles of the battleground.

> "The choices now facing us are three," he said. "(1) Damming the stream for hydroelectric generation, (2) Damming the stream for pumpback storage to irrigate lands to the south, or (3) Preserving the stream as it is—a nearly natural river. . . . My newspaper believes that the first of the three alternatives: a hydroelectric dam—is the least likely to pan out as a responsible use of this resource. . . .
>
> "That leaves the two remaining options of reclamation and conservation. The choice between those two courses cannot responsibly be made at this moment—by anyone."

Therefore, Hall said, his paper favored the Moratorium bill. So did a large percent of Idaho people, he added, quoting a recent poll taken by a professional research company, whose results showed 65 percent of the Idahoans contacted in favor of the bill, 13 percent opposed, and 22 percent undecided. When Senator Jordan reminded him that the *Tribune* long had supported building the dams below Lewiston, which soon would create slack water for navigation, he answered:

> "That is correct, Senator. We take a position of which is the higher use. With something as important as navigation, it is pretty hard not to put down your fishing rod and cry a little, and let them go ahead. . . ."[18]

Unabashedly immoderate, as might be expected, was the redheaded radio and television personality, Arthur Godfrey, who had recently taken a trip upriver from Lewiston into Hell's Canyon with Floyd Harvey. Exuberantly, he had written a letter to Secretary of the Interior Hickel, which he insisted be placed in the hearing record. The letter rhapsodized:

> "This is the heart of Paradise, believe me. I would willingly attempt to swim the entire 96 or 97 miles up that cold river from Lewiston just to see it again. . . ." Comparing slack-water areas behind the dams to the free-flowing river, he went on: "In its place a deep sluggish polluted lake full of hordes of faint-hearted outboard motor nuts spewing ⅓ of their fuel—unburned!—into the waters along with their beer cans and other people droppings!
>
> "Please go and see it! I believe no one who has ever beheld its priceless, irreplaceable beauty would dream of building another dam there. . . ."[19]

A few months later, Secretary Hickel, Arthur Godfrey, and the popular actor, folk-singer, Burl Ives, did journey into the "heart of Paradise . . ." on an expedition highly praised by conservationists and viewed with "underwhelming" enthusiasm by the dam builders.

One newspaper editorial favoring the latter referred to Arthur Godfrey in such ungenteel terms as: "slightly nauseating" and "pompous" in posing as "an ecology-saviour of Hell's Canyon," putting the "soap salesman" in the same category as Justice Douglas, who "threw out the federal permit for Mountain Sheep Dam and meddled in the legislative and administrative field. . . ."

How deeply Mr. Godfrey's feelings were wounded by the editorial is unknown; but it seems safe to assume that, as a lover of puns, he chuckled at the editorial's concluding line, which pithily summed up what may be called differing points of view:

> "We cherish neither Radio City white knights nor a prospect of Northwest black nights. . . ."[20]

During the hearing, when witness Annette Tussing of Clarkston, Washington, mentioned the giant sturgeon that spawn in the Middle Snake, Senator Church was put in a reminiscent mood. The first job he ever held, he said, was pounding stakes with an Idaho survey crew. The fellow that carried the transit used to go around singing a little song that went:

15. S. 940, p. 27.
16. S. 940, p. 70.
17. S. 940, p. 73.
18. S. 940, pp. 50-53.
19. S. 940, p. 126.
20. Editorial, *Union-Bulletin*, Walla Walla, May 27, 1970.

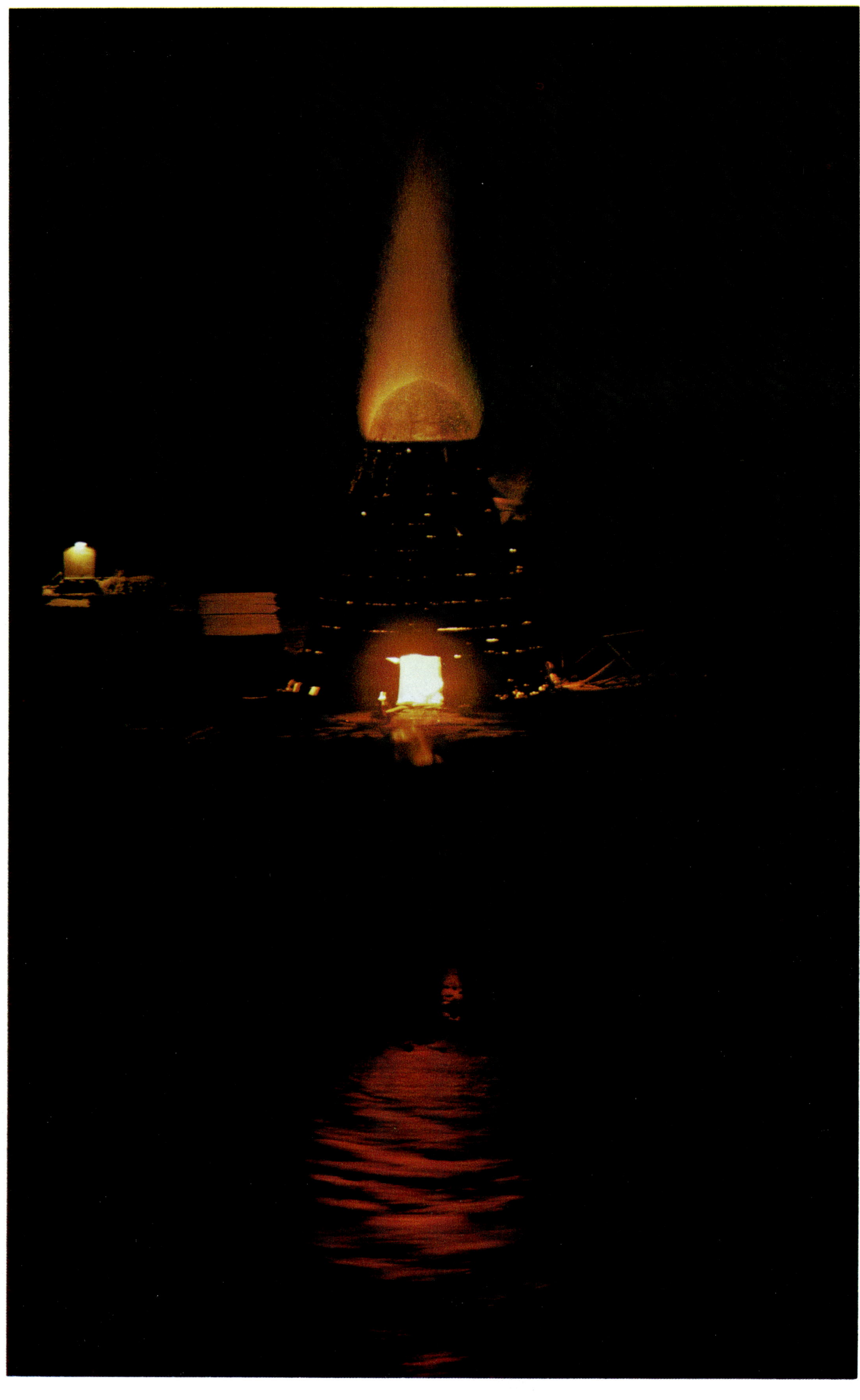

"The virgin sturgeon is a very rare fish,
And that is why caviar is a very dear dish."

Whether the Idaho senator sang or recited the words is not recorded in the transcript. But Mrs. Tussing was surprised.

"Arthur Godfrey used that on his broadcast. I thought how clever he was. Now you reveal this."

Even as the hearing drew to a close, Pacific Northwest Power—the combine of eighteen public and four private utilities—was preparing for yet another hearing before the Federal Power Commission, which the Supreme Court had ordered to examine all aspects of the Middle Snake dam proposals—including the case for no dam at all. After reviewing the long history of controversy in the area, the Power Company attorney said:

"I assure you, sir, that if the moratorium bill is adopted, the Wilderness Society and the Sierra Club will have prevailed. We will not return to this kind of battle ten years from now."[21]

Several months later, after due consideration, the 10-year Moratorium on dam building in the Middle Snake River was approved by the United States Senate. It has not yet been acted on by the House. Since it has Administration approval, the odds would seem to favor its eventual passage.

In October, 1970, Federal Power Commission attorneys recommended against building *any* dam in the Middle Snake. Their voluminous report concluded:

"High Mountain Sheep is economically feasible but should not be built because of dangers indicated by fishery biologists to the anadromous fish runs in the Salmon, Imnaha and Snake River.

"Neither Pleasant Valley nor Appaloosa should be developed because neither would be economic."[22]

A week later, a statement protesting the FPC staff finding was issued by spokesmen for Pacific Northwest Power. The adverse recommendation, they said, was "just a skirmish . . ." in their sixteen-year battle "to obtain a source of economical power for our 1.5 million customers and others in this power-hungry region. . . ."[23]

There, for the time being, the matter rests.[24]

* * *

3.

Between Lewiston and its confluence with the Columbia —a distance of 140 river miles—the Snake flows through a grain-growing region whose productivity is unequalled. Since the area's population is small, almost all the wheat, rye, and barley raised in it is shipped to Portland, on the lower Columbia, or to Seattle, on Puget Sound. From these tidewater ports, 90 percent of the grain is marketed overseas.

Fifty bushels of wheat, which is the average per-acre yield of a farm in the Palouse Hills, weighs 3,000 pounds, and the average farm is 1,000 acres. Assuming that half of his land is planted to wheat in a given year, the farmer has 1.5 million pounds of the staff of life to ship and sell. Since his net return is based upon the per-bushel price at tidewater, less rail freight charges from his shipping point, he is deeply concerned with shipping costs. For example, a 25 percent rail freight reduction proposed and hotly debated during the 1960s would have put an extra $7 million in the pockets of the region's farmers.[1]

This most welcome windfall was related to the building of dams on the Columbia and Lower Snake and the extension of tug and barge traffic inland. But it did not materialize. Instead, it set off a controversy called the Grain Rate War.

Though not as dramatic or colorful as the Hell's Canyon battle, this struggle inspired an equal amount of editorial fireworks, legal maneuvering, hearings by Federal Commissions, and rulings pro and con. In our limited space, all we can do is identify the disputants, summarize what was at stake, and then step out of the ring.

So far as rail freight rates go, the Lower Snake River Country is "parity territory"—that is, grain shipment rates from points within it are supposed to be the same to either Seattle or Portland. Currently, about 70 percent of the grain goes to Portland by rail, truck, barge or a combination thereof, while 30 percent goes by rail across the Cascades to Seattle.

The main argument set forth in favor of developing upriver navigation has been that barge line competition would have a beneficial effect on rail freight rates. But when that very thing happened in 1960, in the form of a grain rate slash by five Northwest railroads that would have made their

Left: Night View of a Wigwam Burner, near Riggins, Idaho. In many parts of the Pacific Northwest these burners, which dispose of sawmill wastes, are being banned because of their air pollution effects. The fact that uses are being found for former waste products is hastening the day when these colorful but outmoded monsters will exist no more.

21. S. 940, p. 172.

22. *Spokesman-Review,* Spokane, Oct. 25, 1970, p. 7.

23. Ibid., Oct. 31, 1970.

24. In a bill sponsored by Senators Jordan and Church and recently passed by the Senate, the Moratorium period has been set at seven years, which makes it expire in 1978. The measure now is under study by a House committee.

1. *Oregonian, Portland,* August 31, 1960.

charges competitive with truck-barge fees, the truck-barge companies protested violently.

Gist of their argument was that the railroads were trying to destroy them.

Not at all, replied the railroads. We are only being competitive.

The Portland Dock Commission, anxious to keep downriver traffic coming their way, backed the truck-barge companies. The Seattle Port Authority, eager to gain traffic, cheered for the railroads. Farmers upriver, who long had promoted navigation development with this very aim in mind, watched with interest—and hoped for the best.

Referee and judge for the contest was the Interstate Commerce Commission, which sets rates on carriers operating between states. One principle involved in the dispute was that of "compensatory" freight rates. Simplified as much as such a highly complex subject can be, this means that after taking all cost factors into consideration a railroad may not transport a certain commodity at a loss just because other carriers are taking business away from it.

The railroads argued:

> "(1) The barge lines do not have to construct or maintain their own rights of way, nor pay taxes on them (as the railroads do); and they pay nothing for the use of expensive waterway improvements provided by the taxpayer.
>
> "(2) The rates charged by the barge lines are not subject to governmental regulation, as are those of the railroads. Since the barge lines on the Columbia operate in interstate commerce, even when hauling between Oregon points, they are not subject to State regulation; and the bulk cargo exemption in the Instate Commerce Act relieves them from Federal regulation. Consequently the barge lines can set any rate they wish, whether compensatory or not, and the railroads have no way of objecting. For the most part, barge rates are not even known to the public. Similarly, truck rates are not subject to governmental control when the trucks are hauling agricultural commodities. . . ."[2]

On their part, the truck-barge interests were quick to point out:

> (1) The immense land grants given the railroads for building into the West.
>
> (2) Historically, use of the nation's rivers always has been free.
>
> (3) Electric power users in the Columbia-Snake region eventually will pay off all dam construction, navigation facility, and irrigation benefit costs.
>
> (4) Even though the truck-barges were taking some grain-hauling business away from the railroads, Rail still was carrying 60 percent of the wheat tonnage to tidewater, while Trucks carried only 15 percent and Barges only 24 percent.[3]

Did the railroads want *all* the business? asked the truck-barge lines. After they had "destroyed" their competitors, would they not raise their rates far above what they had been before, leaving the shipper worse off?

Of course not! answered the railroads. Strictly regulated as they are by the ICC, they could not possibly do such a thing.

So the battle raged.

Angered by Portland's opposition to the proposed slash in rail freight rates, wheat farmers in eastern Washington, Oregon, and Idaho accused the city of "declaring war . . ." against them, to which Portland replied uncomfortably:

> "If a seven-million-dollar yearly reduction in freight rates is possible, grain growers should get it, certainly. But the ports whose barge services forced the cut to be made should not suffer for it. . . ."[4]

In October, 1963, the ICC issued an order disallowing the 1960 rail grain rate reduction, calling it "unjust and unreasonable. . . ." The five railroads petitioned for a rehearing.

In November, 1964, ICC hearing examiner William J. Sweeney reversed the previous finding, calling the lower rail rates "just, reasonable, and lawful. . . ."[5] The truck-barge interests appealed.

The Grain Rate War still goes on, with the rulings and reversals of rulings at times confusing the news media of the region to such a degree that the same ICC order is interpreted in opposite ways. For example, compare these two stories, both of which were based on the same ruling:

> (1) "The Portland Freight Traffic Association reported victory Tuesday in its battle against grain rate increases which would have diverted large amounts of Eastern Washington grain from the Columbia River ports to the Puget Sound area. . . .
>
> "The present rate for shipment of single carloads of wheat to Columbia River ports is 21 cents a hundred pounds. The Milwaukee Railroad had proposed a rate from Rosalia, Wash., north of Pullman, to Puget Sound of 12 cents a hundred pounds in 10-car shipments. . . ."[6]
>
> (2) "An Interstate Commerce Commission hearing examiner has rejected lower rates proposed by the Chicago, Milwaukee, St. Paul & Pacific Railroad for

2. Letter from Randall B. Kester, chairman, Oregon Railroad Assn., to Raymond M. Kell, chairman, Portland Commission of Public Docks, Aug. 8, 1960.

3. These are 1960 figures.

4. *Oregonian*, Portland, Editorial, Aug. 31, 1960.

5. Ibid., Nov. 26, 1964.

6. *Union-Bulletin*, Walla Walla, Jan. 29, 1970.

Right: Salmon River Valley, near Riggins

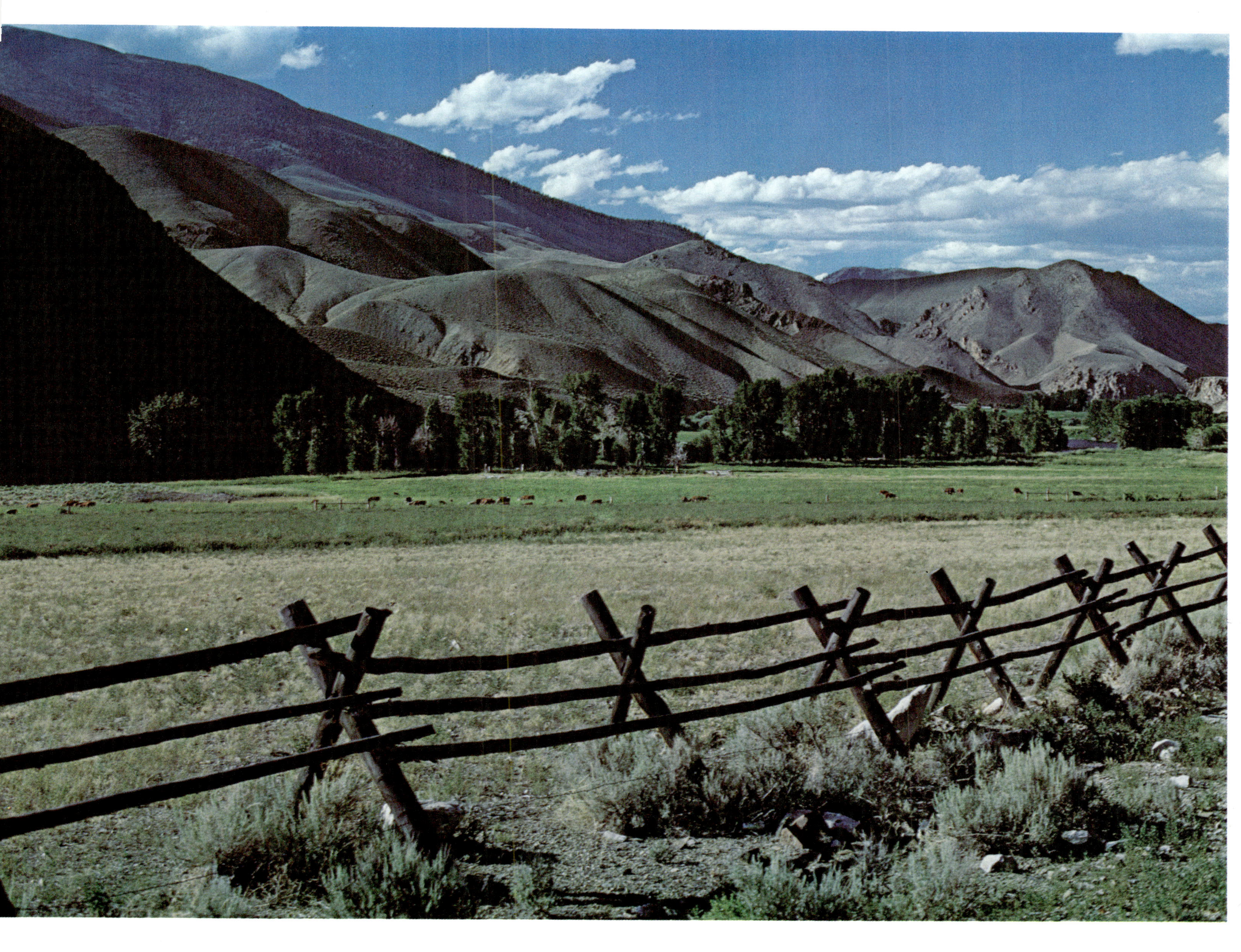

grain shipments between eastern Washington and Puget Sound. . . .

"Under the rate proposal, the Milwaukee would have charged 12 cents per hundredweight . . . substantially lower than the 21 cents charged by other carriers . . .

"The examiner held that a major portion of the wheat traffic would have been diverted to the Milwaukee because of the reduced rates and, at the same time, this would 'undoubtedly adversely affect' other competitive carriers such as truckers and barge lines. . . ."[7]

As slack-water navigation moves up the Snake toward Lewiston and competition between truck, barge, and rail intensifies, it would appear that the farmer eventually will be its beneficiary. But he needs all three carriers—and to continue to exist, all three must stay healthy. How any regulatory body can achieve that worthy goal is a question only the future can answer. . . .[8]

We can give only brief mention to two other areas of controversy involving the use of Snake River water: large-scale irrigation projects developed by private capital; and water diversion to the Pacific Southwest.

According to the ground rules laid down many years ago by the Bureau of Reclamation, a farmer using water stored behind a federal irrigation dam can own no more than 160 acres of land (320 acres for husband and wife). The original intent of this restriction was to encourage development of the family farm; but, like the "Five Acres and Independence" dream of the 1930s, that concept of farming is as outdated as the walking plough.

In southwestern Idaho and southeastern Washington, the Snake runs through deep canyons which contain little tillable land at water level, while, eight hundred feet above, hundreds of thousands of fertile acres need only moisture to produce abundantly. With the advance of technology in high-speed pumps, lightweight pipe, and automated sprinklers, water can be lifted from pools behind dams and put upon vast areas of land with very little labor. But the cost of 1,000-horsepower primary and 500-horsepower booster pumps, added to the expense of self-propelled sprinkler systems—each of which can irrigate a circle containing 138 acres untouched by human hands—is far too great for the family farmer on a limited acreage. To be profitable, corporate financed and operated tracts of 4,000 acres or more must be put into production as units. But if the Bureau of Reclamation restriction is enforced, how does the corporation get its water?

In 1969, when a Bureau official ruled that the restriction *did* apply to waters impounded behind a federal dam on the upper Missouri River, interests attempting private development of large-scale irrigation projects in the Snake and Columbia river areas protested strongly.

"To place the use of water from these rivers in the control of the federal government will do inestimable harm to the development of arid areas in this state," said one Washington State Congressman. "It is a foregone conclusion that much of our marginal land will not be developed that has the 160-acre limitation."[9]

The question currently is under study by the Department of the Interior. Since the dams on the Lower Snake are primarily for power generation and navigation benefits, with no planned storage space for irrigation water, the Bureau of Reclamation recently has indicated that the restriction does not apply. But because of the capital investment required to develop these large farms, the corporate interests involved are pressing for something more binding than indications.

So far as water diversion from the Snake River watershed to the Pacific Southwest is concerned, this extremely touchy question presumably is shelved for a few years. The word "presumably" is used because Congress has authorized the National Water Commission to study and report on *all* the nation's water problems, including interbasin water transferral. Since the Colorado River Basin states have agreed to a ten-year moratorium preventing them from "initiating studies of water importation" before 1978, many Snake River residents and public officials complacently assume that no pressures for water diversion from Northwest to Southwest will be applied until the moratorium has expired.

But Senator Len Jordan, who long has kept a watchful eye on Idaho's water and who knows from practical experience what one night's work by a badger can do to an irrigation canal bank, already is warning his constituents that they must make long-range plans to protect their priceless resource. In a recent speech in Boise, he said:

"Your comprehensive plans—based upon sound and current data, responsive to the present-day needs of our region, and able to elicit support from the broadest possible spectrum of our citizens—must be available to insure our region's interests are not subordinated to emotional cries of crises in the Southwest. . . ."[10]

At the moment, the cloud of future controversy over water diversion to the Southwest is only a hand-sized shadow in the blue, wide horizon of the Northwest sky. But it is growing. The storm it seems likely to bring to the Snake River Country in the not too distant future may make all past atmospheric disturbances look very mild indeed.

-----

7. *Spokesman-Review*, Spokane, Jan. 29, 1970.

8. In 1970, 400,000 tons of wheat were transported by barge from the Lower Snake grain-growing region to Columbia River tidewater ports. This totals 13.3 millon bushels. Figures supplied by Inland Empire Waterways Assn., courtesy H. Calvert Anderson, executive vice president.

9. Statement by Vaughn Hubbard, *Union-Bulletin*, Walla Walla, November 30, 1969.

10. *Spokesman-Review*, Spokane, December 3, 1970.

4.

When the Boston iceman, Nathaniel Wyeth, "rolled a stone into the garden of the Rocky Mountain Fur Company" in 1834 by building Fort Hall, the man he left in charge of the trading post was a saltwater sea dog named Captain Joseph Thing. Whether the landlocked sailor yearned for the bounding main as he traded with Indians and tended his vegetable garden in the dry, windswept valley near present-day Pocatello, Idaho, is unknown. Whether he dreamed of once again commanding a ship headed for distant ports is unrecorded. If such were his yearnings and dreams, he surely must have felt that he was as high and dry as a sea captain could possibly get.

In location, he was. But if he had hung around a while, he could have swapped yarns a century and a quarter later with the skipper of an epoch-making vessel—the submarine *Nautilus*—without leaving his post. Over their rum toddies, the two captains could have exchanged tales of rounding the Horn under full sail in the 1830s and of cruising at full speed underwater for sixty-six days in the 1950s—while still in Idaho. After hearing his visitor tell *that* big windy, Captain Thing no doubt would have cut off his rum, for the idea of sailing anywhere underwater—especially in the deserts of Idaho—would have seemed to him as preposterous as the notion of cruising from the Pacific to the Atlantic under the ice of the North Pole.

America's nuclear navy was born in the desert of southeastern Idaho. Established in 1949 as a place where the Atomic Energy Commission could build, test, and operate various types of reactors with maximum safety, the bleak, remote site of the Nuclear Testing Station 55 miles north of Pocatello and 30 miles west of Idaho Falls looks to be more suited to rattlesnakes, coyotes, and antelope than to the research of scientists. Indeed, the men whose careers require them to perceive the unseeable still watch where they plant their feet when outside their desert laboratories, for rattlers still coil in the shade of clumps of sagebrush, and the sophisticated security network of electronic eyes—which makes fencing the 894 square mile station unnecessary—still has not learned to distinguish between coyote, antelope, or human intruder.

With over $500 million invested in facilities, the Nuclear Testing Station is one of the United States' principal centers for developing peacetime uses of atomic energy, has the world's largest and most varied collection of reactors, and can boast of many "Firsts." These include:

(1) Producing the first usable quantities of electricity from nuclear sources.

(2) Proof-testing the feasibility of nuclear propulsion for both submarines and surface ships.

(3) Demonstrating the principle of breeding nuclear fuel.

(4) Plant-scale conversion of highly radioactive liquid wastes to solid form for safer storage in 90 percent less space.[1]

1. *Thumbnail Sketch,* National Reactor Testing Station, 1969.

Every reactor now in existence owes some debt to knowledge gained here, the experts say. In 1951, Experimental Breeder Reactor No. 1 produced the first useful amounts of electricity from nuclear heat; in 1953, the prototype of the *Nautilus* was "launched"; in 1955, a reactor called BORAX-III supplied all the electricity needed to meet the demand load of the city of Arco, Idaho, seven miles west of the reserve; in 1956, the feasibility of powering a turbojet engine by nuclear heat was demonstrated; in 1958, the first of two ship reactors sustained criticality, heralding the feasibility of using nuclear power to propel large naval and commercial vessels. Research is also being done here on the use of radioactive particles in the treatment of cancer and other diseases.

Indicative of the incredibly rapid pace at which nuclear research moves today is the fact that EBR-I—which between 1951 and 1964 was used in experiments perfecting the technique of "breeding" nuclear fuel—already has been retired and dedicated as a National Historic Landmark. It has been replaced by EBR-II—which carries on the work of its predecessor toward even more distant research horizons.

To the layman who feels it unjust that an inanimate object should become a Historic Landmark before he was aware it even existed, let alone knew what it *did,* we offer sympathy—and a minimum of enlightenment.

The basic principle upon which EBR-I operated is that a reactor is capable of "breeding," meaning it can create more fuel than its operation consumes. This is what the research physicists say:

> "Projections indicate the possibility of 1.2 and 1.5 breeding ratios for uranium-235 and plutonium-fueled power plants, respectively."[2]

Beyond that quoted statement, we have neither the space nor the expertise to go. We do know that reactors produce heat; that heat can be transformed into electric energy; and that the earth's supply of certain types of easily used nuclear fuel is limited. The conventional reactor is able to convert only a small portion of its fuel's potential into usable heat. Breeder reactors can do much better.

Therefore, insofar as the generation of electricity is concerned, they are our hope for the future.

° ° °

5.

Until this final chapter, I have attempted to tell the life story of the Snake and the country through which it flows in an objective manner from all possible viewpoints. How successful the attempt has been is not for me to say. But now

2. Ibid., p. 24. Though many problems are yet to be solved in producing electricity with breeder reactors, Charles Luce, chairman of the National Water Commission and top executive for Consolidated Edison of New York, has said: "Nuclear plants are our best possibility for the power we need with the least damage to our ecology. The Sierra Club? More power to them."

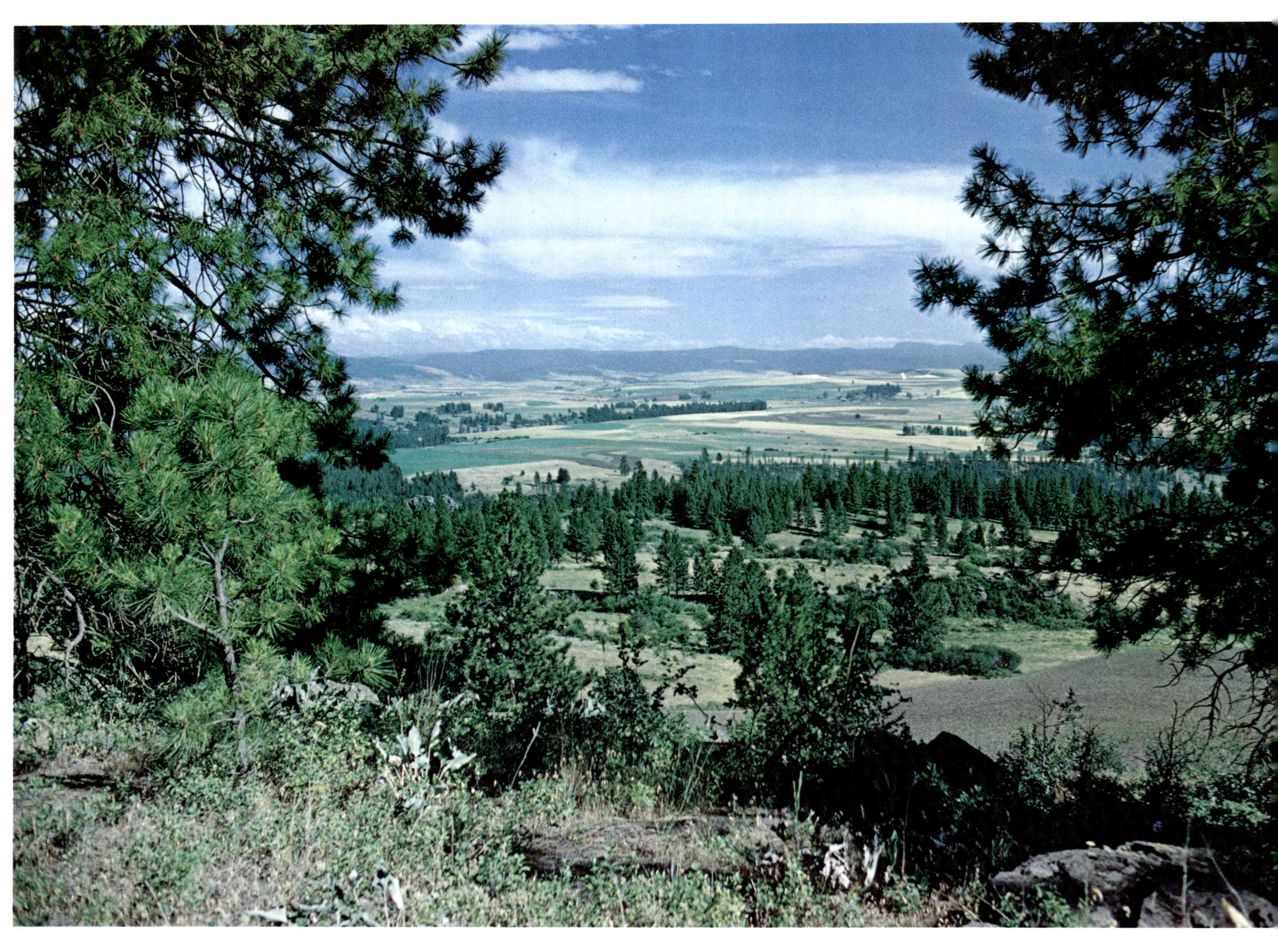

Above: Grande Ronde Valley, near Elgin, Oregon

Right: A Young Mule Deer photographed in Eastern Oregon

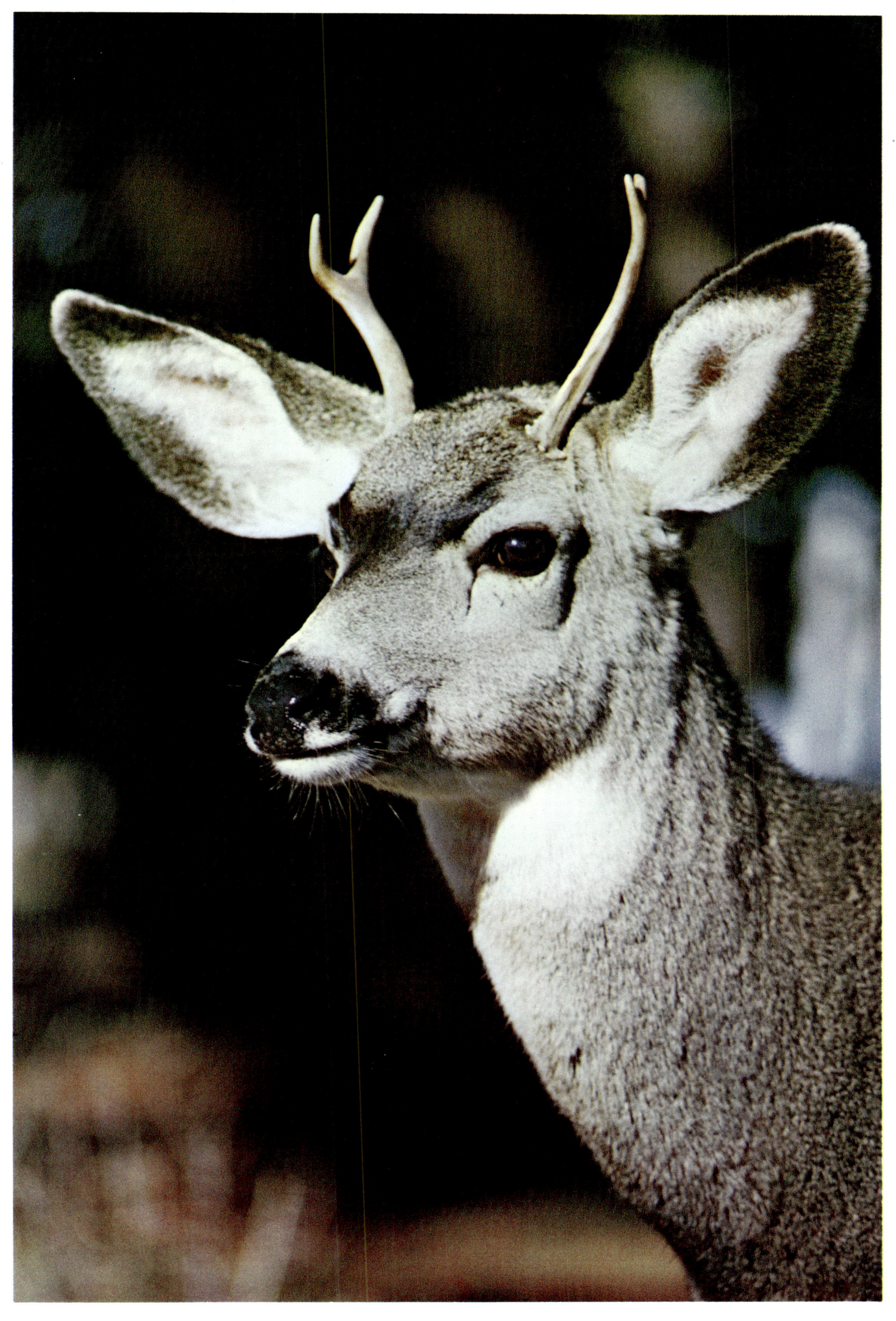

as a personal reward for this self-imposed discipline I would like to conclude with a few subjective impressions picked up during the years, miles, research, and personal encounters required to put this book together.

On one occasion, I was invited to join a group of experts on an inspection ride of the watershed from which a city of 25,000 obtains its water supply. Since the day-long trip was made on horseback and covered some fourteen miles of extremely rough mountain trails, my first impression was physical and wore off in a few days. My second was mental and remains with me: namely, that if water users were as meticulous about enforcing standards for downstream release as they are for upstream intake, we would have no water quality problems.

Logging is allowed in this heavily timbered watershed reserve only at those times and with those methods that will keep erosion at an absolute minimum. Wheeled vehicles are banned over most of the area. Hunting is permitted only under careful controls. The elk and deer population is kept down to the number of animals that can be supported by the natural vegetation. Since it is the habit of elk to congregate in certain spots on certain nights, these areas of destroyed grass are closely watched for signs of spreading erosion. If erosion does approach the danger point, it is the duty of the watershed patrolman to force the elk to change their playground.

As a result of this care, the city receives pure, soft, naturally filtered water requiring a minimum of treatment at minimum expense. Since a supply of good water is a basic requirement to food processors, the city has attracted several canneries and frozen food plants. Waste products from these industries at times are too voluminous for the city's sewage treatment plant to handle, so agreements have been made with downstream onion farmers for delivery of the waste water for irrigation use. During the pea-processing season, this waste water becomes so overly enriched with nitrogen and other fertilizer elements that it cannot be used by the farmers, who turn it into the nearby creek. The waste effluents at times are equal to those of a city of 600,000, the experts say. Thus, below the city, the pure, clear stream, whose headwaters are guarded so zealously, degenerates into what has been called the most polluted stream in the state.

A facility to correct this condition will cost three million dollars, I was told, and it must be built if the food-processing plants are to continue their operations.

Here, on a reduced scale, the water quality problems of the Snake River Country as a whole may be seen. With farsighted care, a community can insure itself a fine water supply at relatively little cost. With nearsighted neglect, it merely postpones the inevitable day when it must pay for its lack of vision.

Compared to older, more heavily populated regions of the nation, water quality problems in the Snake River Country have not reached the crisis stage. Some ecologists warn of the long-range effects of sedimentation and algae growth in the pools behind the dams. Mining interests operating under laws passed when the miner was king and could do no wrong despoil wilderness areas despite conservationists' efforts to stop them. Forest products industries, artificial fertilizer plants, food processors, and municipalities pour inadequately treated wastes into the river, which, at times of low flow, make it unsafe for water contact pursuits.

But the residents of the region have long been accustomed to an abundance of pure water; thus, they have far less tolerance for pollution than people living in urban areas. City fathers, county commissioners, industrialists, state and federal representatives, and public-relations-conscious agencies like the Bureau of Reclamation, Corps of Engineers, and Bonneville Power Administration are extremely sensitive to public opinion. When the people speak, they are heard. Not heeded, always—but they are heard.

As the Chairman of the National Water Commission, Charles Luce, recently pointed out, the "sleeper" in the pollution problems of the Snake River Country may turn out to be the use of chemicals on farms and forests of the region. The sources of municipal and industrial waste discharges can be pinpointed and controlled, he said. But farmlands and forest slopes cover vast areas, which must be treated with a wide variety of chemicals and insecticides to maintain food and fiber production and insure pest supression. This facet of pollution control may pose our knottiest problem.[1]

My final impression as I look back on what I have seen, heard, read, and experienced is that "The whole new ball game" set up by recent decisions regarding the Middle Snake may be a re-defining of the word "Progress." In the blind worship of that once holy word, we have despoiled much of the land, air, and water of our once beautiful nation. The monumental task of environmental rehabilitation facing the rest of the country is comparatively small in the Snake River watershed. We have not ruined our land, air, and water yet. While there is still time to save these priceless resources, we have taken a break in the contest and now are engaged in a close scrutiny of the rules.

When the ball game resumes, I suspect that some of the rules will be changed. If this book inclines those changes to favor quality rather than quantity, to encourage wise development rather than mindless expansion, and to favor balanced rather than special-interest use of our resources—then I shall have accomplished my aim in writing it.

Nothing on the face of the earth is as fascinating as a living river. To live, it must run free. So "balanced use" to me means that a portion—preferably several portions—of the Snake must be left in a natural state forever. As Oliver Wendell Holmes said long ago:

> "A river is more than an amenity. It is a treasure. . . ."

-----

1. Charles Luce, Speech, Walla Walla, Oct. 20, 1969.

Right: Hell's Canyon near Copperfield, Oregon

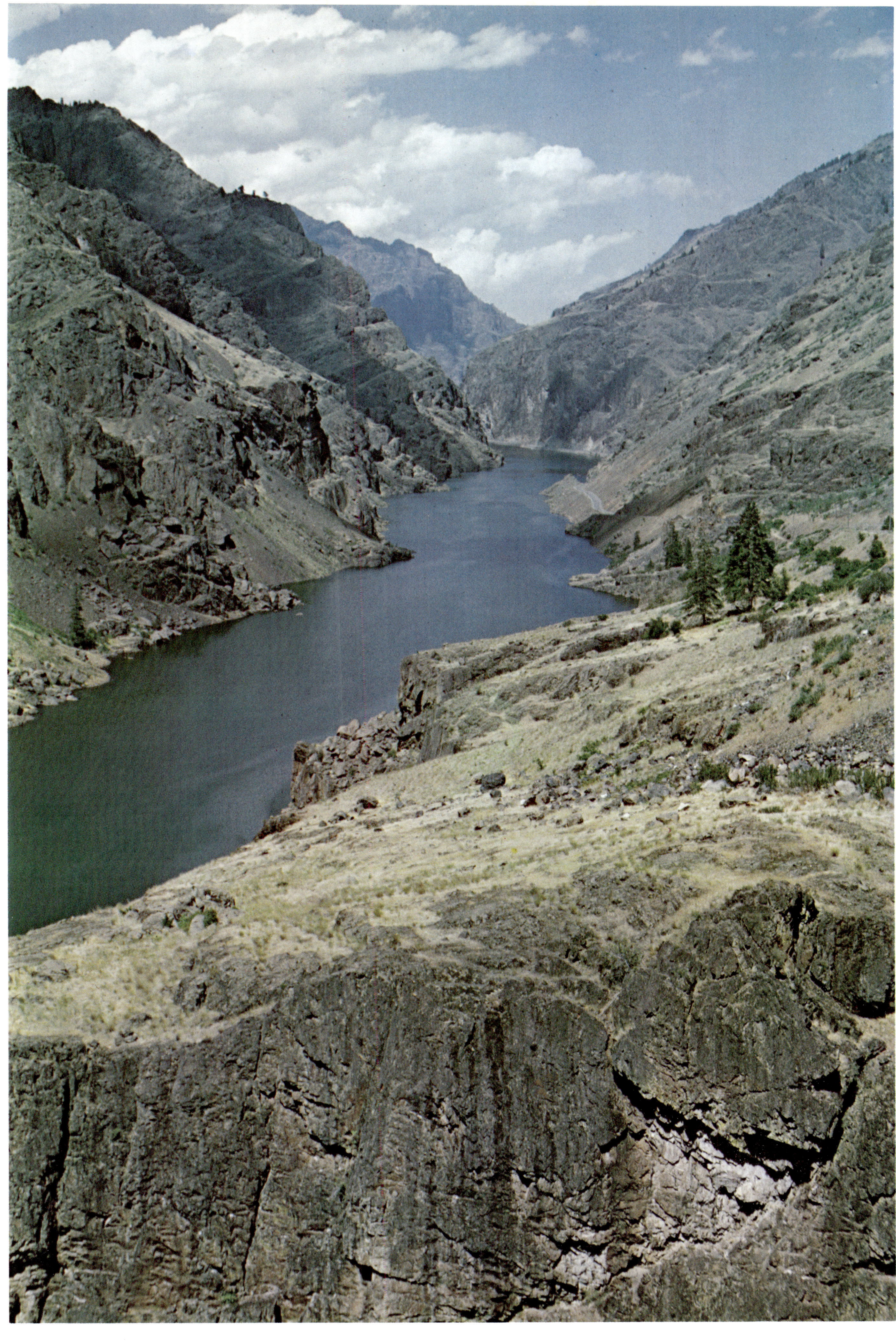

Bibliography

AUTHORS

Applegate, Jesse. *A Day with the Cow Column.* Chicago: Caxton Club, 1934.

Bailey, Robert G. *River of No Return.* Lewiston, Idaho, 1947. Revised edition. First published, 1935.

Baker, W. W. *Forty Years a Pioneer.* Seattle: Lowman & Hanford, 1934.

Ball, John. *Autobiography,* comp. by his daughters, Kate Ball Powers, Flora Ball Hopkins, Lucy Ball. Grand Rapids, Mich.: Dean-Hicks Co., 1925.

Ball, R. F. *Idaho Power Company, a History, 1887-1943.* Boise, 1943.

Bancroft, H. H. *History of the Northwest Coast. Works,* vols. 27, 28, San Francisco, 1884.

———. *History of Oregon. Works,* vol. 29. San Francisco, 1886.

———. *History of Washington, Idaho and Montana. Works,* vol. 31. San Francisco, 1890.

Binns, Archie. *Peter Skene Ogden.* Portland, Ore., 1968.

Bird, Annie Laurie. *Boise, the Peace Valley.* Caldwell, Idaho: The Caxton Printers, Ltd., 1934.

Blankenship, Russell. *And There Were Men.* New York: Alfred A. Knopf, 1942.

Bowles, Samuel. *Across the Continent.* New York, 1866.

Brattain, Ross R. "Wagon Wheel Blood," Unpublished MS, edited by W. D. Guernsey, excerpts courtesy Dr. Walter H. Brattain, Walla Walla. Original MS Archives, Penrose Library, Whitman College, Walla Walla, Washington.

Brown, Jennie Broughton. *Fort Hall on the Oregon Trail.* Caldwell, Idaho: The Caxton Printers, Ltd., 1932.

Cannon, Miles. *Toward the Setting Sun.* Portland, Ore.: Columbian Press, 1953.

Carr, Braxton B. *American Waterways Operators.* (Barge Navigation figures quoted in *Tri-City-Herald,* Pasco, Washington, Sept. 26, 1968.)

Chittenden, Hiram Martin. *American Fur Trade.* 2 vols. Stanford, Calif.: Academic Reprints, 1954. First published 1902.

Clark, W. P. *Indian Sign Language.* L. R. Hamersly & Co., 1885. Reprint by Rosicrucian Press, San Jose, Calif., 1959.

Coe, L. W. "Up Snake River." *Overland Monthly,* August, 1886, vol. 8, 2nd Series.

Davies, K. G., ed. *Peter Skene Ogden's Snake Country Journal, 1826-27.* London: Hudson's Bay Co., 1961.

DeVoto, Bernard, ed. *The Journals of Lewis and Clark.* Boston: Houghton Mifflin Company, 1953.

———. *Across the Wide Missouri.* Boston: Houghton Mifflin Company, 1947.

Drimmer, Frederick. *The Animal Kingdom, Mammals.* New York: Greystone Press, 1954, vol. 1.

Drury, Clifford Merrill, ed. *The Diaries and Letters of Henry H. Spalding.* Glendale, Calif.: The Arthur H. Clark Company, 1958.

———. *First White Women Over the Rockies.* Glendale, Calif.: The Arthur H. Clark Company, 1963.

———. *Henry Harmon Spalding.* Caldwell, Idaho: The Caxton Printers, Ltd., 1936.

Elliott, T. C. "The Strange Case of Jonathan Carver and the Name Oregon." *Oregon Historical Quarterly,* Dec., 1920.

———. "Jonathan Carver's Source for the Name Oregon." *Oregon Historical Quarterly,* March, 1922.

———. "Earliest Travelers on the Oregon Trail." *Oregon Historical Quarterly,* March, 1912.

Elsensohn, Sister M. Alfreda. *Pioneer Days in Idaho County.* Vol. II. Caldwell, Idaho: The Caxton Printers, Ltd., 1951.

Estes, George. *The Rawhide Railroad.* Troutdale, Ore., 1916.

Evans, Elwood. "Annual Address." Oregon Pioneer Assn., 1877.

Fuller, George W. *A History of the Pacific Northwest.* New York: Alfred A. Knopf, 1931.

Gilbert, Frank T. *Historic Sketches of Walla Walla, Whitman, Columbia and Garfield Counties, Washington Territory,* Portland, 1882.

Gray, Capt. William Polk. "Reminiscences," by Fred Lockley. *Oregon Historical Quarterly,* December, 1913.

Hailey, John. *History of Idaho.* Boise: Syms-York Co., 1910.

Hawley, James H. *History of Idaho.* Chicago: S. J. Clarke, 1920.

Idaho Power Company. *Bulletin,* 1966. Boise.

———. *Bulletin,* August, 1962. Boise.

The Idaho Story. Vol. 2. Idaho Pioneer Assn., 1968.

Irving, Washington. *Astoria.*

———. *Adventures of Captain Bonneville.*

Johansen, Dorothy O., and Gates, Charles M. *Empire of the Columbia.* New York: Harper & Brothers, 1957.

Jermann, Thomas C. "It's Time To Defuse Population Explosion." *National Observer,* July 27, 1970.

Jones, Nard. *The Great Command.* Boston: Little, Brown and Company, 1959.

Jordan, Grace E. *Home Below Hell's Canyon.* New York: Thomas Y. Crowell Co., 1954.

Josephy, Alvin M., Jr. *The Nez Perce Indians and the Opening of the Northwest.* New Haven, Conn.: Yale University Press, 1965.

Lavender, David. *Land of Giants.* New York: Doubleday & Company, Inc., 1960.

———. *Westward Vision.* New York: McGraw-Hill, Inc., 1963.

———. *The Fist in the Wilderness.* New York: Doubleday & Company, Inc., 1964.

Lever, W. H. (Publisher, no author named). *History of Whitman County,* 1901.

Matthews, Mitford M., ed. *A Dictionary of Americanisms on Historical Principles.* Chicago: University of Chicago Press, 1951.

McCaig, Robert. *Electric Power in America.* New York: G. P. Putnam's Sons, 1970.

McConnell, William J. *Early History of Idaho.* Caldwell, Idaho: The Caxton Printers, Ltd., 1913.

———. "The Idaho Inferno." Deposition, 1879, microfilm from Bancroft Library, University of California.

Mills, Randall V. "Frontier Humor in Oregon." *Oregon Historical Quarterly,* December, 1942.

———. *Stern-wheelers Up the Columbia.* Palo Alto, Calif.: Pacific Books, 1947.

Morgan, Dale L., ed. *The West of William H. Ashley.* Denver: Old West Publishing Company, 1964.

Reynolds, Helen Baker. *Gold, Rawhide, and Iron.* Palo Alto, Calif.: Pacific Books, 1955.

Rich, E. E., ed. *Peter Skene Ogden's Journals, 1824-25 and 1825-26.* London: The Hudson's Bay Company Record Society, 1950, Vol. 1.

Romig, Robert L. "The South Boise Quartz Mines, 1863-92." Microfilm of M. A. Thesis, University of California, 1950.

Ross, Alexander. *The Fur Hunters of the Far West.* London, Smith, Elder, 1855; reprint edited by Kenneth A. Spaulding, University of Oklahoma Press, 1956.

Russell, Carl P. *Firearms, Traps and Tools of the Mountain Men.* New York: Alfred A. Knopf, 1967.

Russell, Osborne. *Journal of a Trapper.* Boise, 1915. Reprint by Oregon Historical Society, 1955.

Schmitt, Martin F., ed. *General George Crook, His Autobiography.* Norman: University of Oklahoma Press, 1946.

Smith, Arthur D. Howden. *John Jacob Astor.* New York: Cornwall Press, 1929.

Smith, Henry Nash. *Virgin Land: the American West as Symbol and Myth.* Cambridge: Harvard University Press, 1940.

Spalding, Eliza. "Diary." Original at Penrose Library, Whitman College, Walla Walla, Washington.

Spaulding, Kenneth A., ed. *Robert Stuart's Journey of Discovery, 1812-1813.* Norman: University of Oklahoma Press, 1953.

———. Reprint of *The Fur Hunters of the Far West,* by Alexander Ross. Norman: University of Oklahoma Press, 1956.

Splawn, A. J. *Kamiakin, The Last Hero of the Yakimas.* Portland, Ore., Kilham Stationery & Printing Co., 1917.

Stegner, Wallace. *Beyond the Hundreth Meridian.* Boston: Houghton Mifflin Company, 1954.

Stevens, Hazard. *Life of Isaac Ingalls Stevens.* 2 vols. Boston: Houghton Mifflin Company, 1901.

Strahorn, Carrie Adell. *Fifteen Thousand Miles by Stage.* New York: G. P. Putnam's Sons, 1911.

Sullivan, Maurice S. *Jedidiah Smith, Trader and Trailbreaker.* New York: Press of the Pioneers, 1936.

Talkington, Henry L. *Heroes and Heroic Deeds of the Pacific Northwest.* Caldwell, Idaho: The Caxton Printers, Ltd., 1929.

Terrell, John Upton. *Black Robe: The Life of Pierre-Jean De Smet.* New York: Doubleday & Company, 1964.

Thompson, Erwin N. *Shallow Grave at Waiilatpu.* Portland, Ore.: Oregon Historical Society, 1969.

———. "The Lower Snake River in History," MS, 19 pp., 1960. Penrose Library, Whitman College, Walla Walla, Washington.

Victor, Frances Fuller. *The River of the West.* Hartford, Conn., 1870.

Wheeler, Harry E., and Cook, Earl F. University of Washington and University of Idaho. "Structural and Stratigraphic Significance of the Snake River Capture, Idaho-Oregon." *Journal of Geology,* Vol. 62, No. 6, November, 1954.

Whitman, Narcissa. "Diary." Original at Penrose Library, Whitman College, Walla Walla, Washington.

Wells, Merle W. "Steamboat Down the Snake." *Idaho Yesterdays,* Vol. 5, No. 4, Winter, 1961-62.

———. "She Will Strike About There. . . ." *Idaho Yesterdays,* Summer, 1957.

PERIODICALS

Boise News, Idaho City, Nov. 10, 1863.
Boise News, Idaho City, Feb. 13, 1864.
Boise News, Idaho City, Feb. 20, 1864.
Boise News, Idaho City, March 26, 1864.
Boise News, Idaho City, June 25, 1864.
Idaho Statesman, Boise, Nov. 26, 1864.
Idaho Statesman, Boise, Feb. 17, 1865.
Idaho Statesman, Boise, Nov. 2, 1865.
Idaho Statesman, Boise, Nov. 7, 1865.
Idaho Statesman, Boise, June 24, 1970.
Idaho World, Idaho City, Nov. 4, 1865
Lewiston Teller, Lewiston, March 31, 1877.
New York Tribune, Oct. 28, 1854.
Oregon Argus, May 19, 1855.
Oregon Argus, Nov. 24, 1860.
Oregon Historical Quarterly, Dec., 1913.
Oregon Historical Quarterly, Sept., 1917.
Oregon Historical Quarterly, Dec., 1920.
Oregon Historical Quarterly, March, 1922.
Oregon Historical Quarterly, Dec., 1942.
Oregonian, Sept. 23, 1854.
Oregonian, Aug. 31, 1960.
Oregonian, Nov. 26, 1964.
Owyhee Avalanche, Silver City, Idaho Terr., May 5, 1866.
Spokesman-Review, Spokane, Jan. 29, 1970.
Spokesman-Review, Spokane, Oct. 25, 1970.
Spokesman-Review, Spokane, Oct. 31, 1970.
Spokesman-Review, Spokane, Dec. 3, 1970.
Tri-City Herald, Pasco, Wash., Sept. 26, 1968.
Union-Bulletin, Walla Walla, Dec. 7, 1965.
Union-Bulletin, Walla Walla, Nov. 30, 1969.
Union Bulletin, Walla Walla, Jan. 29, 1970.
Union-Bulletin, Walla Walla, May 27, 1970.
Walla Walla Statesman, Feb. 16, 1866.
Walla Walla Statesman, April 20, 1866.
Walla Walla Statesman, April 27, 1866.
Washington Historical Quarterly, Vol. II, No. 2, April, 1908.
Weekly Oregonian, Aug. 25, 1855.
Whitman College Quarterly, Vol. II, No. 2, June, 1898.

PUBLIC AGENCY DOCUMENTS

Bonneville Power Administration. *The Treaty With Canada for Joint Development of the Columbia River,* Dec. 1, 1965.

———. *1965 Report, U.S. Columbia River Power System.*

———. *The Story of Bonneville Power 1936-1968-1987,* by Gordon D. Friedlander, Nov., 1968.

———. "Building the Pacific Intertie," *Bulletin,* August, 1968.

———. *Pacific Northwest Economic Base Study for Power Markets,* Vol. I, Summary, 1970.

———. *Energy Requirements and Hydropower Generation in the Northwest,* Henry R. Richmond, Dec. 4, 1969.

———. *Conference Proceedings, Regional Advisory Council,* Portland, Jan. 9, 1970.

———. *A Ten Year Hydro-Thermal Program For the Pacific Northwest,* Jan., 1969.

———. "Electricity and the Environment: Enemies or Allies?" Remarks by H. R. Richmond, BPA Administrator, Richland, Wash., May 14, 1970.

Bureau of Reclamation. *The Columbia River: A Comprehensive Report on the Development of the Water Resources of the Columbia River Basin for Irrigation, Power Production, and Other Beneficial Uses in Idaho, Montana, Nevada, Oregon, Utah, Washington, and Wyoming,* February, 1947.

———. *Upper Snake River Basin, Source to Powder River, incl.,* Vol. I, Summary Report, 1961, joint publication with Corps of Engineers.

House Executive Document, 2nd Sess., 33rd Congress, Part I, 1854/55.

———. 46, 36th Congress, 2nd Sess., Oct., 1860.

Pacific N.W. River Basins Commission. *Irrigation,* Appendix IX, Jan., 1970, Preliminary Report, Vancouver, Wash.

———. *Electric Power,* Appendix XV, Dec., 1969, Preliminary Report, Vancouver, Wash.

———. *Water Resources,* Appendix V, March, 1969, Vancouver, Wash.

Senate, 940, *Middle Snake River Moratorium Hearing,* 91st Congress, 2nd Sess., Feb. 16, 1970.

U.S. Army Corps of Engineers. Detailed maps, charts, proposals for projects, and statistical data covering the entire Snake River watershed.

U.S. Atomic Energy Commission. *Thumbnail Sketch,* National Reactor Testing Station, Idaho Falls, 1969.

———. *Nuclear News,* Vol. 12, No. 5, May, 1969.

———. *Argonne National Laboratory,* 1969, Annual Report.

———. *Miscellaneous Fact Sheets, EBR-II and Related facilities.*

———. *Hydrology of the National Reactor Testing Station, Idaho, 1966.* U.S. Geological Survey, Water Resources Division.

U.S. Department of the Interior. *Resources Study of the Middle Snake, April, 1968.* Agency reports by:
Bureau of Reclamation
Fish and Wildlife Service
Federal Water Pollution Control Administration
Bonneville Power Administration
Bureau of Outdoor Recreation
National Park Service
Bureau of Mines
Bureau of Land Management

Appendix Material by:
U.S. Army Corps of Engineers, Letter Dec. 14, 1967.
U.S. Supreme Court Decision, June 5, 1967.

Index

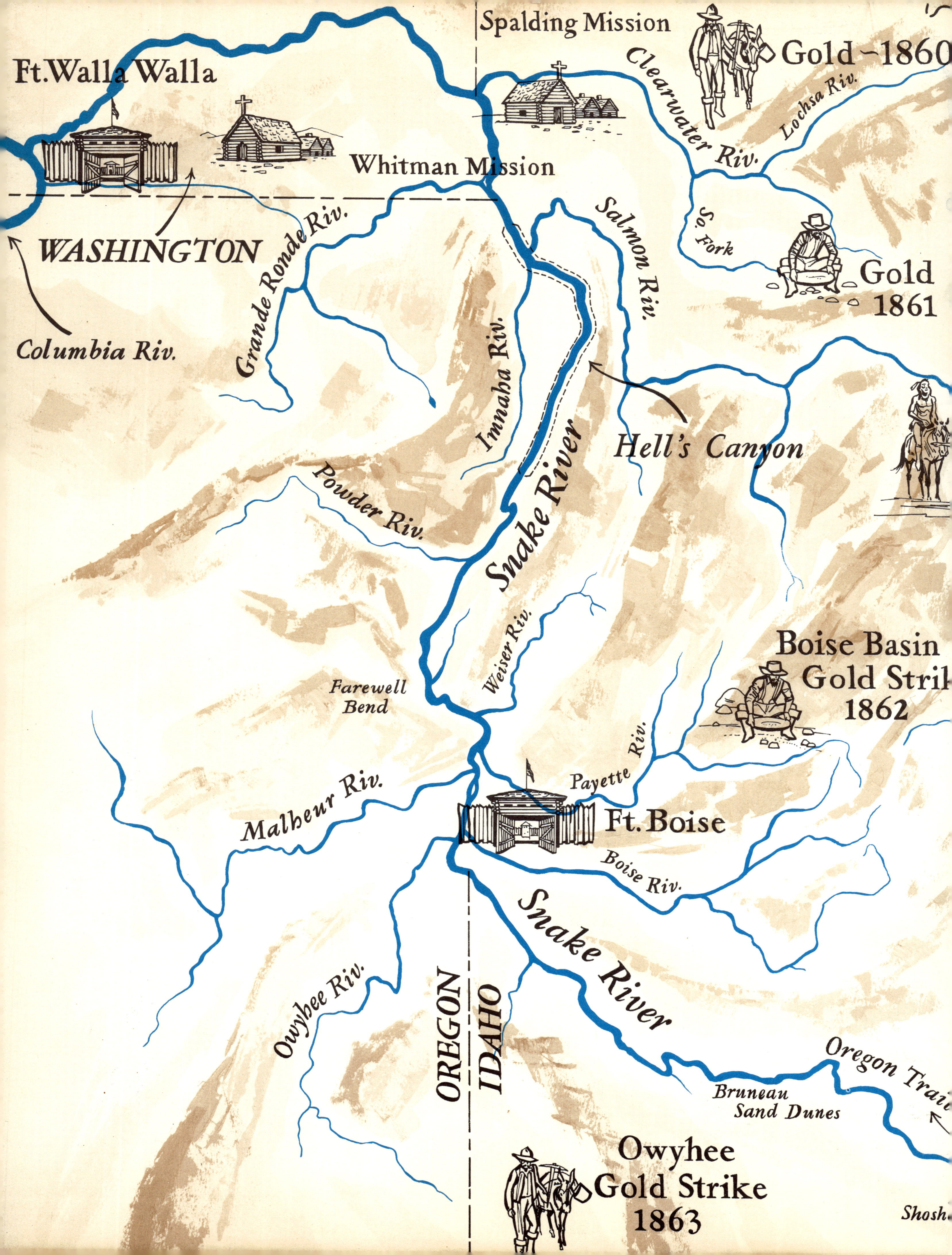
Spalding Mission
Gold - 1860
Ft. Walla Walla
Clearwater Riv.
Lochsa Riv.
Whitman Mission
So. Fork
Salmon Riv.
Grande Ronde Riv.
WASHINGTON
Gold 1861
Columbia Riv.
Imnaha Riv.
Hell's Canyon
Snake River
Powder Riv.
Weiser Riv.
Boise Basin Gold Stri
1862
Farewell Bend
Payette Riv.
Malheur Riv.
Ft. Boise
Boise Riv.
Snake River
Owyhee Riv.
OREGON
IDAHO
Oregon Trai
Bruneau Sand Dunes
Owyhee Gold Strike 1863
Shosh